AF717066

Baris Karaagac (Ed.)

Accumulations, Crises, Struggles

Politik, Gemeinschaft und Gesellschaft in einer globalisierten Welt

herausgegeben von

Thomas Faist (Universität Bielefeld)

Band 15

LIT

Accumulations, Crises, Struggles

Capital and Labour in Contemporary Capitalism

edited by

Baris Karaagac

LIT

Cover picture: Jenna Pope

Bibliographic information published by the Deutsche Nationalbibliothek
The Deutsche Nationalbibliothek lists this publication in the Deutsche Nationalbibliografie; detailed bibliographic data are available in the Internet at http://dnb.d-nb.de.

ISBN 978-3-643-90411-9

A catalogue record for this book is available from the British Library

Klosbachstr. 107
CH-8032 Zürich
Tel. +41 (0) 44-251 75 05
Fax +41 (0) 44-251 75 06
E-Mail: zuerich@lit-verlag.ch
http://www.lit-verlag.ch

LIT VERLAG Dr. W. Hopf
Berlin 2013
Fresnostr. 2
D-48159 Münster
Tel. +49 (0) 2 51-62 03 20
Fax +49 (0) 2 51-23 19 72
E-Mail: lit@lit-verlag.de
http://www.lit-verlag.de

Distribution:
In Germany: LIT Verlag Fresnostr. 2, D-48159 Münster
Tel. +49 (0) 2 51-620 32 22, Fax +49 (0) 2 51-922 60 99, E-mail: vertrieb@lit-verlag.de

In Austria: Medienlogistik Pichler-ÖBZ, e-mail: mlo@medien-logistik.at
In the UK: Global Book Marketing, e-mail: mo@centralbooks.com
In North America: International Specialized Book Services, e-mail: orders@isbs.com
e-books are available at www.litwebshop.de

For my grandparents, Mehmet and Mediha (Melahat) Karaağaç

TABLE OF CONTENTS

Acknowledgements

This project is finally done. It has taken much longer than it should have due to several unforeseeable obstacles and at times, sheer misfortune. However, I am very happy with the end result, as this collection has been able to bring together research of the highest caliber that will, without any doubt, contribute significantly to the literature on contemporary capitalism. I would like to thank the Canadian Centre for German and European Studies at York University and Prof. Leo Panitch for their generous contributions. I would also like to extend my cordial thanks to Yasin Kaya and Adam Schachhuber for their help and contribution in different phases of the editing process. I am grateful to all of the contributors, who were generous in both their labour and patience with me. My special thanks go to Shaghayegh Tajvidi, the language editor of the book. It would not be possible to finish this project without her tireless editing and consistent support since the very beginning. Finally, I would like to express my gratitude to my professor, supervisor and mentor, Greg Albo, who, over the years, has introduced me, as well as countless students, to political economy and set the best example as an educator, human being and socialist.

Introduction

Barış Karaağaç

This is a book about capitalism. To be more specific, it is about the most recent phase or stage of capitalist development: neoliberal globalization. Neoliberalism, as much a political project as an economic one, is still pervasive, and it continues to provide the general framework for politics and political imagination across most of the globe. Even the recent financial crisis – the worst since the Great Depression of the 1930s – and its aftermath have not changed this state of affairs in any substantial way. While the ongoing Great Recession has led to significant social trauma and turmoil, expressed in the numerous opposition movements that have emerged around the world, the crisis is still far from being the crisis *of* neoliberalism. It is, rather, still a crisis *within* neoliberalism (Saad-Filho, 2011).

The Great Recession is entering its sixth year and there still seems to be no end to it, at least not in the near future. At the 2010 IMF summit in Istanbul, the infamous financial institution (infamous, at least, for billions of people around the world, if not for bankers and industrialists) heralded the end of the crisis and concluded with a call to focus on how to handle or administer the upcoming recovery. Only two years later, the chief economist of the same institution crushed all hope when he told the entire world to forget about recovery for another ten years! This pessimistic forecast, coming in the immediate aftermath of such widespread optimism, reveals a deeply shaken faith in austerity policies and their ability to pull the world economy out of recession.

Nevertheless, austerity is still what defines the policies that have been put in place to address the economic crisis in the Global North. The socialization of the debt through an assault on the gains made during the period of embedded liberalism in the interior periphery of the North has significantly eroded the living conditions of millions of people in countries such as Greece, Spain and Portugal. In fact, when we look at the numbers provided by the IMF, we see a general deterioration over most of the Global North (IMF 2013). Between 2007 and 2012, the general trend is that of contraction or stagnation of the economy in all of the major capitalist countries. (The exceptions have been Germany and the United States, both of which have achieved some modest growth.) Moreover, based on the population trends, all countries except Germany have become poorer on a per capita basis. As the majority has become poorer, a small percentage of the population has become wealthier, indicating the persistence of the badly skewed distribution of wealth over the past three decades. Austerity has emerged as the major cause of deteriorating living conditions for the masses in this period. As Boratav (2012) asks, how else can we explain the fact that impoverishment has become as pervasive in the UK as it has in Portugal or Spain, in spite of the absence of a banking crisis and the ability to borrow cheaply in the former country? As Schmidt makes clear in this volume, the periphery of the European Union has been part of this process of increasing poverty as a result of the socialization of the consequences of the banking crisis and the implementation of austerity based on strict financial discipline as dictated by Germany. The case of Greece, where GDP per capita has fallen by 18 per cent (according to the estimates of the IMF) between 2007 and 2012, can be compared to post-1990 Russia and post-2000 Zimbabwe as the worst cases of impoverishment in the history of capitalism (Boratav 2013). Despite some attempts to revise or loosen neoliberal recipes, such as Shinzo Abe's promises of more public spending and a looser monetary policy to revive the Japanese economy after more than twenty years of stagnation, the FED's recent 'pegging' of monetary policy to the unemployment rate, or the IMF's recognition of the detrimental effects of the current degree of austerity on growth, a possible exit from the current crisis is not in sight, as these weak attempts at stimulus have had minimal impact on production and growth in the core of world capitalism. Their immediate effect has been an increase in speculation and short-term financial flows into the Global South, where quick and higher gains can be made.

When we look at the Global South, the picture is more variegated compared to the Global North. If we restrict our discussion, following Boratav (2013), to the largest non-oil exporting economies in this part of the globe, we can see that these economies have recorded growth in the wake of a short period of crisis and contraction. Furthermore, we can see that external dependence on financial flows is a decisive factor in how much the crisis has affected and continues to affect individual peripheral economies. Countries like Mexico, Turkey and South Africa, which opted for growth based on short-term inflows of capital before the crisis, have experienced a more pronounced slowdown in the aftermath of the crisis, as compared to countries like China, Indonesia and Argentina. This is important, as it casts a harsh light on the prospects for sustained growth based on financial inflows in the periphery. Another important point is that the reduction in the US current account deficit and the financial inflows into the periphery provided by the recent loosening of monetary policy in core economies do not seem to have affected the Global South in a positive way. While a smaller US current account deficit has translated into shrinking surpluses or a re-emergence of deficits in some parts of the periphery, the recently created liquidity has entered into the Global South not as productive capital (i.e. foreign direct investment) but as speculative capital. While speculative inflows might provide some relief for economies like Mexico and Turkey, it does not and will not address the core causes of the current malady, and it will definitely not contribute to the further 'development' of these peripheral economies. These inflows will create higher levels of debt that could easily trigger a deeper crisis in the future.

The core of the contemporary capitalist system is still suffering from the recent crisis, which is itself the product of the contradictory dynamics of a regime of accumulation that was put in place after the structural crisis of the 1970s. With the policies implemented and the discourse dominant in policy-making circles, there does not seem to be an exit in the near future, as the chief economist of the IMF confirmed. Neoliberalism as a class project does not seem to be ready to exit the stage yet, despite the discrediting of its intellectual foundations and the increasing opposition to its material effects. Of course, this will continue to be the case until or unless there is an agency that demands such a change and, at the same time, has the capacity to effect that change. Such an agency and its actions should be informed by an accurate analysis of capitalist social relations and their various and concrete manifestations in different social contexts in particular phases of development.

Both neoliberalism and the recent crisis have been experienced differently around the world. This variation in experience cannot be reduced to a single factor and can only be explained by focusing on the interplay of objective and subjective factors. The decisive factors seem to have been the levels of development, configurations of class forces, and particular forms of state and of integration into the global circuits of capital in each national context. This volume brings together the work of a group of scholars of the neoliberal experience and the most recent global crisis. It aspires to contribute to the literature on analyses of neoliberalism as well as on crises of capitalism. It also aspires to contribute to the debate on the possible exits from the current neoliberal phase and, maybe, capitalism itself, which would give us the possibility of achieving a truly democratic organization of social life as well as emancipation from all forms of oppression.

In his critique of the mainstream debate between neoliberals on the one hand and Keynesians or institutionalists on the other, Gregory Albo draws our attention to the pressing need for alternative perspectives on the capitalist state and economic policy in contemporary capitalism. Neither of these two mainstream approaches has been able to provide a satisfactory theoretical and conceptual framework to understand the neoliberal phase and its contradictions, which culminated with the current crisis. While privatization and deregulation have not led to smooth functioning of global markets with increasing prospects for prosperity for all – as the rising tide lifting us all – the bastions of the welfare state, particularly in Western Europe, have not been able to withstand the neoliberal tide, as opposed to the predictions by the mainstream dissenters. This has led, in Albo's words, to the emergence of 'varieties of neoliberalism'. In such a global context, where the ideological discrediting of neoliberalism has failed to shake its dominance as a guide to economic policy, anti-capitalist movement and programmes have also proved unable to shift the balance of social forces and provide alternative visions of economic and democratic possibilities. In his piece, which should become a standard reference for all students of political economy, Albo provides a thorough and thought-provoking alternative framework to understand the state, its centrality and its relationship to economic policy. This is a framework that could inform the search for an exit from the current crisis, from the crisis of theory as well as from capitalism itself.

Anna Agathangelou offers a poetics drawing upon Epicurean and contemporary feminist Marxist-(neo)colonial theories to understand and challenge 'security' in the so-called 'Near East' in the age of neoliberal globalization. In developing this poetics, she disrupts the dominant epistemes and their 'necessary' ontological insights in understanding the "war on terror" and the way it has and continues to unfold in Eurasia. Defining it as "a practice embodied in different terrains," she studies the "war on terror" as part of the larger practice of the creation of a particular world order and within that world order, the production of state identities, and gendered sexualized, classed, and racialized subjects. Her piece goes beyond many of the critical analyses of the global political economy through its focus on the foundationally gendered, classed and racialized violence that is constitutive of the imperial order. Agathangelou's intervention in the debate on 'empire' and the notion of 'security' that is constitutive of it is critical. She draws our attention to the need to question and disrupt the dominant discourses that enable capital accumulation, violence and (in)securities and that allow us to place ourselves outside of the terroristic practices of imperialism while placing coloniality at the centre of our attempts to analyze and then challenge the global hegemonic model of power. The dissection and analysis of the different institutions controlling different spheres of social existence, while recognizing their interdependence and tension-ridden nature, can inform the struggles aimed at transforming the existing modalities of power.

If the Arab Spring and the recent civil war in Syria have filled the first pages of the international news sections of newspapers over the past two years, the other hot international topic has been the Euro-crisis, or the crisis of neoliberalism on the European continent. Ingo Schmidt looks at what went wrong in Europe, which seemed to be going quite strong only a decade ago with the European Union having launched its common currency and aspiring to become the most competitive and fastest-growing region in the world. This rosy picture has been transformed within a very short period of time into one that is marked by conflict, pessimism and tragedy for the poor. Taking a longer historical approach and questioning the recently emerged 'common-sense' based on the mainstream analyses that effectively blame the victim for the crime, Schmidt deploys a Marxian framework to explain why and how the recent financial crisis translated into the numerous economic and political crises plaguing Europe to this day. Schmidt concludes with a discussion of the crisis of legitimacy at the centre of the present problem(s) in Europe today, as well as the left- and right-wing alternatives to the existing neoliberal model.

An issue that has taken on greater urgency in the context of the Great Recession, is working hours. While there was a trend toward reduced working hours in the advanced capitalist world throughout the period of 'embedded liberalism (Ruggie 1982)' or Fordism in the US and even in the early years of the post-Fordist period in the case of Europe, this has been decisively reversed under neoliberalism as a result of capital's desire to extract an increasing surplus from the production process so as to restore profitability. The struggle over working time has been crucial to addressing the problem of high levels of unemployment as one of the constituent characteristics of the present crisis, as shorter working times have proven to be an effective tool to ease the problem of unemployment. However, despite several attempts to reduce working time temporarily in crisis-ridden countries, permanent reductions are nowhere on the political agenda. Christoph Hermann, in his work on the state of working hours in the age of neoliberalism, examines the struggle over and trajectory of working hours through a critical lens that draws on the French Regulation School. Focusing on the experience of North America and the leading economies of the European continent, the chapter presents a thorough analysis of changes in working time in different periods of capitalist development over the past century. Pointing to the relationship between the recent surge in working hours and the role of capitalist competition, Hermann emphasizes the political significance of the struggle for a shorter working day, as this means a struggle for the limitation of competition through working class solidarity. The author's main argument – that any progressive force confronting neoliberalism today should focus not only on shortening working time but also on competition – is quite timely in the midst of a period of high unemployment rates.

Besides the debates on the origins of and exits from the recession, one of the most controversial international topics as this book goes to print is the conflict in Syria. The Syrian Baathist regime has proved to be not immune to the demands for more democracy in the Arab world, which has come to be known as the 'Arab Spring'. The protests against the Assad regime, however, soon after assumed a different character with the involvement of foreign actors under the umbrella of the so-called 'Free Syrian Army'. The interesting characteristic of this diverse group of rebels is that it has been funded and provided logistical and military support by a number of countries in the region such as Turkey, Qatar and Saudi Arabia. The Gulf states with significant Shia minorities and their fear of increasing influence of Iran in the region have not hesitated to rally behind the rebels and to tout a regime change in Syria. However, except for their authoritarianism, oil wealth and almost unconditional support for the US presence in the region, little is known or discussed in mainstream circles about the internal processes of accumulation and class formation in these countries, and their specific integration into the global markets, i.e. the internationalization of their capitals. What is even less discussed is the quite specific role and weight of temporary migrant labour in capital accumulation in the Gulf. The growth of a migrant labour force,, which is made up of individuals who move for the purpose of work and whose right to stay in their country of destination is usually connected to an employment contract, is one of the striking characteristics of neoliberal globalization.

In a theoretically and empirically rich piece that questions the prevailing methodological nationalism that encloses class and class formation in fixed national boundaries, Adam Hanieh explores the relationship between temporary migrant labour, space and class formation in the six states of the Gulf Cooperation Council, which arguably constitute the most extreme case of temporary labour flows of any region in the global economy. Applying David Harvey's spatialization framework, Hanieh shows how the specific spatialization of class relations in the Gulf through the flows of temporary migrant labour between the region, South Asia and the rest of the Arab world has provided a special spatial fix for Gulf capitalism; this makes possible an increased appropriation of value stemming from spatial differences in the costs of the reproduction of labour power, establishing and maintaining a powerful system or means of social control and also allowing the Gulf states to displace the impact of the recent crisis.

One of the important points made by Hanieh regards the nature of generational reproduction of class in the case of temporary migrant workers and their capacity to resist and transform the prevailing social relations. Class memory and bonds of solidarity among these labourers tend to be weak and collective action is often difficult. Capitalist social relations, contrary to the expectations of Marx and Engels about 160 years ago, have not been able to transform and simplify the contradictions of the world by creating two dominant social classes with transformative capacity of their own. While capitalism is dominant and its logic has penetrated every inch of the globe today, the transformation along with the simplification of class lines it has brought about remains incomplete in vast territories of the Global South. In this process of incomplete transformation, 'precarious' work as a specific form of employment has become increasingly salient. John Saul enquires into the implications of precarious work and the "precariat" it has created for understanding the class or classes of working people in contemporary capitalism, but particularly in the Global South. In his discussion of the emergence of the precariat in Africa, he highlights the increasing ambiguity of the term 'working class' and questions its homogeneity with the rise of a large group of workers with precarious employment, co-existing with and sometimes overtaking in numbers the traditional 'working class'.

There is no doubt that Latin America has been the centre of focus for anti-neoliberal forces and analyses in the past decade or two. This should not come as a surprise given the disastrous impact of neoliberal policies since the early 1980s, particularly with the Debt Crisis and the ensuing 'Lost Decade', which generated a wave of anti-neoliberal politics across the continent. This wave managed to bring to power left-wing and/or populist governments led by charismatic leaders who, in theory or practice or both, challenged the dominance of neoliberalism and espoused alternative forms of development and social organization. This challenge, arguably, culminated with the creation of the Bolivarian Alliance for the Peoples of Our America under the leadership of Venezuela as a response to the Free Trade of the Americas proposed by the United States. With Venezuela and Bolivia -and Ecuador- at the centre of media and scholarly attention recently, mostly due to the personalities of Hugo Chavez and Evo Morales respectively, another important Latin American country that has drawn analysts as well as activists interested in post-neoliberal politics since the beginning of the new century is Argentina. After a period of military government that was devastating for organized labour, followed by the institutionalization of neoliberalism in the 1990s leading to the crisis of 2001, the reforms implemented since 2003 have been seen by many observers as a decisive move away from neoliberalism. Ruth Felder and Viviana Patroni, however, argue that it is too early to announce the end of neoliberalism based on these reforms that ended the austerity policies and led to a reduction in the unemployment rate. Nor does this period correspond to mere continuity marked by the persistence of policy and institutional arrangements coupled by patterns of wealth distribution associated with the neoliberal framework of the 1990s. The authors respond to the existing analyses by presenting a picture that is more nuanced and complex than is usually depicted. By placing the articulation between structural transformation, economic policies and the balance of forces between the two major social classes at the centre of their analysis, Felder and Patroni argue that while we can observe critical discontinuities in terms of what workers have experienced in the past two decades, there is also evidence pointing towards continuity with the 1990s. The most recent phase of Argentine development since 2003, thus, has been marked by tensions between continuity and change. One of the most important arguments made by the authors is that while the economic growth has had a positive impact on the overall employment situation, this impact has been felt differently by various sectors of the working class. The economic recovery and the change in the political framework have not been able to address effectively the fragmentation of the working class as precarious work remains to be a significant problem for the working people of the country. The authors are not optimistic about the capacity of the current political and economic paradigm to solve this pressing problem for the working class.

Among the rather pessimistic and bleak accounts of neoliberal capitalism and its most recent crisis from a working class perspective, Minqi Li's eclectic Marxian analysis stands out as a piece projecting a possibly optimistic future based on the pending economic, social and ecological crisis in the world in general, and in China, in particular. In his provocative analysis, Li, one of the leading figures in the Chinese New Left, argues that in the upcoming years the semi-periphery could become the centre of global capitalist contradictions, as the recent accumulation strategy based on the super exploitation of the labour force in the semi-periphery, exploitation of material resources, abuse and destruction of the environment as well as exports to the markets in the Global North is no longer sustainable. This unsustainable accumulation strategy will end in shrinking markets in the core, increasing working class struggle, and an increasingly grave ecological crisis. As a result, Li foresees the breakdown of capitalist regimes in the semi-periphery leading to potentially a general revolutionary crisis. In this scenario, he assigns a central place to China, which, given its economic size, its key position in the global division of labour and its role in the global ecological crisis, is likely to become the key battleground within the semi-periphery. A revolutionary revolt by the Chinese working class, according to the author, has the potential capability to challenge and destroy not only Chinese capitalism, but also the global capitalist division of labour as a whole, which could lead to a radical change in the global balance of power in favour of the working classes of the world.

Another prominent country in the semi-periphery of global capitalism that has figured often in the headlines in recent years is Turkey. Its active and controversial foreign policy and its ability to achieve economic 'stability' after three decades of economic and political tumult, including three major economic crises, have secured this country a place on the global and regional agendas as well as in scholarly analyses. Much of the work on this country has, however, failed to go past skin-deep observations or apologetic platitudes utilized to legitimate either Turkish foreign policy in the Middle East or the ongoing neoliberal economic restructuring which started in the early 1980s. As part of a global trend, this has started to change with the onset of the global capitalist crisis, which has led to a revival in critical studies focusing on the political economy of Turkey. The dominant theoretical framework in these studies has been Keynesian/institutionalist, whose main unit of analysis is the national economy. Sebnem Oguz responds to and presents a critique of this line of thinking that is dominant in critical studies of Turkish political economy. Taking an historical approach supported by rich empirical research, she argues that the Turkish state, as a key actor, has managed to 'turn the crisis into opportunity'. In contrast to the neoliberal and national/developmentalist conceptualizations of 'turning the crisis into opportunity', she uses a Marxist interpretation or understanding of it, which refers to the 'adoption or consolidation of certain capitalist and/or imperial state strategies.' In the specific case of Turkey, according to the author, this means the state addressing and putting in place the structural requirements of an accumulation strategy based on increasing orientation of Turkish capitalism toward global integration and new mechanisms of labour control. The 'neoliberal authoritarian state form' that has been developed further and utilized by the AKP government is more relevant today as it has been used not only to address the requirements of global integration of Turkish capital but also to understand the attempts to silence all forms of opposition to the AKP project, encompassing all spaces of social, economic, and political life from the parliament to the unions and universities.

Maria de Lourdes Rollemberg Mollo explores the role of financialization in the outbreak of the most recent crisis, focusing on another so-called 'emerging market', Brazil. This country has been hailed as a major economic player recently despite its relatively slow economic growth since the onset of liberalization in the late 1980s. The process of financialization that several analysts have identified as the *differentia specifica* of neoliberal capitalism is presented in this piece as the driving force of the global economy and its crisis. Embedding her analysis within a Marxist theory of capital accumulation and the relative autonomy of circulation in relation to production, de Lourdes Rolle places the development of so-called *fictitious capital* at the centre of financialization and its subsequent crisis. She argues that this term, which draws our attention to the "decoupling of profit in circulation from its creation in the process of production", provides a starting point for the theoretical analyses not only of this particular crisis but of financial crises in general. Grounded in this theoretical framework, the author lays bare the fallacy of the neoliberal orthodoxy regarding financial markets and monetary policy that exposed Brazil to the vagaries of speculative capital and rendered the country vulnerable – despite its relatively strict regulatory framework – once the subprime mortgage crisis hit the United States, leading to a contraction in liquidity around the world. She also shows clearly that counter-cyclical policies, such as poverty reduction programs and low interest rates, implemented by the second Lula government have been able to reverse the earlier neoliberal process and secure a relatively rapid recovery from the crisis. The Brazilian experience is important in terms of providing a blueprint amidst the debates on the ongoing recession to address the pressing problems of slow growth and increasing marginalization of significant segments of labouring masses both in the Global North and South.

The relationship between capitalism and food provisioning has become an increasingly important subject, as the greater commodification of food in the era of globalization has conditioned and restricted access to this basic necessity of life.

While worldwide food production has continued to increase and we are still far from exceeding the carrying capacity of the planet, access to food remains, at times, an insurmountable problem for hundreds of millions of people. The dominant discourse that has addressed this problem and defined the conditions of food provisioning in modern capitalist societies since the 1970s is 'food security'. The dominance and respectability of the concept both within civil society and the policy-making circles have been matched by the multiplicity of its definitions and the ends to which it has been put to use. Mustafa Koc, in his critique, argues that contrary to the prevalent discourse and the promises, the concept has, over the course of its evolution under neoliberalism, not only defined the conditions of food provisioning in capitalist economies but also come to legitimize social inequalities in access to the means of production as well as food. As successful as it has been in addressing some of the pressing and practical issues related to food provisioning, such as lack of availability, accessibility and effective utility of food, the discourse of 'food security' has failed utterly in analyzing, and meaningfully and radically challenging the everyday practices, structures and institutions of the current neoliberal food system that create food insecurity. Koc warns that the ongoing recession will exacerbate the food insecurity that is already being experienced by hundreds of millions, and that the 'food security' paradigm has failed to address the causes of the problems around food provisioning, which compels us to challenge the dominant capitalist social relations as the only way of getting to the root of the problem while inviting us to consider food sovereignty as an alternative and a more democratic approach that puts people before the interests of global corporations.

The last piece in this book addresses an aspect of social life under neoliberalism that, despite its significance, has not been addressed much in either the mainstream or critical literature. This aspect is the production of knowledge and the spaces in which it takes place. Situating his discussion within the broader context of the neoliberal emphasis on knowledge in the service of achieving growth and the 'knowledge economy', Eric Newstadt argues that while neoliberalism has been an utter failure in creating the desired 'knowledge commodities' or quality research in higher education, it has succeeded in increasingly commodifying 'knowledge' as well as creating the socio-economic and political conditions necessary for highly flexible labour markets, which extends to universities as sites of knowledge production. Newstadt's analysis exposes the pathologies and contradictions of a new form of thinking and its implementation in knowledge production in higher education. The neoliberal attempt to create competitive markets for educational and research commodities has definitely created new opportunities for big capital and a group of venture capitalists to secure significant amounts of profit, but, as the author powerfully argues, it has brought neither the promised economic well-being (for both the educators themselves and students) nor enlightenment, fulfillment and happiness, which should be the end-goals of education. Both students and an increasingly large segment of educators have become victims of the neoliberal higher education through felixibilization, higher tuition fees and stagnant or worsening quality of education that is assessed by dubious criteria and shaped by corporate concerns. The worrisome fact is that this process of neoliberalization of production and dissemination of knowledge is not confined to a small group of countries but extends to a much larger geography from Canada to New Zealand.

References:

Boratav, Korkut. "2012'de Dünya Ekonomisi: Metropol." *Sol Portal*, 15 January 2013. Accessed 24 January 2013. http://haber.sol.org.tr/yazarlar/korkut-boratav/2012de-dunya-ekonomisi-metropol-66181

Boratav, Korkut. "Dünya Ekonomisi 2012: Çevreden Bakışlar." *Sol Portal*, 22 January 2013. Accessed 24 January 2013. http://haber.sol.org.tr/yazarlar/korkut-boratav/dunya-ekonomisi-2012-cevreden-bakislar-66640

Ruggie, John G. 'International Regimes, Transactions, and Change: Embedded Liberalism in the Postwar Economic Order,' *International Organization* 36, no.2 (Spring 1982): 379-415.

Saad-Filho, Alfredo, 'Crisis in neoliberalism or crisis of neoliberalism?,' in *The Crisis This Time: Socialist Register 2011*, edited by Greg Albo, Vivek Chibber and Leo Panitch, 242-259. London: The Merlin Press, 2010.

Capital, Crisis and State Economic Policy: A Neoliberal Exit?

Greg Albo

Since the 1980s, students of comparative political economy have characterized 'neoliberal globalization' as a particular phase of capitalism with a unique economic policy framework. Drawing on a conception of distinctive temporalities internal to the history of capitalism, the neoliberal period is contrasted with the postwar era of national Keynesian welfare states and Fordist industrial production, and distinguished further from an earlier phase of monopoly capitalism and classical imperialism. As summarized by Andrew Glyn (2007 24-25), a postwar 'golden age' was succeeded by: "a counter-revolution in macroeconomic policy which saw tight monetary policy and fiscal austerity imposed in the name of defeating inflation. This was followed rapidly by the unwinding of much of the detailed government intervention into particular sectors and markets which had characterized the previous decades. Privatization, and the deregulation of the industries concerned, the substitution of private sector sources of supply for public sector in-house provision and the deregulation of labour markets are all aspects of this process." Neoliberal thinkers such as Martin Wolf (2004) and Jagdish Bhagwati (2004) argue that these changes were a necessary adaptation to competitive imperatives that imposed a globalised 'free market logic', anchored by liberal democratic institutions that guaranteed contracts, as the foremost means to organize economic activity.

A battery of dissenters, however, spanning from Keynesians in economics to institutionalists in sociology, have pointed to multiple 'worlds of welfare states' and 'varieties of capitalism'. In contrast to a singular path of capitalist development, the dissidents contend that political and institutional differentiation allows alternate distributional outcomes and spatial variation in the national, regional and local forms of capitalism (Esping-Anderson 1990; Hall and Soskice 2001; Coates 2005). The dissident thesis has fared rather poorly in practice, however. The models of development invoked, whether in the geographical space of the European Union (EU), North America or East Asia, have incorporated features of the neoliberal economic policy framework and pattern of growth. In political terms, social democracy has moved from political impasse in the 1980s to retreat in the 1990s under a 'third way' programme. The market precepts of neoliberalism became part of the policy platforms and governmental practices of social democracy. With further financialization, internationalization of capital and geopolitical relations after 2001 reinforcing market imperatives, neoliberalism became systematically internalized into the apparatuses of the state and economic policy across world capitalism. It became hard not to tout these alternate development models as so many 'varieties of neoliberalism', particularly as social democratic parties became defenders of austerity in 'common fronts' with the centre-right (Albo 2005). Alternative policy frameworks, not to speak of alternatives to capitalism, moved to the margins of public discourse.

The economic crisis that erupted in the core capitalist economies in 2008 is, however, re-invigorating theoretical and political debate about neoliberalism and its contradictions. Serious questions about capitalism as a whole are even being raised by some of its foremost defenders (*Financial Times* 2012). Back on the research agenda are a series of concerns about the limits of capitalism: the competitive imperatives and dynamic processes which form financial instability and economic crisis; the particular ways neoliberalism has been institutionalized in national and local economies and in particular production systems; the nature, form and modes of state economic policy attempting to construct an exit from the crisis; and the political movements that might fuse into a viable anti-neoliberal alternative.

The depth, duration and complexity of the crisis make it impossible to draw anything resembling a definitive balance-sheet on these debates. Like the crisis itself, these contentions are irresolvable at this point. Many of the post-Keynesian theorists on the Left immediately declared the end of the neoliberal phase of capitalism and an opening for a state-led progressive economic policy. This has proven to be a premature, if not wholly misguided, judgement. The discredit of neoliberalism as an ideological framework has not marginalized it as a guide to state economic policy for a new 'age of austerity'. The neoliberal state is now, paradoxically, the central terrain – and strategic agency – in the struggle over 'permanent austerity' and an exit from the crisis.

There is little comfort to be taken from all this for more radical agendas. Resolutely anti-capitalist movements and programmes, informed by Marxism, have fared no better, and often worse, in shifting the balance of social forces and horizons of economic and democratic possibilities. Even as the fifth year of the economic crisis ends, it is too early to draw a close to the neoliberal phase of capitalism. Additional perspective on the capitalist state and economic policy in contemporary capitalism is required, then, before we return to the question of exits from the current crisis.

Capitalist States and the World Market

In institutionalist analyses of the current economic crisis, it is suggested that neoliberal policies have caused a mismatch between national economic regulation and the internationalization of capital. The policies of austerity being advocated by the global financial institutions and most governments, they argue, compound these problems. The challenge for a 'progressive' exit from the crisis is to build new regulatory mechanisms, from the local to the global scales, to re-embed capital in new institutions of governance. The suppression of finance would, in turn, re-establish the institutional foundations for Keynesian expansionary policies. For this project, the crisis is a 'battle of ideas' over the perfectibility of markets and the scale, scope and capabilities of liberal democratic states (Krugman 2012). If the appropriate policy matrix can be re-asserted, a variety of democratic capitalisms can re-emerge, with the state providing a forum for advancing a general 'societal interest' without discarding the efficiencies and freedoms that capitalist markets provide.

There is any number of theoretical and political objections to this assessment. Not least is the stance that an anti-neoliberal project is essentially a technical one of replacing bad policies with good ones (a point returned to in the conclusion). Here it is necessary to raise a number of alternate conceptual points on capitalist states in the world market. This will help situate the *political* foundations for the economic policies of neoliberal austerity.

For one, in its very origins capitalism is constituted within a world market with distinct interacting political divisions based on claims of sovereignty and territory forming modern states, whether they emerge out of absolutist monarchies, emergent parliamentary states or tributary state empires. In the *Grundrisse*, Marx (1973) notes that,

> ...while capital must on one side strive to tear down every spatial barrier to intercourse, i.e. to exchange, and conquer the whole earth for its market, it strives on the other side to annihilate this space with time...The result is: the tendentially and potentially general development of the forces of production...as a basis; likewise, the universality of intercourse, hence the world market as a basis. (539,542)

This is a unique proposition to Marxian analysis: the accumulation of capital is at once an intensification and internationalization of both labour processes and capitalist social relations. Particular places of production – as both class relations and state forms – are always implicated in a wider set of social relations, exchange flows and competitive imperatives constituted within a world market.

This conceptualization, positing seeming oppositions as part of a single process of capital accumulation, is the basis for Marx's aphorism that "the tendency to create the world market is directly given in the concept of capital itself" (ibid., 408). David Harvey (1982) has pointed out that the tendency to capital expansion across the space of the market bears a fundamental contradiction. The expanded reproduction of capital must attain a 'materialization' and 'coherence' in time and space if capital is to be produced and valorised; but the circulation of capital across time is continually transforming space by shifting production processes, 'condensing' distances from new transportation and communication methods and ceaselessly seeking out new markets. The valorization and devalorization of fixed capital complexes and social relations are constant as productive capacities, exchange relations and competitive positions evolve.

The capitalist state is thus constituted as, on the one hand, a historically-specific, geographically-situated institutionalization of class relations; and, on the other, as mediator of the wider set of relations of differentiated accumulation established by the world market. This is the sense that the state, for Marx (1970, 80), is "the form of organization which the bourgeois necessarily adopt for internal and external purposes, for the mutual guarantee of their property and interests." But if the state is central to establishing the framework of property relations for the reproduction of capital, the valorisation, devaluation and internationalisation of capital also draw the state into more concrete interventions. The effects of crisis on capital devaluation or credit relations, for example, are partly displaced into the sphere of politics. As a result, the state necessarily defends the interests of capital that has been invested in its territorial domain so that these capitals, and their attendant social relations, can be valorised. The state does so not to secure an enclosed 'national space', but to safeguard particular capitalist interests whose home base forms within its territorial space in both their local and global dimensions. In Marxian analysis, the competitive imperatives that tend to equalisation of profits and wage rates and the internationalisation of capital in the world market also constitute a differentiated network of concrete labour processes, wage grids, competing capitals and hierarchically organized states.

The world market imperatives that form within capitalist social relations do so across all scales of human activity and governance, and simultaneously constrain and develop states and their administrative capacities to support accumulation. In trying to understand the dynamics of the classical age of imperialism, Nikolai Bukharin (1972, 25-6, 80) suggested that the "world economy as a system of production relations and, correspondingly of exchange relations on a world scale" produced not one but two tendencies forming imperialism. As he put it, "together with ... the internationalisation of capital, there is going on a process of 'national' intertwining of capital, a process of 'nationalising' capital." Bukharin's notion of the 'nationalising' of capital has multiple implications for what occurs as capital accumulates: there is a territorial deepening of capitalist labour processes in particular places even as capital simultaneously internationalizes; and this intensification of markets occurs through a process of 'state-building' of the functions and roles of capitalist states. Bukharin's thesis effectively extended Marx's intuition that capitalist states materialized on a national basis are crucial mediators between local and globalized markets. Indeed, the internationalization of capital is entwined with the particular institutionalization of capitalist states. The state apparatuses and policy capacities are being continually re-organized according to different phases in the world market to support – and attract – internationalizing capitals. The contradiction between the spatial materialization of labor processes and states and the fluidity of international exchange flows takes a more concrete form in the contradiction between competitive rivalry and interdependence between the hierarchically ordered states (the 'imperialist chain') of the world market. This is why neoliberal and institutionalist understandings of states as external to markets, from opposite vantage points, are so fundamentally flawed: capitalist competition does not occur against or apart from states, but through states.

The differentiation of capitalism into a multiple system of territorial states has a second important implication for the way capitalist states and economies are conceived. Institutional and political differentiation arises directly from the specificity of the class relation and labour processes necessary for the production of value. But these places of production are immediately integrated into a wider social system from the very strategies that both capitalists undertake to expand their scale of action and the circulation of capital. Capitalists thereby create encompassing social structures – in conflict with workers – that are not reducible to their individual social actions or the institutions and resources they command, or to the strategies of class struggle they engage. These structures take the forms of the law of value, the dependence of workers on the market for their self-reproduction as a class and as individuals and the imperatives of endless capital accumulation. The state is indispensible to all these processes. As Ellen Wood (2005: 24-5) comments:

> ..... capitalism has never been able to dispense with territorial states... Capitalist appropriation still requires the support of extra-economic coercion, and a state operating at arm's length is still required to supply the administrative order and the ultimate coercive forces that capital needs but lacks... Capitalism also depends on extra-economic practices and institutions to compensate for its own disruptive tendencies.

The specific institutional autonomy of the state, with the concentration of legitimate and armed power at the national scale, separates it from the direct control of the relations of exploitation of capitalist labour processes (although the state presence is still found in all kinds of legal and political forms). This does not mean that the capitalist state takes a 'neutral' stance toward the class divisions of civil society. Rather, whether in parliamentary-democratic or exceptional forms of the capitalist state, the mechanisms of rule, deliberative bodies, organization of state apparatuses, branches and agencies, and policy matrixes are specifically de-limited in their content and functional role in reproducing capitalist social relations. More specifically, capitalist states are subordinated to the rule of money and the rule of law as embedded in constitutional states within an international state system (Clarke 1988). As such, capitalist states always assign some of their functions and administrative mechanisms to different governance scales, from the global to the local.

But the indispensible nodal role of the national state in organizing capitalist social relations, and in unifying and advancing the political interests of domestic capitalist classes (with their complex political divisions), cannot be marginalized. Indeed, as capitalism evolves and becomes increasingly complex in its social and organizational relations, both integration (a tendency to convergence) and differentiation (a tendency to divergence) can be expected to increase: as capitalist social relations become more generalized and the mass of capital to be valorised accumulates, the actions of social agents will tend to be progressively structured by market imperatives. The increasing complexity of socio-economic processes will also mean that social agents are organized into evermore differentiated workplaces, territories and state systems. As capitalist development forms 'national models of capitalism', with the escalating imperatives of the law of value in the world market, capital accumulation will have a tendency to become ever more dependent on the extra-economic coercive and coordinative capacities of states.

This raises a third point in Marxian theory: the national form of the capitalist state contains a series of inherent contradictions in relation to its role in economic regulation. The production of value, for example, is dependent upon the local particularity of labour processes and working classes. These 'internal relations' always overdetermine class struggles. The accumulation and realization of new value, however, is within a world market. These 'external relations' are always a critical determination of the character of local and national capitalist classes, the structure of the power bloc and the form of the state as they are located in a particular phase of capitalism and place in the international hierarchy of states. This is to insist that states, in their function of organizing the capitalist class and disorganizing the subordinate classes, are necessarily involved in enhancing the domestic accumulation of capital to secure its revenue, while at the same time facilitating the insertion of domestic capital into international circuits of capital.

The contradiction can be stated another way with respect to crises. Crises are always situated, at the most abstract level, between the localized production of value in specific relations of exploitation *within the limits of profitability*, and the global circulation and accumulation of capital *without limit*. Individual capitalist states are charged with managing the class struggles enflamed by the crisis while also attempting to find an exit from it. This often entails, on the one hand, an attempt to spatially displace the crisis internationally via the unequal relations of the inter-state system; and, on the other, an effort to politically displace the crisis nationally onto the state, different regions and the working classes via the unequal relations between the dominant and popular classes. This is what gives class struggles a contradictory character in their scalar dimensions: unavoidably formed in the localized spaces of value production and organized class capacities that are always implicated in a series of internationalized value flows and political relations; but ultimately settled within the national form of the state where political power is concentrated, legitimated and relations to the world market mediated.

A fourth theme is how the contradiction between the internationality of capital accumulation and the nationality of the state system is manifested in the uneven development of the world market. If the competitive imperatives to accumulate by 'capital as a whole' implies the circulation of commodities in the world market, the transformations within and between places of production are a consequence of competition between 'many capitals'. This forms the material basis for interdependency, through the different moments in the circuit of capital, and competitive rivalry, over the share of the economic space in the world market, between states. But from the outset, the inter-state system is marked by inequality and uneven development. The international circulation of capital, for example, 'dissolves' pre-capitalist societies and leads to differentiated forms of colonialism, varying in their forms of coercion and settlement but integrated into a world market increasingly governed by capitalist imperatives (Ahmad 2001). Marx looked at this process as the 'historical mission of the bourgeoisie'. What unfolds, however, is that "a new and international division of labour, a division suited to the requirements of the chief centres of modern industry springs up, and converts one part of the globe into a chiefly agricultural field of production, for supplying the other part which remains a chiefly industrial field" (1967, 451). Moreover, 'unequal exchange' within this global division labour tends to accentuate geographical differentiation as trade between countries of different productivities of labour and compositions of capital entails transfers of value, surplus profits and labour-power to core countries.

Uneven development is, therefore, a core feature of the capitalist world market. But this does not mean it takes the same historical form. The primacy of 'internal relations' – modes of extracting value, modes of capital accumulation, state forms – mean that the phases of capitalist development will produce a varying configuration of value flows and relations between states. The tendencies to intensification, concentration and centralisation of capital, for example, all increase the scale of operations, the technical division of labour and the territorial complexity of capitalist firms. Multinational corporations will still have a 'home' base in that the dominant agents who possess and allocate these assets have a specific location. They also become important agents of accumulation in the places they invest in. This inter-penetration of capitals does not lessen international competition, although its form changes as each place of production must compete for funds internally allocated by firms. Individual states, moreover, gain an interest in protecting and attracting fixed capital investments while advancing an interest in inter-state co-ordination to sustain the international circulation of capital. In such a market configuration, Nicos Poulantzas (1975) argued that foreign capital should not be thought of as an 'external' imposition on an integral 'national bourgeoisie' organizing a national economic space for itself. Rather, foreign capital becomes aligned with domestic capital in forming an 'internal bourgeoisie' within the power bloc with also a stake in the internationization of capital. The state actively reproduces – ideologically, politically and through competitive supports – both domestic and foreign capital.

This theoretical point bears further emphasis. The contradiction between competitive rivalry and interdependence is integral to the international circulation of capital. This means inherent in inter-state relations is a contradiction between conflict and cooperation. This can be characterized as an uneven interdependence between states in the world market. To the extent that the circuits of capital in states are internationalised, and thus dependent on the world market for their self-expansion and realisation, the spatial displacement brought on by an economic crisis will become a point of both conflict and coordination in inter-imperial relations. It will also appear in the governance and administration of the economic policy functions that have been allocated to international state apparatuses (such as the European Union or the International Monetary Fund). It is thoroughly economistic reasoning to expect that crises will necessarily spill over into imperial rivalry in the sense of a rupture in inter-state coordination and over political leadership of the imperialist bloc. This is contingent on the international correlation of forces, alternate strategies being available and political relations becoming militarized.

This raises a further, fifth, theme with respect to the organization of capitalist states in the world market. The relationship between the 'national' state economic apparatus and the 'national economy' is riddled with contradictions. The internationality that is at the core of the capital relation means there is no simple direct correspondance between a 'national bourgeosie', a national economy and a material interest singularly focused on protecting the domestic market. Foreign (and imperialist) capital may be completely internalized within the national economic space, and thus become a key component of the alliances of the power bloc. This 'intertwining of national capitals' occurs, if unevenly, across the chain of states in the inter-state system. The political basis for and organized national bourgeosie narrowly focused on the national state is squeezed in two directions:

from foreign capital establishing labour processes and value chains in the national economic space; and from domestic capital's internationalizing its circuits of capital. This does not mean that the domestic capitalist class has no national basis or concerns. It is to stress, however, that these classes and their allies form a material interest in sustaining the international flows of capital in all its forms. Given the hierachies of the inter-state system, dominant states enforcing policies of 'structural adjustment' and debt payments will have a basis of support from the internal bourgeosies of weaker states. The latter will seek out the international protection of private property, support for increasing the exploitation of the popular classes and the preservation of their own positions in international capital circuits. And the internal bourgeoisie will express much less strategic sympathy for Keynesian reflation (especially as expected by institutionalist economic theory), national industrial policies and the like that prioritize national, community and social needs.

The internationalisation of capital, therefore, fundamentally alters the social form and organisation of the state. The economic policy apparatuses will become increasingly dominated by those branches supporting the internationalisation of capital, particularly to ensure the stability of the currency and its position and access to the international circulation of 'world money'. Indeed, the entire state will tend to be conditioned by international competition, what Leo Panitch (1994) has referred to as the internalisation and mediation of international accumulation by the state. The capacities of each state to mediate international competition will be determined by its administrative and diplomatic capacities, its place in the imperialist chain and internal class relations.

The regulatory mechanisms and forms of state economic intervention do not transform the fundamental tendencies of capitalism. But they do constrain and modify these tendencies making them always complex in their historical patterns. This is partly what makes each crisis of capitalism historically unique in its formation, trajectory and resolution. The real barriers to capital accumulation are not abstract laws but historically situated class struggles over the labour process, state power and insertion into the world market. This is why it is necessary to insist that crises, whether global or local in their scale, are always settled on the terrain of the state.

State Economic Policy and Crisis

The economic policy debate today in the central capitalist states continues to be dominated by a division between neoliberals and institutionalists (or Keynesians). This is, in essence, a dispute over the miscalculations of governments based on limited knowledge and the salutary disciplines of markets, as opposed to the policy and learning capacities of states and the tendencies to instability of financial markets. It divides further into market-led or state-guided policy strategies for building capitalism, with a range of more specific approaches polarized around the two. They share, however, a common ontological departure in conceptualizing markets and states as enclosed entities each external to the other. In this, an external state acts as a subject, via a global economic policy unifying various economic apparatuses, branches and agencies, on the economy as a specific object-process. For neoliberals, state intervention produces inefficiencies and decline, as the concentrated knowledge of states can never match the decentralized decisions of agents in markets; while for institutionalists, the state has the potential, given the right policy mix, to provide the extra-market governance necessary to stabilize systemic market failures.

These themes can, at one level, be dismissed out of hand as particular ideological defences of capitalism. But they emerge from the fact that state economic policy in capitalism has its own institutional specificity, appearance of 'technical neutrality' and, hence, national characteristics. As such, the state plays a formative role in the reproduction of capital as an integral aspect of the economy in providing both the necessary political conditions and a range of direct supports to accumulation. This does not mean that the state 'controls' the capitalist economy as it is institutionally autonomous from the relations of exploitation. The powers of surplus extraction and allocation rest with the capitalist classes subject to the market imperatives encased in the law of value. State economic policy is, however, critical to managing the valorization-devalorization of capital, helping form and convert capitalist class strategies into state economic practices (Poulantzas 1978; Jessop 1985, ch. 4)

The institutional matrix and form of state economic policy continually adapts, therefore, to the balance of class forces and changing national and local patterns of capital accumulation. This is why there can be no 'essence' to national models of capitalism embedded in state economic policy as posited, for instance, by the 'varieties of capitalism' thesis. Similarly, it is not possible to define a single institutionalization of a form of economic policy, whether that is Keynesian budgetary policy or neoliberal inflation targeting, across a specific phase of capitalism. State economic policy is constantly adapting its modes and rules to the minor crises and class struggles inherent in capitalism. Major crises, moreover, may represent critical turning points in the form, fields and modalities of state economic intervention. Major crises represent moments when explicit political decisions need to be made in facilitating capital restructuring and forging the political compromises, and exercise of state coercion as needed, to find an 'exit' to the crisis and a new foundation for expanded accumulation. The particular institutional separation of the politics from the economy characteristic of capitalist societies does not mean that political power is not integral to the economic relations of capitalism. As de Brunhoff (1976, 5) notes, "Capital always requires the existence of a state power."

It is the historical and spatial differentiation of state economic intervention that is, then, of analytical interest. State intervention takes the social form of 'economic policy'. That is, the mediation of the accumulation of capital via economic policies managing: the money form and interest rates adjudicating the inter-temporal and inter-sectoral allocation of money; taxation and subsidies regulating the stocks and flows of investment; the production and reproduction of labour-power; the ecological and energy pre-conditions for production; and so forth. The essential function of 'economic policy' is supervising and disciplining social relations for the expanded reproduction of capital. But the precise institutional and policy form this takes varies across space and time; and it entails intervention across the entire circuit of capital, from the local conditions of value production to the international circulation of capital (Poulantzas 1978, 191).

In theoretical dispute, state economic policy has several definitions. In classic political economy, from Adam Smith to J.S. Mill, economic policy is implicitly interpreted as simply the summation of the areas where the state intervenes in the economy. But as with the theoretical core of classical political economy, this generalizes state economic policy across history and does not help us understand the specifically capitalist form of economic policy, its historical social forms of state intervention or its shifting modalities (Clarke 1988). This is necessary to situate some of the predominant capitalist economic policy frameworks adopted by states.

Institutionalist theory, for example, embraces Keynesian economic policy and adopts an instrumental conception of economic policy consistent with its view of a rational managerial state socially external to the economy. This was given its initial formulation by Jan Tinbergen (1964, v and 3; 1966), in many ways the founder of modern economic policy, as follows: "...we define policy as the action taken by government in pursuit of certain goals... All these goals have, in varying degrees, an economic aspect. Economic policy is the economic aspect of overall governmental policy: it consists of deliberate government intervention in economic affairs in order to realise certain goals." Neoliberals, in contrast, take their lead from Hayek and define economic policy normatively with reference to the state guarantee of private contracts and market exchange through a rules-based governance system (Tanzi 2011; World Bank 1997). These are generalized definitions of economic policy that can be equally applied to capitalist and non-capitalist modes of production.

The state economic policy specific to capitalism can be delineated, first, in the abstract sense, as the political role of state economic intervention in the reproduction of capital governed by the primacy of fields of the management of the money-form and labour-power (de Brunhoff 1976, 7). In more concrete terms, economic policy is the social form of intervention to manage the valorization of capital in its money, productive and commodity forms over the economic cycle and the availability of labour-power, in terms of skills and labour reserves, for exploitation. The historical forms of state economic policy also have complex determinations in their guiding ideological framework, the fields and matrix of policy practices, and the regulatory modes and rules for intervention.

The particular fields and practices of state economic policy are always distinct. This leaves a degree of policy incoherence across the branches of the state given their particular objects and correlated material interests. Political struggles and market imperatives ensure a certain degree of 'disunity' in economic policy. But global economic policy directed by the dominant central state apparatuses attempts to provide some strategic unity across the array of departments, agencies, corporations, commissions and so forth that constitute economic policy as a whole. This is the importance of the economic discourses and theoretical concepts provided by, for example, monetarism, Keynesianism, post-Keynesianism and so forth. These discourses suggest quite distinct forms of co-ordination, organizations of state apparatuses and modalities and rules for state intervention. It is the concentration of political power in these central economic apparatuses, which always reside at the apex of power in capitalist states, which deploys and modifies these discourses to organize ideologically a framework for state intervention. In particular, the central economic apparatuses work out the political strategies and compromises that define the economic policy for 'exit strategies' from economic crises.

Neoliberal economic policy, for example, does not mean that the state withdraws from intervention in the market and supplying the political supports for the relations of exploitation of capitalism. But it does mean that neoliberalism emerges out of specific class struggles, adopts particular discursive interpellations as a key moment in the construction of ideological hegemony, and deploys distinctive policy modalities (de Brunhoff 1976, 95-6; Clarke 1988, ch. 11; Peck 2010, ch. 3).

Economic policy is always characterized, then, by a particular institutional autonomy, policy capacities and 'national' characteristics. National states are always integral to the accumulation and internationalization of capital, but are never reducible to the law of value. This can be put another way. If crises recur as a consequence of the market imperatives of capitalism to increase capital investments beyond their capacity to be valorized, the resolution of crises never resides in a self-contained autonomous process of capital devalorisation. This can only occur via a restructuring of class relations, the destruction of 'fictitious capital' formed in credit markets, the centralization, concentration and intensification of capital and the re-organization of value chains. This cannot occur apart from state economic policy – and the class struggles over that policy – to restore the disciplinary conditions necessary for the production of value. This includes facilitating the devaluation of unproductive capitals and re-establishing the money-form so it can function as means of consumption and measure of value.

This contradiction between the necessity of state intervention to support accumulation and its institutional externality becomes more important through time from the tendency to the socialization of capital as fixed capital grows in its complexity and its needs for extra-market supports. Indeed, the technical composition or mass of the dominant capitals and the extra-market support needed to co-ordinate capital investments will, in good part, be an indirect index of state intervention. The accumulation of capital renders national and local state economic intervention in the management of crises more crucial, as well as inter-state coordination due to the internationalization and inter-penetration of capitals. This involves crucial political struggles over the displacement of the crisis into the future through the public sector and spatially across the inter-state system. The law of value becomes a crucial mechanism forming the uneven development of the inter-state system as peripheral states unequally bear the consequence of the crisis (Burnham 2011).

The restructuring of state apparatuses, as well as the scalar allocation of functions, is integral to the political compromises and administrative techniques integral to resolving the crisis. But even as crises become more general and encompassing in their dynamics and logic across the world market, the particularities of national forms of economic policy become accentuated. There are a few mechanisms in the re-organization of the fields and modalities of state economic policy to note in general. But it is necessary to avoid invoking these mechanisms in all cases as the very nature of the political settlement of crises on the terrain of the state makes all cases individual and unique.

Specialized economic apparatuses of the state, for example, often become a crucial institutional terrain. The central contradictions of the crisis in their political form are materially condensed here and strategic responses to the crisis negotiated apart from the day-to-day state intervention of the main economic ministries such as the treasury and the central banks. These special apparatuses allow "the creation of uniform networks operating across the boundaries" of individual departments and apparatuses (Poulantzas 1978, 170-1). In the midst of an economic crisis, specialized state economic bodies permit more direct involvement of key representatives of the power bloc in the "accumulation-reproduction process of capital...least subject to conjunctural habits of government policy (ibid., 171)."

Second, the state economic apparatuses charged with securing the money-form will gain in primacy over other apparatuses. Above all, treasuries and central banks will tend to gain bureaucratic insulation from legislative branches of the state and massive operational latitude to facilitate the 'displacement' of the crisis from its source in the sphere of accumulation. In particular, the necessary destruction of fictitious capital in the form of credits that cannot be met shifts from a private relationship between banks and debtors to a relation between the state and private banks. This always entails a politically negotiated socialization and destruction of fictitious capital through the operations of state economic policy.

Third, the political supervision of specialized economic commissions and central economic ministries, the various industry branches of the state, which cover the entire spectrum of economic output, will follow a pattern of 'structural selectivity'. According to political negotiated 'economic criteria', they will force industry consolidation of ownership of productive assets, the rationalization of the technical composition of capital, and further the internationalization of the circuits of capital.

Fourth, the array of state apparatuses governing the regulation of labour-power will be mobilized to facilitate new economic conditions for exploitation and the extraction of value (Hanieh 2013). This re-organization of state labour policies can take contradictory form given the increasing complexity of the social and technical divisions of labour. The crisis raises this contradiction to a new level. On the one hand, labour policies will adopt new modalities to instrumentalize and flexibilize labour market, training, education and welfare policies to facilitate restructuring of workplaces; and, on the other, labour policies may have to make political concessions to contain class struggles over the economic policy being adopted for exit out of the crisis.

The resolution of economic crises, therefore, concentrates power in the centres of the state. The crisis cannot be resolved internally to some self-enclosed and self-regulating 'economy'. The state is central, for example, to efforts to re-establish the legitimacy and hegemony of the leading fractions of the power bloc. The internal organization of the state must also adjust to the new dynamics of class struggle as articulated into the state. The state economic policy managing the valorisation-devalorisation of capitalist social relations is an intensely political process. It needs to be presented as 'technical', whether it is neoliberal or Keynesian, and beyond politics and social struggle. The struggle over state economic policy is crucial to the course of the crisis. If economic policy is successfully 'depoliticized' there is no necessary transmission of the economic crisis into a crisis of the political regime, not to speak of a crisis of the state or of world order (Jessop 1985, 89; Poulantzas 1978, 184). Even major crises can be politically de-limited if working class organization fails to consolidate and form an independent political strategy. The most debilitating political contention of the Left is to see in every crisis the seeds of the transition to socialism, rather than undertake a sober assessment of the balance of forces.

Reconstructing Neoliberalism

The course of the economic crisis that has unfolded since 2008 has lent itself to a great deal of confusion in understanding state economic policy. Even in many Marxist accounts, the most common interpretation has been to suggest that the state rediscovered state power and Keynesian policies as part of the rescue strategies to control market instabilities after the financial collapse. But now the state is seen to be regressing and again losing power as neoliberal strategies of austerity are adopted due to the imperatives being imposed by financial markets. This analysis is quite misleading. It leaves the impression that fiscal austerity represents a weakening of the state relative to market actors. And it implies that current political struggles need to be oriented toward re-establishing a 'strong state' to sustain the stimulus measures and to ensure that a regulatory regime to 'repress' finance is adopted.

Such arguments profoundly misread the political conjuncture and the tactics being deployed to reconstruct the neoliberal state and stabilize the power bloc, with the dominant role of finance capital within the bloc. The state is not the subject of economic policy. State intervention cannot be gauged by the level of expenditures or size of fiscal deficit. These are by no means direct indices of the capacity for state intervention into the economy. Such measures tell us nothing about the form the interventions take, the kinds of class strategies being advanced, and what alternate strategies must confront. The politics of the cuts needs to be assessed, not in the crude terms of more state or more market, but with respect to the social forms of state power and market disciplines, their political viability and class strategies (O'Connor 1973; Gough 1979).

Current state economic policy needs to be scrutinized for multiple ways it is consolidating exit strategies for the current crisis. It is necessary to first point out that, in both the initial rescue and now the exit strategies, economic policy has been foremost designed to stabilize and sustain a privately controlled, liberalized financial system. This has been the crucial parameter for state policy. From the outset, it has required that banks be insulated from paying for the crisis, irrespective of how much 'moral hazard' this causes or the benefits the financial sector directly received through the rescue strategies. It is inconceivable that the massive volume of fictitious capital that the financial sector generated could be absorbed within the financial system once a crisis emerged. This always meant 'displacing' the crisis into the public sector in one form or another to destroy its 'value'. This has occurred through a number of mechanisms that increased the power of the financial branches of the state and giving them larger operational mandates with limited parliamentary scrutiny. These administrative modes include: shifting the bad loans onto the balance sheets of central banks; temporary nationalizations of banks and that will then 'strand' bad debt in the public sector when privatized; absorbing the bad debt directly into the public accounts; and providing various public supports to improve bank balance sheets. The nationalizing and then collectivizing the banking system has, of course, been ruled out of bounds of acceptable policy options, even if this has both popular appeal and strong theoretical backing (Buiter 2009). As in past financial crisis, the crucial question has turned around 'distributional conflicts': the 'haircut' that the financial sector would take for the bad loans and the new taxes they might face; the distribution of the debt burden within the public sector in terms of how public sector funds would be raised between taxes and long-term bond floatation (held by either central banks, public pension funds or bond markets); and the allocation of cuts between state activities (Reinhart and Rogoff 2009; Wolff 2010).

Given the still precarious state of the recovery at the end of 2012, the balance sheets of banks are only slowly improving, and 'stress tests' still suggest a great deal of weakness. Market disciplines in the financial sector are, therefore, only slowly being re-imposed. Many of the emergency state measures for the financial sector have remained in place, with the astonishingly low interest rates for borrowing from central banks and the associated loose monetary policy being the most visible. This has shaped a crucial component of the general exit strategy of avoiding the imposition of any *systematic* restructuring and writedowns of government loan obligations to private banks even over debts dumped into the state sector. The financial sector is seen as simply not able to accommodate this. Whatever 'haircuts' may be negotiated with the financial sector, particularly for the more desperate cases of sovereign default risk, this is not a general policy orientation for the capitalist core as a whole (Roubini and Mihm 2010, ch. 7: IMF 2012).

Yet, even while money markets have been slow to re-establish their full liquidity and depth, the core states have been moving to re-assert the primacy of financial disciplines over government finances (Nersisyan and Wray 2010). The specific state policy mechanism to do so is to require a return to government bond markets, and a withdrawal of relying on credit supplied by central banks. How governments fund their deficits is an administrative decision that has important consequences. It bears briefly spelling out, as it is also the means by which the financial markets re-establish their disciplines over government finances. The financial sector solvency crisis is, first, transferred into the finances of the public sector, from the bailout of the financial system and the drop in state revenues and expansion of expenditures. In other words, public deficits replace private ones. Governments can fund their deficits via the private banking system or their own central banks, and in responding to an emergency economic crisis, the government will turn to the central bank. But as the financial crisis eases, neoliberal banking precepts and concerns for inflation require the placing of government bonds in the financial system. This also serves as another measure to provide the financial system with stable returns and liquidity; but the increase in public debt also raises, for private bankers, the concern for sovereign debt default. In other words, the bailed-out financial sector lenders now demand guarantees that their sovereign loans will be repaid with reasonable returns. The higher returns demanded by the financial system, in turn, amplify the public sector deficit. And if these become too large, a public sector crisis explodes onto the political scene. Private investors start demanding austerity, particularly if increasing government revenues through taxes is blocked. Thus the administrative decision to alter the mechanisms to fund public deficits is also a means to re-establish the political authority of financial capital and its disciplines over public finances.

It is a complete nonsense, then, to see the public sector crisis as caused by a fiscal 'weakening' of the state – a state living beyond its means (in the terms the neoliberals have been invoking). It is the product of a particular ruling class strategy to impose austerity on the working classes and the public sector to pay for the financial crisis. It arises from the reassertion of the financial and market disciplines of neoliberalism. In contrast to every day perceptions, the exit strategies represent a more radical interventionist economic policy on the part of capitalist states – certainly more so than post-war Keynesianism, and even the rescue strategies – to try to restore 'market regulation' (Albo, Gindin and Panitch 2010). And they attempt to reproduce, more generally, the political relations that have constituted capitalist states in the period of neoliberalism (Oguz 2013).

The attempt to return to neoliberal financial disciplines is re-asserting a further distributional dynamic that is framing the exits to austerity. The payment of debt is partly to come out of tax revenues from growth resulting from the driving up of exports over imports via attacking the wage and regulatory components of unit labour costs. It is also to occur from a net transfer from the state sector, drawn from income support programmes, the incomes of public employees and public asset sales, to the capitalist sector through debt and interest payments, in the context of an overall decline in the level of government expenditures. The consequences of this fiscal strategy is quite transparent: the working classes, directly through wage repression to boost international competitiveness, and indirectly through tax increases and public sector cuts, should pay for the crisis and for the restoration of the economic viability of capitalist control over the financial system.

This logic is embedded in the concrete forms that fiscal strategies for the state sector are taking. In aggregate, the neoliberal 'golden rules' for limits on government borrowing over the business cycle are being re-stated as the overarching budgetary guideline. In practice, this translates into deficit and debt targets in the transition to austerity. Following positions already emerging in the EU and from IMF advisories, the Toronto G20 communiqué forwarded targets (with some variations for different countries and zones) of cutting budgetary deficits by half by 2013, and phasing in reduction of gross debt as a percent of GDP by 2016 (G20 2010, 3). This fiscal strategy has continued to frame the economic policy of the core states despite continued stagnation (IMF 2012). In terms of taxation, the exit strategies are consistent with core neoliberal positions: an emphasis on shifting the burden of taxes away from capital toward workers, with the weight of tax increases skewed toward VAT taxes; only modest efforts at financial taxes (largely limited to Europe, and as very muted versions of the varied calls for a 'Robin Hood tax'); and often include proposals for further corporate tax cuts. The austerity exits nowhere advance anything like a systematic 'crisis tax' levied on the capitalist sector or on high income groups.

A re-organizing of state apparatuses is also evident in the strengthening of neoliberal administrative modes and the primacy given to 'cuts' across all branches of the state. This is to establish fiscal control at the apex of the state, where it can be controlled by the core of the political and administrative executive (where political and policy control is also being concentrated, apart from elected deputies and full cabinet). Fiscal control is often taking the form of a 'specialized administrative apparatus' such as the British 'Office for Budget Responsibility', to oversee the cuts, with special sanctions enforced by the state executive and a capacity to probe departmental budgets (Burke 2010). Such bodies bear some resemblance to the review boards and commissions set up in the first phase of neoliberalism at the end of the1970s and into the 1980s (CSE 1979; Savoie 1994). But not only are the current cuts more severe, there are some important administrative differences. The new fiscal control apparatuses are being given greater powers over departments; tend to be more insulated from parliamentary oversight; have greater freedom to by-pass public sector unions and challenge collective agreements; and are mandated to explore asset sales, commercialization and other modes of administration of policies. They reflect a general 'hardening of the state' over the course of the crisis, and a further distancing of state administration from parliamentary accountability – both being consistent features of neoliberalism.

Within the enhanced capacities for fiscal control by the senior executive of the state, a number of characteristic neoliberal administrative norms are being restated. The bulk of deficit reduction is to come from expenditure cuts as opposed to tax increases; public sector wage freezes or cuts are to be directly legislated if concessions cannot be negotiated; government employment levels are to be lowered via layoffs, contracting-out, flexibilizing the labour process and even mass off-shoring of work; pension plans for public employees are to be constrained; and cuts are to be implemented such that the branches of the state supporting welfare, public education and cultural activities are disproportionately rolled-back, departments facilitating accumulation are marginally hit, and the coercive apparatuses largely maintain their budgets (police, prisons and security in particular, although shifts in military budgets due to the ramped up spending from the Middle East wars are likely to suffer) (KPMG International 2009; Hermann and Flecker 2011; Peters and Pierre 2004).

In summary, the exit strategies impose a punitive austerity of wage repression and public sector cuts within an increasingly authoritarian neoliberalism. It is the working classes that bear the cost of the financial crisis and the burden of adjustment in the recovery. It is financial capital, and the capitalist sector as a whole, that is to be the beneficiary. The Toronto G20 communiqué of 2010 boasted that "[w]hile the global economic crisis led to the sharpest decline of trade in more than seventy years, G20 countries chose to keep markets open to the opportunities that trade and investment offer." And now "fiscal consolidation plans... are essential to sustain recovery, provide flexibility to respond to new shocks... and avoid leaving future generations with a legacy of deficits and debt" (G20 2010, 5, 2). This has captured the guiding thread to state economic policy since.

The spectrum of conservative and social democratic parties adopting some form of austerity strategy has been all but encompassing. Moreover, the stability in the political alignments inside the core capitalist states has been paralleled in the international correlation of forces. In the wake of the crisis, an unprecedented degree of coordination between states sprang forward in the expanded form of the G20 Washington meeting of 2008, and agreement on a global fiscal stimulus. The US was at the centre of this coordination, and the crisis has strengthened its role in the world market relative to both Japan and the EU. The austerity exits have again raised the quandary of rebalancing the world market between surplus and deficit zones in international trade. This is a dilemma that has spanned the neoliberal epoch, and bred competitive rivalries in the world market, as the US has played the central role as both 'consumer of last resort' to supply effective demand to the world market and as 'safe haven of first resort' for hedging global financial flows. The uncertainty of how to resolve this contradiction reflects underlying national political arrangements and class alliances re-enforced by neoliberal policies. It underlies the distinct possibility of a long period of stagnation, and the IMF's prognosis of permanent austerity for the public sector.

Exits Left?

It is a central insight of Marxian political economy that the economic instability of capitalist economies is neither a consequence of misguided states intervening in a self-regulating economy nor of a failure to repress finance and allow it to escape state control. Capitalist crises recur as the limitless drive for accumulation continually runs up against the limited basis for producing and realizing profits. But if this fundamental contradiction of capitalist social relations inexorably leads to overaccumulation, each crisis is singular – a particular historical conjuncture of economic turbulence, class struggles and state interventions. A crisis can only be analyzed in the concrete and resolved in the concrete. If left at the abstraction of determinate laws, or in the more abstract empiricism of secular movements of particular ratios, an economism tends to be produced – in theory and politics – that eclipses the historical movement of capital and the form and role of the state as the decisive point in the concentration of power and the settlement of crises (Clarke 1994; Ercan and Oguz 2007). It is in the analysis of the conjuncture, where historical social structures meet the contingencies of class struggle and social agency, that Marxism demonstrates its theoretical creativity and makes a contribution to the strategic dilemmas confronting the Left.

Current Marxist analyses have offered far more penetrating insights than other theoretical paradigms on the ways that the state is reconstructing the scaffolding of neoliberalism – on a more authoritarian basis. But these interventions have insisted that it remains open whether this will be sufficient for an exit from the crisis. The sources of overaccumulation remain in the structure of bank balance-sheets, in the leverage of debtors in credit markets, in government fiscal positions and in the imbalances in the world payments system. A protracted period of turmoil and stagnation cannot be ruled-out (Panitch, Albo and Chibber 2010).

The crisis has, however, left the Left in a paradoxical setting. On the one side, the Left's critique of capitalism has re-gained a resonance it has not had for decades in parallel to the deep fractures in neoliberal ideology. This is the source to the claims of a 'Marx revival'. The political imprint is noticeable in anti-austerity struggles, the Occupy movement and the revolts and strikes that keep bursting across the central capitalist states in Europe. On the other, the Left – and certainly the radical Left – has failed strategically to intervene with any demands of any depth or credibility, apart from the most general of slogans – 'stop the cuts', 'we won't pay for the crisis', 'occupy the banks' (Panitch, Albo and Chibber 2011). Anything as ambitious as a 'transitional programme' to disengage from subordination to the law of value has been, it is safe to say, utterly absent. Indeed, for all the different emphasis on the Marxian analytics of the crisis, it would be difficult to extract essential programmatic divisions over alternative transformative exits from the crisis. This has contributed to limiting the reverberations from the economic crisis being a systemic crisis of capitalist rule, rather than a particular crisis of state economic policy.

A deeper political crisis, where exits not just from neoliberalism but out of capitalism become visible fractures across the state, has yet to emerge. It is a striking political fact that social democratic parties in Europe and elsewhere, with their substantial hold on unions and working class voters, have offered almost nothing in the way of opposition in programme or mobilization to neoliberal policies. Indeed, they have administered austerity and defended the private banking system as vigorously as their conservative counterparts. Across the European periphery, the social democratic parties have been particularly reactionary, even supporting 'exceptional' measures to affirm 'technocratic' governments or to work in quasi 'grand coalitions' to back austerity. The social democratic movement has not been able to unite even for implementation of the most minimal of financial constraint in the form of a financial transactions tax, not to speak of a more generalized 'crisis tax' (Lehndorff 2012).

The platforms that have emerged out of the broader socialist movement have been informed by heterodox political economy (and often Marxism via the theories of capitalist stagnation from Michal Kalecki and Paul Sweezy), and often associated with the union movements allied to the social democratic parties. They have, however, remained on the margins of public debate. These strategies have sought wage-led 'high-road' exits to the crisis. The sources have been diverse including interventions by Robert Pollin (2011), Robin Blackburn (2011), Thomas Palley (2012), the International Trade Union Confederation (2010), and the Political Economy Research Institute (2008). There has been a brace of ideas which have informed these platforms – repressing finance, boosting effective demand through a coordinated international expansion and strengthened wage and pension policy, and a high-valued added industrial strategy.

The political metrics to evaluate these progressive exits are not entirely clear. Although emerging, in a sense, out of the social democratic milieux, they command almost no sympathy from the social democratic parties in practice. To the extent they have a base of support, it is over the degree of agreement on the continued need, as with the 'exceptional' economic policy of 2009-10, of stimulus measures to reverse the spiral of collapsing demand. But the remaking of state economic policy tends to look backward: to the regulatory structures of 'financial repression' of the postwar period; and to the 1990s moment of 'post-Fordism' of the high-value added, high-skilled worker alternative to an ascendant neoliberalism (Albo 1994; 1997). It is hard not to conclude that this project remains the illusionary exit of re-embedding capitalist institutions within national models of 'competitive corporatism' in conditions of more stable world effective demand as an alternative to neoliberalism. Yet, for the most part, these have served as the Left responses to the crisis in the anti-austerity opposition.

As trenchant as the Marxian explanation of the crisis may be, there has been little in the way of more radical programmes to speak of. If there has been an overarching intervention, it has been the traditional formulation of the left that financial instability, waste and commodification of the surplus necessitate not just nationalization of the banking system but its socialization. In the current crisis, a number of commentators have staked this claim on the 'moral hazard' integral to the financial crisis that has bankers gaining the unseemly rewards of speculation but effectively off-loading the risks through the bail-outs into the public sector. As banks pose 'systemic risk' from this mismatch, and also perform indispensible functions with respect to money, credit and the allocation of the social surplus, finance needs to be treated as a 'public utility' and come under democratic control. This is a position that gained support from a diverse group of Marxist theorists, among them Peter Gowan (2009), Leo Panitch (2008) and Alex Callinicos (2012).

The variations on the proposal for socialization of finance have largely been in isolation from any wider programme of exits from the Left. The Party of European Socialists, for example, has not offered anything resembling an alternate programme and focused its efforts largely on an alternate EU reflation programme to the austerity coming from the European Central Bank and the European Council (the closest being the EuroMemorandum 2012). The depth of the crisis in Southern Europe, however, is beginning to raise additional ideas such as debt audits, debt default and withdrawal from the euro – the last being a point of sharp contention on the European Left. The most developed position in this vein has come from the Research on Money and Finance Group located at SOAS in the University of London (Lapavitsas 2011). The RMF group has carefully documented why remaining in the Eurozone is a dead loss for the Greek working class, and re-asserted the case for a wider 'alternate economic strategy' that makes central control over capital central (recalling some of the 1970s programmatic departures to resist the international restructuring of capital that followed). This view has been countered in the premise that this strategy requires an exit from the euro in the writings of Ozlem Onaran (2011) and Michel Husson (2011), whose positions bear an association with the long-standing view, from Ernest Mandel, of a 'United States of Europe', and also Elmar Altvater (2011), writing partly out of the position of Attac-Germany.

Other alternate agendas have been supplemental to the core demand around extending public ownership over the banking system. A reflationary 'green new deal', for example, has been advocated by David Harvey (2010) and the climate justice movement (Dawson 2010). Others such as Greg Albo, Sam Gindin and Leo Panitch (2010), Michael Lebowitz (2010), the People Before Profit Alliance (2011) in Ireland, and a scattering of the European radical left parties have placed greater emphasis in alternatives on some of the traditional demands of the Left around worktime reduction, capital controls, and democratizing the state and workplaces. But these more ambitious programmes lack a political base to advance them, although the course of the crisis is bringing such dialogue back into circulation after being vanquished from respectable circles for two decades (Panitch, Albo and Chibber 2012).

None of these transformational proposals are being forwarded as strategies of rupture and exit from capitalism. They are emerging out of the balance of forces and crisis of neoliberalism specific to this conjuncture. Reformist – never mind radical – agendas are marginal to the centres of state power. But it is one of the most important insights of Marxist debates about capitalist instability is that the crisis can never be resolved internal to an autonomous economic circuit of capital. Economic relations become 'politicized' inside the state and social relations across the economy. This is the importance of penetrating the political form and organization of state economic policy. Transitional strategies emerging from the social and anti-capitalist movements may neither be politically viable, nor even fully coherent. But they further 'politicize' economic relations and challenge the precedence of profits over meeting the concrete needs of workers in 'economic policy'. They force a confrontation with how alienated 'politics' and the 'state' are from substantive democratic power. In the political conjuncture opened up by the current crisis, this is what is being posed, on the one hand, by the strikes and street battles against the exceptional 'technocratic' governments across Southern Europe, and, on the other, by the Occupy movement in North America: a democratic exit for the majority, or an authoritarian neoliberal exit being forged to protect the interests of the banks and the 1%.

References:

Ahmad, Aijaz, ed. *On the National and Colonial Questions: Selected Writings of Marx and Engels*. New Delhi: Leftwords Books, 2001.

Albo, Greg. "Competitive Austerity and the Impasse of Capitalist Employment Policy." In *Between Globalism and Nationalism: Between Globalism and Nationalism: Socialist Register 1994,* edited by Ralph Miliband and Leo Panitch, 144-170. London: The Merlin Press, 1994.

Albo, Greg. "A World Market of Opportunities? Capitalist Obstacles and Left Economic Policy." In *Ruthless Criticism of All that Exists: Socialist Register 1997,* edited by Leo Panitch, *5-47*. London: The Merlin Press, 1997.

Albo, Greg. "Contesting the 'New Capitalism'." In *Varieties of Capitalism, Varieties of Approaches* edited by David Coates, 38-55. New York: Palgrave, 2005.

Albo, Greg, Sam Gindin and Leo Panitch. *In and Out of Crisis: The Global Finacial Meltdown and Left Alternatives*. Oakland: PM Press 2010.

Altvater, Elmar. "From Sub-Prime Farce to Greek Tragedy: The Crisis Dynamics of Financially Driven Capitalism." In *The Crisis and the Left: Socialist Register 2012,* edited by Leo Panitch, Greg Albo and Vivek Chibber, 271-287. London: Merlin Press, 2011.

Bhagwati, Jagdish. *In Defense of Globalization*. New York: Oxford University Press, 2004.

Blackburn, Robin. "Crisis 2.0." *New Left Review*, no. 72 (2011): 33-62.

de Brunhoff, Suzanne. *The State, Capital and Economic Policy*. London: Pluto Press, 1976.

Buiter, Willem. "Time to Take the Banks into Full Public Ownership." *Financial*

Times (2009). Accessed 16 January 2009. http://blogs.ft.com/maverecon/2009/01/time-to-take-the-banks-into-full-public-ownership/.

Bukharin, Nikolai. *Imperialism and World Economy*. London: The Merlin Press, 1972.

Burke, Michael. "Fake Independence of the 'Office for Budget Responsibility'." *Socialist Economic Bulletin*, 15 June 2010. http://socialisteconomicbulletin.blogspot.com.

Burnham, Peter. "Towards a Political Theory of Crisis: Policy and Resistance across Europe." *New Political Science* 33, no. 4 (2011): 493-507.

Callinicos, Alex. "Contradictions of Austerity." *Cambridge Journal of Economics* 36, no. 1 (2012):65-77.

Coates, David, ed. *Varieties of Capitalism, Varieties of Approaches*. New York: Palgrave, 2005.

Clarke, Simon. *Keynesianism, Monetarism and the Crisis of the State*. Aldershot: Edward Elgar, 1988.

Clarke, Simon. *Marx's Theory of Crisis*. Basingstoke: Macmillan, 1994.

CSE State Group. *Struggle Over the State: Cuts and Restructuring in Contemporary Britain*. London: CSE Books, 1979.

Dawson, Ashley. "Why We Need a Global New Deal." *New Politics* 12, no.4 (2010).

Ercan, Fuat and Sebnem Oguz. "Rethinking Anti-Neoliberal Strategies through the Perspective of Value Theory: Insights from the Turkish Case." *Science and Society* 71, no.2 (2007):173-202.

Euro Memorandum. "European Integration at the Crossroads: Democratic Deepening for Stability, Solidarity and Justice." *Transform! European Journal for Alternative Thinking and Political Dialogue*. Brussels: Transform Europe, 2012.

Financial Times. "Series: Capitalism in Crisis." January-February (2012).

G20. "The G-20 Toronto Summit Declaration." June 26-27, 2010.

Glyn, Andrew. *Capitalism Unleashed*. Oxford: Oxford University Press, 2007.

Gough, Ian. *The Political Economy of the Welfare State*. London: Macmillan,1979.

Gowan, Peter. "Crisis in the Heartland." *New Left Review*, no. 55 (2009): 5-29.

Hall, Peter and David Soskice, ed. *Varieties of Capitalism: The Institutionalist Foundations of Comparative Advantage*. Oxford: Oxford University Press, 2001.

Hanieh, Adam. "Rethinking Class in the Gulf Arab States: The Spatial Structuring of Temporary Migrant Labour." In *Accumulations, Crises, Struggles: Capital and Labour in Contemporary Capitalism,* edited by Baris Karaagac. Berlin: LIT, 2013.

Harvey, David. *The Limits to Capital*. Chicago: University of Chicago Press,1982.

_____. *The Enigma of Capital*. Oxford: Oxford University Press, 2010.

Hermann, Christoph and Jörg Flecker, ed. *Privatization of Public Services:*

Impacts for Employment, Working Conditions, and Service Quality, London: Routledge, 2011.

Husson, Michel. "Exit or Voice? A European Strategy of Rupture." In *The Crisis and the Left:Socialist Register 2012,* edited by Leo Panitch, Greg Albo and Vivek Chibber, 298-306. London: Merlin Press, 2011.

International Trade Union Confederation. *Take Action on Jobs to Sustain the Recovery: Global Unions' Statement*. 2011. www.ituc-csi.org.

International Monetary Fund (IMF). *World Economic Outlook: Coping with High Debt and Sluggish Growth*. Washington: IMF, October, 2010.

KPMG International. *Tough Choices Ahead: The Future of the Public Sector*. Ottawa: KPMG, 2009. www.kpmg.com.

Krugman, Paul. *End This Depression Now!*. New York: Norton, 2012.

Jessop, Bob. *Nicos Poulantzas: Marxist Theory and Strategy*. London: Macmillan, 1985.

Lapavitsas, Costas. "Default and Exit from the Eurozone: A Radical Left Strategy." In *Socialist Register 2012,* edited by Leo Panitch, Greg Albo and Vivek Chibber, 288-297. London: Merlin Press, 2011.

Lebowitz, Michael. *The Socialist Alternative: Real Human Development*. New York: Monthly Review Press, 2010.

Lehndorff, Steffen. *A Triumph of Failed Ideas: European Models of Capitalism in the Crisis*. Brussels: ETUI, 2012.

Marx, Karl. *Capital, Volume 1*. New York, International Publishers, 1967.

_____. *A Contribution to the Critique of Political Economy*. New York: International Publishers, 1970.

_____. *Grundrisse*. New York: Vintage, 1973.

Nersisyan, Yeva and Randall Wray. "Deficit Hysteria Redux?" *Real-World Economics Review*, no. 53 (2010):109-128.

O'Connor, James. *The Fiscal Crisis of the State*. New York: St. Martin's Press, 1973.

Oguz, Sebnem. "Turning the Crisis into an Opportunity: The Turkish State's Response to the 2008 Crisis." In *Accumulations, Crises, Struggles: Capital and Labour in Contemporary Capitalism,* edited by Baris Karaagac. Berlin: LIT, 2013.

Onaran, Ozlem. "An Internationalist Transitional Program towards an Anti -Capitalist Europe." *International Viewpoint Online*, no. 435 (2011). www.internationalviewpoint.org.

Palley, Thomas. *From Financial Crisis to Stagnation*. Cambridge: Cambridge University Press, 2012.

Panitch, Leo. "Globalisation and the State." In *Between Globalism and Nationalism: The Socialist Register 1994,* edited by Ralph Miliband and Leo Panitch, 60-93. London: Merlin Press, 1994.

_____. "The Financial Crisis and Democratic Public Finance." *The Bullet*, no. 157

(2008).
http://www.socialistproject.ca/bullet/bullet157.html.

Panitch, Leo, Greg Albo and Vivek Chibber, ed. *The Crisis This Time: Socialist Register 2011*. London: The Merlin Press, 2010.

_____. *The Crisis and the Left: Socialist Register 2012*. London: The Merlin Press, 2011.

_____.*The Question of Strategy: Socialist Register 2013*. London: The Merlin Press, 2012.

Peck, Jamie. *Constructions of Neoliberal Reason*. Oxford: Oxford University Press, 2010.

People Before Profit Alliance. *An Alternative Economic Agenda*. Dublin: PPBA, 2011.
http://www.peoplebeforeprofit.

Peters, B. Guy and Jon Pierre, eds. *Politicization of the Civil Service in Comparative Perspective: The Quest for Control*. New York: Routledge, 2004.

Political Economy Research Institute. *A Progressive Programme for Economic Recovery and Financial Reconstruction*. Amherst: PERI, 2008.

Pollin, Robert. "Back to Full Employment." *Boston Review*, January-February (2011).
http://bostonreview.net/forum/back-full-employment.

Poulantzas, Nicos. *Classes in Contemporary Capitalism*, London: Verso, 1975.

_____. *State, Power, Socialism*. London: Verso, 1978.

Reinhart, Carmen and Kenneth Rogoff. *This Time is Different*. Princeton: Princeton University Press, 2009.

Roubini, Nouriel and Stephen Mihm. *Crisis Economics*. New York: Penguin Press, 2010.

Savoie, Donald. *Thatcher, Reagan, Mulroney: In Search of a New Bureaucracy*, Toronto: University of Toronto Press, 1994.

Tanzi, Vito. *Government versus Markets: The Changing Economic Role of the State*. Cambridge: Cambridge University Press, 2011.

Tinbergen, Jan. *Economic Policy in Our Time, Volume I*, Amsterdam: North -Holland, 1964.

_____. *On the Theory of Economic Policy*. Amsterdam: North Holland, 1966.

Wolf, Martin. *Why Globalization Works*. New Haven: Yale University Press, 2004.

Wolff, Rick. 'Austerity: Why and for Whom?' *MRZine*, 4 July 2010.
http://www.monthlyreview.org/mrzine/

Wood, Ellen. *Empire of Capital*, London: Verso, 2005.

World Bank. *The State in a Changing World: World Development Report*. Washington: World Bank, 1997.

Impolite (Dis) Articulations of Originary Accumulation, Terror and Transnationalized Securities: Eurasia as a Site of Multiple Contestations

Anna M. Agathangelou

I. Introduction

> I write down what I think is true, because the stories told by the Greeks are, in my opinion, ridiculous and countless.
>
> Hecataeus

One of the major themes in Hecataeus' *Geneologies* is the emergence of Persia as a new empire. The text traces the rise of the Greek Empire and its links with other peoples outside the context of Greek cities. Because of his extensive travels (paradoxically made easier by the formation of the Persian Empire) Hecataeus was able to question the "Greek view of early history by showing that thc generations of Greek heroes reached back only a few hundred years, as opposed to the thousands of years found among some eastern peoples".[1] (Similarly, during today's neoliberal moment, I argue that for those who support empire and imperialism as well as those who do not, "security" constitutes the decisions of top-tier capital agents (i.e., the market, the corporation, the state) in the world economy. Such practices consolidate imperial dynamics and politics as heroic and masculine.[2] The "descrip-

[1] Hecataeus of Miletus, *Hecataei Milesii Fragmenta*: *Scylacis Caryandensis Periplus*, ed. Rud Klausen (Oxford: Oxford University Press, 1954).
[2] Neferti Tadiar, *Fantasy-Production: Sexual Economies and Other Philippine Consequences for the New World Order*, (Hong Kong University Press/ Ateneo de Manila University Press, 2004), 10.

tive realist deployments of the term [empire][3] eclipse" the work of the women, working class people, and people of color worldwide "necessary to produce and maintain the very political and economic structures comprising the world".[4] Above all, these realist deployments collapse violence with life-generating activities and relations.

I focus on Eurasia as a region of contestation in the (re) production of multiple worlds (and not merely the imperial global system). I examine the "war on terror" as a practice embodied in different terrains as part of the larger practice of the creation of a particular world order and within it the production of state identities, and gendered, sexualized, classed, and racialized subjects. I bear witness to the foundational gendered, classed, and racialized violence constitutive of the US and global (neo) imperialism. I trace how the "war on terror," including security practices, has become a significant technology of empire[5] and imperialist deployment by consolidating the power of those "economies" and transnational blocs interested in sustaining modalities and regimes of accumulation and ontologies of (in) security and profit. It does so, I argue, by mythologizing the tensions generated out of forces, that on one level are interested in infinite expansion with no limit to capital's penetrations, and on another level, disrupt what they depend on, national sovereign-class-racialized-gendered relations, to secure expansion in the name of global and regional security.

I use the crises in Eurasia to track the aspirations and the activities which draw on existing gendered, racialized, sexualized, nationalized, and regionalized asymmetries and power relations to consolidate their profit-seeking practices. In addition, I examine the unleashing of a series of transnational economic and other policies, only some of which we might label "neoliberal" and profit-seeking. These are far from uniform, occasionally working in a contradictory manner to consolidate (neo) colonial capital powers and produce new kinds of subjects to respond to emerging social relations.

I draw on policy texts such as the US National Security Strategy (March 2006) and Iraq Benchmark Assessment Report (September 2007)[6] to expose the tensions between the ontological priorities in the contestations of socio-economic relations. I argue that recent contestations and wars within Eurasia represent the newer mo-

---

[3] See for instance, the now well-known book by Hardt and Negri, *Empire* (2000).
[4] Tadiar, *Fantasy-Production*, 10.
[5] See Anna M. Agathangelou et al., eds. *Technologies of Empire and (In) Secure Possibilities* (York University: Centre for International and Security Studies, 2007) for an explanation of the technologies of empire.
[6] George W. Bush, *The National Security Strategy* (Washington D.C.: The White House, March 2006). http://georgewbush-whitehouse.archives.gov/nsc/nss/2006/; Council on Foreign Relations, *September 2007 Benchmark Assessment Report*, accessed January 28, 2012, http://www.cfr.org/iraq/iraq-initial-benchmark-assessment-report-july-2007/p13802.

dalities that the US as a leader is trying to formulate – these are leading to the build-up, articulation, and (re) consolidation of a neoliberal new world war (dis) order. By examining these modalities, we can see how "security" as constituted in Eurasia has a much longer history than that discussed since September 11 and the unleashing of the "War on Terror." This analysis will allow us to situate what is unfolding in Eurasia at this moment within a context of empire making practices over a longer period of time.

I conclude by articulating a (neo) anti-colonial-marxist-postcolonial-feminist framework, insights of which are borne out by the history of philosophical and feminist international relations, nuanced by Greek theory sensibilities. This allows us to gesture to disjunctures of the dominant onto-epistemes in social relations of power while simultaneously articulating other multi-faceted possible relations beyond freedom from necessity (that is, structures of violence, including exploitation and war).

II. Genealogies of the New World (Dis) Order: Unfettered Accumulations and Militarizations?

> The Strong Do What They Can and the Weak Suffer What They Must.
>
> Thucydides

> Al Qaeda is to terror what the mafia is to crime. But its goal is not making money; its goals is remaking the world-and imposing its radical beliefs on people everywhere.
>
> George W. Bush, September 11, 2001

Securing the Segmented World and Its Consolidation Requires Militant "non-terror" Violence

Globalism as a Force of Restructuring and Deterritorialization

In *Genealogies*, Hecataeus spoke scathingly of the short-sightedness of Greek aristocrats and questioned their commonly accepted view of history which featured Greece at the centre. But he was also concerned with highlighting the landscapes and worlds that such stories made invisible. I want to do the same thing, disrupting the dominant idea in world politics and international relations that a single concept such as "empire" can explain contemporary global crises.

Empire as an explanatory framework seems to require strong and heroic peoples and "marginal regions of the world as…simply [the slaves and labourers and] producers of [labour and] data for the theory mills of the North" (Appadurai 1999, 230). As Tadiar says:

> Locating their hero, information labor, in the financial and media entertainment sectors, [heroic politics] elide the service and affective work extensively performed by women. Heroic politics is masculinist politics, even in the name of anti-empire.... what descriptive realist deployments of the term [empire] eclipse is precisely this kind of work necessary to produce and maintain the very political and economic structures comprising the world.[7]

These politics, I argue, mythologize the past as devoid of conflict. They require a myth of the political that includes possibilities crucial for averting war and makes invisible (1) war/conflict among the capitalist classes, and (2) struggles and contestations of these re-structurings. Such mythological productions have acted through the privileged voices of a (neo) imperial's imaginary to disenable us from examining those forces of conflict that found the political (in this particular case, the New World Order out of which the "War on Terror" emerges) at least as much as they destroy it.

Stories about Eurasia: "Social chauvinism," religious clashes, and/or the expansion of the military-industrial-financial capital?

Lenin and Luxemburg addressed the geopolitical struggles between Britain and Germany and their shifting allies for European supremacy in the early 20th century. The second half of the century was dominated by the Cold War between the US, which emerged as the world's leading industrial-military power, and the former Soviet Union and its bloc of protectorates. Since the 1990s, the US has ushered in a new phase, namely the industrial geopolitical struggle to control Eurasia and its lands/labour/energy resources.[8] Heinberg says: "Modern global geopolitics, because it implies worldwide transportation and communication systems rooted in fossil energy resources, is ... a phenomenon unique to the industrial era.9 He argues that because the US is driven by its desire for resources, Eurasia, a large geographical site with many resources, especially energy resources, is a site of contestation in the larger global geopolitical power politics (what Kipling calls the "great game" in Kim (2002)).

For example, Zbigniew Brzezinski, former National Security Advisor to US President Jimmy Carter says Eurasia should be at the centre of US efforts to "project its own power globally":

---

[7] Tadiar, *Fantasy-Production*, 10.

[8] Richard Heinberg, *The Party's Over: Oil, War and the Fate of Industrial Societies* (British Colombia:New Society Publishers, 2003).

[9] Heinberg, *The Party's Over*, 2.

> The chief geopolitical prize is Eurasia. For half a millennium, Eurasian powers and peoples who fought with one another for regional domination and reached out for global power dominated world affairs. Now a non-Eurasian power is preeminent in Eurasia-and America's global primacy is directly dependent on how long and how effectively its preponderance on the Eurasian continent is sustained.[10]

This realist-liberal epistemology calls on the US to project its power in the Eurasian context. Domination of this land is necessary for those who want to be the tech-(neo) imperial leaders. In the past, those who emerged as leaders fought one another and dominated this region; as a result, they were able to dominate world affairs. Today, the US is present in this region and must devise strategies to preclude the emergence of any other leader.

Yet the American people are not "accustomed to imperial responsibilities".[11] "The pursuit of power is not a goal that commands popular passion, except in conditions of a sudden threat or challenge to the public's sense of domestic well-being").[12] With the September 11 attacks, the American people felt a "sudden threat...to the public's sense of domestic well-being".[13] Consequently, business and state leaders found the opportunity to articulate the global imperial desire to act unilaterally as noted by Paul Wolfowitz in 1992 in the Defense Planning Guidance: "Our strategy [after the fall of the Soviet Union] must refocus on precluding the emergence of any potential future global competitor...Russia will remain the strongest military power in Eurasia and the only power in the world with the capacity of destroying the United States."[14] (This call to arms set up "hegemony of a new type," a "global supremacy" with the US as "the first and only truly global power").[15] This call to secure the Eurasian perimeter stretched from Africa to Eastern Europe:

> NATO under the leadership of the United States bombed [Kosovo] for 11 weeks and then landed ground troops, leading to the establishment of permanent military bases in the area that had formerly been part of the Soviet sphere of influence. In the Persian Gulf Iraq was faced with an economic embargo and daily bombings by the United States and Britain.

---

[10] Zbigniew Brzezinski, "The end of the American Century: The Grand Chessboard: US Geostrategy for Eurasia," *Harvard International Review*, Winter (1997): 30.
[11] Heinberg, *The Party's Over*, 3.
[12] Brzezinski, "The End of the American Century," 36.
[13] Heinberg, *The Party's Over*, 3.
[14] Paul Wolfowitz, "Defense Planning Guidance," *New York Times*, March 8, 1992. See also "Excerpts from Pentagon's Plan: 'Preventing the Re-Emergence of a New Rival,'" *New York Times*, March 8, 1992; "Keeping the U.S. First," *Washington Post*, March 11, 1992; Dorrien, Imperial Design, 40–41.
[15] Brzezinski, "The End of the American Century," 3, 10, 30-39.

> Meanwhile, the United States sought military bases in Central Asia in areas surrounding the oil-an-natural-gas-rich Caspian Sea basin; formerly part of the Soviet Union.[16]

These calls to arms are not arbitrary. In the name of protecting the "homeland," Bush calls for a world order where militarism and violence are "procreative acts":

> We are a Nation blessed with unprecedented liberty, opportunity, and openness – foundations of the American way of life. Our principal terrorist enemies – al-Qaida, its affiliates, and those inspired by them – seek to destroy this way of life. ... The United States, through a concerted national effort that galvanizes the strengths and capabilities of ...governments; the private and non-profit sectors; and regions, communities, and individual citizens – along with our partners in the international community – will work to achieve a secure Homeland that sustains our way of life as a free, prosperous, and welcoming America. In order to realize this vision, the United States will use all instruments of national power and influence – diplomatic, information, military, economic, financial, intelligence, and law enforcement – to achieve our goals to prevent and disrupt terrorist attacks; protect the American people, critical infrastructure, and key resources; and respond to and recover from incidents that do occur.[17]

The text articulates the major principles guiding the US. Embedded within it is a major epistemological articulation of world relations which calls forth a pioneering, heroic, venturist and masculine US leader who can gloss over any anxiety about the "other," those phantasmic others – invisible women and brown bodies who build comfortable places for the US military and government in Iraq, as well as insurgents, who from an instrumentalist and quantitative perspective have no ontological existence. This episteme articulates "a way of life as a free, prosperous, and welcoming America" and juxtaposes it to the desires of the empire which have gendered, racialized, and class implications. Its "fantastical" vision articulates a geopolitics necessary to secure "our Nation." The text also points to the NWO strategy that will secure the re-division of the world, and articulates the role required of the free, welcoming, and prosperous American citizens in the face of encroachment by those who risk its economic and political well-being, including immigrants, workers from South East Asia, women's labour, and insurgents.18 The US must ensure that al-Qaida does not disrupt this "Nation" of freedom, opportunity, and openness, code words for neo-liberal enterprise, politics, security relations, and subject formations.

Of course, Bush's idea of freedom and opportunity gestures once more to an imperialist strategy. Lenin and Luxemburg articulate that such liberal ideas about

---

[16] John Bellamy Foster, "The New Geopolitics of Empire," *Monthly Review* 57, no.8 (2006): 9.

[17] George W. Bush, *Our Vision and Strategy for Homeland Security* (Washington D.C.: Homeland Security, 2007).

[18] Bush, *Our Vision and Strategy for Homeland Security*; See also Agathangelou, Anna, M., Daniel Bassichis, and Tamara Spira "Intimate Investments: Homonormativity, Global Lockdown, and Seductions of Empire," *Radical History Review* 100 (2008): 120-144.

freedom and opportunity are rather constitutive elements of an imperialist strategy whose goal is the plundering of colonies and oppressing other nations. In the words of Lenin, it seems to become " 'right' of one or another of the 'great' powers [our partners in the international community] to plunder colonies and to oppress other nations".[19] The US (i.e., the Bush administration) has argued for the protection of the "homeland" while working to ensure the privatization of all resources in Afghanistan and Iraq, not to mention the lands formerly under the control of the Soviet Union.[20] The privatizations of these countries through the "thefts" of major national resources (i.e., oil) have been articulated as the embodiment of a free world and its contingent securities. The world's essential constituents are geopolitical regionalist imaginaries, pointing to the contradictory creation, syncretism, and collaboration of worlds vying for a place for their goods and their financial markets, and the creation of the conditions necessary to sustain such relations.

These worlds and social relations have to be brought about instead of merely accepted as given. To grant this possibility is quite apart from saying this is the best way to think and do social relations.[21] Even the greatest proponent of the global-geopolitico-regional imaginary (the US, aka George W. Bush) recognizes this point and moves to educate different subjects, including US citizens, that it knows what it is doing in Eurasia, making it a powerful agent of tech-(neo) colonial-imperial project(s). Its militant and violent projects become the "New Way Forward."

The "New Way Forward": (Un) Making and (Re) Making the Imperial World

The Iraq Benchmark Assessment Report says the following of the "New Way Forward":

> Current U.S. strategy -- the New Way Forward -- recognizes that the fulfillment of commitments by both the U.S. and Iraqi Governments will be necessary to achieving our common goal: a democratic Iraq that can govern, defend, and sustain itself, and be an ally in the War on Terror. The building of a strong strategic partnership with the Iraqi Government will be an important part of the effort to achieve this end state, which remains a long-term goal, and requires the application of all elements of national power, including especially diplomatic, economic, and political power.
>
> (http://www.whitehouse.gov/news/releases/2007/07/20070712.html)

---

[19] Vladimir Ilich Lenin, *Imperialism the Highest Stage of Capitalism* (Australia: Resistance Books, 1999), 7.

[20] Jeremy Scahill, *Blackwater: The Rise of the World's Most Powerful Mercenary Army* (New York: Nation Books, 2007).

[21] Anna Agathangelou et al., "Intimate Investments," *Radical History Review* 100 (2008).

The New Way Forward lays out the paradigmatic principles behind securing the American role as the dominant power in Eurasia, including its intervention and preeminence in Iraq. While the "overarching strategy continues to emphasize a transition of responsibility to the Iraqi Government and its security forces," shaping Iraq into an "end state" requires Coalition forces to play a greater role albeit in "conjunction with the Iraqi Security Forces" created by the US to "secur[e] the Iraqi population."

Clearly, this report is a message to the world that American fantasies will be preeminent in Eurasia. The US role in the formation of a new Iraq is one of many such possible interventions in (re)constituting and redrawing Eurasia as a geopolitical site. In essence, the report is, in the words of Loraux (2006, 14), who spoke of Greek imperial power in ancient Greece, "a political genre in which, governed by civic laws, the logos becomes in turn a civic norm for speaking" by the US.[22] An idea that the US wishes to have of itself emerges, one that stretches far beyond the needs of the contemporary moment. Yet there is a disjuncture between what the report claims the US to be and what the US does daily: the restructuring and killings of Eurasians, the imprisonment of and violence to marginalized bodies within the borders of the US; the exploitation of the brown and black bodies who labour to re-build Iraq and Afganistan.[23]

The report outlines the benchmarks (i.e., actions) that will ensure the creation of a "new" Iraq, a reconciled, conflict-less site for capital relations, one that will be secure, provide services to its population, and achieve economic well-being. These activities would ensure, according to this public report, US and Iraqi collaborative actions for the "New Way Forward," namely, the accomplishment of a "democratic Iraq that can govern, defend, and sustain itself, and be an ally in the "War on Terror." This text draws on structures already in place: the US is necessary to (re) constitute global relations of power and ensure security in the region by securing the "end state:" what must proceed in the United States (i.e., funds for the Coalition Forces in Iraq must be raised) and what must occur in Iraq (i.e., the Iraqi security forces and the ruling classes must support the War on Terror).[24]

These reports offer a glimpse into the epistemological work of imagining this New Way Forward as part of the strategy of the new secure world which itself depends extensively on a World War (dis) Order. They provide insight into the heterogeneous and uneven activities that constitute what we might call neoliberal-

---

[22] Nicole Loraux, *The Invention of Athens: The Funeral Oration in the Classical City*, trans. Alan Sheridan (New York: Zone Books, 2006).

[23] Agathangelou et al., "Intimate Investments."

[24] For a detailed analysis of the contestations between the ruling classes see: Sabbah Alnasseri, "Understanding Iraq," in *Global Flashpoints: Socialist Register 2008*, ed. Colin Leys and Leo Panitch (London: The Merlin Press, 2009), 77-100.

imperial-global security state politics. The reports also imagine an empire that is omnipresent; they bracket conflict and disassemble *polemos* and other violence. This signals to an imaginary that makes the New World Order appear as an achieved state. And yet this bracketing requires more than just an imaginary. The *salus* of this community, its well-being, welfare, security and immunity from risk, cannot be guaranteed by the expiation fantasies of the military/police powers who would manage peace in the world.It seems that entry into this New World Order requires that we forget what has been done if we wish to participate in an economy of *soteriology* or salvation (Plato, 1980) when peace and war become one and the same (Heidegger 2000, 83; 150-51).[25]

The US Military as the World's Hypermasculine Military/Police Officer

> Now what about someone who brings harmony to the city? Would he order its way of life with a view more to external war or more to that internal war called stasis, which occurs from time to time and which everyone would wish never to come to pass in his city and, if it does, would wish to end as soon as possible? The best, however, is neither *polemos* nor stasis…but rather peace (*eirene*) and at the same time goodwill towards one another. Moreover, it is likely that even that victory of the city over itself belonged not to the best things (*ariston*) but to the necessary things (*anangeion*).
>
> Plato 1980, 628a8-628e.

In *Laws*, Plato articulates a crucial epistemology, raising questions about the foundations of the city-state and the strategies the subject must consider to secure harmony in the city. This is, of course, central to IR's more general questioning of necessary or compulsory things. What is crucial here is that the New World Order (a geopolitical imaginary) coined by George Bush Senior became a central explanatory framework which allowed its proponents (mostly located in the US and the UK) an entry point into other worlds and the opportunity to make a foothold in Eastern Europe, the Balkans, and moving into Caucasus and Central Asia. Since 1991 (not 2001), the US has participated in a number or New World Order Wars: the Kosovo war was waged and decided as a NATO war; the Afghanistan war was waged mostly as a US war; the current war in Iraq is the war of the "coalition of the willing".[26] As it moves into these different places, with the support of international organizations and international financial organizations, along with strategic bypassing, the US is turning itself into the world's military police force.

---

[25] Martin Heidegger, *Introduction to Metaphysics*, trans. G. Fried and R. Polt (New Haven, CT.: Yale University Press, 2000).

[26] Steve Schifferes, *"US names 'coalition of the willing',"* *BBC*, March 18, 2003.

Clearly, the US is interested in a "secured military foothold in Central Asia" and for the first time is based in a territory historically considered "untouchable".[27] The dramatic global-geopolitical-regional shifting of social, economic and power dynamics and of roles in the world does not just *happen*. It is a result of intentional politics and practices of powers who are interested in establishing their preponderance in Eurasia: (re) drawing the socio-economic and political boundaries to secure socio-economic-political and territorial access to resources in the name of accumulation. These same powers are re-mapping the world to secure access to resources, including land, cheap labour, and bodies for their reconstructions.

While mega-capital's push to expand anywhere, anytime enables the integration of the world economy (while demanding "economic regulation"), there is simultaneously a fracturing of capital into national and/or regional units. The need for a world government emerges from this contradiction; at the same time, this seems impossible, as governance at a global level is nascent and requires much dispersion of power. In the absence of a world government and its contingent governance institutions, regulation becomes military officialdom with the US in charge. For instance, the invasion of Iraq has been explained as a moral and strategic imperative as if it had nothing to do with the US regulation of Eurasia:

> Our nation's moral and strategic imperatives in Iraq are one: we must help Iraq defeat those who threaten its future – and also threaten ours… The success of a free Iraq is critical to the security of the United States – if we withdraw prematurely, violent extremists would be emboldened, and we would leave to our children a far more dangerous world.[28]

In this Benchmark report, the Bush administration seems to be one with Iraq. Of course, the Iraq being discussed constitutes mostly the ruling class interested in the formation of a state whose role is to mediate the various forces in ways that profit them. In this way, the (re) articulation of an ontology of (neo) modernity, albeit with neo-liberal cues, is made possible. Colonial forms of rule are reactivated in the social forces emerging in these newly created conditions.[29]

---

[27] Sungur Savran, "Globalisation and the New World Order: The New Dynamics of Imperialism and War," in *The Politics of Empire: Globalisation in Crisis*, ed. Alan Freeman and Boris Kagarlitsky (London: Pluto Press, 2004), 117-150.

[28] The White House, *Iraq Benchmark Assessment Report* (Washington D.C.: Council on Foreign Relations, 2007); Leaving American children a far more dangerous world becomes a masculinist fable circulated by the media and international organizations of security such as NATO and the Organization Security Council Europe (OSCE).

[29] Pinar Bilgin, "'Is the 'Orientalist' Past the Future of Middle East Studies?' *Third World Quarterly* 25, no.2 (2004): 423-433.

The War(s) in Eurasia: Resources and/or the Promises of Neoliberal Capitalism(s)

The new imaginaries about Eurasia state that the war in Afghanistan began because of the September 11 attacks in the US, and the war in Iraq started because Saddam Hussein failed to follow the UN Security Council's articles on weapons of mass destruction. Yet these fables make invisible certain elements central to its constitution. Consider Suleyman Demirel's comment at an OSCE conference where he addressed the geography that has been delineated since 1989: "Following the Cold War a new political geography was formed which was named 'Eurasia'...This new geography covers a vast area from the Balkans to Chinese Wall and embraces millions of people who had been desiring freedom for decades.[30] Although Eurasia as a region has a much longer history than the one assigned by the current global powers, [31] attributing a particular coherency to it, either material or imagined *vis-à-vis* the world system, is a way of knowing it and thus containing it. Many newer names given to the region have to do with the dissolution of the former Soviet Union; now it is divided into many independent nation-states with specific economic, political, ethnic and religious elements.

The introduction of the New World Order as a global-geopolitical-regional imaginary and a set of articulated strategies and practices about global security activates a set of practices, including acts of conflict, reconsolidation, and realignment. Eurasia, as the geopolitical-epicenter of realignment, allows us to ask on what ontological grounds such geopolitical-regional reconsolidations have taken place before and (in an intensified way) after September 11. Could a security that counts make possible a world that is one and without conflict? Could a security that counts lead to the best regime where its oneness of property and imaginaries preclude comparisons and, hence, divisions and segmentations? (Plato, *Laws*, 739b8-e and *Republic,* 462b-c). Could the United States see itself as moving to secure in itself that best regime?

The conflict in Eurasia began in Yugoslavia in the 1990s.[32] In Yugoslavia, the consolidation of the New World Order and the re-alignment of power relations in the world did not happen easily; rather, they required what I call the New World

---

[30] Suleyman Demirel, "President Demirel Speaks at 10th Antalya Security and Cooperation Conference: "An Undivided, Democratic, Prosperous Europe is no longer a dream," Anadolu News Agency March 10, 2000 *http://www.hri.org/news/turkey/ anadolu/2000/00-03-10.anadolu.html.*

[31] Eurasia has a much longer history and this concept was usually used to denote the unity between Europe and Asia that "spread as they were in a contiguous manner across the gigantic land mass that stretches from the Atlantic on the West to the Pacific on the East" (Demirel 2000, cited in Savran, 2004, 145).

[32] Anna M. Agathangelou, *The Global Political Economy of Sex: Desire, Violence and Insecurity in Mediterranean Nation-States* (New York: MacMillan/Palgrave, 2004).

War (dis) Order. Yugoslavia's history and its location linking Central and Eastern Europe[33] did not collapse at the same rate as did other socialist states. The "dismemberment" of Yugoslavia began with a series of diplomatic responses by the Western countries, including Germany, Austria, and the Vatican to the secessionist states of Slovenia and Croatia in 1991; the American support of Bosnian Muslims led to further violence between 1991 and 1995 (Woodward 1995). These soteriological (i.e., sacrifices by the West) opened up space for NATO penetration and European Union involvement which resulted in the consolidation of the New World Order's newly acquired power and territories in that region.

Yugoslavia marks the entry point and the "forgetting to remember" of a specific political, that is, the link to the gendered, racialized, and class international conflicts with the socialist "East" (the former Soviet Union and other bureaucratic worker-states) and the struggles of the Third World as expressed through the Non-Aligned Movement (beginning with Bandung). Indeed, this conflict intertwined internal and Western forces seeking to secure stability in Europe for capitalist social relations, even when that white hyper-masculine invincibility was projected through theatrical militarism.[34] Yugoslavia became the site, albeit small in comparison with Russia and China, to (re) consolidate imperialism in its newer neoliberal formation. This conflict, essentially a containment of war, was necessary for what happened in Eurasia.

Why Eurasia? Why is it important in the New World War (dis) Order? Since the dissolution of the former Soviet Union, Eurasia as a geographical site with a specific internal coherence, imagined and otherwise, has had much to do with natural gas and petroleum. For instance, Azerbaijan, Kazakhstan and Turkmenistan contain energy resources, along with gold and mineral reserves. Some theorists argue that there is an emerging energy-producing region (Iran, the Caucasus, Central Asia, etc.) extending from Saudi Arabia and the Persian Gulf in the south to Kazakhstan in the north. Statistics show resources such as natural gas, oil, gold, and other mineral reserves to be important economically, but the region is significant in other ways as well, specifically its geopolitical and geographic location in relation to struggles over Asian land, labour, and economic structures. The United States and Western Europe have used NATO and US military forces to secure their role in the processes of "capitalist restoration" beginning with Yugoslavia in the Balkans and extending to China. Russia and China have played significant roles in the Eurasian region historically, economically, politically, and militarily; now the US and the EU have joined the struggle over "Asia."

---

[33] Yugoslavia was also a major European country to border Greece – two major (antagonistic) NATO countries – thus indicating the socialist possibility that capitalist-centric Europe could not be contained (Agathangelou 2004).

[34] Pepe Escobar, "The US and Eurasia: Theatrical Militarism," *Asian Times*, December 2, 2002.

Of course, one could ask: "Which Asia?" It is crucial to recognize that the war in Yugoslavia, the Gulf War, the intifada, the Afghanistan and Iraq wars, the contestations and tensions with Iran, and the Georgian wars are manifestations of struggles over which world view to foreground. The many bases erected by the US in Uzbekistan and Kyrgyzstan during the Afghanistan war are significant, as Russia and China are nuclear powers and a direct war against either may not be the wisest strategy.

In short, Eurasia is a site of immense importance; "Asia" is a site, a region-specific place and an imaginary.[35]

Eurasia, I argue, is an articulated site and space and a discursive set of regimes that bring together disparate histories and world orders to secure what the imperium (led by the US and other dominant imperial powers such as Russia, Germany, and Japan) would like: lands, labour, and extraction sites for profit. The notion of national, social, political, and economic formations as embodied through national cultural identities are under pressure. The kind of regionalization being articulated at the moment is the symptom of an imperium within the discursive spaces of what comes to be constituted as Eurasia, a world of many religions (Orthodox Christianity, Islam, etc.) and many ethnic groups living side by side for centuries. While the imperium knows the radical existence of multiple worlds, it still works with strategies that do not recognize it.[36] The insistence of "survivors" and "terminators" to flatten lands and social relations and to create sedimented and layered disjunctive orders of the world through the fables and narratives of a "neo-imperial vision" that spatially roots the world in the "West" points to the limits of the epistemes – namely their failure to think the ontological grounds that such dominant colonial powers embody. Indeed, the enduring effect of this "neo-imperial vision" is that "the United States arrogates to itself the global role of setting standards, determining threats, using force, and meting out justice" to fulfill its "new goal" which is "to make these advantages permanent- a *fait accompli* that will prompt other states to not even try to catch up".[37]

The "complex overlapping disjunctive order" defies a "hard-line imperial grand strategy".[38] For instance, the Turkic republics in Central Asia lived under Russian rule from the 19th century until recently, and emergent ethnic clashes are not out of the question. The geopolitical worlds that have emerged as a result of the National

---

35 Arjun Appadurai, *Modernity at Large: Cultural Dimensions of Globalization* (Minneapolis: University of Minnesota Press, 1996), 32.

36 For a description and articulation of multiple worlds we coin "worldism." See: Anna M. Agathangelou and L.H.M. Ling, *Transforming World Politics: From EmpireTo Multiple Worlds* (New York: Routledge, 2009).

37 John G. Ikenberry, "America's Imperial Ambition," *Foreign Affairs* 81, no. 5 (2002): 44, 55.

38 Appadurai, *Modernity at Large*, 32; Ikenberry, "America`s Imperial Ambition," 59.

World Order strategy, the regional project of Russia the imperial ambitions of Japan, the many national struggles and conflicts (that is, remembering struggles seen as "localized" and individual and forgetting structural forces and social relations that secure further conflicts), the disrupting of national sovereignty as possible strategies of engaging conflicts and class structures, and the setting up of international colonies (i.e., Afghanistan and Iraq) are major aspects of these neo-imperial strategies with plenty of ethnic, religious, racial and other tensions to draw on for legitimacy.[39]

III. The "War on Terror" or a Permanent War?

Beginning with a series of wars in Europe (i.e., Yugoslavia) and the Gulf War in 1991, we have seen a reconstruction of the world and an attempt to implement neoliberalism(s) worldwide. The September 11, 2001, attacks on two major symbols of economic and political power, the World Trade Center and the Pentagon, made apparent that first-world countries are sites of conflict and insecurity. Although rendered apparent by events following the September 11 attacks, the accelerating pace of securitizing and militarizing the social has deeper roots.

The post-Cold War world of neoliberal, economic globalization provided a fertile seedbed for what is now coined the "War on Terror." With the fall of the former Soviet Union and the Eastern European bloc, the US emerged as the leader of the global capitalist system. Shifts in extractive accumulation regimes required changes in transnational organizations and their contingent embodied intelligibilities; thus, the World Trade Organization (WTO), the World Bank and the International Monetary Fund (IMF) have mediated mega-capital moves and investments by pushing for structural adjustment in the name of stability (i.e., certainty) and prosperity. But stability and prosperity for whom?

IMF policies in the wake of Asia's financial crisis (1997-98) provoked riots, widespread strikes, and ethnic violence. The IMF paved the way for Western corporations to buy out Asian ones at "fire sale" prices (Ling 2002). The promises of globalization that more and more people would have access to the economic benefits of the global economy ("free trade," mass privatization, deregulation, and short-term profits) did not come to fruition. Once open protests of these market rules mobilized, proponents of neoliberalism realized that a push to privatize nationalized spaces and territories could not just happen: people are socialized into these relations. Thus, securitizations and militarization became central in consolidating these projects.

---

[39] Igor Torbakov, "The West, Russia and China in Central Asia: What kind of game is being played in the region?" *OAKA* 1, no. 2 (2006).

Attempts by the imperial armies of the US and the EU to stay in the fragmented capital formations/spaces have intensified. With a series of wars beginning in Europe to exploit the power gaps left by the shifts in the worker-states and the former Soviet Union and China, and in order to amass capital, these countries socialized their peoples in practices of terror and surveillance. For instance, the United States National Strategy for Homeland Security (October 2007) acts as a securitizing tool and articulates the US desire to consolidate itself as the Global State in the New Global Political Order. It reads:

> The purpose of our Strategy is to guide, organize, and unify our Nation's homeland security efforts. It provides a common framework by which our entire Nation should focus its efforts on the following four goals: Prevent and disrupt terrorist attacks; Protect the American people, our critical infrastructure, and key resources; Respond to and recover from incidents that do occur; and continue to strengthen the foundation to ensure our long-term success (1).... Since the turn of the millennium, our Nation has endured history's deadliest attack of international terrorism and the most destructive natural disaster to strike American soil.... [but] today we are safer, stronger, and better prepared to address the full range of catastrophic events, including man-made accidents and natural disasters. ...Working together our nation will secure the Homeland in order to sustain our way of life-now and for generations to come (53).... The first principle of our Culture of Preparedness is a shared acknowledgement that creating a prepared Nation will be an enduring challenge. ...We will continue to emphasize the responsibility of the entire Nation to be flexible and ready to cope with a broad range of challenges. (41)

This strategy outlines those sets of knowledge required to socialize people into thinking of themselves as flexible and yet fixed to the homeland, distinguishing the domestic (American and secure) from the foreign (international terrorists, destructive natural disasters, and man-made accidents). It articulates practices of terror deemed necessary by transnational leaders and managers of capital to consolidate the New World Order.

This text and its previous permutations mark a reinsertion of war with impunity in the name of national and individual security. These unfettered imperial hypermasculine and always "white" and "white but not quite armies are centralizing war (that is, the right of equals in the global arena) to maintain their sovereignty and secure their value.[40] However, this global war cannot happen in the old way. Much depends on outsourcing corporate warriors and creating privatized military and prison industries.[41] The current privatization of the military is a worldwide industry

---

[40] Agathangelou et al., "Intimate Investments,"120-144.

[41] Agathangelou, ibid.; Gearoid Ó Tuathail, "Just Out Looking for a Fight: American Affect and the Invasion of Iraq," *Antipode* 35, no.5 (2003): 856-870; Jennifer Hyndman, "Feminist Geopolitics revisited: Body Counts in Iraq," *The Professional Geographer* 5, no. 1(2007): 35-46; Simon Dalby, "Environmental Insecurities: Geopolitics, Resources and Conflict" *Economic and Political Weekly* 38, no.48 (2003): 5073-5079; Ben Kiernan, *Blood and soil: a world history of genocide and extermination from Sparta to Darfur* (New Haven:Yale University Press, 2003).

generating \$200 billion per year; it depends on the gendered, racial labour of peoples at the peripheries who work as private warriors:

> While reliable figures are difficult to come by and governmental accounting and monitoring of the contracts are notoriously shoddy, the US army estimates that of the \$87bn (£50.2bn) earmarked this year for the broader Iraqi campaign, including central Asia and Afghanistan, one third of that, nearly \$30bn, will be spent on contracts to private companies.... The myriad military and security companies thriving on this largesse are at the sharp end of a revolution in military affairs that is taking us into unknown territory - the partial privatisation of war.[42]

These practices of terror are ways to secure accumulation. Echoing Rumsfeld, we see warriors becoming "venture capitalists." The proving ground for this venture is Eurasia, with its major access to oil, people, and Asia itself.

In the 1930s, colonial and imperial powers carved up the region into nation-states to secure their interests, accessing oil and gas as well as money.[43] It is not coincidental that once Baghdad was invaded by the United States, the American troops guarded the Ministry of the Interior and the Ministry of Oil. Since that time, as Gregory notes:

> [F]lows of capital in and out of Iraq leave a trail of death and destruction followed by reconstruction: one of several key decisions in the innumerable meetings in post war Iraq between American and British officials and the shaky interim "government" of Iraq had to do with the establishment of "Iraq Inc." involving the privatization of Iraq's state industries and the allocation of reconstruction contracts to mainly American and British corporations.[44]

Klein adds:

> Any movement serious about Iraqi self-determination must call not only for an end to Iraq's military occupation, but to its economic colonisation as well. That means reversing the shock therapy reforms that US occupation chief Paul Bremer has fraudulently passed off as "reconstruction," and canceling all privatisation contracts that are flowing from these reforms.[45]

---

[42] Ian Traynor, "The Privatisation of War," *Guardian*, December 10, 2003.
[43] These include the "seven sisters" major companies, Exxon (formerly Standard Oil of New Jersey, then Esso), Mobil (formerly Standard Oil of New York, which merged with Vacuum Oil), Chevron (formerly Standard Oil of California), Texaco, Gulf Oil (controlled by the Mellons), Shell (Royal Dutch Petroleum), British Petroleum (Anglo-Iranian). Today, there is a shift in these relations leading to what the Financial Times has called the new seven sisters; see Modern History Project "OPEC, The Seven Sisters, and Control of the Petroleum Industry." http://www.modern historyproject.org/mhp/Article Display.php?Article=FinalWarn08-4#OPEC and Carola Hoyos, "The new Seven Sisters: oil and gas giants dwarf western rivals," *Financial Times*, March 11, 2011.
[44] Derek Gregory, *The Colonial Present: Afghanistan, Palestine, Iraq* (Oxford: Wiley-Blackwell, 2004).
[45] Naomi Klein, "Iraq is not America's to sell: International law is Unequivocal- Paul Bremer`s Economic Reforms are Illegal," *The Guardian*, November 7, 2003.

Using the ontologies of unlimited access to all spaces, territories, bodies, and epistemes of colonial cartographies, Baghdad was redrawn into zones. Of the "Green Zone," one interpreter said: "It's like I never left America. They serve peanut butter, lobster and ice cream. The cell phones have a 914 area code [White Plains, New York]. The television sets show Monday Night Football. The people speak English".[46]

Yet not all zones ensure access to particular commodities for all bodies. Some bodies, like other industries of colonization and slavery[47] are more valuable than others, as Pugliese eloquently articulates:

> Where the 9/11 New York dead will be individuated at Ground Zero through the inscription of all their names on a memorial wall, the Iraqi civilian dead are dispatched to this electronic morgue as so many anonymous numerals...What occurs in that spectral cyberspace marked by the bar between the Minimum and Maximum? What flickers and wavers between this discrepancy of numbers? Who inhabits this macabre space marked by the suspensive hiatus of the dead and the undead? In this indeterminate space are to be found the Iraqi dead who are also undead, lost souls denied even the most minimal conditions of signification.[48]

Pugliese continues his analysis by describing the "necrological tabulating machine" in a reference to the number of private contractors killed.

Outsourcing is another socializing technology of security in the "War on Terror," what I call a productive concept of the global war with a goal to move boundaries, territorial and otherwise, to ensure the major ontology of capitalism: access to anything, anywhere and anytime, with no limitations. There has been an increase in the hiring of soldiers by Privatized Military Firms (PMFs), and private contractors operate prisons in Guantanamo Bay and in Iraq, Afghanistan, Turkey, and the Balkans. Major corporations, including defense contractors, are receiving million-dollar contracts to provide security services and reconstruct Eurasia.[49] These contractors hire migrant labor from the Philippines, Nepal, Pakistan, India and Sri Lanka to do dangerous and dirty "grunt jobs." The racialized and gendered international division of labour is profitable for peripheral states and for corpora-

---

[46] Gregory, *The Colonial Present*, 247

[47] Agathangelou, Anna M. *The Global Political Economy of Sex* (New York: MacMillan-Palgrave, 2004).

[48] Joseph Pugliese, "Asymmetries of Terror," *Borderlands* 5, no.1 (2006). http://www.borderlands.net.au/vol5no1_2006/pugliese.htm

[49] According to Hartung and Berrigan (2007), the biggest winners of Pentagon Prime Contracts in 2005 and 2006 have been 1) Kuwait Petroleum Corp. to $1,011.2 million in 2006 from $330.4; 2) Harris Corp to $1,339.1 from $736.7 in 2005; 3) Tetra Tech to $493.8 from $299.5 in 2005; 4) American Body Armor and Equipment (Armor Holdings) to $634.9 from $419.9; 5) Battelle Memorial Institute to $519.1 from $358; 6) Electronic Data Systems to $2,008.0 from $1,450.5; 7) Renco Group (AM General) $1,994.1 from $1,406.3; 8) Lockheed Martin $26,619.7 from $19,447.1; 9) Thales $656.9 $481.6; 10) Johns Hopkins University $524.7 from $394.2.

tions involved in outsourcing the war on terror and other reconstruction projects. The bodies of these Third Country Nationals carry the marks and embody terrorist neo-liberal capitalist practices, even as their labour generates significant profits for imperial sovereignties. But records of how many have been killed are nowhere to be found.

The outsourcing of war and the global rise of the privatized military industry is not a new phenomenon.[50] Private Military Companies (PMCs), Private Security Companies (PSCs), and contractors and firms in adjacent business sectors have played a greater role in the implementation of the defense, development, and security agendas since the end of the Cold War.[51] It is a global industry operating on every continent except Antarctica.[52] This new site of the corporation has become crucial in deciding the "right to take life or let live."

The "sovereignty" granted postcolonial states and corporations has shifted with the push for the privatization of security and the development of terroristic neo-libero-capitalism. These corporations are active participants in the terror industries and have no accountability. PMFs and PSs sell their services to the highest bidder: nation states, other multinational corporations, international organizations, non-governmental organizations. Of course, such hirings are rife with contradiction: corporations can be hired to "protect" the very people they were hired to kill earlier, as in Angola.[53]

The privatization of war and peace are guided by the epistemes and ontologies of the market. A major and enduring effect of this *polemos* (i.e., war) is the erection of frames of intelligibility within which the neo-liberal imperium no longer refers to racialized modes of capital accumulation, to racialized divisions of labor, to specific forced distributions of land, peoples, and worlds, to certain exhaustive epistemic formations, to particular social relations of power, to projects of terror and genocide in the name of security; in short, it no longer refers to deliberations over lands, grounds, regions, racial, class, gender, sexual, knowledge and spatial

---

[50] Peter W. Singer, *Corporate Warriors* (New York: Cornell University Press, 2003).

[51] These include risk advisory, training of local forces, armed site security, cash transport, intelligence services, workplace and building security, war zone security needs, weapons procurement, personnel and budget vetting, armed support, air support, logistical support, maritime security, cyber security, weapons destruction, prisons, surveillance, psychological warfare, propaganda tactics, covert operations, close protection and investigations, combat operations, strategic planning, asset protection, support and training. See Singer, Peter W. Corporate Warriors; Lize Mogel and Mario Azzellini, "The Privatization of War: Colombia as Laboratory and Iraq as Large-Scale Application,"
Critical Spatial Practice, 2006. http://criticalspatialpractice.blogspot.com/2006/09/privatization-of-war.html.

[52] Ibid.

[53] Singer, *Corporate Warriors*.

formations. Instead, our debates in international relations about empire, the war on terror, and security instantiate the neoliberal imperium's violence and terror as merely external threats to the viability of the structures in place; they become the constitutive antagonisms of the neo-imperial, neo-colonial world whose ontology is fear, expendability, and profit.

IV. Greek Theory and Indiscernible (In) Security?

> I cannot help laughing at the absurdity of all the map-makers – there are plenty of them – who show the Ocean running like a river round a perfectly circular earth, with Asia and Europe of the same size.
>
> Herodotus 1972, 4.282

In the above passage, Herodotus, echoing other Greek writers, including Hecauteus of Miletus, articulates the narrative as a contested paradigm about the worlds (visible and invisible) in which he finds himself. Such writing contests the dominant narratives that represent the existing worlds and are written to enclose structures of inquiry within dominant and conquering relations. International relations theorists have consistently drawn on Greek thought to justify conquest and destruction; this pushes us to recognize the need to rethink theory and our reading of theory. How do we use this to disrupt the dominant but "flat narratives" of world politics, when social, national, and personal security are the bywords of the day?

Kavafis' "Ithaca" signals to a collective solidarity, asking us to "rethink thinking itself" and the choices we make daily in constituting our multiple journeys:

> As you set out for Ithaca
> hope your road is a long one,
> full of adventure, full of discovery.
> Laistrygonians, Cyclops,
> angry Poseidon – don't be afraid of them:
> you' ll never find things like that on your way
> as long as you keep your thoughts raised high,
> as long as a rare excitement
> stirs your spirit and your body.
> Laistrygonians, Cyclops,
> wild Poseidon - you won't encounter them
> unless you bring them along inside your soul,
> unless your soul sets them up in front of you.[54]

---

[54] Constantine Kavafis, "Ithaca," http://cavafis.compupress.gr/index2.htm.

As Kavafis' poem indicates, life embodies multiple journeys. It is never the dominant "Western" imaginary of security couched in "taking-care" imaginaries. These imaginaries make us invisible and render our choices invisible. We are no longer active participants who create our world but those lacking choices. We are seduced into believing that choices are made by leaders whose primary ontological interest is us and our well-being. We become spectators, judging those who generate insecurity. Flat narratives of security and peace, narratives of our terminators terminating the terrorists, do not implicate us; they do not permit us to account for our roles in creating those conditions that make possible terrorism and other insecurities. Our multiple journeys are resolved into a narrative of "securitization as discursive practice….[one that] synchroniz[es] security, safety, and certitude. It depicts all three as co-temporal occurrences. To be secure is to be safe is to be sure. To secure is to protect from danger is to know the danger and how to go about doing the protecting".[55]

These imaginaries make invisible the roles we play and the living flesh and the labour "we" and others contribute to the formation of our dominant neoliberal imperium. Engagement with those whose labour and "unsafe" lives due to exploitation and accumulation regimes is being elided in studies of security. Yet this labour enabled the rise of industrializing economies and militant regimes, including the sex industries which sustain the massive military presence in South Korea and elsewhere. The postcolonial feminist critique unpacks these flat narratives; it questions dominant thinking and its effect on Asian security and asks, "What kind of Asian and what kind of security?" What is our role in constituting and consolidating such imaginaries which silence antagonism and violence? How can our labour contribute to the formation of our present?

In his poem, Kavafis pushes us to disrupt the tracking of empire, while postcolonial feminists such as Tadiar (2004) remind us that security in Asia has meant a dependence on "living labor" (56). Speaking of the Philippines, Tadiar says:

> Living labor means the labor of living, which is often the main labor of disposable, surplus people. The cheapness of Filipina labor in the domestic labor export industry as well as in the urban service economy depends on them being disposable, surplus people, which means before they can serve as cheap labor. …they first must expend work to survive. Indeed, what most have had to survive are the consequences of the developmentalist, counter-insurgency war in the countryside that has for more than half a century been and continues to be waged by the Philippine state. …The Philippine war of "security" that began during the Cold War, one might argue, itself serves as an industry that produces disposable, surplus people.[57]

"Living labor" points to the dominant socio-ontology of exploitation, profit, and

---

[55] Costas Costantinou, "Poetics of Security," *Alternatives: Global, Local, Political* 25, no. 3 (July-September 2000): 287-306.
[56] Tadiar, *Fantasy-Production*, 15.
[57] Ibid.

accumulation.

A feminist postcolonial critical approach to "security" begins by articulating ways to disrupt the ontology of exploitation and profit accumulation regimes that enable capitalist accumulations, wars, and (in)securities. Such a critical approach gestures to the blurring of the line between security/insecurity and notes the spectrum of (in)security – as experienced in the home, society, and across conflict lines. In the economy of new imperialism, terroristic practices are embodied in mobility and the extraction of surplus under stringent conditions of national security and war (i.e., the "War on Terror" is a measure of security). This is central in sorting out the security-capable from the (in) secure. Yet globalization, or the free and fragmented nature of capitalist extractive regimes and the "War on Terror," renders them unsustainable. The biggest contradiction of these terroristic practices is the disjuncture between their vision of measurement and containment and their desire to link all peoples (who occupy different social locations in terms of gender, race, class, nationality, regionalism).

When we recognize this investment and our role in it, we begin to ask questions. From whose perspective do we enter the conversation on (in)security and war? Outside the terroristic practices of capitalism (i.e., labour relations, wars, state security), what kind of worlds/communities may we imagine? Surveillance, monitoring, and tracking are not merely technologies of terror; they are also social relations of intervention, and our revolutionary work requires us to argue points and positions and to tease out content that could not be expressed otherwise. For instance, as the neoliberal imperium moves to consolidate itself, it is not enough to argue for "old" ways of change. As new geometries of terror, voyeurism, pleasure, and fear shape our spatial relations, what would it mean for us to confront our own affective investments in violence? It is important that we look at this living labour and think about how to create the conditions necessary to disrupt the dominant practices.

Which Euro-Asian stories of the everyday do we bring to bear on our shaping of worlds that do not centralize the dominant vision of security of capital and state powers as we have come to know it through the United States, Russia, Japan, and now China? How do we imagine belonging without a security of capital and state powers? What does that security look like?

To Epicurus, this belonging is not the instrumental security of the present bolstered by the vision of empire. Rather, the socio-ontology of Epicurus exceeds the multiple worlds we are now part of[58]; it speaks to a globality which begins with social existence as historico-onto-structurally heterogeneous, with intersubjective

[58] Frantz Fanon, *The Wretched of the Earth* (New York: Grove Press, 1965), 12-13.

being as primary to all other relations (even work relations), and including the tensions generated in the constitution of the hegemonic model of power whose primary assumption is property relations (modernity).[59] While there is a trajectory toward "a common value orientation," including a set of "common" social practices and hegemonic institutions in all aspects of social existence, this trajectory is always contested – even when hegemonic institutions of social existence are universal but not necessarily global.[60]

This socio-ontological approach helps us to read frameworks in international political economy and to problematize them. If this is our point of departure from other IPE theorists and we acknowledge those who re-situate crucial questions in coloniality, we can argue that the globally hegemonic model of power presupposes an element of coloniality with race as a politico-ontological structuring project.[61] Any critical theorizing of security in Asia must begin with a global model of power which centralizes coloniality.

Starting with this insight, we could analyze the security institutions that articulate the segregation of the global world system and a model of power which constitutes itself as global by bringing together all spheres of social existence under the hegemony of an institution produced within that same model of power. Different institutions control different spheres. For instance, the capitalist enterprise controls labor and its resource, the bourgeois family controls sex, its resources and products, the nation-state controls and manages authority, resources and its products, and Eurocentrism controls and manages intersubjectivity. They are interdependent and rife with tension.[62] Recognition of this structuring requires *a poetics of socio-ontology/social existence* which Epicurus defines as the relationships of accompaniment in struggle and deliberation, a collective linked by mutual support of a life-giving cooperative struggle that ontologically validates one's existence and creative life-activity.

A project of revolution points to the disruptions already taking place. It disrupts that which is very familiar (and often predicated on promises), articulating frames that interrupt our daily terroristic practices. It is crucial to articulate feminist pro-

---

[59] Anna M. Agathangelou, "Necro- (neo) Colonizations and Economies of Blackness: Of Slaughters, 'Accidents,' 'Disasters' and Captive Flesh," in *International Relations and States of Exception: Margins, Peripheries and Excluded Bodies,* ed. Sheila Nair and Shampa Biswas *(New York: Routledge*, 2009), 186-209.
[60] Anna M. Agathangelou, "Bodies of Desire, Terror and the War in Eurasia: Impolite Disruptions of (Neo) Liberal Internationalism, Neoconservatism and the 'New' Imperium," *Millennium—Journal of International Studies* 38, no. 3 (2010): 698.
[61] Anna M. Agathangelou, "Bodies to the Slaughter: Slavery, Reconstruction, Fanon's Combat Breath, and Wrestling for Life," *Somatechnics Journal* 1, no. 1 (2011): 230
[62] Anibal Quijano, "Coloniality of Power, Eurocentrism, and Latin America," *Nepantla* 1, no.3 (2000): 545; Agathangelou, *The Global Political Economy of Sex*, 15.

jects that critique contemporary politics and its frames of reference. But how does one intervene in production and framing projects? We need a political project that disrupts militarization and the everyday by allowing us to recognize that we already inhabit the social relations of terroristic practices. We are already part of the politics of capital and war; the everyday is part of it, not marginal to "political" militarization. We need a politics, a series of critical strategies and political engagements that play out and that, along with art and poetry, are political in their orientation. Entering into the articulation of hitherto unacknowledged conditions of our existence, we must ask why we are invested in annihilation. Whom are we entertaining?

References:

Agathangelou, Anna M. *The Global Political Economy of Sex: Desire,Violence and Insecurity in Mediterranean Nation-States*. New York: MacMillan/Palgrave, 2004.

_____. "Necro- (neo) Colonizations and Economies of Blackness: Of Slaughters, 'Accidents,' 'Disasters' and Captive Flesh." In *International Relations and States of Exception: Margins, Peripheries and Excluded Bodies*, edited by Shampa Biswas and Sheila Nair, 186-206. New York: Routledge, 2009.

_____. "Bodies of Desire, Terror and the War in Eurasia: Impolite Disruptions of (Neo) Liberal Internationalism, Neoconservatism and the 'New' Imperium." *Millennium—Journal of International Studies* 38, no. 3 (2010): 693-722.

_____. "Bodies to the Slaughter: Slavery, Reconstruction, Fanon's Combat Breath, and Wrestling for Life." *Somatechnics Journal* 1, no. 1 (2011): 209-248.

Agathangelou, Anna, M. and L.H.M. Ling *Transforming World Politics: From Empire To Multiple Worlds*. New York: Routledge, 2009.

Agathangelou, Anna, M., Daniel Bassichis, and Tamara Spira "Intimate Investments: Homonormativity, Global Lockdown, and Seductions of Empire." *Radical History Review* 100 (2008): 120-144.

Agathangelou, Anna, M. Anna Kim, Abhinava Kumar, Nelson Lai, Derek Maisonville, Emily Rosser, and Melissa White, ed. *Technologies of Empire and (In) Secure Possibilities*. York University: Centre for International and Security Studies, 2007.

Alnasseri, Sabah. "Understanding Iraq." In *Global Flashpoints: Socialist Register 2010*, edited by Colin Leys and Leo Panitch, 77-100. London: The Merlin Press, 2009.

Appadurai, Arjun. *Modernity at Large: Cultural Dimensions of Globalization*. Minneapolis: University of Minnesota Press, 1996.

Appadurai, Arjun. “Grassroots Globalization and the Research Imagination.” *Public Culture* 12, no. 1 (1999): 1-19.

Aziz, al-Azmeh. “Postmodern Obscurantism and 'The Muslim Question'.” *JSRI* 5 (Summer 2003):21-47. Accessed November 18, 2011. http://www.jsri.ro/old/html%20version/index/no_5/aziaalazmeh-articol.htm

Bilgin, Pinar. “ ‘Is the ‘Orientalist’ Past the Future of Middle East Studies?” *Third World Quarterly* 25, no.2 (2004): 423-433.

Brzezinski, Zbigniew. *The Grand Chessboard*. New York: Basic Books, 1997.

_____. “A Geostrategy for Eurasia, Foreign Affairs, The Council on Foreign Relations.” *Foreign Affairs* 76, No. 5 (September/October 1997). Accessed October 2011. http://www.comw.org/pda/fulltext/9709brzezinski.html.

Bush, George W. *Speech before a Joint Session of Congress*. (Speech, White House: Washington D.C., September 20, 2001.

Bush, George W. *Our Vision and Strategy for Homeland Security*. Washington: Homeland Security, 2007.

Caldwell, Anne. “Empire and Exception.” *New Political Science* 28, no. 4 (2006): 489 –506.

Chin, Larry. “A six-part series, The United States in the Philippines: Post-9/11 imperatives.” Online Journal (17 July 2002). Accessed November 2, 2011. http://globalresearch.ca/articles/CHI207A.html

Costantinou, Costas. “Poetics of Security.” *Alternatives: Global, Local, Political* 25, no.3 (July-September 2000): 287-306.

Dalby, Simon "Environmental Insecurities: Geopolitics, Resources and Conflict." *Economic and Political Weekly* 38, no. 48 (2003): 5073-5079.

Escobar, Pepe “The US and Eurasia: Theatrical Militarism.”*Asian Times*, December 2, 2002. Accessed October 17, 2011. http://www.atimes.com/atimes/Front_Page/DL04Aa01.html

Fanon, Frantz. *The Wretched of the Earth*. New York : Grove Press, 1965.

Foster, Bellamy John. “The New Geopolitics of Empire.” *Monthly Review* 57, no. 8 (2006). http://monthlyreview.org/2006/01/01/the-new-geopolitics-of-empire

Gregory, Derek. *The Colonial Present: Afghanistan, Palestine, Iraq*. Oxford: Wiley-Blackwell, 2004.

Hardt, Michael and Antonio Negri. *Empire*. Cambridge: Harvard University Press, 2000.

Hartung, William D. and Frida Berrigan. “Top Pentagon Contractors, FY2006: Major Beneficiaries of the Bush Administration’s Military Buildup.” A World Policy Institute Special Report. 2007.

Heidegger, Martin. *Introduction to Metaphysics*. Translated by G. Fried and R. Pol. New Haven, CT: Yale University Press, 2000.

Heinberg, Richard. *The Party's Over: Oil, War and the Fate of Industrial Societies*. British Colombia: New Society Publishers, 2003.

Heinberg, Richard. “The US and Eurasia: End Game for the Industrial Era?” 2003.

Accessed March 25, 2011.
http://www.manifeste.org/article.php3?id_article=182

Hecataeus of Miletus. *Hecataei Milesii Fragmenta: Scylacis Caryandensis Periplus*. Edited by Rud Klausen. Oxford: Oxford University Press, 1954.

Herodotus. *The Histories*. Edited by Aubrey de Selincourt. New York: Penguin Books, 1972.

Hoyos, Carola. "The new Seven Sisters: oil and gas giants dwarf western rivals." *Financial Times*, March 11, 2011.

Hyndman, Jennifer. "Feminist Geopolitics revisited: body counts in Iraq." *The Professional Geographer* 59, no.1 (2007): 35-46.

Ikenberry, John, G. "America's Imperial Ambition." *Foreign Affairs* 81, no. 5 (2002): 44-60.

Kavafis, Constantine. *Ithaca*. 1911. http://cavafis.compupress.gr/index2.htm.

Kiernan, Ben. *Blood and Soil: A World History of Genocide and Extermination from Sparta to Darfur*. New Haven: Yale University Press, 2003.

Kipling, Rudyard. *Kim*. Edited by Zohreh T. Sullivan. New York: Norton, 2002.

Klein, Naomi. "Iraq is not America's to sell: International law is unequivocal - Paul Bremer's economic reforms are illegal." *The Guardian*, February 7, 2007.

_____. "Iraq is not America's to sell: International law is Unequivocal – Paul Bremer`s Economic Reforms are Illegal." *The Guardian*, 7 November 2003.

_____. "Iraq: Privatization in Disguise." *Thunder Bay Indymedia*, April 15, 2003.

Loraux, Nicole. *The Invention of Athens: The Funeral Oration in the Classical City*. Translated by Alan Sheridan. New York: Zone Books, 2006.

Lenin, Vladimir Ilich. *Imperialism the Highest Stage of Capitalism*. Australia: Resistance Books, 1999.

Ling, L.H.M. "Cultural Chauvinism and the Liberal International Order: "West versus Rest" in Asia's Financial Crisis." In *Power, Postcolonialism, and International Relations: Reading Race, Gender, Class*, edited by Geeta Chowdhry and Sheila Nair, 115-141. London: Routledge, 2002.

Luxemburg, Rosa. *Selected Political Writings of Rosa Luxemburg*. Edited by Dick Howard. NewYork and London: Monthly Review Press, 1971.

Mahdi, Kamil. "Privatisation won't make you popular. Resistance has forced a military rethink- but not an economic one." *The Guardian*, November 26, 2003.

Mogel, Lize and Azzellini Mario. "The Privatization of War: Colombia as Laboratory and Iraq as Large-Scale Application." *Critical Spatial Practice*, 2006. Accessed October 3, 2011.
http://criticalspatialpractice.blogspot.com/2006/09/privatization-of-war.html

Modern History Project "OPEC, The Seven Sisters, and Control of the Petroleum

Industry." Accessed November 11, 2011. http://www.modernhistoryproject.org/mhp/ArticleDisplay.php?Article=FinalWarn08-4#OPEC

Ó Tuathail, Gearoid. "Just Out Looking for a Fight: American Affect and the Invasion of Iraq." *Antipode* 35, no.5 (2003): 856-870.

Plato. *The Laws of Plato*. Translated by T. Pangle. Illinois: Chicago: University of Chicago Press, 1980.

_____.*The Republic*. Translated by Benjamin Jowett. University of Adelaide, 2004.

Pugliese, Joseph. "Asymmetries of Terror: Visual Regimes of Racial Profiling and the Shooting of Jean Charles de Menezes in the Context of the War in Iraq." *Borderlands* 5, no.1 (2006). Accessed November 1, 2011. http://www.borderlands.net.au/vol5no1_2006/pugliese.htm

Quijano, Anibal. "Coloniality of Power, Eurocentrism, and Latin America." *Nepantla* 1, no.3 (2000): 545.

Savran, Sungur. "Globalisation and the New World Order: The New Dynamics of Imperialism and War." In *The Politics of Empire: Globalisation in Crisis*, edited by Alan Freeman and Boris Kagarlitsky, 117-150. London: Pluto Press, 2004.

Scahill, Jeremy. *Blackwater: The Rise of the World's Most Powerful Mercenary Army*. New York: Nation Books, 2007.

Schifferes, Steve. "US names 'coalition of the willing'." *BBC*. March 18, 2003.

Singer, Peter W. *Corporate Warriors*. New York: Cornell University Press, 2003.

Tadiar, Neferti. *Fantasy-Production: Sexual Economies and Other Philippine Consequences for the New World Order*. Hong Kong: Hong Kong University Press/ Ateneo de Manila University Press, 2004.

Torbakov, Igor. "The West, Russia and China in Central Asia: What kind of game is being played in the region?" *OAKA* 1, no.2 (2006): 27-37.

Traynor, Ian. "The Privatisation of War." *The Guardian,* December 10, 2003.

Tuazon, Bobby. "Current US Hegemony In Asia Pacific." Accessed 10 October 2011. http://www.converge.org.nz/abc/pr28-84.html

The White House. *Iraq Benchmark Assessment Report*. Council on Foreign Relations, Washington, September 14, 2007.

_____. *The National Security Strategy of the United States of America*. March 2006. Accessed October 2, 2011. http://georgewbush-whitehouse.archives.gov/nsc/nss/2006

_____. *Benchmark Assessment Report*. September 2007. Accessed October 2, 2011. http://merln.ndu.edu/archivepdf/iraq/WH/20070914.pdf.

Wolfowitz, Paul. "Defense Planning Guidance." *New York Times*. March 8, 1992.

Woodward, Susan, L. *Balkan Tragedy: Chaos and Dissolution after the Cold War*.Washington: The Brookings Institution, 1995.
Zizek, Slavoj. "Slavoj Zizek: On war in Iraq, Zionism and Palestinian terror." *From Occupied Palestine,* 2004. Accessed November 4, 2011. http://www.fromoccupiedpalestine.org/node.php?id=1266.

Unmaking Neoliberal Europe: Capitalist Crisis and the Search for Alternatives

Ingo Schmidt

About a decade ago, Europe was going strong. Its leaders had launched the common currency in 1999, prepared the accession of Eastern European countries, and, at the Lisbon Summit 2000, declared that the European Union (EU) would become the world's most competitive and fastest growing region over the next ten years. It did not work out that way. Even before the Great Recession, economic growth in the EU was lagging behind the US, not to mention growth stars like China and India. All that was growing fast in the EU were imbalances between creditor and debtor countries, the polarization between the rich and the poor and distrust among ordinary Europeans vis-à-vis their leaders. When the recession eventually hit in 2008/9, it was really just the last straw that broke Europe's back. As elsewhere, a mix of bank bailouts and fiscal stimulus turned the crisis of the private economy into a fiscal crisis of the state. Unlike elsewhere, this transformation was accompanied by a sovereign debt crisis in some of EU debtor countries, which, in turn, challenges the very existence of the Euro, if not of the EU as a whole. Business and political elites are torn between austerity plain and simple and a mix of austerity for the poor and the continued injection of money into financial markets. They are also divided over the question of transferring more decision making power to the EU-level or strengthening national sovereignty vis-à-vis Brussels. This issue is further complicated by growing frustrations among governments of small member states over the dominance of large countries, namely France and Germany, and quarrels between insiders and outsiders of the Euro-zone. The political crisis at the top corresponds with a crisis of legitimacy at the bottom. As the voting patterns show, this crisis was looming for a long time. Turnout at national elections has always been higher than at European elections and both have been declining more or less steadily over the last decades. Over the course of the economic and political crises in Europe these legitimation problems became much more acute, though. In the creditor countries of the Euro-zone, the crisis of legitimacy is mostly expressed by growing support for right-wing populists and their anti-European propaganda. This kind of anti-Europeanism is mostly fuelled by a sense that the EU unjustly transfers hard earned money to undeserving idlers in the deficit countries. Such sentiments scale up pressures on the governments of creditor countries to impose harsh austerity measures onto deficit countries. The actual and future losses of jobs, social security, and public services that such measures cause triggered a series of mass protests and strikes in deficit countries like Greece, Portugal and Spain. The social agenda of these struggles is complemented by resentment against subordination of their countries to the dictates of creditor states, EU-institutions, and the IMF. The Europe that was progressing strongly down the neoliberal road a decade ago is now pulled apart by centrifugal forces. The search for alternatives to neoliberal Europe has begun. This article tries to explain why the world recession of 2008/9 translated into a variety of economic and political crises in Europe. Against this background, left- and right-wing alternatives to neoliberal Europe will be discussed. At first, though, the theoretical principles that guide the analyses of crises and alternatives in Europe will be introduced.

Theoretical Starting Points

Accumulation is the lifeblood of capitalist economies; when it stops some companies go bankrupt, their previous owners may even fall down the social ladder and join the growing ranks of unemployed workers. Thus, the only way to maintain social status, profits and wages is to keep accumulation going. However, there are two threats to doing so. One threat is that efforts to spur profits and accumulation by slashing wages cut into workers' consumer spending. In this case, higher profits cannot be realized because of a decline of companies' sales. The other threat is that wage raises, even though they may boost sales, squeeze profit rates.

The installation of labour-saving technologies may appear as a way out of the deadlock between the Scylla of insufficient consumer spending[1] and the Charybdis of a profit squeeze.[2] Labour costs will decrease because less labour power has to be

---

[1] Michael F. Bleaney, *Underconsumption Theories: A History and Critical Analysis* (New York: International Publishers, 1976). Radhika Desai, "Consumption Demand in Marx and in the Current Crisis," In *Research in Political Economy* 26 (2010): 101-143.

[2] Andre Glyn and Robert Sutcliffe, *British Capitalism and the Profit Squeeze* (London: Penguin Books, 1972). Richard M. Goodwin, "A Growth Cycle," in *Socialism, Capitalism, and Economic Growth: Essays Presented to Maurice Dobb*, ed. C. H. Feinstein et al. (Cambridge, MA: Cambridge University Press 1967), 54-58.

bought to produce a given amount of commodities, and because lower employment levels eventually lead to lower wages per working hour. Higher investment spending will compensate sale shortfalls that are caused by the decreased wage bill. After all, without such investments no labour-saving technology could be installed. However, the replacement of human labour impairs accumulation in its own ways. If the costs of labour-saving technologies exceed associated increases in labour-productivity, the profit rate will actually fall instead of rise. This is Marx's famous, and highly controversial, law of the tendency of the profit rate to fall.[3] Yet, even if the character of new technology is not such that it will lead to a falling profit rate, the accumulation process runs into problems. Investments in new technology, like any other net investments, create additional demand in the short term but cannot stop the long-term build up of overcapacities. Under competition from other companies, firms do not only seek to lower production costs at a given level of output, but also aim to increase their sales and output. One way of doing this is to add to already existing production capacity to serve a growing market. Individual capitalists may not care much whether they sell investment goods to other companies or consumer goods to private households. The capitalist economy as a whole, though, cannot rely on an increasing share of investment demand just because companies try to slash their wage bills and thus workers' purchasing power, which, despite the wasteful lifestyles of the rich, is still the main source for consumer spending. After a detour via investments in new technologies and additional production capacity the capitalist economy is back to its original deadlock between insufficient demand and profit squeeze.

Historically, the way accumulation within the capitalist economy was kept alive was by expanding into "non-capitalist social strata at home and in the outside world."[4] Some of these strata are engaged in simple commodity production but are still outside of the capitalist process of accumulation. They can be integrated into the accumulation process, and thus create additional demand for commodities produced within it, because capitalist production tends to be cheaper than simple commodity production. Thus, competition between the capitalist economy and

---

[3] Karl Marx, "Capital, Vol. III," in *Marx Engels Collected Works*, Vol. 37. (New York: International Publishers, 1998 (originally published in German in 1894)), 209-238. For the recent controversy on this law see, among others: Gerard Duménil and Dominique Lévy, "The Profit Rate: Where and How Much Did it Fall? Did it Recover?" *Review of Radical Political Economics* 34 (2002): 437-461. Chris Harman, "The Rate of Profit and the World Today," *International Socialism* 115 (2007), http://www.isj.org.uk/?id=340. Michel Husson, "The Debate on the Rate of Profit," *International Viewpoint* 425 (2010), http://www.internationalviewpoint.org/spip.php?article1894. Fred Moseley, "The Rate of Profit and the Future of Capitalism," *Review of Radical Political Economics* 29 (1997): 23-41.

[4] Rosa Luxemburg, *The Accumulation of Capital* (London, New York: Routledge, 2003 [1913]), 447.

non-capitalist strata leads to an expansion of the former at the expense of the latter. Where non-capitalist economies do not use money or, if they do so, cannot be integrated into the circuits of capital accumulation as fast as is necessary to find sufficient demand for capitalist firms, a mix of credit and violence is be used to open new markets for capitalist expansion.[5]

The role of financial and military power in opening new markets is illustrated by the neoliberal wave of accumulation, which began in the early 1980s and reached its limits with the Great Recession.[6] One of the products of the preceding, Keynesian, wave of accumulation was fiscal crises of Western welfare states and debt crises of development states in the South. Western government, turning from Keynes to Friedman, used these crises effectively to enforce the privatization of state-owned companies, public services like health care and education, and pension systems. Ruling elites in the South that were either too weak or unwilling to turn to neoliberalism received support from Western-controlled institutions, namely the IMF, World Bank, WTO, and Western military, in privatizing the commons in those countries. Another product of the Keynesian wave of accumulation further fuelled the neoliberal wave. Encouraged by high levels of employment and job security during the Keynesian wave, workers had begun to demand not only higher wages, but also a say in job design and company management. Groups that had been on the periphery of welfare capitalism, such as women, ethnic minorities, and immigrant workers, also began raising their voices, just like the cross-class coalitions that built the developmental states in the South. Thus, there was a real threat that profits would be squeezed by wage increases in the North and jacked up prices that resource-exporters in the South would charge. Yet, the bargaining power of Northern unions and Southern exporters was broken by dispersing production processes, which hitherto had been concentrated in the industrial districts of the North, into global and regional supply networks[7] that could be rearranged as soon as workers at one of the networks junctions began organizing. Part of this restructuring process was the integration of comprador-bourgeoisies of the South into the neoliberal international. Without political support from labour or other progressive movements from the North, Southern middle and working classes proved too weak to resist the turn from import-substitution to world market integration. The road to global production was open – but it had to be built. Massive investments in logistics and production sites around the globe spurred accumulation beyond the levels made possible by the aforementioned privatizations. Yet, the further privatizations

---

[5] Luxemburg, *Accumulation*, Section III: The Historical Conditions of Accumulation.

[6] Ingo Schmidt, ed., *Spielarten des Neoliberalismus*. Hamburg: VSA-Verlag, 2008. Ingo Schmidt, "Rosa Luxemburg's Accumulation of Capital: New Perspectives on Capitalist Development and American Hegemony," *Socialist Studies* 6 (2010): 92-117.

[7] Alan M. Rugman and Alain Verbeke, "A Perspective on Regional and Global Strategies of Multinational Enterprises," *Journal of International Business Studies* 35 (2004): 3-18.

and industrial restructuring went, the smaller were the stimulating effects they had on aggregate demand. At the same time, a complementary explosion of debt and speculation, which boosted consumer demand while it lasted – ushered in the unravelling of neoliberal capitalism once the financial house of cards fell apart.

The economic crisis of neoliberal capitalism soon raised the spectre of unruly masses interfering with the crisis management of business and political elites. The crisis of legitimacy[8] that began soon after governments told their electorates that they had to tighten their belts while financial markets acquired unlimited access to state money shows clearly that the Great Recession was more than a cyclical crisis. Like other major crises in the past – namely the Depression of the 1870s-90s, the Great Depression of the 1930s, and the Stagflation of the 1970s – it called into question not only the accumulation strategies and political systems under which capitalism had developed prior to these crises, but also, capitalism itself.[9] A major crisis is one in which accumulation halts; political capacities to re-start it fail; and, subordinated classes, or sections of them, seek major changes of the economic and political system. Subordinate classes appear as autonomous social actors only when the store of legitimacy of the existing economic and political system has been exhausted. The next step after moving from an economic crisis to a crisis of legitimacy is the search for alternatives.

Neoliberalism is now in a state of crisis that Keynesianism was facing in the 1970s. In that decade, a series of recessions, currency crises, fiscal crises, accelerating inflation and unemployment contradicted the Keynesian promise that state intervention was able to maintain full employment along with continually rising wages and profits. At the time, Marxists offered a multiplicity of explanations for the crisis of Keynesian capitalism[10] whereas neoliberals offered just one. The welfare state, they argued, diverts economic activity from hard work and innovation to rent seeking. Efforts to acquire already existing wealth through redistribution, rather than the production of additional wealth, lead to stagnation.[11] Keynesian efforts to counteract stagnation and the unemployment that accompanies it, by means of expanding money supply and government spending, fuel inflation instead of aggregate demand and employment.[12] Job creation schemes are guided by the false

---

[8] Jurgen Habermas, *Legitimation Crises* (Boston: Beacon Press, 1975).

[9] Ingo Schmidt, "Große Krisen seit den 1930er Jahren," *Prokla – Zeitschrift für kritische Sozialwissenschaften* 39 (2009): 523-540.

[10] For a short overview see: James O'Connor, *The Meaning of Crisis – A Theoretical Introduction* (Oxford, New York: Basil Blackwell, 1987), 49-107.

[11] Kevin M. Murphy, Andrei Shleifer, Robert W. Vishny, "Why is Rent-Seeking so Costly to Growth?" *American Economic Review* 83 (1993): 409-414.

[12] Milton Friedman, "The Role of Monetary Policy," *American Economic Review* 58 (1968): 1-17.

belief that workers are involuntarily unemployed, while according to neoliberal theory, they are lured into voluntary joblessness by an overly generous welfare state. Marxist and other heterodox economists charged this theory for its reliance on unrealistic and overly simplified assumptions, as well as a lack of empirical validity.[13] Other critics pointed to the huge ideological apparatuses that promoted academic theories, which were considered rather obscure even within economics departments until the early 1970s, to an almost unchallenged common sense status over the course of the 1980s and early 1990s.[14] As true as these critiques may be, they almost invariably fail to recognize that neoliberalism was not attractive because of its scholarly qualities or its support from rich sponsors and corporate media, but because it made sense to people from different classes who were struggling with impudent state bureaucrats, job loss and the negative effects of inflation on their current and future incomes. Neoliberalism had not only served as an explanation for these concerns, but also provided a simple solution: to let people develop their enthusiasm for work and innovation unburdened by taxes and government regulations. This recipe was all the more attractive since it also incorporated some of the New Left zeitgeist of the early 1970s. A critique of capitalism and the Keynesian welfare state that was originally meant to open pathways from the withering of the capitalist state to communism was successfully turned into a strategy of melting the welfare state into the thin air of global capitalism. Neoliberalism promised to lift the burden of taxation and government regulations for everybody and thus improve peoples' opportunities for self-fulfilment. However, it did not take too long until people found out that some of them, dependent on their class-, race-, and gender-statuses, had more opportunities than others. While the lucky few at the top, who were increasingly symbolized by Wall Street and other financial centres, became increasingly wealthier by a few mouse-clicks, others toiled away fearing they would soon join the growing ranks of the working poor. In the late 1990s, growing discontent with neoliberalism led to a wave of international protest movements like the anti-WTO protests in Seattle and the World Social Forum, which defiantly declared that another world is possible and called for increasing support for social democratic parties. However, street protests petered out in the early 2000s and social democrats took the neoliberal road as soon as they were elected into office, as opposed to campaigning for the "other world" that their supporters, along with many protestors, were waiting for. It was not until the series of economic and political crises that started with the Great Recession that the crisis of legitimacy deepened enough to reach the core of neoliberal hegemony. Divisions

---

[13] Alfredo Saad-Filho and Deborah Johnston, ed., *Neoliberalism – A Critical Reader* (London, Ann Arbor: Pluto Press, 2005).

[14] Richard Cockett, *Thinking the Unthinkable – Think Tanks and the Economic Counter-Revolution, 1931-1983* (London: Fontana Press, 1995). Kim Phillips-Fein, *Invisible Hands – The Businessmen's Crusade Against the New Deal* (New York, London: W. W. Norton, 2009).

within the ruling neoliberal bloc are so deep now and popular discontent is so profound that it seems most unlikely that the neoliberal hegemony can be restored.

Neoliberal Europe and its Economic Crisis

Neoliberalism in Europe, just as in other parts of the world, developed as a response to the economic and legitimation crises of Keynesian welfare states in the 1970s; it became a hegemonic project after progressive alternatives to Keynesianism, such as the Alternative Economic Strategy in Britain or the Common Program advocated by a socialist-communist alliance in France, were defeated.[15] The election of Margaret Thatcher in Britain and François Mitterand's turn from left-Keynesianism to neoliberalism were arguably the two key events that set Europe on the path to neoliberalism. West Germany, which had rebuilt its economy after World War II on the principles of balanced budgets, tight money, and world market integration[16], had exerted diplomatic and economic pressures on its European neighbours all through the post-war boom, but it was only after the crises of the 1970s that other major countries followed this lead. Since then, pressure on countries where domestic forces were too weak to establish their home-grown versions of neoliberalism came increasingly under external pressure to adopt the new economic model. The EU, and more precisely its predecessor European Community (EC)[17], were instrumental in institutionalizing the advancements that neoliberalism had made on the domestic level, as well as extending them to countries where such advancements were lagging behind.

The EC was well positioned as a promoter of neoliberalism in the 1980s since it had advanced neoliberal ideas right from its beginnings in the 1950s. Those years are commonly, and rightly so, associated with Keynesian welfare states and macroeconomic demand management. Yet, instead of diagnosing a clear break between a Keynesian era in the 1950s and 1960s and a neoliberal era following the period of crises and political reorientation in the 1970s it seems appropriate to mention that neoliberal policies were already pursued in the shadow of the Keynesian hegemony during the post-war decades. US companies, for example, already began relocating production from unionized workplaces to non-union shops during the heyday of the post-war boom and took advantage of anti-union legislation in some of the US-

---

[15] Ingo Schmidt, "There Were Alternatives: Lessons from Efforts to Advance Beyond Keynesian and Neoliberal Economic Policies in the 1970s," *Working USA* 14 (2011): 473-498.

[16] Ingo Schmidt, "German Labour Experiences Since World War Two: A Suggested Interpretation," *Labour/Le Travail* 63 (2009): 157-179.

[17] For an overview on the EU's history, its institutional make-up and policy areas see: Steven P. McGiffen, *The European Union – A Critical Guide* (London, Sterling: Pluto Press, 2005).

states.[18] On the international level, US policies were quite contradictory. On the one hand, they supported an "embedded liberalism"[19], namely through the Bretton-Woods-System, which allowed national governments to pursue Keynesian policies without negative interference from international capital flows or exchange rate fluctuations.[20] On the other hand, they prepared the way to international trade integration through the General Agreement on Tariffs and Trade (GATT). The anti-Keynesian philosophy of free trade and unrestricted capital mobility also drove the process of European integration that was supported by the US.[21] The neoliberal seeds were already sown during the post-war era but it took the economic and political crises of the 1970s to really shift the balance from Keynes to Hayek. Milestones in this direction, as far as Europe is concerned, included the Single Market (SM), based on the Single European Act (SEA) of 1986[22], and the European Monetary Union (EMU), which was initiated with the Treaty of Maastricht of 1992.[23]

The single market brought the unrestricted movement of goods, services, and capital across the EC; only labour migration continued to be, and in some cases still is, restricted after the SM was officially completed in 1992. It is important to remember, though, that the SEA was not the first outburst of emergent neoliberalism in the 1980s but a re-launch of the common market principles that were already enshrined in the founding document of the EC, the 1957 Treaty of Rome.[24] However, under the reign of Keynesian hegemony governments were not willing to surrender control of economic activity entirely to private companies and never moved beyond a customs union, which was completed in 1968, but still kept restrictions on capital flows across borders. Such restriction were removed by the SEA and the introduction of the Euro fuelled cross-border flows of goods, services and capital even further. The common currency lowered transaction costs of cross-border economic activities and eliminated exchange risks within the Euro-zone. Like the single, or "common market" as it was called in the Treaty of Rome, monetary union was not a new idea either. It was first projected in the late 1960s when tensions in the international monetary system began to appear – notably current

---

[18] Michael Goldfield, *The Decline of Organized Labor in the United States* (Chicago: University of Chicago Press, 1987).

[19] John G. Ruggie, 'International Regimes, Transactions and Change – Embedded Liberalism in the Postwar Economic Order,' *International Organization* 36, no. 2 (1982): 379-415.

[20] Peter A. Hall, ed., *The Political Power of Economic Ideas – Keynesianism Across Nations* (Princeton: Princeton University Press, 1989).

[21] Bernard H. Moss, *Monetary Union in Crisis – The European Union as a Neo-liberal Construction* (Houndmills, Basingstoke: Palgrave Macmillan, 2005).

[22] European Community: *The Single European Act*, 1986. http://www.eurotreaties.com/singleuropeanact.pdf.

[23] European Community: *The Maastricht Treaty,* 1992. http://www.eurotreaties.com/maastrichtec.pdf.

[24] European Community: *The Treaty of Rome*, 1957. http://www.eurotreaties.com/rometreaty.pdf.

account deficits in the US and respective surpluses in Germany and Japan – but the fixed exchange rate regime of Bretton Woods was still in place.[25] When this regime was abandoned and international financial instability increased in the early 1970s, the initial plans for a monetary union in the EC were abandoned. In 1979 a less ambitious plan, the European Monetary System (EMS), was launched, which reinstituted some form of fixed exchange rates – allowing for minor fluctuations – on the EC level.[26] The EMS limited exchange risks to some extent and put pressure on governments and central banks across the EC to adopt German austerity policies in order to defend agreed upon exchange rates. Failure to do so would most likely lead to domestic inflation, capital flight a deterioration of the balance of payments and ultimately sovereign debt and currency crises. This was the first step to the institutionalization of the regional hegemony that Germany's export-oriented economy had achieved over the post-war period. EMU took this institutionalization to the next step by adding a commitment to tight monetary and fiscal policy to the introduction of a common currency. These measures were meant to keep inflation rates down and avoid the crowding out of private investment by public spending. Thus, a kind of neoliberal constitutionalism was created wherein political discretion was either replaced or subjugated to the overarching goals of price stability, balanced budgets and unrestricted trade and capital flows.[27] On that basis, advocates proclaimed, rent seeking and its stifling effects on economic growth would become impossible and thus give way to prosperity based on entrepreneurialism and the profit-motif. The making of neoliberal Europe went hand-in-hand with the extension of the original six EC member states to the current total of twenty-seven EU members.

The combined processes of the neoliberalization of the EC and EU, respectively, and the extension of its geographical reach allowed companies to establish European supply chains. The locations along these chains are differentiated by available technology and skill endowments, which allow specialization on the production of different parts of a final product.[28] The SM and EMU enabled this process by

---

[25] European Community: *Report to the Council and the Commission on the Realization by Stages of Economic and Monetary Union in the Community, 1970.* http://ec.europa.eu/economy_finance/emu_history/documentation/chapter5/19701008en72realisationbystage.pdf.

[26] On the EMS and European monetary integration more generally see: John Grahl, *After Maastricht – A Guide to European Monetary Union* (London: Lawrence & Wishart, 1997).

[27] Stephen Gill, "European Governance and New Constitutionalism: Economic and Monetary Union and Alternatives to Disciplinary Neoliberalism in Europe," *New Political Economy* 3 (1998): 5-26.

[28] Rob Van Tulder and Winfried Ruigrok, "European Cross-National Production Networks in the Auto Industry: Eastern Europe as the Low End of the European Car Complex" (working paper, BRIE Working Paper Series, no. 121, University of California, Berkeley, CA, 1998). John

lowering the costs of cross-border investments, which are required to set up branches in different locations, and of cross-border trade without which parts cannot be moved from one location to another and final products could not be distributed to customers all over Europe and beyond. The attraction of European supply chains grew with the accession of Southern European countries in the 1980s – Greece joined the EC in 1981, Portugal and Spain followed in 1986 – and Eastern European countries since 2004. Southern and Eastern enlargement of the EC and EU, respectively, allowed companies in the North-Western core of Europe to tap into pools of cheap labour that, unlike even cheaper labour in the Global South, could be exploited under a common legal system and with little (under the EMS) or no (under EMU) exchange rate risks.

There is little evidence that companies were constantly shopping for the lowest wages, taxes, or government regulations in Europe[29], but it is quite clear that the restructuring of production processes under the reign of neoliberalism led to a deepening of the centre-periphery divisions that had already existed during the Keynesian wave of accumulation.[30] These divisions correspond to the splits between countries running surpluses in their capital and current accounts and those having deficits.[31] The former group comprises Germany, Austria, the Benelux-countries, and Scandinavia; and the latter, the Mediterranean and most of the Eastern European countries. Britain and France, even though they are political heavyweights in the EU, are also struggling with current account deficits and sovereign debt.

When the neoliberal restructuring of the European economy began, peripheral regions attracted capital from core regions that was seeking cheap labour. These capital imports added to the sovereign debt of peripheral countries. Theoretically, the new production capacities that were set up with the help of foreign capital should have boosted exports and thus allowed the repayment of this sovereign debt. These pay-offs did not happen in practice, or only on a minor scale, because

---

Zysman, Eileen Doherty, and Andrew Schwartz, "Tales from the 'Global' Economy: Cross National Production Networks and the Re-organization of the European Economy" (working paper, BRIE, University of California, Berkeley, CA, no. 83, June 1996).

[29] Franz Traxler and Birgit Woitech, "Transnational Investment and National Labour Market Regimes: A Case of 'Regime Shopping'?" *European Journal of Industrial Relations* 6 (2000): 141-159.

[30] Helen Caraveli and John Darzentas, "Centre-Periphery and Specialization in the EU: An Analysis from a New Economic Geography Perspective," (conference proceeding, 46th Congress of the European Regional Science Association, University of Thessaly, Thessaly, 2006).

[31] Costas Lapavitsas, A. Kaltenbrunner, D. Lindo, J. Michell, J.P. Painceira, J. Powell, A. Stenfors, and N. Teles, "Eurozone Crisis: Beggar Thyself and Thy Neighbour." *Research on Money and Finance, Occasional Report* (London, 2010), accessed on November 11, 2011, http://www.researchonmoneyandfinance.org/media/reports/eurocrisis/fullreport.pdf.

workers in the periphery turned out to be more militant than those in core countries. And they had to be: commodity and capital imports from core countries along with relatively high growth in the course of the build-up of new industries, led to higher inflation rates so that higher increases of nominal wages were needed just to defend existing real wages. Workers' taste for rising wages in the periphery was further stimulated because European integration and its promise of equal living standards led them to compare their much lower wages to those of their counterparts in the core countries. The latter, on the other hand, felt squeezed between the introduction of labour-saving technologies and the relocation of production to low-wage areas. Therefore, union leaders and employers did not have much difficulty dragging workers in the European core toward wage restraint. This was the basis of constant or even decreasing unit labour costs in the core, where wage restraint was complemented by strong productivity growth in export-industries. In the periphery, though, relatively strong wage growth and sluggish productivity development led to increasing unit labour costs and thus a loss of competitiveness compared to exporters from the core. Under conditions of, more or less, fixed exchange rates of the EMS, not to mention the common currency since 1999, these divergent trends in unit labour costs could not be compensated by respective currency revaluations. The competitiveness of peripheral countries deteriorated and current account deficits became permanent. Another factor that contributed to these deficits was the continued dependence on imported investment goods. Industrial restructuring in Europe had developed some consumer goods and parts industries in the periphery, but the production of investment goods remained pretty much monopolized in core countries.

For quite some time, though, current account deficits could be financed through continued capital imports from the core where industrial restructuring led to a combination of high profits and sluggish growth. This means that there was an overabundance of capital that did not find profitable investment opportunities in the core and eventually found its way to peripheral countries. Capital exports from the core to the periphery were particularly strong when EMU led to a convergence of peripheral interest rates to the low level of core countries, notably the economic hegemon, Germany. Investment financing in the periphery thus became relatively cheaper than in the core countries. However, the money that kept flowing from core to periphery failed to finance much further productive investments because preceding investments had already created sufficient production capacity to satisfy market demand. Increasingly, capital imports blew up housing bubbles and thus, contributed to the combination of upward spiralling real estate prices and consumer credit that is well known from the bubble economies of capitalist core countries such as Britain, the US, and, back in the 1990s, Japan.[32]

The turn from productive investment booms to bubble economies in the European periphery points to a larger problem of the neoliberal wave of accumulation mentioned above. The combined processes of introducing new technologies and relocating production sites was very successful in outmanoeuvring union strongholds that had developed in old industrial districts. Thus, they also helped to lower wage rates and boost productivity. Yet, they also deepened centre-periphery relations in Europe and beyond and led to macroeconomic imbalances. Industrial restructuring also contributed to the build-up of overcapacities.

As long as it lasted, the installation of new capacities creates investment demand and thus spurs accumulation. Machines were sent to new production sites, roads and railroads were built and communication technologies installed. All this required a certain number of workers whose pay checks increased consumer good sales. Moreover, privatization in the West and the integration of former communist countries in the East allowed capitalism to expand into non-capitalist economies. Once these social and geographical spaces were integrated into the circuits of capital accumulation, the demand stimulus of such expansion petered out. The explosion of debt and speculation[33] that had accompanied, and indeed driven, the neoliberal wave of accumulation right from the start turned more and more into a self-serving spiral with little connection to the accumulation of productive capital. The accumulation of fictitious capital[34] stopped because relatively moderate increases in interest rates pushed a fair amount of private households, whose credit-financed consumption had kept accumulation afloat prior to the Great Recession, beyond their ability to service outstanding debts. With the amount of bad debt rising, it became undeniable even to the most hazardous financial speculators that they had been banking on fantasies rather than the actual valorisation of surplus value through market sales. Adherents and beneficiaries of neoliberal accumulation had to learn that, contrary to what their economics textbooks say, supply does not automatically equal demand. Thus, the housing crisis of 2007, passing through the stage of a financial crash, soon transpired into a general crisis of overproduction.[35]

Governments were able to contain this crisis and calm down the nerves of panicky financial investors with a combination of fiscal stimulus packages and bank

---

[32] Graham Turner, *The Credit Crunch – Housing Bubbles, Globalisation and the World Economic Crisis* (London: Pluto Press, 2008).

[33] John Bellamy Foster and Fred Magdoff, *The Great Financial Crisis – Causes and Consequences* (New York: Monthly Review Press, 2009), ch. 2.

[34] Marx, *Capital, Vol. III*, 397-411.

[35] Foster and Magdoff, *The Great Financial Crisis – Causes and Consequences*, ch. 6; Schmidt, *Große Krisen seit den 1930er Jahren*.

bailouts. Central banks injected practically unlimited amounts of cheap money into the world financial system. However, the price of these rescue measures was the transformation of the financial and economic crisis of the capitalist world economy into a fiscal crisis of the state and the bloating of central bank balance sheets with high-risk assets. At first, this shift of crises from markets to the state was convenient for financial investors and the propertied classes in general but their comfort did not last long. The austerity measures they are now demanding are pushing the world economy back to recession and thus more debt defaults and financial turbulence.[36] The spectre of an all-out debt-deflation[37] that was successfully chased away by large-scale state intervention when the Great Recession hit in 2008 came back with a vengeance with the Euro-crisis since 2010.[38] Many, if not most, corporate leaders, political elites, and economists fear that governments and central banks will not have enough financial firing power to contain another recession. Such fears haunt ruling classes all over the world.[39] What is special about the crisis in Europe is that it laid bare the macroeconomic imbalance between its core and periphery that, until recently, was hard to see behind the tight-nit network of EU-institutions. These institutions and the common market and currency they created, Euro-propagandists tirelessly told the public in EU member countries, would not only enhance competitiveness but also produce social cohesion and overcome regional disparities. With the onset of the crisis it turned out that all that European integration had accomplished was an increase in competitiveness (and even that was much less impressive than in other countries or world regions), but that this had happened at the expense of a loss of social cohesion and deeper regional disparities.

However, the divisions and imbalances within the EU are not the cause of the current crisis, at least not directly. More appropriately one should say that they determine the form the crisis takes with its combination of fiscal and sovereign debt crises in the periphery and governments in core countries imposing austerity packages on the periphery, even at the risk of pushing the whole EU into the next recession if not outright depression. The current division between debtor and creditor countries in the EU has actually the same origin as the general economic crisis that broke out in 2008 and has found different expressions since than. The seeds for this general crisis were sown in the 1980s when capitalists began pushing for redistri-

---

36 International Monetary Fund. *World Economic Outlook: Slowing Growth, Rising Risks.* (Washington D.C., September 2011). http://www.imf.org/external/pubs/ft/weo/2011/02/pdf/text.pdf.

37 Irving Fisher, "The Debt-Deflation Theory of Great Depressions," *Econometrica* 1 (1933): 337-357.

38 Ingo Schmidt, "European Capitalism: Varieties of Crises," *Alternate Routes* (2011): 71-86.

39 *The Economist*, "Lessons of the 1930s: There Could be Trouble Ahead," December 10-16, 2011.

bution from wages to profits. Under these conditions effective demand growth became increasingly dependent on credit and rising asset prices. This financialization of the economy laid the basis for today's fiscal and sovereign debt crises as much as the shortfalls of effective demand that followed the 2008 stock market crash. However, increasing numbers of Europeans of different class backgrounds and across the political spectrum are as much concerned about economic crises as about the capacities of the EU or its member states to address these issues in any way. The economic crisis of neoliberal Europe has also produced a crisis of legitimacy of the political system in general and the EU in particular.

Legitimation Crisis and the Search for Alternatives

The need for, and legitimacy of, European integration has been in question right from the start. Some circles in European resistance movements against the Nazis had developed the idea to build a socialist Europe that would, simultaneously, transcend nation-states and the nationalism that had contributed so much to the rise of Nazism and the outbreak of World War II and would also represent an alternative to Stalinism in the East and American-style capitalism in the West.[40] Unsurprisingly, though, neither the Americans nor the Soviets liked these ideas; the turn from the Anti-Hitler-coalition to the Cold War rang their death-knell. The communist and social democratic mainstreams of the labour movement, rather than fighting for an autonomous political space that could have included support for a socialist Europe, willingly integrated into the emergent Cold War-order. The communists followed Moscow's foreign policies slavishly and suppressed any opposition to this course in its own ranks. Immediately after the war, the Soviets sought to establish political regimes that would rely on cross-class alliances, so-called People's Democracies, and remain neutral between Soviets and Americans. These policies, it seemed, left open the door for an independent road to European socialism. It closed when the formation of an anti-communist bloc in the West increased Soviet willingness to install communist regimes in Eastern Europe despite a lack of popular support for them.[41] On the other side of the Iron Curtain, the majority of social democrats adopted an Atlanticism that was instrumental in integrating West European labour into the Cold War bloc against Soviet communism.[42] From the late 1940s onwards, European integration was crucially shaped by Cold War conditions, which included the consolidation of US hegemony in the West and the con-

---

[40] Frank Niess, *Die europäische Idee – Aus dem Geist des Widerstands* (Frankfurt: Suhrkamp, 2001).

[41] Ivan T. Berend, *Central and Eastern Europe 1944-1993: Detour from the Periphery to the Peripher (Cambridge*: Cambridge University Press, 1996), ch. 1.

[42] Donald Sassoon, *One Hundred Years of Socialism – The West European Left in the Twentieth Century* (New York: The New Press, 1996), ch. 9.

tainment of long-standing rivalries among the European powers. In full contrast to the ideas of building a socialist Europe from the bottom up, European integration from the European Coal and Steel Community, the 1951 predecessor of the EC, to today's EMU became an elite project of the European ruling classes and their allies in the US and other capitalist countries.

For a while, however, this did not cause problems of legitimacy because the integration process was of little interest to ordinary people. One of the paradoxical outcomes of European integration was the rescue of the nation state from the setbacks it had suffered during two world wars and the interwar period.[43] Part of this rescue was the extension of welfare states that had only existed in embryonic form before. Rising levels of real incomes and social security for the majority of its populations earned European nation-states a level of allegiance from their citizens that appeals to national pride during the preceding era of great power conflicts were unable to achieve. The forces of market integration, which turned out to be a decisive factor of welfare state retrenchment since the 1980s, unfolded more or less unnoticed behind the veil of welfare state extension during the Keynesian wave of accumulation. Ironically, it was the legitimation crisis of the welfare state – itself unfolding in tandem with the economic crises of the 1970s – that shifted the political balance from the Keynesian welfare state to neoliberalism after protracted struggles between left- and right-wing alternatives.[44]

One important aspect of the struggles of the 1970s that still resonates today is the embrace of the nation-state by progressive currents that aimed at a socialist transformation of the Keynesian welfare state. These currents included left-wing social democrats as much as an array of New Left groupings and most of the communist parties in Western Europe. These currents did not have much in common, but they shared the recognition that multinational corporations and supranational governance structures such as the EC were major forces pushing for the neoliberal turn against labour. This observation led them to an extremely negative outlook on European integration. As in the late 1940s and early 1950s when the Cold War order emerged, right-wing social democrats were the force on the left, broadly understood, that embraced the EC even if this included welfare state retrenchment. Understandable as left-wing Euro-scepticism is, its downside is that the void of progressive internationalism, apart from abstract declarations of international solidarity, remained empty – and could successfully be filled by the social forces supporting neoliberalism. The proletarian internationalism that the left failed to bring about in the 1970s was redefined as internationalism of free trade and capital mo-

---

[43] Alan S. Milward, *The European Rescue of the Nation-State* (London, New York: Routledge, 2000).

[44] Schmidt, *There Were Alternatives*.

bility beginning in the 1980s and culminating in neoliberal globalization after the end of the Cold War.

Some circles in member state governments and the EC-bureaucracy recognized that the dual process of welfare state retrenchment on the national level and market integration on the European level might cause legitimation problems. They sure had a point. The further national welfare states were downsized, the more attractive they became among the subordinate classes. In the 1970s, progressive movements had mobilized against the far-reaching exclusion of women, immigrants, and ethnic minorities. They also took issue with the subjugation of the welfare state to capital accumulation and its detrimental impact on the environment. Yet, in the face of unfolding neoliberalism, the left-wing challenge of the welfare state increasingly went into oblivion. In a mix of realism and nostalgia the welfare-state expansion of the post-war era became seen as the best subordinated classes can expect under capitalism. Conversely, those at the bottom of the social ladder saw European integration with growing suspicion while the legitimacy it did gain was concentrated among the propertied and professional middle classes.[45] Under these conditions it became increasingly difficult to get consent from the subordinate classes for further steps towards integration. The idea to complement market integration, i.e. the economic union, with a social union was an attempt to overcome this problem. In practice, this meant to either create European institutions that could stabilize national welfare states or shift the provision of social securities of different kinds from the national to the European level. These questions became particularly urgent in the 1990s when the EU was moving forward from single market to common currency, an issue that is as important economically as it is symbolically, and to integrate the post-communist countries of Eastern Europe.

The deepening and widening of EU raised concerns from Ireland to Bulgaria, from Latvia to Portugal and in any other country in-between. Many people in Western Europe feared competition from Eastern European countries as a consequence of Eastern enlargement. They also felt that the fiscal and monetary policy guidelines enshrined in the Maastricht Treaty and the Statute of the European Central Bank (ECB)[46] would intensify already existing pressures on social protections. At the same time, the Euro, rather than representing European commonalities, became a symbol for the rendering of national sovereignty to remote and elitist EU-

---

[45] Neil Fligstein, *Euro-Clash – The EU, European Identity, and the Future of Europe* (Oxford: Oxford University Press, 2008).

[46] European Central Bank, *Statute of the European System of Central Banks and of the European Central Bank,* 1998.
http://www.ecb.int/ecb/legal/pdf/en_statute_from_c_11520080509en02010328.pdf.

institutions. Rising Euro-scepticism[47] fed into a more general discontent with neoliberalism that spread across the world in the late 1990s, it paved the way to large-scale demonstrations at EU-summits and the European Social Forum-movement as part of the wider World Social Forum movement.[48] At the same time, the resurgence of social democratic governments in Western Europe indicated that voters wanted an alternative to the neoliberalism wielded by conservative and liberal parties.[49] With 15 out of the then 18 EU member states under social democratic governments by the end of the 1990s a short period of institution building began that gave the impression that the deepening of the economic union and the widening of EU membership would eventually be complemented by a social union, the so-called European Social Model (ESM).[50] As it turned out, contrary to the institutions governing the SM and EMU, institutions of the ESM had no binding powers. On the one hand, unhindered mobility of goods, services, and capital and fiscal policy guidelines became enshrined in the EU governance structure, which is overseen and enforced by the EU Commission, EU Council and EU Court of Justice. On the other hand, the tripartite Social and Macroeconomic Dialogues, the only institutions in which unions can voice their opinions, are limited to moral persuasion but have no capacities to introduce or monitor EU law.

Moreover, when the economic boom of the 1990s ended in the 2001 recession, social democrats that had been elected under the vague banner of Third Way policies openly turned to neoliberalism. This turn led social democrats back to opposition benches in most EU countries and ended the interlude of ESM-building. Euro-scepticism reached new heights when the planned EU Constitution[51] was defeated by Dutch and French referenda in 2005. Four years later, Irish voters accepted the Lisbon Treaty[52], a redrafted version that dropped the ambitious title constitution, but consolidated the existing EU-regulations under a new legal umbrella. Yet, this approval required a second round of voting since the first round did not yield the results EU governments were hoping for. By that time, the Great Recession had already thrown Ireland into a severe banking and sovereign debt crisis. The full-

---

[47] Robert Harmsen and Menno Spiering, ed., *Euroscepticism: Party Politics, National Identity, and European Integration* (Amsterdam, New York: Editions Rodopi, 2005).
[48] Donatella Della Porta and Manuela Caiani, *Social Movements and Europeanization* (Oxford: Oxford University Press, 2011).
[49] Bryan Evans and Ingo Schmidt, eds., *Social Democracy after the Cold War* (Athabasca: Athabasca University Press).
[50] Ingo Schmidt, "New Institutions, Old Ideas: The Passing Moment of the European Social Model," *Studies in Political Economy* 84 (2009): 7-28.
[51] European Union, "Treaty Establishing a Constitution for Europe," 2004, http://www.eurotreaties.com/constitutiontext.html.
[52] European Union, "The Lisbon Treaty," 2008, http://www.eurotreaties.com/treatytexts.html#lisbon.

blown Euro-crisis was just about to begin and with it a looming legitimation crisis broke out that paved the way for the search for alternatives to the current European order.

As a matter of fact, at this point there is not only a growing taste for alternatives to the present EU-order among the subordinate classes, but among their rulers as well. The latter had to recognize that common monetary policies without common fiscal policies further add to the problems already caused by the economic crisis. To solve at least this governance problem, major forces in the EU, led by French president Sarkozy and German chancellor Merkel, push for the transfer of fiscal policies from member state governments to the EU-level. They seek to combine this transfer with policy guidelines that would squeeze any room for discretionary spending of the kind used to contain the Great Recession out of the political system. However, such plans are contested. Some governments, with British Prime Minister Cameron being the most vocal, reject the idea of a further transfer of decision-making powers from member states to EU institutions. A number of governments of smaller member states agree with this view but do not dare to openly challenge the dominant position of France and Germany in European affairs. Small circles in the political apparatuses of member states, more often in debtor than in creditor countries, and the EU also question the push for austerity while the European and, possibly, global economy is on the brink of another recession. They argue for more relaxed fiscal and monetary policies instead. Such conflicts over governance structure and economic policy orientation show an unprecedented level of disunity in the neoliberal bloc that ruled Europe for about the last three decades. Deepening cracks among the rulers entice the ruled to articulate their discontent more openly and explore alternatives to the faltering neoliberal Europe.

Such articulations and explorations take different directions. In Southern European debtor countries a series of mass strikes and protests erupted in opposition to austerity imposed by domestic governments, creditor countries, the EU and the IMF.[53] On the other hand, many of the Eastern European debtor countries and Western European creditor states have witnessed an upsurge of right-wing populism since the Great Recession struck.[54] This upsurge only accelerates previously existing right-wing populism that had developed in Western Europe on the fringes of neoliberal hegemony since the 1980s. It expresses national resentments against the kind of internationalism represented by European integration and, more recent-

---

[53] Andy Durgan and Joel Sans, "'No One Represents Us': The 15 May Movement in the Spanish State." *International Socialism* 132 (2011), http://www.isj.org.uk/index.php4?id=757&issue=132. Stathis Kouvelakis, "The Greek Cauldron,"*New Left Review* 72 (2011): 17-32.

[54] Nora Langenbacher and Britta Schellenberg, eds., *Is Europe on the "Right" Path? Right-wing Extremism and Right-wing Populism in Europe* (Berlin: Friedrich Ebert Stiftung, 2011).

ly, growing fears that the EU may develop into a transfer union that would subsidize self-indulgent lifestyles in the European South. These right-wing populists fully support the imposition of austerity measures on creditor countries but think that the EU waters them down. Underlying such sentiments, is the fact that creditor countries successfully pursued beggar-thy-neighbour policies over the last several years, if not decades, and were thus able to shift some of the social costs of neoliberal adjustments onto the very countries that were driven into debt by these policies.[55] The sovereign debt crisis of Southern debtor countries places the continuation of these policies at risk. Attempts to save outstanding credits and current account surpluses in core countries through stepped up austerity will only make the crisis worse and lead to income and job losses in creditor and debtor countries alike. Considering the underdevelopment of progressive alternatives that could possibly avoid such losses, the appeal to the perceived strength of one's own nation seems an obvious alternative to the neoliberal internationalism represented by the EU. However, such economic nationalism, i.e. disconnecting from foreign markets that, until now, absorb a significant share of creditor countries' overproduction, would propel the current crisis onto an entirely new level of economic collapse and political disintegration.

The context in which right-wing populism developed in Eastern Europe is radically different from the West. Economically, Eastern European countries are as much debt-ridden as their counterparts in Southern Europe. That only three of them — Estonia, Slovakia, and Slovenia — adopted the Euro does not ease the dependence of their economies on continued capital imports. In fact, the Euro-crisis hit Eastern Europe even before it found its way to Southern Europe.[56] Yet, the austerity measures that followed in the wake of the crisis did not trigger mass unrest as they did in the South. Much rather, they boosted the support for right-wing organizations and parties. One of the reasons for the absence of mass mobilizations against austerity is that unions, who played a crucial role in the respective mobilizations in Southern Europe without being the only organizing force in that regard, hardly exist as an autonomous social force in Eastern Europe. In most countries they did not develop after the collapse of Soviet-style systems that had unions firmly integrated into their power structures. On the other hand, Poland's Solidarność, which has been key in overturning this system, moved sharply to the right during the new capitalist order.[57] Activist networks that were also important in the anti-austerity mobilizations in Southern Europe, also only exist in embryonic

---

[55] Lapavitsas et al., *Eurozone Crisis: Beggar Thyself and Thy Neighbour*.

[56] Özlem Onaran, "The Crisis of Capitalism in Europe, West and East," *Monthly Review* 62 (October 2010): 18-33.

[57] David Ost, *The Defeat of Solidarity – Anger and Politics in Postcommunist Europe* (Ithaca, London: Cornell University Press, 2005).

forms in Eastern Europe and the electoral left is in a state of depression. In most Eastern European countries, formerly ruling communist parties transformed themselves into social democratic parties in the early 1990s. As such, they had unexpected electoral successes later in the decade, leading them into government in the Czech Republic, Hungary and Poland around the time of the social democratic resurgence in Western Europe.[58] However, governing the transition from Soviet communism to neoliberal capitalism was a thankless job. Vast majorities of Eastern Europeans had rejected, or even hated, communist regimes and thus welcomed the new capitalist order that promised liberty and prosperity. Many were also hoping to maintain the equalities that communism had instituted. Yet, such hopes vanished quickly in the face of economic decline and sharp inequalities that allowed liberties for a small number of new rich people and left masses of people totally disempowered. Without going through a period of welfare capitalism that so many people in Western Europe were regretting in the 1990s Eastern Europeans had to adjust from Soviet-style paternalism and soft budget constraints to the neoliberal constraints of international competitiveness in a very short time. Post-communist social democrats who governed during parts of this transition period soon found themselves in the curious situation of representing the equally dismayed regimes of communism and neoliberal capitalism. With communism, which was equated with Soviet communism and understood as the only form non-capitalist economies could take, and capitalism, at least in its neoliberal form, being equally tainted, a political turn to right-wing nationalism and authoritarianism seemed the only way people who were not beneficiaries of the new, capitalist regime could go.[59]

The recent upturn of right-wing populism in East and West represents a truly European phenomenon that has the potential, if its policies of economic nationalism, authoritarianism, and xenophobia pursued, to deepen the crisis brought about by neoliberal capitalism even further. The question, then, is whether there are left alternatives that could cater to the desire to end neoliberal rule and avoid the catastrophic outcomes right-wing populism has in store.

Social democrats, who attracted voters looking for an alternative to neoliberalism in the 1990s, are almost completely identified with neoliberal policies today. And rightly so, over their Third Way turn they lost whatever left or Euro-sceptic currents they had in the past and are more firmly committed to Atlanticism, the EU, and austerity than ever before. Rather than challenging austerity, social democratic parties in Europe ask for a fair sharing of the burden of austerity measures. This burden sharing includes, as a maximum, the claim for slightly more progres-

---

[58] Peter Gowan, "The Post-communist Socialists in Eastern and Central Europe," in *Looking Left – Socialism in Europe After the Cold War*, ed. David Sassoon (New York: The New Press, 1997), 143-176.

[59] *Journal of Democracy*, "Is East-Central Europe Backsliding?," *Special Focus* 18 (2007): 5-63.

sive tax systems and financial market regulations. The identification of social democracy with the, albeit disintegrating, neoliberal regime in Europe does not necessarily hinder social democrats from winning elections as the 2011 elections in Denmark and Ireland show. Fed up with the conservative governments that were in office when the Great Recession of 2008/9 was followed by the Euro-crisis beginning in 2010, voters elected a social democratic majority in Denmark or at least allowed a social democratic party to join a coalition government for the first time ever, as happened in Ireland. Yet, the opposite took place in countries where social democrats were in office when the crisis struck as the British elections in 2010 and the Portuguese and Spanish 2011 elections show; all three produced solid conservative majorities. What this indicates is that elections during the current crisis are not lost or won over alternative political platforms. Much rather, whoever was in government when the crisis struck had good chances to be voted out of office in the next election. It seems that voters are discontent with markets, financial markets in particular, and expect governments to overcome market-triggered crises through whatever kind of political intervention. Governments are part of the neoliberal regime rather than countervailing powers to it. Therefore they cannot deliver upon voters' expectations and lose approval as soon as they get elected. Electoral politics, and certainly not the catch-all parties that dominate this space, do not offer the kinds of alternatives people are looking for. Obviously, the essentially conservative character of electoral politics is anything but new. In fact, growing discontent with neoliberal Europe and Third Way social democracy, whose emergence was itself part of the then existing hegemony of neoliberalism, produced a whole series of new left formations across Europe from the early to the mid-2000s.[60] All of them promised to straddle the line between electoral and activist politics with some of them, like the German *Die Linke*, aligning closer with the former, and others, such as the French *Noveau Parti Anticapitaliste*, leaning towards the latter. Moreover, all of them advance alternatives to neoliberalism, which range from updated welfare statism to vaguely defined socialisms of different kinds. Although the more radical groups among these new left formations deem a revolutionary break with capitalism as ultimately necessary, they nonetheless align themselves, to different degrees in different countries, with more moderate groups in the defensive struggles against austerity. However, contrary to what many of the people active in all of these groups expected, their role in these struggles was very limited compared to that of unions and grassroots activists. Yet, the mobilization successes that the latter enjoyed in some Southern European countries also have their weaknesses. They draw their mobilizing capacities from the immediate efforts of workers, the unemployed and student youth to ward off the next onslaught of

---

[60] Daniel Bensaid, *New Parties of the Left – Experiences from Europe* (London: IMG Publications, 2011). Birgit Daiber, Cornelia Hildebrandt and Anna Striethorst, ed., *Von Revolution bis Koalition – Linke Parteien in Europa* (Berlin: Karl Dietz Verlag, 2010).

austerity policies on their living and employment conditions. Without developing alternatives to these policies, however, they peter out and leave participants of strikes and protests increasingly disoriented and unmotivated. At some point, despite that their desire for an alternative economic model may actually have grown, people will fail to come out to the next rally or picket line. This is exactly what national governments and the EU bureaucracy are banking on. Sooner or later, they speculate, opposition to austerity will wither away and leave the field to the old neoliberal model no matter that it lost the attractiveness it once had.

To avoid such an outcome the left needs to develop a strategic vision that takes anti-austerity struggles as its starting point for building a progressive bloc of power around the ongoing conversation about the contours of alternatives to neoliberalism and the way to achieve these. More concretely, what is needed is not only the rejection of neoliberal capitalism or the idea to take over the existing economic model from today's ruling classes but a vision of a society in which economic and ecological crisis can be avoided and social divisions, let alone antagonisms, along the lines of class, race, and gender can be avoided. Essentially, this is a conversation about socialism.[61] And, considering the negative reputation of socialism due to its equating with Soviet communism, it is still a difficult conversation to have, as the absence of any notable left politics in Eastern Europe shows. On the other hand, any future socialist project can draw on experiences of past attempts to build socialist societies.[62] A related question is how to realize such an alternative vision in practice, which includes the question for how long and for which purposes left organizations can operate in the institutions of existing state apparatuses. At the European level, we may ask whether EU membership can facilitate progressive change[63], including a remake of the current neoliberal design of the EU, or whether the EU is inextricably mired in the neoliberalism it has helped to build over decades so that exit from the EU is a prerequisite for progressive change.[64] And finally, in order to attract and mobilize the people who are seeking alternatives to neoliberal Europe, the debate about them needs to converge around simple strategic formulas that are easy to grasp and link the present with a possible future. Neolib-

---

[61] Michael Lebowitz, *The Socialist Alternative – Real Human Development* (New York: Monthly Review Press, 2010).

[62] Michael Lebowitz, *The Contradictions of "Real Socialism" – The Conductor and the Conducted* (New York: Monthly Review Press, 2012).

[63] Michel Husson, "Exit or Voice? A European Strategy of Rupture," in *The Crisis and the Left: Socialist Register 2012,* ed. Leo Panitch, Greg Albo and Vivek Chibber (London: The Merlin Press, 2011). Gerassimos Moschonas, "The European Union and the Dilemmas of the Radical Left: Some Preliminary Thoughts," *Transform! European Journal for Alternative Thinking and Political Dialogue* 9 (2011): 8-20.

[64] Costas Lapavitsas, "Default and Exit from the Eurozone: A Radical Left Strategy," *The Crisis and the Left: Socialist Register 2012,* ed. Leo Panitch, Greg Albo and Vivek Chibber (London: The Merlin Press, 2011).

erals were very successful in organizing their political project around the simple message of markets as a venue for self-realization; currently right-wing populists attract people who seek protection from these markets in the name of the nation. The left is still miles away from the time when the 8-hour-day or, in a more radical fashion, Soviet power and electrification attracted mass followings for the 2nd and 3rd Internationals, respectively. We've got work to do.

References:

Bensaid, Daniel. *New Parties of the Left – Experiences from Europe*. London: IMG Publications, 2011.

Berend, Ivan T. *Central and Eastern Europe 1944-1993: Detour from the Periphery to the Periphery.* Cambridge: Cambridge University Press, 1996.

Bleaney, Michael F. *Underconsumption Theories: A History and Critical Analysis.* New York: International Publishers, 1976.

Caraveli, Helen, Darzentas, John. "Centre-Periphery and Specialization in the EU: An Analysis from a New Economic Geography Perspective." Conference Proceeding, 46th Congress of the European Regional Science Association, University of Thessaly, Thessaly, 2006.

Cockett, Richard. *Thinking the Unthinkable – Think Tanks and the Economic Counter-Revolution, 1931-1983*. London: Fontana Press, 1995.

Daiber, Birgit, Cornelia Hildebrandt, and Anna Striethorst, eds. *Von Revolution bis Koalition – Linke Parteien in Europa*. Berlin: Karl Dietz Verlag, 2010.

Della Porta, Donatella and Manuela Caiani, M. *Social Movements and Europeanization*. Oxford: Oxford University Press, 2011.

Desai, Radhika. "Consumption Demand in Marx and in the Current Crisis." *Research in Political Economy* 26 (2010): 101-143.

Duménil, Gerard and Dominique Lévy, "The Profit Rate: Where and How Much Did it Fall? Did it Recover?" *Review of Radical Political Economics* 34 (2002): 437-461.

Durgan, Andy and Joel Sans. "'No One Represents Us': The 15 May Movement in the Spanish State." *International Socialism* 132 (2011). Accessed November 20, 2012. http://www.isj.org.uk/index.php4?id=757&issue=132.

European Central Bank. *Statute of the European System of Central Banks and of the European Central Bank,* 1998. Accessed November 13, 2011. http://www.ecb.int/ecb/legal/pdf/en_statute_from_c_11520080509en02010328.pdf.

European Community. *The Treaty of Rome*, 1957. Accessed November 13, 2011. http://www.eurotreaties.com/rometreaty.pdf.

_____. *Report to the Council and the Commission on the Realization by Stages of Economic and Monetary Union in the Community,* 1970. Accessed November 14, 2011. http://ec.europa.eu/economy_finance/emu_history/documentation/chapter5/19701008en72realisationbystage.pdf.

_____. *The Single European Act*, 1986. Accessed November 13, 2011. http://www.eurotreaties.com/singleuropeanact.pdf.

_____. *The Maastricht Treaty,* 1992. Accessed November 14, 2011. http://www.eurotreaties.com/maastrichtec.pdf.

European Union. *Treaty Establishing a Constitution for Europe*, 2004. Accessed November 13, 2011. http://www.eurotreaties.com/constitutiontext.html.

_____. *The Lisbon Treaty*, 2008. Accessed November 14, 2011. http://www.eurotreaties.com/treatytexts.html#lisbon.

Evans, Bryan and Ingo Schmidt, eds. *Social Democracy After the Cold War.* Athabasca: Athabasca University Press, forthcoming.

Fisher, Irving. "The Debt-Deflation Theory of Great Depressions." *Econometrica* 1 (1933): 337-357.

Foster, John Bellamy And Fred Magdoff. *The Great Financial Crisis – Causes and Consequences.* New York: Monthly Review Press, 2009.

Friedman, Milton. "The Role of Monetary Policy." *American Economic Review* 58 (1968): 1-17.

Gill, Stephen. "European Governance and New Constitutionalism: Economic and Monetary Union and Alternatives to Disciplinary Neoliberalism in Europe." *New Political Economy* 3 (1998): 5-26.

Glyn, Andrew and Robert Sutcliffe. *British Capitalism and the Profit Squeeze.* London: Penguin Books, 1972.

Goldfield, Michael. *The Decline of Organized Labor in the United States.*Chicago: University of Chicago Press, 1987.

Goodwin, Richard M. "A Growth Cycle." In *Socialism, Capitalism, and Economic Growth: Essays Presented to Maurice Dobb*, edited by C.H. Feinstein, 54-58. Cambridge, MA: Cambridge University Press, 1967.

Grahl, John. *After Maastricht – A Guide to the European Monetary Union.* London: Lawrence & Wishart, 1997.

Habermas, Jurgen. *Legitimation Crises.* Boston: Beacon Press, 1975.

Hall, Peter A., ed. *The Political Power of Economic Ideas – Keynesianism across Nations.* Princeton: Princeton University Press, 1989.

Harman, Chris. "The Rate of Profit and the World Today." *International Socialism* 115 (2007). Accessed November 22, 2011. http://www.isj.org.uk/?id=340.

Harmsen, Robert and Menno Spiering, ed. *Euroscepticism: Party Politics, National Identity, and European Integration.* Amsterdam, New York: Editions Rodopi, 2005.

Husson, Michel. "The Debate on the Rate of Profit." *International Viewpoint* 425 (2010). Accessed November 23, 2011, http://www.internationalviewpoint.org/spip.php?article1894.

Husson, Michel. "Exit or Voice? A European Strategy of Rupture." In *The Crisis and the Left: Socialist Register 2012,* edited by Greg Albo, Vivek Chibber and Leo Panitch, 298-306. London: The Merlin Press, 2011.

International Monetary Fund. *World Economic Outlook: Slowing Growth, Rising Risks*. Washington D.C., September 2011. Accessed December 2, 2011, http://www.imf.org/external/pubs/ft/weo/2011/02/pdf/text.pdf.

Journal of Democracy, "Is East-Central Europe Backsliding?" Special Focus18 (2007): 5-63.

Kouvelakis, Stathis. "The Greek Cauldron." *New Left Review* 72 (2011): 17-32.

Langenbacher, Nora and Britta Schellenberg, eds. *Is Europe on the "Right" Path? Right-wing Extremism and Right-wing Populism in Europe*. Berlin: Friedrich Ebert Stiftung, 2011.

Lapavitsas, Costas, A. Kaltenbrunner, D. Lindo, J. Michell, J.P. Painceira, J. Powell, A. Stenfors, and N. Teles. "Eurozone Crisis: Beggar Thyself and Thy Neighbour." Research on Money and Finance, Occasional Report. London, 2010.

Lapavitsas, Costas. "Default and Exit from the Eurozone: A Radical Left Strategy." In *The Crisis and the Left: Socialist Register 2012,* edited by Greg Albo, Vivek Chibber and Leo Panitch, 288-297. London: The Merlin Press, 2011.

Lebowitz, Michael. *The Socialist Alternative – Real Human Development*. New York: Monthly Review Press, 2010.

Lebowitz, Michael. *The Contradictions of "Real Socialism" – The Conductor and the Conducted*. New York: Monthly Review Press, 2012.

Luxemburg, Rosa. *The Accumulation of Capital*. London, New York: Routledge, 2003.

Marx, Karl. "Capital, Vol. III." *Marx Engels Collected Works, Vol. 37*. New York: International Publishers, 1998 (originally published in German, 1894).

McGiffen, Steven P. *The European Union – A Critical Guide*. London, Sterling: Pluto Press, 2005.

Milward, Alan S. *The European Rescue of the Nation-State*. London, New York: Routledge, 2000.

Moschonas, Gerassimos. "The European Union and the Dilemmas of the Radical Left: Some Preliminary Thoughts." *Transform! European Journal for Alternative Thinking and Political Dialogue* 9 (2011): 8-20.

Moseley, Fred. "The Rate of Profit and the Future of Capitalism." *Review of Radical Political Economics* 29 (1997): 23-41.

Moss, Bernard H. *Monetary Union in Crisis – The European Union as a Neo-liberal Construction*. Houndmills, Basingstoke: Palgrave Macmillan, 2005.

Murphy, Kevin M., Andrei Shleifer and Robert W. Vishny. "Why is Rent-Seeking so Costly to Growth?" In *American Economic Review* 83 (1993): 409-414.

O'Connor, James. *The Meaning of Crisis – A Theoretical Introduction*. Oxford, New York: Basil Blackwell, 1987.

Onaran, Özlem. "The Crisis of Capitalism in Europe, West and East." *Monthly Review* 62 (October 2010): 18-33.

Phillips-Fein, Kim. *Invisible Hands – The Businessmen's Crusade Against the New Deal*. New York, London: W. W. Norton, 2009.

Ruggie, John G. 'International Regimes, Transactions and Change – Embedded Liberalism in the Postwar Economic Order.' *International Organization* 36, no. 2 (1982): 379-415.

Rugman, Alan M. and Alain Verbeke. "A Perspective on Regional and Global Strategies of Multinational Enterprises." *Journal of International Business Studies* 35 (2004): 3-18.

Saad-Filho, Alfredo and Deborah Johnston, eds. *Neoliberalism – A Critical Reader*. London, Ann Arbor: Pluto Press, 2005.

Sassoon, Donald. *One Hundred Years of Socialism – The West European Left in the Twentieth Century*. New York: The New Press, 1996.

Schmidt, Ingo, ed. *Spielarten des Neoliberalismus*. Hamburg: VSA-Verlag, 2008.

______."German Labour Experiences since World War Two: A Suggested Interpretation." *Labour/Le Travail* 63 (2009): 157-179.

______."Große Krisen seit den 1930er Jahren." *Prokla – Zeitschrift für kritische Sozialwissenschaften* 39 (2009): 523-540.

______. "New Institutions, Old Ideas: The Passing Moment of the European Social Model." *Studies in Political Economy* 84 (2009): 7-28.

______. "Rosa Luxemburg's Accumulation of Capital: New Perspectives on Capitalist Development and American Hegemony." *Socialist Studies* 6 (2010): 92-117.

______. "European Capitalism: Varieties of Crises." *Alternate Routes* (2011): 71-86.

______. "There Were Alternatives: Lessons from Efforts to Advance beyond Keynesian and Neoliberal Economic Policies in the 1970s." *Working USA* 14 (2011): 473-498.

The Economist, "Lessons of the 1930s: There Could be Trouble Ahead," December 10-16, 2011.

Traxler, Franz and Birgit Woitech. "Transnational Investment and National Labour Market Regimes: A Case of 'Regime Shopping'?" *European Journal of Industrial Relations* 6 (2000): 141-159.

Turner, Graham. *The Credit Crunch – Housing Bubbles, Globalisation and the World Economic Crisis*. London: Pluto Press, 2008.

van Tulder, Rob and Winfried Ruigrok. "European Cross-National Production Networks in the Auto Industry: Eastern Europe as the Low End of the European Car Complex." BRIE Working Paper Series, No. 121, University of California, Berkeley, CA, 1998.

Zysman, John, Eileen Doherty and Andrew Schwartz. "Tales from the 'Global' Economy: Cross National Production Networks and the Re-organization of the European Economy." BRIE, Working Paper No. 83, University of California, Berkeley, CA, 1996.

Neoliberalism and the surge in working hours

Christoph Hermann

Introduction

On the onset of the 1970s crisis, the United Autoworkers still won a reduction of the retirement threshold to 30 years of service, a fourth week of paid vacation and an additional six days off as part of the Paid Personal Holiday Program (PPH). The UAW leadership planned to gradually increase the amount of personal holidays to 48 days a year resulting in the establishment of an effective 36-hour working week. UAW-president Douglas Fraser noted in 1978, that "[t]he four-day week is inevitable [...] The only question is how fast do we get there" (Diss Greis 1984, 47). The union managed to increase the amount of personal holidays to nine days in 1979, but the development came to sudden end in 1980. In the wake of a looming economic crisis and a struggling American auto industry – Chrysler was on the verge of bankruptcy and had to be bailed out in 1979 – the UAW agreed to accept cutbacks to help automakers to regain profitability. Yet while the concessions were widely advertised as measures to secure jobs, one of the major 'give backs' was the PPH program. Hence instead of sharing work through a reduction of working hours, a key demand of trade unions during the Great Depression, the UAW accepted an effective extension of work time to safeguard jobs. The ongoing contract with Chrysler was opened in 1980. The union not only waved the entitlement to existing personal holidays, but also future paid holidays already included in the contract. In terms of working time, the total 'give back' at Chrysler amounted to 17 days per year. Ford and General Motors followed suit and demanded for similar concessions in the early 1980s. In both cases, the UAW agreed to eliminate about two weeks of paid vacation (ibid., 273-276).

While American unions conceded to what some authors have called concession bargaining, German unions were still demanding for shorter working hours. The metal workers' trade union IG Metall went on strike for a 35-hour week in 1978 and 1984 and actually won the 35-hour week for large parts of the metal sector workforce in the first half of the 1990s. However, 20 years later IG Metall and other German unions found themselves in a similar situation as the American unions in the early 1980s. In 2004, two western German employers, symbols of Germany's corporate power and the corporatist approach of German capital, gained temporary exemptions from the 35-hour standard after they had threatened to relocate production to cheaper locations. Siemens was able to extend the working week at its production sides in Kamp-Lintfort and Bocholt from 35 to 40 hours without a raise in wages. In exchange the company promised to maintain production for the two-year duration of the agreement (Funk 2004; Bispinck 2006, 125). In the same year DaimlerChrysler (now only Daimler) introduced a general 40-hour week for its research and development department staff, as well as a stepwise implementation of the 39-hour week for all service and support workers. Here the company agreed to maintain production until 2011(ibid.). Siemens and DaimlerChrysler are no exceptions: In 2004 IG Metall signed the Pforzheimer agreement with the metal sector employer organisaiton. Accordingly IG Metall accepts temporary deviations from existing collective standards if the deviations safeguard or create jobs, or improve the competitiveness of the company, the capacity for innovation and the conditions for new investments. Until the end of 2006, 850 'opening agreements' have been concluded. 58.8 per cent included a temporary extension of working hours beyond the collectively agreed limits (Haipeter 2009, 239-245).

This paper discusses the development of working hours through the lens of Marxist theory. It analyses the changes in different periods based on the contentious relationship between necessary working hours and those actually worked, resulting in predominantly extensive and intensive accumulation regimes. To understand the recent surge in working hours, as one of the main arguments goes, one has to account for the role of competition as driver of capitalist development and as a mode of social dominance. Conversely, the struggle for working time must be understood as a struggle for the limitation of competition through working-class solidarity and the manifestation of a political economy of the working class.

The paper starts with a clarification of essential Marxist terms and theoretical assumptions, including necessary working time, surplus working time, extensive/intensive accumulation, the role of competition and the political economy of the working class. The following section discusses the emergence of the Fordist working-time compromise and its major weaknesses, before the flexibilisation of working hours is analysed as a major component in the shift towards a post-Fordist accumulation system. However, flexibilisation was only a first step towards an extension of working time in neoliberal capitalism. The last section describes major changes in working hours since the mid 1970s. The main argument is that neoliberalism pushes for an extension and multiplication of working days in an aim to increase surplus labour. While institutionalists have emphasised national differences, including the significant differences in working hours put in by US and German workers, we show that Germany experienced similar developments as the US, only twenty years later. The chapter ends with a brief conclusion arguing that in neoliberal capitalism the struggle for shorter working time cannot only focus on the length of the working day. In order to free time the struggles must also address the problem of accelerating competition.

The political economy of the working class

The struggle over working time evolves from the difference between the working time that is necessary to reproduce society at a given standard of living (in the remainder of the paper simply called necessary working time) and the working hours which are effectively expended for the production of goods and services in a capitalist society.[1] While capital tends to expand this difference – the surplus labour time – because it is the source of profits, the working class aims to limit it. There are different ways in which surplus labour time can be restricted. Apart from the shortening of the working day, additional methods include the slowing down of the pace of work, which amounts to a lowering of work intensity and the rise of the living standard. The latter takes primarily the form of the struggle for higher wages. However, the struggle for shorter working hours varies from the struggle for higher wages insofar as it has the potential to go beyond distribution matters. Inasmuch as working-time regulation becomes a basic condition for the organisation of production, it can have a lasting impact on the mode of surplus-value creation and therefore on the emergence of a specific historical system of accumulation.

Regulation Theory distinguishes two basic forms of accumulation regimes. Although absolute and relative surplus-value production are always intertwined with each other, the extensive accumulation regime is predominantly based on the extension of absolute surplus value, while in the intensive accumulation regime the expansion of relative surplus value is more important (Boyer 2004, 52ff). In historical terms, the extensive accumulation regime stands for the time before the introduction of mass-production methods, while the intensive accumulation regime refers to the years following the spread of the Talyorist-Fordist mode of production (ibid). However, the era of post-Fordism is characterised by a simultaneous increase in working hours and productivity without one of the two modes of surplus

---

[1] This should not be confused with socially necessary abstract working time as measurement of the value of commodities.

value-creation having a dominant position (see further below). Hence instead of focusing on the increase in absolute surplus value, the widening gap between necessary and actually laboured working time can be taken as an indication for the current shift towards a predominantly extensive mode of surplus value creation.

Capital's "werewolf hunger for surplus-labour" (Marx 1968, 265) makes capital reckless of the health and life expectancy of the workers, even though extra-long working hours threaten the reproduction of the working class and with it of capital itself. From this perspective the struggle for shorter working hours, as long as it does not exceed certain limits, can serve the interest of capital as capital as whole (*Gesamtkapital*). Shorter working hours not only secure the reproduction of the working class, they also spur companies to improve the efficiency of work organisation and to invest in new labour-saving machinery. The role of working time reduction as 'productivity whip' has been emphasised by a number of authors and has repeatedly played an important role in the trade-union argumentation for shorter working hours (including the discussions predating the introduction of the 35-hour week in France). However, radical working-time reductions at least in principal also point to the possibility of a human existence beyond exploitative capitalistic social relations.

Yet capital's disregard of the condition of the working class is not a question of morality. As Marx notes, "Free competition brings out the inherent laws of capitalist production, in the shape of external coercive laws having power over every individual capitalist" (ibid., 270). Competition in several regards plays a crucial role in the struggle for working time: First of all, competition compels the individual capitalist to extend the working day in order to broaden the basis for profit-making; at the same time it forces him to reduce the working time embodied in capitalistically produced commodities to the smallest possible extent. However, competition between individual capitalists is also important to preserve the power of capital over working time. Although the employment contract gives the capitalist the power to dispose over the working time of his employee (after the introduction of the normal working day in certain statutory or collectively agreed limits), only competition makes sure that workers actually subordinate their own working-time interests to the interests of capital. This is because competition not only forces capitalists to compete with each other; also the respective workforces become competitors in the race for markets and profits. By putting in long hours, workers hope to contribute to the economic success of their employers and thereby protect their jobs (although, as recent examples from Germany show, long working hours do not necessarily translate into high profits and secure work places). Unless in times of an economic boom, the fact that some workers put in extra-long working hours leaves others with only a few hours of work while others again have no job at all.

The struggle over working time therefore not only concerns the length of the working day. As Marx (1983, 362) pointed out, it is about "the great contest between the blind rule of the supply and demand laws which form the political economy of the middle class, and social production controlled by social foresight, which forms the political economy of the working class." In a similar way, Karl Polanyi (1957) has argued that society needs to be protected from the excesses of market-mediated competition. This includes most notably the protection of labour power. Polanyi primarily refers to the limitation of competition on labour markets, but he also emphasises that factory working hours should be set independently from market constraints (ibid.). Inasmuch as working hours are determined outside the market (ibid., 251), the establishment of the normal working day implies a gradual decommodification of labour power. Conversely the flexibilization of working hours, if they primarily reflect the interests of the employers and not of the workers, is nothing else than a subjugation of working time under market constraints and therefore an attempt to recommodify labour power (Hermann 2008).

The struggle for the normal working day

While competition ensures sure that working time is subordinated to market constraints, solidarity is the weapon of the working class that enables it to organise working hours according to the needs of human beings. The demand for shorter working hours was not accidentally linked to the expectation that the working day should be the same for all workers. According to Markus Promberger (2005) this was due to the insight that "otherwise the project for significantly shorter working hours . . . would not prevail, as the competition of various sectors, companies and groups of workers would always lead to an upwards adjustment of working hours (17)." Successful campaigns for shorter working hours, on the other hand, strengthened the position of the labour movement and increased the power of trade unions (Bienefeld 1972).

The history of working time reductions is primarily a history of strikes, protests and demonstrations. Despite different working time realities, hundred thousands protesters participating in the May 1 demonstrations in 1890 demanded for the introduction of the eight-hour working day. Yet it was not until the end of the First World War that the demand was met in large parts of the industrialised world. In 1919 most of the participating nations in a conference organised by the newly formed International Labour Organisation in Washington agreed to introduce the eight-hour day. However, the ratification of the agreement remained incomplete. After the economy had slowly recovered, the national bourgeoisies started to take back the concessions made to the revolting masses at the end of the war. In Germany the eight-hour day, which had been introduced as part of the demobilisation laws, was increasingly questioned and was partially abolished in 1923 (Schneider

1984, 83). In part the same forces who argued against the implementation of the eight-hour day were now calling for an extension of working hours to defend the competitiveness of the national economies.

The economic upturn did not last long. By the end of the 1920s the world economy had slipped into the Great Depression, followed by a wave of unemployment, which continued for large parts of the 1930s. In the wake of mass unemployment, shorter working hours suddenly became a public issue again. The shortening of the working week was put on the table by progressive forces as a strategy to redistribute the remaining work among a larger number of workers, thereby reducing the number of those out of employment. In the United States trade unions fought for the introduction of the 30-hour week in the early 1930s. The campaign failed, yet with the adoption of the National Industrial Recovery Act (NIRA) the 40-hour week was implemented in a large number of sectors by the mid 1930s. The NIRA was subsequently revoked by the Supreme Court, but in 1938 the Roosevelt Administration passed the Fair Labor Standard Act, which apart from establishing a minimum wage also included the gradual introduction of the 40-hour week (Hunnicutt 1988, 246-7). Yet in contrast to earlier regulations the 40-hour week no longer imposed a maximum working-time limit. Instead the law only called for the payment of overtime supplements for hours exceeding the 40-hour threshold. By introducing the obligation for overtime pay, the legislation already included the main ingredients of what retrospectively can be called the Fordist working-time compromise.

A similar development took place in France. Here the Front Populaire had introduced the 40-hour week starting in 1936 (Chatriot, Fridenson, and Pezet 2003). The government adopted detailed timetables for the different sectors. Critics argued not such much against the 40-hour week as against the rigid application of the new working-time standard. After the fall of the Blum government, his successor, Balladier, responded to the criticism by allowing a large number of exemptions and by introducing the possibility to work overtime. This arrangement was reestablished after the end of the Second World War and it lasted until the 1960s, when for the first time a legal limit was imposed on overtime hours.

In Germany the Federation of German Trade Unions failed to reach 40-hour legislation in the 1930s, yet the earlier struggle for the eight-hour day had strong similarities with the fight for the 40-hour week in France and the United States. Initially, the statutory regulation only allowed for a few exemptions in which the eight-hour limit could be exceeded. However, from 1923 onwards, employers succeeded in relaxing and eroding the eight-hour norm, which they had repeatedly criticised as being too schematic. The working-time emergency act of 1927 reduced the number of exemptions but at the same time it allowed for a general deviation from the eight-hour standard if workers were rewarded with overtime bonuses for additional hours (Schneider 1984, 85). With the acceptance of deviations, even if bought dearly by overtime supplements, working time was re-subordinated to the power of capital. Hence, as Rudi Schmiede (1984) notes in an essay on the "schematic eight-hour day", "the question of working time more than any other issue is suited to decide who has decisive societal power and which organisational principles dominate society (372-3)."

The Fordist working-time compromise

The Fordist working-time compromise included a number of significant concessions from the labour movement. First of all, the 40-hour plus overtime trade-off gave companies the possibility to temporarily increase working hours – in the US without a maximum working-time limit, in Germany up to 60 hours a week. This means that working time was only partially sheltered from market-mediated competition (Hermann 2008). In fact employers frequently made use of this possibility and ordered millions of overtime hours at the height of the post-war boom. In Germany, for example, the number of average overtime hours per employee increased from 95 hours in 1960 to 157 hours in 1970 (Bosch 1994, 133). This corresponds to an additional month's work per year. Hence the Fordist working-time compromise was much more flexible than is often thought. However, flexibility came at a price: overtime supplements ranged from 50 to 100 per cent of the regular wage.

Secondly, during decades of full-employment the 40-hour week became an almost universal working-time standard. Yet this was only possibly because a large part of the population was actually excluded from paid employment. In many countries women at some point were forced to choose between an employment career and a family. Not surprisingly, the vast majority opted for marriage and children. As full-time housewives and mothers they became responsible for unpaid and unregulated reproductive work. Accordingly, the unequal and unfair distribution of paid and unpaid labour was not questioned or altered in the Fordist working-time compromise. Only at the height of the Fordist expansion and the related expansion of the welfare state, unpaid but socially indispensable activities such as childcare or the care of the elderly were gradually transformed into paid labour. Yet to a significant degree this was only the case in the developed welfare states in northern Europe, where since the 1960s an increasing number of women have found jobs in education and health care. But in this case, too, this has hardly changed the unequal distribution of unpaid work.

Thirdly, although most developed countries had introduced the 40-hour week at the end of the post-war expansion, the Fordist working-time compromise essentially remained a national compromise. The year the 40-hour week was implemented differed considerably from country to country, partially reflecting the development in productivity: While in the US the majority of workforce outside agriculture enjoyed the 40-hour week in the mid 1950s, in Europe workers had to wait until the mid 1960s or 70s to achieve the same standard. Conversely, the US in the mid 1960s increasingly came under pressure because the Europeans were closing the productivity-gap while still working significantly longer than the Americans (as discussed in the following pages, the US responded to the decreasing competitiveness of its major industries by extending working hours).

In addition, the Fordist working-time compromise led to a massive intensification of work. The obligatory overtime supplements created a strong incentive to invest in relative surplus value production. With the combination of a more and more fragmented work process divided into simple motions and a moving and increasingly mechanised production process, a new production model was invented in the first two decades of the 20th century allowing for a radical reduction of the working time expended in industrially produced goods. Henry Ford not only combined the various elements that are essential for the mass-production system and developed the Model T, the first mass-produced automobile. He also introduced the eight-hour day and later on the 40-hour week at a time when twelve-hour working days were no exception in the American steel industry.[2] However, Ford's working-time reduction remained an exception and in the wake of mounting competition on the automobile market the company abandoned the 40-hour week in the late 1930s.

While Ford's working time initiative fell victim to competition, the introduction of a general and mandatory working-time standard in the 1930s and after the Second World War helped to consolidate the Fordist mode of production. Even though companies had previously managed to achieve substantial productivity gains through the application of new technology, it was only after the establishment of the 40-hour week or the obligation to pay overtime supplements that less efficient corporations would invest in the modernisation of their machinery rather than pressuring their workers into working longer hours to compensate for the technological backwardness. The shorter working hours therefore helped to expand the Fordist production model into a truly comprehensive technological paradigm. Hence the 40-hour week more than anything else symbolised the shift from an extensive to an intensive accumulation regime. A precondition, however, was the failure of laissez-faire capitalism, growing state interventionism (New Deal), mass protests and the formation of militant industrial trade unions in the 1920s and 30s.

---

[2] Ford's reduction of working time was not free of self-interest: Firstly by granting his workers shorter hours than his competitors he hoped to lower the fluctuation rate which had reached a costly level. Secondly he wanted to prevent his workers joining the International Workers of the World which was organising autoworkers in Detroit by demanding the introduction of the eight-hour day.

In the Fordist period of capitalist development the augmentation of surplus value was primarily based on the extension of output per unit of working time, rather than the reduction of working time per unit of output. The result was on the one hand a relatively stable working day and on the other a dramatic fall in working time expended on the production of individual commodities. In fact, the productivity gains inherent in the Fordist production system had the potential for a radical cut in necessary working time. Yet because necessary working time does not only depend on social progress but also on the collective standard of living, the reduction in working time inherent in industrially fabricated goods has to some degree been compensated by a multiplication of the number of goods produced. Instead of putting in shorter working hours, workers started to buy cars, houses and other consumption goods. This was only possible, however, because a wage relation had been established that ensured that income would rise in line with productivity gains. Yet occasionally workers were also willing to put in overtime hours to take part in the emerging mass consumption culture.

In addition to the rise in living standards, working hours were decreasing continuously although not dramatically. As in the 1920s and 30s, in the post-war decades trade unions argued that productivity gains not only allowed but effectively demanded a reduction of working hours to prevent the re-emergence of unemployment (which had caused so much pain and social dislocations in the inter-war period). American trade unions vainly attempted to achieve the introduction of the 35-hour week in the 1950s. Instead, they succeeded in establishing the legal entitlement to paid holidays for the organised section of the labour force and in the larger industrial enterprises they managed to expand holiday time during the post-war period.[3] In Germany, the General Trade Union Congress increased pressure for shorter working hours in 1950. In 1952 the rallies organised on May 1 focused on the introduction of the 40-hour week; in 1956 the union advertised the popular slogan 'Saturday Daddy belongs to me'. Consequently working hours in the metal industry, which is the leading sector for working-time reductions in Germany, were first reduced to 45, then 44, before the 40-hour week was introduced in several stages during the 1960s. As a result, average collectively agreed working hours (for the whole economy) fell about ten per cent between 1960 and 1974, and by the mid 1970s were just over 40 hours a week (Schudlich 1987, 382). In addition to the shortening of the working week, German workers also achieved the extension of paid vacation. Together, shorter working hours and rising living standards ensured that the gap between necessary working time and that actually worked remained relatively stable during the post-war era.

---

[3] Ford workers, e.g., were entitled to two weeks of paid vacation in 1947, four weeks in 1958 and six weeks in 1968.

Post-Fordism and working-time flexibilization

By the 1970s, the Fordist paradigm had run into a severe crisis. Some authors have argued that the crisis was the result of increasingly saturated mass production markets. Yet the problem was not saturated markets; the problem was that surplus could not longer be increased by producing more of the same product. The solution, accordingly, was not a shift from economies of scale to economies of scope, or mass production to craft production. The solution was a combination of increasing output per unit of working time and reducing working time per unit of output. The invention of flexible technology was instrumental in shifting the focus on reducing inputs rather than extending output. With flexible technology new products or new models need a much lower break-even point to become profitable. Yet in order to fully exploit the new possibilities, the technological innovations had to be combined with changes in work organisation. In a notable departure from the traditional Taylorist-Fordist production paradigm, mass producers started to enrich tasks and install work teams, even on the assembly line. While some observers saw the changes as a reaction to an increasingly disillusioned and dissatisfied workforce who had shown their disapproval through a series of protests and strikes in the 1960s and 70s, task enrichment and team working were not introduced to improve working conditions. To the contrary: Because the goal was the limitation of working time per unit of output the changes were introduced to burden the same amount of work on a smaller number of workers. The result was what popular media described as 'downsizing' – more or the same is done by fewer workers.

The changes not only resulted in a veritable intensification of work. Lean production also demanded for changes in the length and distribution of working hours. While the maximization of output per unit of time facilitated a gradual standardization of work hours, the limitation of time per unit of output demanded for a far-reaching flexibilization. Hence flexible working hours were not only and perhaps not even primarily the result of increasingly volatile markets; they were also the result of systematic constraints in increasingly lean production systems and an advanced rate of surplus extraction. European producers responded to the need for more flexibility by introducing new work time systems, including averaging periods and working time accounts. The introduction of the 35-hour week in the German metal sector in the 1990s was linked to a substantial flexibilisation of working time: While weekly working time was limited to 35 hours, companies received the possibility to avoid the payment of overtime supplements as long as the average hours over a particular averaging period did not exceed the 35-hour limit. Perhaps Volkswagen went furthest in exchanging shorter hours for more flexibility: In order to maintain employment despite a significant fall in demand, the company moved to a 28.8-hour week in 1994. However, part of the new working time arrangement was that management could temporarily extend working time to 38 hours per week without the obligation of pay overtime supplements

(Haipeter/Lehndorff 2005, 273). The result was what VW human-resources director Peter Hartz (1996) has called a "breathing enterprise".

It took about ten year before German companies took full advantage of the flexibility granted by the new working time regulations and negotiated deviations from standard hours with local workforces – part of the flexibilisation project was a shift in the bargaining arena from the sector to the company level. In addition to the spread of averaging period, which often last for an entire year, companies have introduced working time accounts for their employees. These accounts are used to deposit overtime hours. In 2004, more than 60 per cent of German companies had introduced work time accounts, affecting at least 37 per cent of the dependent workforce (Groß, Munz and Seifert 2000, 217). The advantage for the company is that it saves overtime supplements which otherwise would be added to the regular pay rates. Workers benefit insofar as they maintain their entitlement to free-time which they can take at a later point. Yet according to a study from 2000, only in a third of the companies excess hours were actually taken as time off in lieu (Bauer et al. 2002, 161). In nine per cent the limits were ignored and the credits extended; in 29 per cent excess hours were paid out and in another 18 per cent they were simply eradicated (ibid.). According to trade union sources, 750,000 deposited hours expired in a single year at Daimler headquarters in Stuttgart (Jänicke, Ohl and Wagner 2008, 105). In combination with a growing number of temporary exemptions, shorter and flexible hours increasingly become flexible and long. Heiner Dribbusch and Thorsten Schulten (2008) summarize the situation as follows: "[T]he proactive approach of reducing weekly work timework time with wage compensation to tackle unemployment, which was prominent among German unions during the 1980s, ended in the early 1990s, and since the mid 1990s employers have succeeded in turning the tide towards longer working hours (127)."

While European manufacturers have pushed for new working time models which grants them more flexiblity without the need to pay overtime premiums, American employers who are not constrained by overtime limits continued to rely on overtime to achieve maximum working time flexibility. Overtime already soared during the postwar boom. However, despite fluctuations average weekly overtime hours put in by US manufacturing workers never exceeded 4.1 hours. The situation started to change in the 1980s: Average weekly overtime hours of production workers increased over an entire business cycle from 3.3 hours in 1979 to 3.8 hours in 1989. And they continued to grow at an even higher pace in the 1990s, taking off at 3.3 hours in 1991 and reaching a record 4.9 hours in 1998. This means that overtime increased by almost 50 per cent over a seven-year period (Hetrick 2000, 33). The surge of overtime beyond the business cycle can also be seen in a growing proportion of American workers putting in extra long work hours. The share of male workers who work more than 48 hours a week grew from 16.6 per cent in 1980 to 24.3 per cent in 2005 (Kuhn and Lozano 2008, 311-312). In 2000,

19.4 of all US workers (men and women) worked more than 40 hours and those who worked overtime on average put in an additional 11.8 overtime hours per week (Golden and Jorgensen 2002, 6).

Neoliberalism and the surge in working hours

Neoliberalism covers roughly the same period as post-Fordism. However, while post-Fordism is mainly a technical term, describing the changes in production systems following the crisis of Fordism, neoliberalism is primarily a political concept. As such it highlights the changes in power and class relations and related changes in the protection of employment and the distribution of wealth, following decades of workers' gains (as can, for example, be seen in a growing wage share). Neoliberalism, in short, is a "ruling-class political program to respond to the challenges from the Left" (Albo 2007, 356). The result was not only a reform of the production model, but also a transformation of reproduction patterns and the development of a "new social rule, specific to neoliberalism" (Albo and Fast 2003, 39). In terms of working time, the new social rule required more people to sell their labor power to gain the means of existence and in sum put in more work hours. Markets and competition in several regards played a crucial role in the neoliberal counter-revolution. Competition is beneficial from a capitalist point of view, even though individual capitalists may go out of business. Overall, competition strengthens the position of the capitalist class, while undermining the strength of the working class because the latter is built on solidarity, the opposite of competition (Flechter and Gapasin 2008, 9-10). There are several ways how capitalists accelerate competition in post-Fordist production systems: With just-in-time production competition was prolonged into the heart of the factory. Just-in-time deliverers not only struggle to meet short-time production targets, but also to undercut their competitors. Globalisation allowed international companies to force local production sites to compete for production volumes. This was complemented by an internal marketisation in which various departments were transformed into cost- or profit centers and subsequently assessed as if they were standalone companies (Hermann 2006). While for workers they are always real, market pressures can be created virtually. When managers, for example, impose particular benchmarks or production targets in order to increase profits, the result is the same: Workers fearing for their jobs tend to accept longer hours and lower wages regardless if the purpose is to increase competitiveness or profits.

In sum neoliberalism slowed down and partly reversed the secular decline in working hours (Hermann 2008; Basso 2003). In some countries the change can be seen in an increase in average working hours, but more often average hours have stagnated while the total number of workers and productivity went up. In the United States the average working week in 2000 was 1.6 hours longer than in 1970

(McGrattan 2004, 17). By the end of the 1990s, American workers were putting in more than an additional week per year than in the early 1980s. In manufacturing where the part-time rate is traditionally low the difference between 1975 and 2000 amounted to more than two weeks. Sweden also shows a strong upward trend in yearly working hours, especially in the 1980s. The difference between 1990 and 2000 is 80 hours. In Britain yearly hours increased substantially in the 1980s (by 70 hours between 1981 and 1989), but fell back in the 1990s. Average yearly hours in 2001 were virtually the same as in 1981. Canada experienced a surge in work hours in the 1990s with the effect that in 1999 workers put in 13 hours more per year than in 1991. In contrast to Britain hours only fell back slightly after 2000. In France and Germany average yearly hours were still falling in the 1980s and 90s, but stagnated or slightly increased between 2003 and 2008.[4]

Average yearly working hours include part-time work. If we only look at full-time hours, working time more or less stagnated between 1992 and 2006 in Germany and between 2003 and 2008 in France.[5] In West Germany average working hours in 2006 were the same as in 1988 – that is before the introduction of the 35-hour week (Kümmerling, Jansen and Lehndorff 2009). Actual weekly working hours in the metal and engineering sector in West Germany reached 39.1 hours in 2006. This means that working hours in the German metal industry have increased by roughly an hour within three years (ibid.). According to Lehndorff, "these work time extensions were not caused by ups and downs of the economy. They were the outcome of a shift in political power relations" (Lehndorff 2009, 10). The 2007-2009 crisis led to a fall in working hours, but overtime working quickly reappeared when growth picked up again in 2010.[6]

The halt of the secular decline in working hours can also be seen in the development of per capita work hours (including those without a job). In the United States per capita hours have increased by 18 per cent between 1985 and 2000, while Canada recorded the same growth for the longer period between 1970 and 2008. In Britain per capita hours virtually stagnated between 1980 and 2008 and in Sweden between 1985 and 2008. Among the few countries which still recorded falling per-capita hours in the 1990s were France and Germany. But in both countries the development came to a halt in the mid 1990s, with per capita hours largely stagnating between 1995 and 2008.[7] Another way of looking at the same development is the comparison of working hours put in by households rather than individ-

[4] Data from OECD.
[5] Data from Eurostat.
[6] The president of the employer-friendly Cologne Institute for Economic Research (which has been mentioned before) argued that Germany would soon face a 45-hour week in Germany to cope with a shortage of qualified personnel (Handelsblatt, November 23, 2010).
[7] Data from OECD, own calculations.

ual workers. The combined (paid) work week of married couples in the United States increased from 52.2 hours in 1970 to 63.1 hours in 2000. This is also an increase by almost 20 per cent (Jacobs and Gerson 2004, 29-31). Together with a 20 per cent growth in productivity, the changes have resulted in a veritable increase in what Marxists call surplus labour.

Conclusion:

In sum, German employers, very much as their American counterpart 20 years earlier, have stepped up pressure to extend work time. The ideological shift can also be seen in how Europe responded to the 2007-9 crisis. While in the crisis several countries also reduced work time temporarily as part of short-time work programs, permanent work time reductions was nowhere on the political agenda, not even in France and Germany which still introduced the 35-hour week in the 1990s and after 2000. This is even more remarkable since short-time work actually proofed that shorter hours are a viable tool to avoid unemployment.[8] While in the past trade unions and progressive parties pushed for shorter working hours to fight growing unemployment, in neoliberal capitalism longer hours are advertised as a measure to safeguard jobs. Even Volkswagen returned to the 33- and 34-hour week without wage compensation in 2006. While initially management cut working hours to safeguard jobs, now they are arguing the longer hours are necessary to protect employment.

However, the neoliberal break with the secular decline in working hours was rarely based on a direct extension of working time. What happened instead was a combination of flexibilisation, temporary exemptions and an intensification of competition. An OECD study found that countries with strong product market regulations tend to have shorter hours than those with more competition (Causa 2009). While the OECD sees this as an argument for more rather than less competition, the finding clearly shows that trade unions can no longer limit their struggle against surplus extraction on labor market regulation. They have to address the problem of accelerating competition in neoliberal capitalism. Still, a return to the Fordist working time compromise with its emphasis on standardization is hardly an option. While male workers received overtime bonuses for hours worked beyond the 40-hour threshold, women who worked part-time were penalized by lower wages and atypical and insecure contracts. To some extent the changes in neoliberal capitalism were possible because workers welcomed more individuality and flexibility in scheduling working time. There is only one alternative to

[8] The Institute for Work, Skills and Training, for example, estimates that short-time work together with a reduction of overtime and the clearing of overtime accounts saved 1.2 million jobs in Germany (Franz and Lehndorff, 2010).

marketisation and standardization – workers' participation. In the long-term the best way to assure a balance of various interests, including the distribution of paid and unpaid work, is the replacement of markets through democratic decision-making processes. Only real and meaningful participation processes guarantee a social production controlled by social foresight propagated by Marx.

References:

Albo, Greg. "Neoliberalism and the Discontented." In *Global Flashpoints: Socialist Register 2008,* edited by Colin Leys and Leo Panitch, 354-362. London: The Merlin Press, 2007.

Albo, Greg and Fast Travis. "Varieties of Neoliberalism: Trajectories of Workfare in Advanced Capitalist Countries." Paper presented at the Annual Meetings of the Canadian Political Science Association Congress of the Humanities and Social Sciences, Dalhousie University, Halifax, Nova Scotia, May 30, 2003.

Basso, Pietro. *Modern Times, Ancient Hours. Working Lives in the 21st Century.* London: Verso, 2003.

Bauer, Frank, Hermann Groß, Steffen Lehndorff, Sebastian Schief, and Georg Sieglen. *Arbeits- Und Betriebszeiten 2001. Neue Formen Des Betrieblichen Arbeits- Und Betriebszeitmanagements. Ergebnisse Einer Repräsentativen Betriebsbefragung*. Cologne: Institut zur Erforschung Sozialer Chancen (ISO), 2002.

Bienefeld, Manfred A. *Working Hours in British Industry*. London: London School of Economics and Political Science, 1972.

Bispinck, Reinhard. "Germany: Working Time and its Negotiation." In *Collective Bargaining on Working-Time. Recent European Experiences*, edited by Maarten Keune and Béla Galgóci, 111-128. Brussels: European Trade Union Institute, 2006.

Bosch, Gerhard. "Federal Republic of Germany." In *Times are Changing: Working Times in 14 Industrialised Countries*, edited by Gerhard Bosch, Peter Dawkins amd François Michon, 127-152. Geneva: ILO, 1994.

Boyer, Robert. *Théorie de la régulation*. Paris: Éditions La Découverte, 2004.

Causa, Orsetta. "The Policy Determinants of Hours Worked Across OECD Countries." *OECD Journal: Economic Studies,* 2009. Accessed May 17, 2011. http://www.oecd.org/dataoecd/17/30/46867013.pdf

Chatriot, Alain, Patrick Fridenson and Eric Pezet. "La réduction du temps de travail en France entre réglementation tutélaire et négociation encadrée (1814-1978)." *Revue de l'IRES* 2, no. 42 (2003):1-33.

Diss Greis, Theresa. *The Decline of Annual Hours Worked in the United States since 1947*. Philadelphia, Wharton School, University of Pennsylvania, 1984.

Dribbusch, Heiner and Thorsten Schulten. "German Trade Unions between Neoliberal Restructuring, Social Partnerschip and Internationalism." In *Labour and the Challenges of Globalization : What Prospects for Transnational Solidarity?,* edited by Andreas Bieler, Ingemar Lindberg and Devan Pillay, 178-198. London: Pluto Press, 2008.

Franz, Christine and Steffen Lehndorff, "Arbeitszeitentwicklung Und Krise - Eine Zwischenbilanz," *IAQ-Report*(2010). http://www.iaq.uni-due.de/iaq-report/2010/report2010-07.pdf

Fletcher, Bill and Fernando Gapasin. *Solidarity Divided: The Crisis in Organized Labor and a New Path toward Social Justice*. Berkeley, CA: University of California Press, 2008.

Funk, Lothar. "Siemens Deal Launches Debate on Longer Working Hours." *European Industrial Relations Observatory on-line* (2004). Accessed May 18, 2011. www.eurofound.europa.eu/eiro/2004/07/feature/de0407106f.htm

Golden, Lonnie, and Helene Jorgensen. "Time after Time: Mandatory Overtime in the U.S. Economy." Economic Policy Institute Briefing Paper 120. Washington D.C., January 1, 2002.

Groß, Hermann, Eva Munz, and Hartmut Seifert. "Verbreitung Und Struktur Von Arbeitszeitkonten." *Arbeit* 9, no. 3 (2000): 217-229.

Haipeter, Thomas and Steffen Lehndorff. “Die atmende Fabrik: Geht der Tarifpolitik bald die Luft aus?” in *Flexible Zeiten in der Arbeitswelt,* edited by Hartmut Seifert, 260-285. Frankfurt a. M: Campus Verlag, 2005.

Haipeter, Thomas. "Kontrollierte Dezentralisierung? Abweichende Tarifvereinbarungen in Der Metall- Und Elektroindustrie." *Industrielle Beziehungen* 16, no. 3 (2009): 232-53.

Hartz, Peter. *Das atmende Unternehmen. Jeder Arbeitsplatz hat einen Kunden. Beschäftigungssicherung bei Volkswagen*. Frankfurt a. M: Campus Verlag, 1996.

Hermann, Christoph. "Laboring in the Network.” *Capitalism, Nature, Socialism* 17, no. 1 (2006): 65-76.

Hetrick, Ron L. "Analyzing the Recent Upward Surge in Overtime Hours." *Monthly Labor Review* 123, no. 2 (2000): 30-33.

Hunnicutt, Benjamin. *Work Without End. Abandoning Shorter Hours for the Right to Work*. Philadelphia: Temple University Press, 1998.

Jacobs Jerry A. and Kathleen Gerson. "Unterstanding Changes in American Work time." In *Fighting for Time : Shifting Boundaries of Work and Social Life,* edited by Cynthia Fuchs Epstein and Arne L. Kalleberg, 29-31. New York: Russel Sage, 2004.

Jänicke, Sophie, Kay Ohl, and Hildegard Wagner. "Es Wird Zeit! Ansätze Einer Neuen Arbeitszeitdebatte in der IG Metall." *PROKLA*, no. 150 (2008): 103-12.

Kuhn, Peter, and Fernando Lozano. "The Expanding Workweek? Understanding Trends in Long Work Hours among U.S. Men, 1979–2006." *Journal of Labor Economics* 26, no. 2 (2008): 311-43.

Kümmerling, Angelika, Andreas Jansen, and Steffen Lehndorff. "Die Veränderung Der Beschäftigungs- Und Arbeitszeitstrukturen in Deutschland 2001 Bis 2006." Accessed May 3, 2011. http://www.iaq.uni-due.de/aktuell/veroeff/2009/kuemmerling01.pdf.

Lehndorff, Steffen. "Zurück zur 40-Stunden-Woche? – Wirksamkeit und Krise der tarifvertraglichen Arbeitszeitregulierung." *WSI-Mitteilungen* 6 (2004): 306-12.

_____. "Before the crisis, in the crisis, and beyond: The upheaval of collective bargaining in Germany." *European Review of Labour and Research* 17, no. 3 (August 2011): 341-354.

Marx, Karl."Inaugural Address and Provisional Rules of the International Working Men's Association." In *The Portable Marx*, edited by Eugene Kamenka, 509-522. New York: Penguin Books, 1983.

Marx, Karl. *Capital. A Critique of Political Economy*. New York: International Publishers, 1968.

McGrattan, Ellen R. and Richard Rogerson. "Changes in Hours Worked, 1950–2000." *Federal Reserve Bank of Minneapolis Quarterly Review* 28, no. 1 (2000): 14–33.

Polanyi, Karl. *The Great Transformation. The Political and Economic Origins of Our Time*. Beacon Hill: Beacon Press, 1957.

Promberger, Markus. "Wie neuartig sind flexible Arbeitszeiten? Historische Grundlinien einer Arbeitszeitpolitik." In *Flexible Zeiten in der Arbeitswelt*, edited by Hartmut Seifert, 9-39. Frankfurt a. M: Campus Verlag, 2005.

Rigaudiat, Jacques. *Reduire le temps de travail*. Paris: Édition Syros, 1996.

Schmiede, Rudi. "Der ‚schematische Achtstundentag' 1918 bis 1923 – Konturen einer arbeitspolitischen Ausnahmeperiode. In *Arbeitspolitik: Materialen zum Zusammenhang von politischer Macht, Kontrolle und betrieblicher Organisation der Arbeit*, edited by Ulrich Jürgens and Frieder Naschold, 365-380. Opladen: Westdeutscher Verlag, 1984.

Schmiede, Rudi. "Die Entwicklung der Arbeitszeit in Deutschland: Eine Übersicht." In *Arbeitskampf um Arbeitszeit. Kritisches Gewerkschaftsjahrbuch 1979/80*, edited by Jacobi Otto, Walther Müller-Jentsch, and Eberhard Schmidt, 71-87. Berlin: Rotbuch Verlag, 1980.

Schneider, Michael. "Der Kampf um die Arbeitszeitverkürzung von der Industrialisierung bis zur Gegenwart." *Gewerkschaftliche Monatshefte* 35, no. 2 (1984):77-89.

Schudlich, Edwin. *Die Abkehr vom Normalarbeitstag. Entwicklung der Arbeitszeit in der Industrie der Bundesrepublik seit 1945*. Frankfurt a. M.: Campus Verlag, 1987.

Rethinking Class in the Gulf Arab States: The Spatial Structuring of Temporary Migrant Labour[1]

Adam Hanieh

Introduction

The world market in contemporary capitalism is marked, as Albo has observed, by a certain 'two-sidedness'.[2] On the one hand, there is a tendency towards the internationalization of capital, signifying the global reach of capitalism as "a social system driven by the encompassing accumulative imperatives of a world market".[3] Within this system, the commodity is – as Christian Palloix remarked in an earlier, highly prescient analysis – "conceptualized, produced, and realized at the level of the world market".[4] Simultaneously, however, the capitalist world market remains "differentiated by temporally and spatially specific processes of accumulation and statification and particular class relations necessary for the production of value".[5] It requires the mediation of distinct institutions – such as individual nation-states and their associated bodies of law, citizenship and repressive apparatuses – to both se-

---

[1] An earlier version of this chapter was presented as a paper to the 3rd International Initiative for the Promotion of Political Economy (IIPPE) Workshop, Ankara, Turkey 14-15 September 2009 and later published as "Temporary Migrant Labour and the Spatial Structuring of Class in the Gulf Cooperation Council," *Spectrum: Journal of Global Studies* 1, no. 3 (2010): 67-88. Many thanks to the coordinator of the IIPPE labour session, Bruno Tinel, and the editors of *Spectrum* for helpful feedback.

[2] Greg Albo, "Contemporary Capitalism" in *Elgar Companion to Marxist Economics*, ed. Ben Fine and Alfredo Saad-Filho (London: Elgar, 2012). January 2010 draft 2, accessed June 3, 2010, http://www.yorku.ca/albo.

[3] Albo, "Contemporary Capitalism."

[4] Christian Palloix, "Conceptualizing the Internationalization of Capital," *Review of Radical Political Economics* 9, no.2 (1977): 20.

[5] Albo, "Contemporary Capitalism."

cure the conditions of reproduction and to articulate the heightened competition between individual capitals that emerges in the feverish scramble for profits.

The implications for labour of this single – yet always spatially-segmented – world market are profound. Forced to operate at a global level, the increased competition between individual capitals has generalized pressures to intensify labour, extract more absolute surplus value through extension of the working day, reduce wages, and shrink the size of the workforce. Under the guise of neoliberal orthodoxy, contemporary capitalism has thus attempted to shift the balance of class power through a decades-long attack on the conditions of labour. De-regulation, flexibilization, casualization, and increased insecurity of employment have become the common experience of workers globally. These policies effectively set workers against one another, and in pursuing their own individual self-interest they "press in the same direction as capital" against "the interests of wage- labour as a whole".[6]

In addition to these downward pressures on wages and conditions, the internationalization of capital that characterizes contemporary capitalism has also been accompanied by the "tendential emergence of a global labour market".[7] This does not mean that all labour is free to move but, rather, that "an increasing proportion of the world population [is integrated] directly into capitalist labor markets" and that "national and regional labor markets [have been locked] into an integrated global labor market".[8] This is, of course, not an entirely new characteristic of capitalism – slavery, indentured work, post-war migration and other forms of international labour flows have long been indicative of certain tendencies towards a 'global factory'.[9] Within contemporary capitalism, however, the world market imposes a logic of reproduction on every concrete manifestation of labour, such that virtually all social relations are 'conceptualized' at the level of the world market.

One striking form of this internationalization is the growth in temporary migrant labour flows. Temporary migrant labour generally refers to individuals who move for the purpose of work and whose right to stay in their country of destination is usually (but not necessarily) connected to an employment contract.[10] Typi-

---

[6] Michael Lebowitz, *Beyond Capital: Marx's Political Economy of the Working Class* (New York: St. Martin's Press, 1992), 83.

[7] Henk Overbeek "Neoliberalism and the Regulation of Global Labor Mobility," *The Annals of the American Academy of Political and Social Science*, no. 581 (2002): 76.

[8] Overbeek, *Neoliberalism*, 78.

[9] Massimo De Angelis, "Trade, the Global Factory and the Struggles for a New Commons" (paper presented at the Conference of Socialist Economists on Global Capital and Global Struggles: Strategies, Alliance and Alternatives, London, July 12, 2000).

[10] The definition of 'temporary migrant labour' is heavily contested in both academic and policy circles. The UN differentiates between short-term and long-term migration for reasons other than recreation, business, religious pilgrimage and medical treatment. The International Labour Or-

cally these contracts are of limited duration (from months to a few years). Within contemporary capitalism, temporary migrant labour has come to acquire a pronounced and definite functionality as a source of cheap workers in both low-skilled and high-skilled sectors.[11] In many cases, these workers face circumscribed rights and conditions – including prohibitions on unions and collective organizing, restrictions on seeking alternative employment, and control of movement within the country. In the OECD, where the public provision of basic services has been significantly eroded, temporary labour programmes have met the demand for workers in the health, aged-care, cleaning and child care sectors. From the perspective of labour-sending countries in the South, the remittance flows associated with temporary migrant labour have been heralded as a means of "harnessing the synergies between migration and development" particularly in the context of a general reduction in bilateral and multilateral aid flows.[12] In 2007 alone, migrant workers sent US$265 billion to the South through remittances, surpassing official global development aid by 60 percent.[13] Many countries have become heavily reliant on these remittances. In some cases – such as Honduras, Haiti, and Guyana – they account for more than 20% of GDP.

This growth in temporary migrant labour should not be seen separately from other types of movement of people, including undocumented migration, permanent migration, forced migration, trafficking and so forth. Despite their significant differences, each of these forms of migration is closely connected to the development of labour markets and the process of class formation, and indicates that the question of class in contemporary capitalism needs to move beyond a prevailing methodological nationalism, in which class is understood as enclosed by fixed national

---

ganization (ILO) focuses on the purpose of migration (employment), rather than its duration. Problems arise when distinguishing between 'illegal' and 'legal' migration (and whether the former should be included in the temporary labour category), and the fact that people may have a variety of reasons for moving across borders – making it difficult to separate, for example, 'forced' and 'labour' migration in some cases. The fluidity of definition should be borne in mind throughout this chapter.

[11] The latter sector is an important, but under theorized, component of migrant flows. It is significant, for example, that the extension of liberalization into services through the 1995 General Agreement on Services (GATS) (a result of the Uruguay round of World Trade Organization negotiations), signified commitments to encourage movement of 'high skilled' temporary migration in areas such as inter-corporate transferees, executives, managers, specialists, business visitors. This is another side to the internationalization of both labour and capital.

[12] Commission of the European Communities. Contribution to the EU Position for the United Nations' High Level Dialogue on Migration and Development, July 14, 2006, accessed November 10, 2010, http://eur-lex.europa.eu/.

[13] The World Bank, "Migration and Development Brief No.8," November 11, 2008, accessed July 3, 2009, www.worldbank.org. Moreover, the financial systems necessary to facilitate these flows of money have been promoted by international financial institutions as a means to deepen the financialization of economies in the South.

boundaries. The internationalization of labour within contemporary capitalism means that class formation necessarily involves internally related sets of social relations that are tied across different geographical areas. Class formation is, in other words, an implicitly spatial process, which thereby demands wrestling with a theorization of space.

This essay employs a Marxist framework to explore this relationship between temporary migrant labour, space, and class formation through the case of the six states of the Gulf Cooperation Council (Saudi Arabia, Kuwait, Bahrain, United Arab Emirates, Qatar and Oman).[14] It is argued that temporary labour flows intertwine geographical spaces (underpinned by the institutional mechanisms that make these flows functional) within a single process of accumulation. They reflect the interlocking of sets of social relations across different zones of the world market. As such, these flows represent a particular spatial structuring, or *spatialization*, of class within contemporary capitalism. Class formation needs to be located and historicized within these spatial structures, which then become critical to interpreting the nature of crises and their possible resolution.

The GCC states possess perhaps the most extreme illustration of temporary labour flows of any region in the global economy (with the possible exception of coastal China). In all of these states the majority of the working population are temporary, migrant workers with no citizenship rights. In some GCC countries, migrant workers exceed 80% of the labour force. These workers perform virtually all of the productive labour in the Gulf economies in addition to service, clerical, retail and domestic work. Neighbouring South Asian countries such as Pakistan, India, Bangladesh, and Sri Lanka are almost fully dependent on the labour markets of the Gulf for their overseas workforce, and remittances from these workers are critical to the survival of millions of people throughout the region.

Most analysis of these workers tends to be sociological in approach – focusing either on the extreme deprivation and exploitation to which workers are subject in the host economies, or the impact of remittance flows on community, village and other social structures in the source countries. This literature contains a wide range of useful and perceptive analysis, and is drawn upon where appropriate below. But the aim of this chapter is not to present a comprehensive analysis of these workers or their labour conditions. Rather, it is to suggest how a focus on the spatial structuring of class formation can deepen an understanding of Gulf capitalism and its mediation of crisis.

---

[14] The GCC was formed in 1981 as a regional integration project that resembled in many ways the European Union. Throughout this chapter, the terms GCC and 'Gulf states' are used interchangeably.

The first section of this essay presents a short outline of Marxist perspectives on space and accumulation, drawing on the work of David Harvey and other radical geographers. The chapter then turns to the development of class structure in the GCC states and describes the nature of temporary migrant labour flows in this context. From the outset, flows of migrant labour have been embedded as a constitutive element of Gulf capitalism. The spatialization of class has acted to mediate patterns of accumulation and avert crisis – a 'spatial fix'. Following an examination of the region's structural reliance on migrant labour and the implications of this for surrounding countries, the essay then explores the 2008 global crisis from the perspective of this class structure. It is argued that while Gulf capitalism may have faced pressure and strain due to the crisis – the spatial displacement of crisis meant that the real impact was shifted to surrounding regions.

2. Marxist Approaches to Space and Accumulation

Over the last few decades, a rich theoretical discussion has developed over the relationship between the different forms of spatiality of capitalism and processes of accumulation. Much of this literature draws upon a particular strand of radical geography that conceives space not as a static 'thing' or 'empty vessel', but rather a product and expression of capitalist social relations that develops through a process of continual contestation and transformation.[15] This understanding of the *spatiality of capitalist social relations* can be found throughout Marx's writings, which frequently link forms of spatial organization to the nature of the social relations (and hence class formation) that characterize different societies. Speaking of the British countryside, for example, Marx argued that the growth of industrial and commercial labour accompanying emerging capitalist social relations was spatially reflected in the separation of town and country.[16] In other words, the changing spatial characteristics of human geography were a reflection of an alteration in the country's social relations and the development of new class structures. In later writings, Marx traced the development of colonialism – i.e. the spatial division of the world market into dominated and dominating countries – to the 'general conditions of

---

[15] Neil Brenner, *New State Spaces: Urban Governance and the Rescaling of Statehood* (New York: Oxford University Press, 2004), 32.

[16] 'The division of labour inside a nation leads at first to the separation of industrial and commercial from agricultural labour, and hence to the separation of town and country and to the conflict of their interests… At the same time through the division of labour inside these various branches there develop various divisions among the individuals co-operating in definite kinds of labour… These same conditions are to be seen (given a more developed intercourse) in the relations of different nations to one another.' Karl Marx and Friedrich Engels, *The German Ideology* (New York: International Publishers Co, 1970), 43.

existence of the manufacturing period'.[17] In comments such as these, Marx consciously stressed the patterning of space as a *form of appearance* taken by a particular set of capitalist social relations.

This understanding of space as a reflection of capitalist social relations was further extended by Henri Lefebvre, a French sociologist who was one of the first to draw out the spatial thematic of Marxism. Lefebvre pointed out the reflexive manner in which spatial forms could act upon and shape social relations, thereby emphasizing space as a social product that could be used as a means of maintaining control and hegemony. Every society produced a certain spatial arrangement and practice, which served to reproduce its own existence. He asked:

'What exactly is the mode of existence of social relationships? ... The study of space offers an answer according to which the social relations of production have a social existence to the extent that they have a spatial existence; they project themselves into a space, becoming inscribed there, and in the process producing that space itself'.[18]

One of the major challenges facing the radical movement, according to Lefebvre, was to demystify the relationship between the structuring of space and the nature of capitalist rule. Contemporaneous with capital's production of space, he argued, social struggles would inevitably emerge against this spatial alienation, attempting to reclaim the urban and the 'right to the city'.

Lefebvre's writing on the 'production of space' sparked a subsequent range of valuable theoretical discussion.[19] A representative example can be found in the work of geographer, Doreen Massey, who stressed the importance of analysing how different types of labour are spatially organized. The spatial placement of controlling, managerial and administrative functions exist in a mutually defining relationship with other controlled areas.[20] She called this relationship a 'spatial structure', and attempted to describe shifts in the accumulation of British capitalism through the different ways that the spatial structure of accumulation shifted.[21] In

---

[17] Karl Marx, *Capital Vol. I* (London: Penguin Classics, 1992), 474.

[18] Henri Lefebvre, *The Production of Space* (Oxford: Basil Blackwell, 1991 [1974]), 129.

[19] See John Carney, Ray Hudson, & Jim Lewis, eds., *Regions in Crisis* (London: Croom Helm, 1980); Doreen Massey, *Spatial Divisions of Labour: Social Structures and the Geography of Production* (London: MacMillan Education, 1984); Doreen Massey, *Global Restructuring, Local Responses* (Worcester, Mass.: Graduate School of Geography, Clark University, 1988); Edward Soja, *Postmodern Geographies* (London: Verso, 1989); Neil Smith, *Uneven Development: Nature, Capital and the Production of Space* (Oxford: Basil Blackwell, 1990); David Harvey, "The Geopolitics of Capitalism," in *Social Relations and Spatial Structures*, ed. Derek Gregory and John Urry (London: Macmillan, 1985), 128-163; David Harvey, *Spaces of Capital: Towards a Critical Geography* (Edinburgh: Edinburgh University Press, 2001).

[20] Massey, *Spatial Divisions*, 112.

[21] Massey, *Global Restructuring*, 252.

this manner, class was imbricated with space, and its active structuring could be understood as a necessary component of the strategy of accumulation by British capital.

These themes were further developed in the work of David Harvey, who linked the 'production of space' to its role in mediating and shaping capitalist crisis. Harvey, following Lefebvre, agreed that the spatiality of capitalism is a product of tendencies and counter-tendencies within the capitalist mode of production. Marx's frequent observation that capitalism tends towards spatial expansion as a means to encompass increasing swathes of human activity implied, however, that space itself needed to be produced. Harvey noted that "spatial organisation is necessary to overcome space" and thus capitalism was driven towards the laying-down of territorial complexes such as factories, transport routes, urban environments, communications networks and regulatory institutions in order to expand and circulate capital.[22] Harvey's key contribution to this theorization of space, however, was his argument that capitalism could switch between different forms of spatiality or spatial structures as a means of averting, displacing, and overcoming, crisis tendencies.[23] He described this crisis-averting utilization of space as a 'spatial fix', which could occur at the level of the individual capital or industry and (most typically) involves the mediation of the state. The production of space and spatial fixes, Harvey pointed out, is a contradictory process, and inevitably reappears as barriers to the future expansion and development of capitalist social relations. When this occurs, capitalism faces a 'switching crisis' as the old spatial structures undergo a devaluation crisis, capital seeks new areas for investment, and new forms of spatiality arise to underpin its flows. This "socio-spatial dialectic" means that space acts to both shape social relations and, contemporaneously, is reproduced within and through those same social relations.[24]

In contemporary capitalism, these insights on the spatiality of accumulation provide a particularly useful framework for understanding the nature of temporary labour migration. If class is understood as a set of social relations that have a concrete spatial materiality – established through relations between different geographical areas – then flows of temporary migrant labour act to alter the spatiality of any specific class formation. A migrant worker may be physically located in a certain country for a period of time, but their reproduction (and that of their family) largely occurs in a different space and within a distinct set of historically-constituted social relations. This spatiality is a necessary form of appearance of the social relations that characterize class, and must thus be integrated into any analysis of concrete reality. Following Harvey, it implies, for example, that contempo-

[22] Harvey, *Geopolitics*, 145.
[23] Harvey, *Limits to Capital.*
[24] Soja, *Postmodern Geographies.*

rary capitalism may re-work the spatialization of class as a means to overcome crisis – a spatial fix implemented through the mechanism of temporary migrant labour.[25]

Confirming the 'two-sidedness' of the world market, this spatial structuring of class also indicates why institutional demarcation and restrictions on the movement of labour are actually accentuated within contemporary capitalism – in contrast to some of the more optimistic predictions of the globalization literature. Control over borders and other institutional mechanisms become ever more significant as a means to establish, manage, and control the spatial organization of labour. In particular, the institution of citizenship takes on a particularly sharp role in delineating the temporary migrant worker from their citizen compatriot. Consequently, while the historical development of institutions such as citizenship and democracy may certainly have "underwr[itten] the creation of workers as isolated abstract persons, cells in the organisms of munificent states",[26] contemporary capitalism sees the equality implicit in that abstraction confined to only certain segments of workers within the same 'national labour market'. Citizenship and the regime of differential rights that accompany it, acts to inscribe the reality of spatial distance within a class located in the *same* geographical space.

3. Temporary Migrant Labour Flows in the GCC

These perspectives on the nature of space help to illuminate the relationship between class formation and temporary migrant labour flows within the six states of the GCC.[27] Temporary migrant labour flows are more central to these states than any other country or zone in the world economy. They differ from the permanent migration flows seen in other areas of the world because they are short-term in nature, lack associated citizenship rights, and are focused on maximizing remittance flows back to the country of origin. Although the use of temporary migrant workers is increasing in many countries across the world, GCC countries are qualitatively different from any other comparable case because of the large proportion of

[25] The spatial structuring of class also raises an interesting question over how transfers of value occur within the contemporary world market, as it suggests that Marx's 'moral and historical' component of the cost of labour power is established external to the space (and thus within a different set of social relations) from which the labour power is actually expended.

[26] Gareth Dale, "Capitalism and Migrant Labour," in *The European Union and Migrant Labour*, ed. Gareth Dale and Mike Cole (Oxford: Berg, 1999), 303.

[27] For a full discussion of class formation in the GCC and its relationship to the development of global capitalism, please see Adam Hanieh, *Capitalism and Class in the Gulf Arab States* (New York: Palgrave-Macmillan, 2011).

their population constituted by these workers.[28] In all of the GCC states, temporary migrant workers represent more than half of the entire labour force and in four of these states (Kuwait, Qatar, Oman and the UAE) the proportion is greater than eighty percent. This heavy reliance on temporary labour flows closely ties the key labour exporting regions (the Middle East and South Asia) to accumulation patterns in the GCC.

The origins of this class structure can be traced back to state formation in the decades from 1930 to 1970.[29] With the slow decline of the British Empire through this period – hastened by India's independence in 1947 – the Gulf sheikhdoms (Kuwait, Bahrain, Oman, Qatar and the seven 'Trucial States' that became the future UAE) transitioned away from the direct control of British colonialism to gain their independence. This period also coincided with the beginnings of oil production and the ensuing struggle between Britain and the United States for regional influence.[30] The revenues that began to accrue from oil, and the arrival of British and American oil companies from the 1930s onwards, acted to sharpen contradictions between various social forces in the Gulf states – different factions in the ruling family, the ruling family and the merchants, nomadic tribes and urbanized settlements, oil workers and the ruling elite, and so forth. At the same time, the immediate over-riding goal of both Britain and the US was to ensure that these states

---

[28] The nearest comparison would perhaps be Singapore, which has around 33% of its labour force made up of migrant workers. In certain economic sectors, however, these flows of temporary migrant labour have become predominant around the globe (examples include Mexican agricultural workers in Canada, Filipina women employed as nurses, teachers and domestic workers in Asia and the Middle East, and undocumented North Africans working in marginal service jobs in Europe). It should be noted that the category of temporary migrant labour does not necessarily mean the worker has a 'legal' status.

[29] See Kiren Chaudry, *The Price of Wealth: Economies and Institutions in the Middle East* (New York: Cornell University Press, 1997); Jill Crystal, *Oil and Politics in the Gulf: Rulers and Merchants in Kuwait and Qatar,* (Glasgow: Cambridge University Press, 1995); Rosemary Said-Zahlan, *The Making of the Modern Gulf States* (Reading: Garnet Publishing, 1998); Alexei Vassiliev, *The History of Saudi Arabia* (London: Saqi Books, 1998); Aqil Kazim, *The United Arab Emirates AD 600 to the Present: A Socio-Discursive Transformation in the Arabian Gulf* (Dubai: Gulf Book Centre, 2000); Daryl Champion, *The Paradoxical Kingdom: Saudi Arabia and the Momentum of Reform* (New York: Columbia University Press, 2003) for surveys of individual GCC states.

[30] The US entry into the Gulf initially occurred through Saudi Arabia, which, as a remote and inhospitable area surrounded by desert, had managed to retain a relative independence from British control. During the early 20th century, Britain's firm hold in the Gulf coastal areas precluded any US penetration. Saudi Arabia's ruling al-Saud monarchy, however, was increasingly in need of external support as a result of the economic crises of the 1920s and 1930s – particularly the collapse of religious tourism that followed in the wake of the Great Depression and the outbreak of World War II. Utilizing these fiscal crises, the US moved to cement its alliance with Saudi Arabia in return for control over the country's oil production (see Vassiliev 1998 for a history of this period).

remained stable and amenable to foreign control of their oil resources as they gained independence.

Initially, the ruling families of the former British dependencies (and Saudi Arabia, which was closer to the US) attempted to ameliorate their own internal divisions through the judicious use of oil revenues. Of particular significance – most notably in Kuwait, Bahrain, and Dubai where merchant classes were strongest and had a history of protest – was the use of oil revenues to consolidate the support of these classes for the ruling regime. There were various mechanisms through which this occurred: granting the largest merchant families contracts for infrastructure, security, and other oil-related activities (although, importantly, never ownership of oil production itself); awarding the merchant class control over import activities through exclusive licensing, agency and distribution rights for foreign produced goods; and giving cheap (and, in some cases, free) land to merchants from which they benefited handsomely following the rise in price as urbanization and infrastructure proceeded. These same policies were also adopted towards different factions within the ruling family (Qatar, where the internal divisions of the ruling al Thani family were particularly acute, stands out in this respect).[31]

But, perhaps more significant than the challenge posed by the merchant classes was the growing anti-colonial sentiment across the Middle East. This became particularly clear during the 1950s, with the emergence of powerful mass struggles in Iran, Egypt, Iraq and elsewhere. Many of these movements were closely tied to large communist parties, operating in an uneasy relationship with military officers and more conservative nationalist forces. In 1951, a significant blow to Western interests occurred with the nationalization of the British-owned and operated Anglo-Iranian Oil Company (AIOC) in Iran by the newly-appointed Prime Minister, Mohammed Mossadegh. Mossadegh, pushed by mass mobilizations across the country, expelled AIOC and took Iranian oil into state hands. Another major turning point was the overthrow of Egypt's King Farouk in 1952, led by the popular military officer Gamal Abdel Nasser. In July 1956, the Egyptian government moved to nationalize the British/French-controlled Suez Canal, a stark confirmation of the growing anti-colonial sentiment within the Middle East.

These nationalist and anti-colonial movements were reflected within the Gulf Arab states. All of these states were rocked by strikes during the 1950s and 1960s, led by oil workers who sought greater control over oil resources and an end to the extreme exploitation that was often found in the work camps of British and American oil companies.[32] Early worker movements were closely linked to the struggles in Egypt and Palestine, and protested the ties between the Gulf monarchies and the

---

[31] Crystal, *Oil and Politics*.

[32] See Robert Vitalis (2007) for a powerful account of these conditions in the case of Aramco, the (then US-owned) oil company that operated in Saudi Arabia.

colonial powers that attempted to exert control over much of the Arab world. Moreover, worker movements intersected with other social struggles throughout the Gulf (e.g. the grievances of Shia in Bahrain, Saudi Arabia and Kuwait; or the guerrilla struggle in the Dhofar region of Oman). Gulf rulers responded to these nascent political and economic struggles with a heavy hand, including exile of leaders, imprisonment and military confrontation.

4. Spatial Structuring of Class in the GCC

These struggles overlapped with the independence of the Gulf states and during this period a complementary strategy to repression emerged that linked state formation with the spatial structuring of class. Initially, Gulf nationals provided the bulk of workers across the region. In Saudi Arabia in the early 1960s, for example, over 90 percent of the workforce was composed of Saudi citizens.[33] But contemporaneous with the expansion of the Gulf oil-industry, increasing numbers of temporary migrant workers were brought to the region from surrounding Arab countries. This was not solely a question of the Gulf's lack of population; most significantly, migrant workers were explicitly denied citizenship rights and their primary spatial identity was constituted through their relationship with their home countries. They may have been physically present in the Gulf (sometimes for many years) but from the perspective of the Gulf states their identity was conceived as residents who were 'Indian', 'Palestinian', 'Egyptian' and so forth. In this manner, class came into being through the re-working of the spatial forms that underpinned accumulation in the Gulf and its relationship with the surrounding region.

Table 1 demonstrates the remarkable extent to which the GCC came to depend on this labour. The migrant population ranges from 24 percent (Oman) to 78 percent (Qatar) of the entire population, a proportion that has generally increased over the last decade. Much of the work is concentrated in construction and manufacturing – in Saudi Arabia and Qatar, for example, these two sectors were employing nearly half of all private sector labor by the mid-2000s.[34] The weight of these sectors explains the large proportion of male migrant workers (about 70 to 80 percent) although large numbers of young Sri Lankan and Filipina women are also employed in the region as domestic and care workers. In 2005 more than two-thirds of the total UAE population was male, despite the fact that the gender-ratio of the Emirati national population was evenly balanced. Within the labour force,

---

[33] Tim Niblock, *The Political Economy of Saudi Arabia* (London and New York: Routledge, 2007), 51.

[34] Saudi Arabia British Bank (SABB), *Saudi Arabia – Thinking Big*, *Fourth Quarter Report* (Riyadh: Saudi British Bank, 2007), 9; Global Investment House (GIH), *Qatar 2008* (Kuwait: Global Investment, 2008), 29.

the migrant proportion is even more highly concentrated than the general population, making up 50 percent of the Saudi labour force to 91 percent of the UAE. Furthermore, reflecting the privileging of citizenship described above, this labour is heavily biased towards the private sector where conditions are generally much worse than the public sector. In both the UAE and Saudi Arabia, migrant workers constitute close to 100 percent of the private sector workforce.[35]

Table 1: Migrant Population in the GCC

Country	Migrant Worker population	Migrant Worker Population as % of Total Population		Proportion of Migrant Worker Population Female	Migrant Workers as % of Total Labour Force	Migrant Workers as % of Public Sector Workforce	Migrant Workers as % of Private Sector Workforce
Year	**2005**	**1995**	**2005**	**2005**	**2005**	**2001**	**Various**
Saudi Arabia	6,360,730	24.7	25.9	30.1	50.2	11.2	95 (2004)
Kuwait	1,668,991	58.7	62.1	31.0	80.3	24	78 (2005)
UAE	3,211,749	70.5	71.4	27.8	91.3	55.5	98 (2004)
Bahrain	295,461	37.5	40.7	30.9	58.8	9.3	79
Qatar	636,751	77.2	78.3	25.8	85.9	33.9	83
Oman	627,571	26.3	24.4	20.9	79	21.9	n.a.

Source: Maitha Shamsi, *Evaluation of Labour Policies in the GCC* (Beirut: Department of Economic and Social Affairs United Nations Secretariat, May 5, 2006).

These labour flows differ significantly from the permanent or settler migration that typifies the advanced capitalist countries. Workers are generally brought to the country under a visa issued by a sponsor (*kafeel)* and obtained through private recruitment agencies in their home country that charge large fees. These fees can take several years to pay off and workers frequently complain that they are paid

[35] It should be noted that these figures likely underestimate the number of temporary migrant workers throughout the GCC. If the numbers of workers who are living and working illegally are included, this figure would rise considerably. Saudi Arabia, for example, deports around 700,000 'illegal' workers on an annual basis, more than 10% of the total number officially recorded as present in the country (Shah 2006, 6). In 2003, around 100,000 non-status workers left the UAE voluntarily as part of one of the regular amnesty programs offered by the government (ibid.).

less than what was initially offered to them or that extra fees are deducted from their salaries.[36] The visa is for a limited duration (usually a few years) but can sometimes be renewed by paying a further fee.[37] Most importantly, these workers have very few political or civil rights in the GCC. In many cases they must surrender their passport to the employer who controls their salary, ability to change work, and even right to leave the country. There is virtually no possibility of gaining permanent residency or citizenship.

A key element to this spatialization of class was thus the institutionalization and delineation of citizenship rights. In all the Gulf states, citizenship carried with it a range of entitlements that were denied to temporary migrant workers. These included access to new jobs in the emerging state apparatus, grants of land, provision of free or cheap housing, and the availability of social services such as health and education. In this manner the class structure became highly stratified –citizens obtained a privileged status vis-à-vis the temporary migrant workers who constituted the bulk of the working class. It was above all a *spatial* process – class materialized through the set of relations established between different geographical spaces, mediated through the institutional arrangements of citizenship and differential laws. This spatial process enabled Gulf regimes to construct a powerful system of control over the vast majority of the resident population, while consolidating and binding citizen support behind the ruling monarch.

Initially, most of these workers were brought from neighbouring Arab countries but by the mid-1980s this non-citizen Arab population was increasingly seeking to settle their families and to win greater rights in the Gulf. It was partially in response to these demands that the Gulf states re-worked this spatial structure: shifting migrant labour flows away from Arab countries towards the Indian subcontinent. Laws were instituted that made it more difficult for Arab families to settle for long periods in the GCC countries (in the UAE, for example, it was made

---

[36] A Human Rights Watch investigation into the Dubai construction industry interviewed a number of construction workers and found that they "paid fees in a range of $2,000-$3,000 to local recruitment agencies in their home countries to obtain employment sponsorship in the UAE… [They] enter into employment contracts for a period of one to three years, subject to renewal, at a monthly wage ranging from $106 to $250; on average a migrant construction worker earns $175 a month (the average per capita income in the UAE is $2,106 a month)" (Human Rights Watch (HRW), *Building Towers, Cheating Workers* (2006), accessed March 15, 2011, http://www.hrw.org/en/reports/2006/11/11/building-towers-cheating-workers-0.)

[37] A large number of fake companies have sprung up in the GCC to sell work permits for which there are no actual jobs attached. Migrants are then forced to find illegal work in precarious conditions. In 2004, it was estimated that 27% of the total workforce of the UAE were sponsored through these companies. The Saudi Ministry of Labour has said that 70% of the visas issued by the Ministry are sold on the black market (Shah 2006, 8).

illegal for Arab non-citizen children to attend public schools). In the wake of the 1990-1991 Gulf War, Arab residents were expelled *en masse* under the pretext that the Palestine Liberation Organization and Yemen had supported Iraq's invasion of Kuwait. In Kuwait, the number of Palestinians fell from 400,000 in 1990 to about 50,000 by the mid-1990s.[38] By 2002, the Arab proportion of migrant workers in the GCC had fallen from 72 percent in 1975 to around 25-29 percent, replaced with cheaper labour from South Asia (see Table 2).[39]

Table 2: The GCC and Key Labour Supplying Zones in South Asia

Country	Proportion of Workforce in the GCC	Type of Work	Further Comments
Bangladesh	In the mid-1990s, around 60-70% of Bangladeshi overseas workers could be found in the Gulf. By 2002, this proportion had risen to 95%.[40] Most of these workers were located in Saudi Arabia, followed by the UAE and Kuwait.	Mostly unskilled and semi-skilled work in construction, agriculture and cleaning. Many of these jobs are dangerous: from January 2004 – August 2008, 6,547 Bangladeshis died on the job while overseas.[41]	Total remittance flows to Bangladesh correlate very closely to the employment of workers in the Gulf – reaching a peak of over US$9 billion in 2008.
Sri Lanka	From 2003-2007, 83-86% of all Sri Lankans departing overseas for work each year went to the GCC countries. Saudi Arabia is the primary destination – nearly one-third of Sri	The workforce is highly feminized. In 2007, 62% of all Sri Lankan overseas workers were female with around 50% of the entire expatriate workforce employed	Sri Lanka is a country that relies heavily on remittance flows – around 7.8% of GDP in 2007.[43]

[38] Nader Fergany, *Aspects of Labor Migration and Unemployment in the Arab Region* (Egypt: Almishkat Center for Research, 2001), 7.
[39] Andrej Kapiszewski, "Arab Labour Migration to the GCC States," in *Arab Migration in a Globalized World* (Geneva: International Organization for Migration, 2004), 123. This shift should not be interpreted as diminishing the importance of the Gulf region for Arab workers. Many Egyptian, Lebanese, Yemeni and Jordanian families are still reliant upon remittance flows from the Gulf region. It was estimated, for example, that in 2007, 30% of Lebanon's labour force resides in the Gulf and the country obtains 24% of GDP from remittance flows.
[40] Data on the Bangladeshi migrant workforce is drawn from the Ministry of Expatriates Welfare and Overseas Employment, Government of the People's Republic of Bangladesh, accessed November 15, 2010, http://probashi.gov.bd/publication/publication.php.
[41] Ain o Salish Kendra (ASK), *Annual Human Rights Report* (2008), accessed June 10, 2010, http://www.askbd.org.

	Lanka's 1.6 million overseas workers can be found in the Kingdom. Significant numbers can also be found in Kuwait and the UAE.	as domestic workers.[42]	
Philippines	At end-2007, more than two-fifths of the total deployed Overseas Foreign Workers (OFWs) were located in the Middle East (43.3 percent), the majority of which were in Saudi Arabia (21.2 percent of total deployed) and the United Arab Emirates (10.5 percent of total deployed).[44] In 2008, more than 50% of new hires and re-hires of Filipino workers were in GCC countries.	Many of these Filipino workers in the Gulf are females who work in sectors such as nursing, teaching, services and domestic work. Seventy-four percent of all new hires of Filipino overseas nurses in 2007 went to Saudi Arabia. Over 54% of new hires of domestic workers went to the GCC states.	The Philippines is heavily dependent upon the export of labour and is consistently within the top four recipients of overseas remittances in the South. The country received US$16.4 billion in 2008 from remittances – equivalent to almost 10 percent of GDP).[45]
India	In 2006, about 4 million Indian workers were estimated to be in the Gulf, mostly in the UAE (2.17 million) and Saudi Arabia (1.26 million, UN 2006) and in 2007, 95% of all labour outflows from India were destined for GCC countries.[46]	Indian workers perform a wide variety of tasks, ranging from skilled engineering, managerial and financial work to construction labour and taxi driving.	In 2007, India was the largest recipient of remittances in the world ($27 billion) and 40% of this total came from workers in the Gulf. Remittances made up 3.3% of Indian GDP in 2007.[47]

[43] World Bank, *Migration and Development Brief No. 10 (*July 2, 2009), accessed June 10, 2010, www.worldbank.org.

[42] Sri Lanka Central Bank (SLCB) *Annual Report 2008* (2009), Statistical Annex, Table 82.

[44] Marianne Domingo, "Deployment Profile and Remittance Patterns of Overseas Filipinos" (Briefing no. 09, Central Bank of the Philippines, June 2, 2009), 4.

[45] Domingo, "Deployment Profile," 1.

[46] Ministry of Overseas Indian Affairs, *Annual Report 2007-2008 (2008),* 62, accessed May 19, 2011, www.moia.gov.in.

Pakistan	In 2003, 97 percent of Pakistanis working oversees were employed in the GCC, mostly in Saudi Arabia and the UAE (59% and 29% of Pakistani overseas workers respectively).	Many of these workers are employed in low-wage construction jobs; Pakistani construction workers underpinned the rapid expansion of Dubai's real estate sector in the early 2000s.	The country is heavily reliant upon remittance flows (in 2007, the US$5 billion flow of remittances was equivalent to around 4.2% of GDP)[48] and these figures are believed to be significantly understated due to the use of undocumented means of remittance transfer.

This spatial structuring of class serves as a 'fix' for Gulf capitalism in a number of ways. It helps to enable, for example, the severe levels of exploitation that most temporary migrant workers face in the Gulf, because wage levels are set relative to the social conditions in the worker's home country rather than the country in which they work. This can be seen in the considerable differences in pay that exists between citizen and non-citizen labour in each sector across the GCC. In Saudi Arabia, for example, a Saudi manufacturing worker was compensated, on average, three times more than a non-Saudi worker in the year 2000. In the transport and communication sector, the difference was four times as great.49 A foreign manufacturing worker in Qatar received one-sixth the average compensation of a Qatari worker in 2003.50 In Bahrain, according to the General Organization for Social Insurance, the general average wage for 2006 in the private sector was BD377 for Bahraini workers and BD170 for foreign labourers.[51] These differences would widen even further if non-wage compensation were included (housing, education and health rights for citizens).

The high levels of exploitation are further indicated by the conditions in which many workers live. Human Rights Watch found, for example, that the labour camps in Dubai housing construction workers were typically 'a small room (12 feet by 9 feet) in which as many as eight workers lived together. Three or four double bunk beds represented the only furniture in each room. The workers used

---

[47] World Bank, *Migration and Development*, note 39.

[48] World Bank, ibid.

[49] Saudi Arabia Ministry of Economy and Planning, *Employment and Wages Survey 1996 and 2000*, accessed June 18, 2011, http://www.mep.gov.sa.

[50] State of Qatar, *Al Nashra Sanawiyya Al Ihsayaht Al Taq'a wa al San'aeya* [Annual Statistical Bulletin on Energy and Industry] *Vol 23* (Doha: General Secretariat for Development Planning, 2004), 127.

[51] http://www.bahrainrights.org

communal bathrooms and showers outside their rooms'.[52] In Bahrain, a Reuters news report described the situation as follows: 'Wooden boards demarcate rooms, bunk beds are stacked from floor to ceiling, corrugated iron covers the roof, and clothes and other personal effects take up every inch of space. Ramusamy [an Indian worker], and others nearby, explained that they had paid up to 1,000 dinars ($2,650), to Indian or Bahraini recruiters who had promised them a monthly salary of about 100 dinars. Most workers, including Ramusamy, borrowed heavily to pay the fee, using their land in India as collateral. Once in Bahrain, they found the average unskilled wage was about 55 dinars. Ramusamy's loan payments are 37.5 dinars, he said. One person at the house had committed suicide, Ramusamy said, and he knew of workers elsewhere who had considered it.'[53]

Conditions such as these are largely made possible because a worker's residency status is directly tied to holding a job. Once they become unemployed they become 'illegal' and are required to leave the country. In other words, because the *right to space* is conditioned on employment – confirmation of the way that class takes a spatial form – employers hold an enormous power differential over the worker. Moreover, generational reproduction of the class is highly fragmented because workers generally return home when they finish their contracts – class memory and bonds of solidarity are weak, and collective action very difficult to undertake. Legal restrictions codify these barriers to class-based action, with unions banned in Saudi Arabia and the UAE and severely restricted elsewhere.[54] Moreover, the limited labour laws that do exist are designed more for cosmetic purposes rather than the worker's well-being. One example of this was the practice in Dubai of transporting construction workers to their work site in cattle trucks. This practice was discontinued with large fan-fare in 2004 because it was felt that it gave the emirate a poor image at odds with its self-perception as a modern, globalized city. Rather than leading to a qualitative improvement, however, workers are now typically transported in old buses that lack effective air-conditioning. In 2006, the Dubai government had only 140 government inspectors responsible for overseeing the labour practices of more than 240,000 businesses employing migrant workers.

---

[52] Human Rights Watch, *Building Towers, Cheating Workers* (2006), accessed June 10, 2010, http://www.hrw.org/en/reports/2006/11/11/building-towers-cheating-workers-0.

[53] Mohammed Abbas, 'Poverty Drives Migrant Indian Workers in Bahrain to Suicide', Reuters, 17 June 2007.

[54] In Kuwait, a national trade union federation exists but for workers to form a union there must be at least fifteen Kuwaiti nationals in the workplace. This effectively prevents unions from forming in the private sector as most workers are migrant workers. In Qatar, non-Qataris are not permitted to form a union. While unions are permitted in Bahrain, strikes are banned in the hydrocarbon, health, education, pharmacy, security, civil defence, airport, port and transport sectors.

The Spatial Displacement of Crisis:

In short, the spatial structuring of class enabled the GCC states to deepen exploitation and ameliorate any potential threats to the status quo. In turn, the countries supplying this migrant workforce became firmly embedded in the reproduction of GCC capitalism. One indication of this has been shown during the recent global economic crisis. The GCC was severely affected by the crisis, particularly in its initial stages. The drop in the price of oil to a low of around US$30 in December 2008 from a peak of $147.27 in July 2008 meant that budget surpluses were significantly reduced.[55] GCC GDP fell from $1.073 trillion in 2008 to $887 billion in 2009, with GDP per capita dropping nearly 18 percent to $23,000 in 2009. Simultaneously, the paralysis of global capital markets and bank lending severely restricted funds for projects in the region, with the GCC real estate sector particularly hard hit due to its reliance on foreign capital and speculative inflows. In the UAE, for example, where a pronounced real estate bubble had developed in the years leading up to the crisis, the value of construction and infrastructure projects plunged from $60 billion in 2008 to just over $10 billion in 2009. By early 2010, 92 percent of all real estate projects that had been put on hold in the GCC were located in the UAE emirate of Dubai, and the US property company, Jones Lang LaSalle, estimated that more than half of all projects in the emirate had stopped.[56] By some estimates, property prices in Dubai dropped by as much as 70 percent and commercial rents by 60 percent.[57] These effects were not isolated to Dubai. A range of massive real estate projects planned across the GCC were put on hold and equity markets plunged as companies faced an uncertain financial future.

The impact of this crisis, however, needs to be understood through the spatial structuring of class outlined above.[58] As the crisis unfolded, two specific trends were noticeable. First, GCC states moved to redirect accumulated surpluses from a decade of high oil prices to private companies, banks and state firms under strain. All bank deposits were guaranteed in Saudi Arabia, Kuwait and the UAE and interest rates were cut in an attempt to encourage lending. In Saudi Arabia, the government placed US$10 billion in the banking system and supported low-income citizens with US$2.7 billion worth of credit. The UAE government also put US$19 billion worth of long-term deposits in local banks and individual emirates invested millions to cover potential losses from large infrastructure projects. The largest

---

[55] From 2007-2008, GCC current account surpluses had reached US$400 billion, equivalent to over 30% of GCC GDP. By 2009, these surpluses had halved and, in the cases of the UAE and Oman, had turned negative.

[56] Bernadette Redfern, "Debt Stalls Hopes of Recovery," *Middle East Economic Digest* 54, no. 5 (29 January – 4 February 2010): 30.

[57] Khaleej Times, "Dubai Property Prices Plunge Up to 70pc," March 30, 2009.

[58] For further discussion of the impact of the crisis on the Gulf see the final chapter of Hanieh (2011).

banks in Qatar received a US$4.12 billion injection of funds to cover real estate investments that had declined in value during the downturn.

Secondly, concurrent with this extension of state support, large state and private companies repatriated temporary migrant workers and slowed new hiring as projects were postponed or cancelled. Precisely because of the spatial structure described above, GCC states could avoid the unemployment crisis that many other countries across the world faced in the wake of the economic collapse. It was very difficult for workers in the Gulf to protest or prevent this from occurring because of their temporary right to space, contracts could simply be terminated or not renewed. Workers were put on a plane and sent home – perhaps following a stint in prison if they were caught working illegally. Once a work visa was terminated it was very difficult to remain in the country to look for alternative work for any length of time. The spatial structure that underpinned class formation in the Gulf meant that the first global crisis of the twenty-first century could be met through another spatial fix.

Migrant job losses were particularly notable in Dubai, which had previously been the core of the region's construction market. Dubai government institutions stated in mid-2009 that they were planning for a one-fifth drop in population as a result of the crisis.[59] In March 2009, UAE construction companies were reportedly block-booking planes and had sent an estimated twenty-thousand construction workers home.[60] The Indian state of Kerala was planning for around 200,000 workers to return from the UAE by the end of summer 2009.[61] Repatriation of workers could be carried out legally and with relatively little protest and, in this manner, crisis was spatially displaced onto the surrounding peripheries of Asia and the Arab world.

By the beginning of 2010 the impact of these job losses was beginning to show in remittance figures.[62] For Sri Lanka, Bangladesh and Pakistan, remittance flows

---

[59] "Dubai Reviews Plans as Population Falls," *Middle East Economic Digest* 53, no. 12 (March 20-26, 2009), 19.

[60] "News in Numbers," *Arabian Business* 10, no. 10 (2009), 13.

[61] Mustapha Karkouti, "Workers Go Home," *The Middle East,* no. 43 (August/September 2009), 25.

[62] With the onset of a severe crisis it is not unexpected to see a temporary rise in remittance flows as long-term migrant workers repatriate accumulated savings in preparation for a return home. This appears to be the case in both India and Pakistan, where remittance levels from the Gulf sharply increased in 2008 and 2009, despite a slow-down in employment. Furthermore, remittance statistics themselves can be highly misleading. In many cases, financial transfers are routed through US banks and therefore appear to becoming coming from the US rather than the actual source country. Moreover, much of the remittance transfers to South Asia occurs through informal channels rather than banks and thus do not show up in official figures. Finally, a thorough assessment of the impact of any drop in remittances needs to differentiate on a sub-national basis

declined or remained essentially stagnant through the first months of 2010.[63] This should be contrasted with annual double-digit growth in remittance flows experienced during the boom years of the previous decade and the pronounced dependency that many countries have on Gulf labour markets. Moreover, as Table 2 suggests, the nature of employment in the Gulf means that the process of spatial displacement is felt in a highly uneven fashion across South Asia. One example of this can be seen in the case of Sri Lanka, where there was a 7% decrease in the number of male Sri Lankans departing for work overseas from 2008 to 2009. This aggregate figure, however, obscures a 17% decrease in the number of unskilled male workers and a simultaneous increase (albeit slight) in the number of departing skilled workers. For this reason, a full appreciation of the spatial displacement of crisis requires data to be differentiated much more precisely than aggregate trends.[64] There is every indication, however, that – coupled with the impact of the global crisis on their own economies – hundreds of thousands of people across South Asia have been profoundly affected by this spatial displacement.

5. Conclusion

In the concluding pages to his *Limits to Capital*, Harvey makes a powerful argument that the configuration of space needs to be understood as an 'active constitutive moment in the dynamics of accumulation'.[65] By this, Harvey means that the configuration of space both enables and expresses the form taken by capitalist accumulation, while simultaneously acting as a possible mechanism of crisis resolution. Capitalism is continually precipitating shifts in the relationships between different spaces – the movement of capital and labour across countries and regions, devaluation of existing fixed capital complexes in specific spaces, the creation of new class fractions and alliances across geographical zones and so forth. Through this incessant reworking of its own spatiality, capitalism lays the basis for new and

---

as labor flows to the Gulf tend to be drawn from specific regions within countries. Remittances, for example, represented over 30 percent of the Indian state of Kerala's net domestic product in 2008, whereas they only represented around 2 percent of total Indian GDP (Zachariah and Rajan 2008, 13).

[63] Remittances to Sri Lanka were two percent less in the first three months of 2009 compared to the same period in 2008. Bangladesh also experienced a two percent decline from Q3 2009 to Q3 2010. Pakistan saw little or no growth through the first three months of 2010 (based on the annual rate of change of three-month moving average of remittance flows).

[64] Moreover, any assessment of remittances should differentiate on a sub-national basis as labour flows to the Gulf tend to originate from specific regions within countries. Remittances, for example, represented over 30 percent of the Indian state of Kerala's net domestic product in 2008, whereas they only represented around 2 percent of total Indian GDP (Kunniparampil Zachariah and Rajan Irudaya, 'A Decade of Kerala's Gulf Connection,' *Migration Monitoring Study*, Kerala: Center for Development Studies, 2008, 13).

[65] David Harvey, *The Limits to Capital* (London: Verso, 1999), 440.

expanded possibilities of accumulation. Simultaneously, contradictions begin to grow within these spatial relations – over time developing into fetters on accumulation that inevitably end in a sharp break and transition to a new configuration of space.

This essay has illustrated Harvey's argument, confirming that processes of class formation need to be understood through a spatial lens. Class, as a set of social relations, is located in concrete spatial configurations – it is spatialized through the relationships that are established between distinct geographical zones in the course of its formation. In the GCC, this spatial structuring of class has been constituted through the flows of temporary migrant labour between the region, South Asia and the rest of the Arab world. This has provided a spatial fix for Gulf capitalism – enabling an increased appropriation of value arising from spatial differences in the costs of the reproduction of labour power, establishing a powerful means of social control, and allowing Gulf capitalism to displace crisis.

This perspective can deeply enrich an understanding of how capitalism in the Gulf region has formed and continues to evolve. It is not possible, for example, to fully understand the stability and adaptability of Gulf capitalism and its ruling elites without an appreciation of the spatialization of class. Political conflicts have generally originated in inter-elite discord (such as between different branches of the ruling family, and the conflict between religious scholars and the monarchy) or Islamist movements based upon the petit-bourgeoisie – not from any popular protest. This relative political calm can be contrasted with the situation in two oil-rich neighbouring countries, Iraq and Iran, where the working class has a long history of mobilization and persistent opposition to Western policies in the Gulf and wider Middle East. In the wake of economic collapse, the Gulf states have seen very little popular protest or anger. It is certainly true that many high-profile projects have been halted, consumer demand has plummeted and businesses have shut their doors – but the citizen population has emerged almost unscathed as Gulf capitalism's spatial fix meant that the real pain of the crisis was felt by the swelling numbers of unemployed across the Gulf's surrounding regions.

This analysis should not be interpreted, however, as implying the continued long-term stability and permanence of the Gulf's spatial structuring of class. Growing unemployment levels in the citizen population – most particularly among youth – are a significant concern to Gulf leaders. Due to the state support of citizenry this does not necessarily translate into the abject poverty seen among the region's migrant workforce, but a pronounced demographic bias towards youth and the cost of maintaining the current structure will place exponentially greater demands on state revenues.[66] Any significant shift in this spatial structure carries with it deep political implications. To proletarianize large numbers of citizens, for example, risks the development of class-based and other social movements that have not been witnessed in the GCC since the pre-independence era. It remains to be seen how these contradictions are solved by Gulf regimes, but it is clear that the spatial fix of Gulf capitalism could well face its own 'switching crisis' in the medium-term future.

At a broader level, the relationship between crisis, migration and space can deepen analyses of contemporary capitalism. During the 2008 crisis, radical commentators frequently cited Lenin's dictum that there is 'no such thing [for capitalism] as an absolutely hopeless situation'– an important reminder that capitalist crises are inevitably resolved in some manner.[67] The question remains, however, of the means by which this resolution takes place. One answer can be found in the relationship between spatiality and the patterns of class formation. The continually evolving process of class formation acts to shape the way that crisis is both mediated and resolved. The spatiality of capitalism is more than an accidental or contingent outcome of accumulation; it is actually constitutive of accumulation itself. In order to understand contemporary capitalism and its crises, it is necessary to grasp this spatialization in its entirety.

---

[66] To date, most Gulf states have responded to this tension with 'Gulf-ization' programs that offer incentives or set quotas for businesses in the hiring of Gulf citizens. These programs, however, have had little real efficacy and have not substantially altered the structure of the labour force.

[67] Vladimir Lenin, "Report on The International Situation And The Fundamental Tasks Of The Communist International July 19, 1920," in *Collected Works*, 4th English Edition, Vol. 31 (Progress Publishers, Moscow, 1965 [1920]), 213-263.

What Working-Class? Non-Transformative Global Capitalism and the African Case[1]

John S. Saul

Everywhere the logic of an ever more globalized capitalist economy has shifted the goal posts – as regards both the nature of on-going capitalist exploitation, and of resistance to it. For starters, we must place centrally the fact that global capitalism, even if still profoundly controlling of the world economy, no longer has the capacity to transform the world and, in effect, simplify its social contradictions as it once promised/threatened to do – and as Marx and Engels, for example, once thought it would, *viz*:

> Our epoch, the epoch of the **bourgeoisie**, possesses…its distinctive feature: it has simplified the class antagonisms. Society as a whole is more and more splitting into two great hostile camps, into two great classes directly facing each other: Bourgeoisie and Proletariat...The bourgeoisie has stripped of its halo every occupation hitherto honoured and looked at with reverent awe. It has converted the physician, the lawyer, the priest, the poet, the man of science, into its paid wage-labourers...The other classes decay and finally disappear in the face of Modern Industry; the proletariat is its special and essential product.[2]

---

[1] This essay, originally prepared for a workshop organized by David Harvey at CUNY in New York, May 2011, will also appear, in much the same form, in *Accumulations, Crises, Struggles: Capital and Labour in Contemporary Capitalism,* ed. Baris Karaagac (LIT Verlag: 2013). It should be read in conjunction with a second, complementary essay, one entitled "On Taming a Revolution: The South African Case" in *The Question of Strategy: Socialist Register 2013,* ed. Greg Albo, Leo Panitch and Vivek Chibber (London: The Merlin Press, 2012).

[2] Karl Marx and Friedrich Engels, "Manifesto of the Communist Party," in *The Marx-Engels Reader, Second Edition*, ed. Robert Tucker (New York: W. W. Norton, 1978), 474, 476, 482. At the same time, of course, they write (ibid., 481) that "the organization of the proletarians into a class, and consequently into a political party, is continually being upset by competition between

Instead, in much of the Global South (and perhaps particularly in Africa, the region of the world that is of my particular interest), the transformation is, at best, incomplete. Global capitalism may indeed have become a dominant reality, one quite capable of imposing upon Africa, for example, a grid of continuing inequality, exploitation and the recolonization of ostensibly liberated and independent peoples in the interests of corporate profit. Yet the global system now in place seems unlikely, either now or in some readily foreseeable future, to produce in Africa (and in many other parts of the world) the kind of relatively straightforward, theoretically proto-revolutionary, social structure – one characterized by an ever clearer polarization between bourgeoisie and proletariat – that many, on both right and left, have tended, in the past, to foresee.

For the fact is that much of the Global South is trapped instead between history's ostensible phases in ways that it will be important to examine below and to specify further. Indeed, one feature of such an "intermediate socio-economic condition" that is particularly worthy of investigation is the ever-increasing saliency of what has come to be termed "precarious work." We will have to explore this reality carefully, but, of even greater importance is the broader reality of penury and of extreme marginalization that has come to define the lives of the "precarious population" more generally: the many who are linked, and in extremely uncertain ways, to the phenomenal growth of this world's urban areas. The meaning and significance of this true "precariat" will have to preoccupy us below.

Of course, such more broadly "insecure" parameters have important implications for our understanding of the "working class" *per se* (in, that is to say, its most organized and its most generic essentials). This will be of especially crucial interest. But so too will be our sense of just what is, under such circumstances, the likely "revolutionary agency" that the "working class" (both the term and the reality that the phrase seem to evoke) can now be expected to have. And what links, if any, can be effectively established – for progressive purposes - between this "proletariat" on the one hand, and the "precariat" on the other. What next, we are forced to ask, what next in terms of any effective challenge from below to the inhuman, inequitable and exploitative capitalist system that continues to dominate Africa and to produce so many graphically unsavoury outcomes?

---

the workers themselves," - adding, however, that "it [the proletariat] ever rises again, stronger, firmer, mightier."

I. Precarious Work in Africa and Beyond: The Ambiguities of the "Working-Class"

Here we will begin by letting the fashionable *Wikipedia* – because in its relevant entry it draws so heavily as it on the estimable scholarly work of Fudge, Owens and Vosko – give us our first lead with regard to "precarious work":

> Precarious work is a term used to describe non-standard employment which is poorly paid, insecure, unprotected and cannot support a household. In recent decades there has been a dramatic increase in precarious work due to such factors as: globalization, the shift from the manufacturing sector to the service sector, and the spread of information technology. These changes have created a new economy which demands flexibility in the workplace and, as a result, caused the decline of the standard employment relationship and a dramatic increase in precarious work. An important aspect of precarious work is its gendered nature, as women are continuously over-represented in this type of work.
>
> Precarious work is frequently associated with the following types of employment: "part-time employment, self-employment, fixed-term work, temporary work, on-call work, homeworkers and telecommuting." All these forms of employment are related in that they depart from the standard employment relationship (full-time, continuous employment with one employer). Each form of precarious work may offer its own challenges but they all share the same disadvantages: low wages, few benefits, lack of collective representation, and little to no job security.[3]

Moreover, in Africa such a definition/description begins actually to describe a very large number of the urban population, so great in their numbers that, as many more flock into the urban areas, they are hard-pressed to find any formal "work" at all, even of the kind most readily defined as being "precarious." Here, indeed, the most orthodox Marxist may be inclined to throw up his/her hands in despair, faced with the reality of an emergent "capitalist" society very different from the kind – one much more straightforward, at least in theory, in terms of revolutionary potential – that Marx and Engels had foreseen, as quoted in our opening paragraph, to be slowly but surely simplifying and clarifying social contradictions.

Should we be surprised that some Marxists are tempted to view with alarm the kind of society that a powerful but nonetheless non-transformative (or, at the very least, not as yet transformative) capitalism does produce in Africa and elsewhere in many parts of the Global South?[4] For such intermediate societies seem – in Africa

---

[3] This Wikipedia entry draws heavily on Judy Fudge and Rosemary Owens, eds., *Precarious Work, Women and the New Economy: The Challenge to Legal Norms* (Toronto: Hart, 2006), especially their introduction, and also on Leah Vosko's chapter in the same book, "Gender, Precarious Work and the international Labour Code: The Ghost in the ILO Closet."

[4] Of course, "precariousness" both with reference, in the "narrow" sense, to those in actual precarious employment (though generally "unorganized" in any trade union sense) as here defined

certainly – very unlikely to alter substantially, and to morph into some entirely straightforward and conventionally "bourgeoisie-proletariat" pattern of polarization, in the near future.

Of course, Marx and Engels themselves speak nervously of the social realities they saw to be scarring the transitional period to a full-bodied capitalism, noting, in particular, the possible resonance of a resultant (in their term) "dangerous class," one defined by them as:

> the social scum, that passively rotting mass thrown up by the lowest layers of the old society, [which] may, here and there, be swept into the movement by a proletarian revolution; its conditions of life, however, prepare if far more for the part of a bribed tool of reactionary intrigue.[5]

As Marx himself writes elsewhere,

> Alongside decayed roués with dubious means of subsistence and dubious origins, alongside ruined and reckless casts of the bourgeoisie, were vagabonds, discharged soldiers, discharged jailbirds, escaped gallery-slaves, swindlers, mountebanks, *lazzeroni*, pickpockets, tricksters, gamblers, *maquereaus* [procurers], brothel-keepers, porters, *literati* [literary hacks] organ-grinders, ragpickers, knife-grinders, tinkers, beggars – in short the whole indefinite, disintegrated mass, thrown hither and thither, which the French term *la bohemia*.[6]

In addition, in a second and related text, he speaks critically of the Mobile Guards, the most assertive strike force mobilized on behalf of France's reactionary Provisional Government, suggesting that:

> they belonged for the most part to the *lumpenproletariat*, which, in all the big towns, form a mass strictly differentiated from the industrial proletariat, a recruiting grounds for thieves and criminals of all kinds, living on the crumbs of society, people without a definite trade, vagabonds, *gens sans feu and sans aveu*, with differences according to the degree of civilization of the nation to which they belong, but never renouncing their *lazzaroni* [hoboes] character.[7]

---

and, in the broader sense, to those - whole segments of the population, especially amongst the youth and unemployed - of the more marked kind of urban "precariousness" discussed below is now also a prominent feature of many of the more well-defined, "advanced" and apparently "successful" capitalist societies; this kind of iteration of precarity and of the complex politics attendant upon it also demands further study.

[5] Marx and Engels, ibid., 482. See also Louis Chevalier, *Labouring classes and dangerous classes in Paris during the first half of the nineteenth century* (New York: H. Fertig, 1973).

[6] Karl Marx, *The 18th Brumaire of Louis Bonaparte* (New York: International Publishers, 1963), 75.

[7] Karl Marx, *Class Struggles in France* (New York: International Publishers, 1964), 50; as he continues, "at the youthful age at which the Provisional Government recruited them [they were] thoroughly malleable, capable of the most heroic deeds and the most exalted sacrifices, as of the basest banditry and the dirtiest corruption."

This litany of not easily "classed" elements does not quite directly evoke African social conditions, though it points at a somewhat similar urban social milieu. To begin with, a much more gender sensitive and diverse listing of urban dwellers would now be required; women, for example, are quite crucial players in Africa both amongst the semi-proletarianized and within the cadre of urban socio-political actors than Marx and Engels' itemization would help us to infer. But note, more generally, that the term lumpenproletariat itself can and should not be so dismissively employed (not least, as we shall see, in South Africa).

Not that the more settled and more organized working class should ever be displaced as a particularly central vector of possible progressive promise, of course. Marx himself was the key thinker in emphasizing – and for good reason – the extent to which the concentration and centralization of this "working class" were crucial determinations of its socialist aspirations and endeavours – and, of course, in Africa and elsewhere their consciousness and organizational presence have often been often crucial both to anti-colonial struggles and to resistances to contemporary recolonization. Yet, as we shall see, the kinds of numbers, and the diversity, that the congested urban settings Africa has increasingly to offer, can also produce vital expressions of political energy in their own right that press the conceptual boundaries of working class action more conventionally defined – political energy that can, potentially, be expressed in particularly dramatic ways (as we have seen most recently in Cairo and in Tunis, for example). To this reality we will have to return.

Nonetheless, note here the stratification – *within* itself, as it were – that this vast mass can evidence. For the reference is not primarily to the most obvious kind of class differentiation, that between the upper and most favoured echelons of Africa's hierarchy (the most affluent of owners, politicians and state functionaries, and enterprise managers and their attendant retinues, as distinct from "the rest"); such class differentiations are clear enough. No, the reference here is to shades of difference – differences that can nonetheless have pertinent socio-political effects – amongst those "below" the elite and affluent: within, that is, the lower tier of society itself.

Such divisions can be quite diverse and can have, for both good and ill, a wide range of expressions: between criminals and victims, for example, between those differently defined in terms of gender, and amongst holders of diverse ethnic, national (think of the recent xenophobic excesses that have scarred South Africa, for example), and religious affiliation. Nonetheless, where full-time employment is a (relative) "luxury" and the availability of working-class organizations of self-defense a rarity, divisions within the urban mass along socio-economic lines can also be important: not least between the fully employed who are generally more effectively organized at the work-site vs. those who are more marginalized, "precarious" and also less well-organized for worker and popular self-defense.[8]

Many decades ago Giovanni Arrighi and I actually employed, albeit somewhat controversially, the term "labour aristocracy" (for want of a better phrase) precisely to distinguish the "upper echelons" of the poor (the relatively stabilized in employment) from those much more marginalized from capital's activities than themselves.[9] So controversial was this application of the term that I soon after (1975) felt myself forced to clarify and to qualify our use of the term, though I first sought to re-establish more clearly our earlier point:

> The "more privileged" and better organized workers have been encouraged to identify upward – to become partners (albeit the most junior of partners) in the jostling for surpluses among the internationally and domestically powerful (including more prominently in the latter category the elites and sub-elites themselves) – rather than to identify downward with the even more "wretched of the earth": the urban marginals and the average inhabitant of the…rural areas.[10]

But, I quickly added, in a capitalism in crisis the "classic strengths of the urban working class" could become "more evident," with the "the upper stratum of the workers [then] most likely to identify downward [to become] a leading force within a revolutionary alliance of exploited elements in the society." And I also conceded that, in any case, the concept "labour aristocracy" - whether its usage had once been "sanctioned" (in his Imperialism: The Highest Stage of Capitalism) by Lenin or not - seemed a harsh one to apply to workers in Africa who remain, to this day, exploited and even more "relatively" disempowered and impoverished vis-à-vis the dominant circles of their societies than they are "relatively" empowered and privileged vis-à-vis their fellow denizens of society's lower orders.

---

[8] Of course, the question of how best to "discipline" these "dangerous classes" arises for the dominant actors within the realms of both capital and the state. Not all "local" initiatives are equally promising for the realization of local empowerment and sustained socio-economic betterment. For example, Veronica Schild – in her "Their Hegemony or Ours? Schild Replies to Barker," *Southern Africa Report* 13, 4 (August 1998) – has, in drawing on her own research in Chile, noted "the way in which the grassroots initiatives and struggles in Chile have been transformed into cultural resources for the neo-liberal state" - with government, NGO and World Bank initiatives coming to harness "grass-roots initiatives" into "projects," including a wide-ranging retinue of programs premised on "competition-based funds," "micro-enterprises," and highly government-orchestrated self-development initiatives, "which have little to do with genuine autonomy and local democracy."

[9] In Giovanni Arrighi and John S. Saul, *Essays on the Political Economy of Africa* (New York: Monthly Review Press, 1973).

[10] See my "The 'Labour Aristocracy' Thesis Reconsidered," in *The Development of an African Working Class*, ed. Richard Sandbrook and Robin Cohen (Toronto and London: University, 1975) and, with the same title but in a somewhat modified version, as chapter 12 in *The State and Revolution in Eastern Africa* (London and New York: Heinemann and Monthly Review Press, 1975).

Indeed, while one of my current South African correspondents notes that there may be "more evidence for the concept's appropriateness now," he nonetheless speaks strongly to this same point, thinking that the concept's use is "misleading because neoliberal globalization is eroding the core of the labour market, making this 'elite' [itself] very precarious." Moreover, "even these core jobs are often below R2000 per month; and, thirdly, almost all workers share their income with a household with an average of five members…" In consequence, any "divergences" of interest and action discernible within the "working-class" must be carefully framed analytically with clear reference to their precise social-economic bases and to such matters as differential remuneration and job security and differing degrees of effective self-organization. Nonetheless, they must also be understood as having, potentially, very real weight. For such differences, as do mark these "lower orders" - as my correspondent adds, "to have job at all in these times may be seen as a privilege rather than a curse" - can also make some difference in terms of divergent "class practices."

In fact, may thus be differences, however subtle, between the "settled" proletariat and the more precariously employed, but also between those of both these categories and the urban "precariat" even more broadly defined – as further examination of the South African case will amply confirm.

Moreover, the politics of the urban dwellers *per se* as distinct from that of the urban proletariat (there is some obvious overlap between categories of course) has a dynamic and thrust of its own (as, again, examination of the South Africa case will demonstrate). For, more generally, we enter here the realm of "street level politics" focused upon so vigorously by Jonathan Barker, among others. A sharp debate has arisen, it might be noted, as to what is the precise import of such "street-level politics"[11] – not so much, be it noted, "workers take to the streets" as "street-dwellers take to the streets." For what we see in such social circumstances is a "people" available for socio-political upsurge (in both township and rural settings), though their actions will perhaps be directed most forcefully at the state and the polity, their programs and their minions, more than, directly, at employers.

Perhaps, too, this does not as readily expand into a socialist challenge as does the workplace-centred confrontations of more formally "proletarian" provenance. But even translating work-place confrontation into socialist-style skepticism about, and hostility towards, capitalism *per se* takes creative political and ideological work for it to begin to happen. How much more such work is necessary to blend the two worlds of working-class/workplace and of urban-rooted protest into resistance at the higher level of clarity and counter-capitalist consciousness – even if these varied resistances can indeed set themselves against the very same broader

---

[11] See Jonathan Barker, *Street-Level Politics* (Toronto: Between the Lines, 1999).

reality of capitalist control over the social milieu that provides the context of struggle.

If we were indeed to expand our sense of progressive resistance to include both working-class and "township" fronts of struggle, we would, nonetheless, have to confront one pressing question: do we run the risk of losing something of essential revolutionary importance by so doing? After all, consider the claims most often made by the left on behalf of the more systemic, more formally "proletarian," confrontations that are most often thought of as being brought into greatest saliency and efficacy at (in the first instance) the level of the workplace itself? How, we must ask ourselves, do these two worlds of resistance and protest (that of workplace and township) link to each other? Can this diversity of resistances (clearly visible in South Africa, for example) be thought to blend into a coherent and cumulative counter-hegemonic project (of possible socialist provenance?) vis-à-vis the status quo? Or is this more "precarious politics" still only, a la Marx and Engels, "dangerous," as one recent analyst of the precariat has apparently concluded?[12]

As to these questions perhaps at least one thing can be forcefully asserted. There are, of course, proletarians and even semi-proletarians in the Global South, who can come to develop their own working-class consciousness sufficiently far as to understand their grievances vis-a-vis their employers as being increasingly against capitalism conceptualized more generally. Yet there has also been produced a "people" - poor people in both urban and rural settings – who are more readily available for socio-political upsurge against state structures of power and repression than are mobilizable for class-confrontation in the work-place. Such a "people" as mobilized along such lines would perhaps be labeled an "under-class" (or, in a sense somewhat more metaphorical than scientific, even a quasi-proletariat or as denizens of the working-class) by some observers. Yet this may be done more to save the hypothesis of class/proletarian centrality to revolutionary discourse, one fears, than to advance effective revolutionary thinking. In any case, the central fact remains that a politics of a broad-based mobilization that includes *both* proletariat

---

[12] As I complete this piece I learn, via the internet, that a new book by Guy Standing entitled *The Precariat: The New Dangerous Class* (London: Bloomsbury Academic, 2011) – thus underscoring in one title both concepts I deploy here: "the precariat" and "the dangerous class" – is set to appear. Clearly, Standing and I are working along some startlingly similar lines since, beyond the title itself, the flyer I have received announcing the book's launch summarizes its content as follows: "The Precariat is a new class, comprising the growing number of people facing lives of insecurity, doing work without a past or future. Their lack of belonging and identity means inadequate access to social and economic rights. Why is this new class growing, what political dangers does it represent and how might these be addressed?" I have yet to read this still forthcoming publication of course, but, while intrigued, I am rather surprised to hear only "dangers" being mentioned in its announcement (above). The reality on the ground is much more complicated (and more promising) in South Africa, as this essay and the complementary one anticipated in footnote 1 will argue.

and precariat will be full of positively revolutionary potential, one that is very broad-gauged and inclusive, economic, political and social – albeit a politics that will be decidedly complex and difficult to martial to revolutionary affect! And this is true, as we shall now see, not least in Africa.

II. Lagos and Beyond: The Politics of "Precarious" Settings

What, in such terms, of Africa then? The continent presents an increasingly urban setting certainly, cities growing exponentially throughout the continent - with the population of cities like Lagos or Cairo already reaching quite staggering proportions. Of course, this is a global phenomenon, as George Packer writes in an article on Lagos entitled "The Megacity", of the Global South more generally:

> Around a billion people — almost half of the developing world's urban population — live in slums. The United Nations Human Settlements Program, in a 2003 report titled "The Challenge of the Slums," declared, "The urban poor are trapped in an informal and 'illegal' world — in slums that are not reflected on maps, where waste is not collected, where taxes are not paid, and where public services are not provided. Officially, they do not exist." According to the report, "Over the course of the next two decades, the global urban population will double, from 2.5 to 5 billion. Almost all of this increase will be in developing countries.[13]

But Packer's main focus in Africa and, particularly, what is, for him, a megacity par excellence: Lagos in Nigeria. In that city, as he reminds us, "in 1950, fewer than three hundred thousand people lived [there]. [However, he continues,] "in the second half of the twentieth century, the city grew at a rate of more than six per cent annually. It is currently the sixth-largest city in the world, and it is growing faster than any of the world's other megacities (the term used by the United Nations Center for Human Settlements for 'urban agglomerations' with more than ten million people). By 2015, it is projected, Lagos will rank third, behind Tokyo and Bombay, with twenty-three million inhabitants."

And it is in such cities that "urban dwellers" can become socio-economic actors that may far transcend the proletarian and semi-proletarian descriptors that in past reality applied to at least some of them – and this can sometimes have quite radical implications. Working-class? Yes and no.

As Freund once wrote of Africa:

> While it might seem at first sight that urbanization and direct subjection to market production would have brought about a class of workers that could be relatively easily understood and subsumed under the categories of capitalist industrial society familiar to Westerners there are problems...in comprehending labour...in the African city. With the exception of South Af-

[13] George Packer, "The Megacity," *The New Yorker*, Nov. 13, 2006.

> rica which needs special treatment precisely for this reason [an issue to which we will have to return]. Only a small section of African workers actually are wage workers operating in the sphere of mass commodity production. Nor is this section growing very significantly.[14]

Indeed, says Freund, "a conservative...estimate of the working population of the Nigerian metropolis of Lagos in the 1970s suggested that only a minority is to be found registered as wage workers." True, this argument does not refer to the more recent and truly mammoth Lagos evoked in a preceding paragraph. But the same point doubtless still holds. What is one to make of this "mass," sometimes epitomized as the "informal sector"? As Freund continues,

> The state in colonial times and often thereafter has taken an ambiguous stance at best towards the 'informal' sector of the economy and those who work within it. Classic development theories focused on industrialization and its consequences in an urban context or the development of a prosperous peasantry in a rural one. The world of shanty towns, of corner stalls and makeshift sweatshops, of women selling little packets of favouring for stew, individual cigarettes and bars of soap do not belong to the structures that it proposed and planned. It is supposed to be a mark of backwardness and a temporary phenomenon only. In reality, though, it is precisely the 'informal sector' that has flourished most in post-colonial Africa and any serious assessment of the African workers has to give it a serious share of attention.[15]

In fact, Peter Gutkind has anticipated this point in an earlier analysis. Under colonialism, he stated, urbanization could only "produce a 'marginal' urban population who live in precarious conditions, exploited in one form or another by the dominant colonial group and relegated ecologically to the peripheries of towns and economically to the peripheries of a producing and consuming society." Indeed, he continued, the African city is best seen as being "made up of three basic population groups, a plebian urban mob, workers and artisans."[16] Gutkind saw fit to characterize this heterogeneous urban population as having a kind of broad-gauged proletarian consciousness. Again, "yes and no" must be the most accurate response, proletarian consciousness becoming, in such a formulation, as much a metaphor as a precise scientific description.

For what, we must ask, does such "proletarian consciousness" actually amount to, especially since post-colonial urban Africa has not been so fundamentally altered structurally from its earlier colonial profile. No wonder that many have felt forced to understand in fresh ways the complexities of an unfinished transition to a cleanly and clearly defined (and polarized) capitalist-based society that might otherwise be thought to merely stymie revolutionary aspiration in present-day Africa.

---

[14] Bill Freund, *The African Worker* (Cambridge and New York: Cambridge University Press, 1988).

[15] Freund, ibid.

[16] Peter Gutkind, *The poor in urban Africa: a prologue to modernization, conflict and the unfinished revolution* (Montreal: McGill University Centre for Developing Areas Studies, 1968).

Thus, observers like Post and Wright have persisted in taking a high road with reference to those social elements set adrift by failed capitalist "transformation." They take a first step in allowing our sense of class contradictions – and of class belonging – to be markedly expanded, especially with respect to Africa and the rest of the Global South. For there, in societies profoundly altered but not transformed by the impact of capitalism, the roster of those exploited (and potentially available for class-based action) is far wider than narrow "classist" categories can hope to elucidate – and this is not just to speak of all those peasants out there! Hence their key formulation:

> The working out of capitalism in parts of the periphery prepares not only the minority working class but peasants and other working people, women, youth and minorities for a socialist solution, even though the political manifestation of this may not initially take the form of a socialist movement. In the case of those who are *not* wage labourers (the classical class associated with that new order) capitalism has still so permeated the social relations which determine their existences, even though it may not have followed the western European pattern of "freeing" their labour power, that to be liberated from it is their only salvation. The objective need for socialism of these elements can be no less than that of the worker imprisoned in the factory and disciplined by the whip of unemployment. The price [of capitalism] is paid in even the most 'successful' of the underdeveloped countries, and others additionally experience mass destitution. Finding another path has...become a desperate necessity if the alternative of continuing, if not increasing, barbarism is to be escaped.[17]

Yet even this may not quite go far enough. Such forces do indeed struggle for equality, but, be it noted, not necessarily and in the first instance for socialism. This is the world of struggles that we have seen Jonathan Barker to epitomize, in the book that he has edited, as "Street-Level Politics"[18] – a world of protest and resistance that stretches beyond the work-place and often elaborates its politics in terms that are not quite so easily recognized as "progressive" in the most conventional of Marxist terms. Yet should we not look for our systemic contradictions where we find them? Indeed, Barker sees the phenomenon he refers to as a "social response to the expansion of market logic into social relationships that have more than economic meaning to people." And elsewhere he speaks of the existence, in Africa and beyond, of "thousands of activist groups addressing the issues of housing, functioning of local markets, availability of local social services, provision and standard of education and abusive and damaging working conditions."[19]

Nor does this mean that there is not a challenge to getting people, both urban and rural, to see their negative situations in effectively proletarian and anti-

---

[17] Ken Post and Phil Wright, *Socialism and Underdevelopment* (London and New York: Routledge, 1989), 151-2.
[18] Jonathan Barker, op. cit., 13.
[19] Jonathan Barker, "Debating Globalization: Critique of Colin Leys," *Southern Africa Report (SAR)* 12, 4 (September, 1997).

capitalist terms. After all, the vectors of oppression they often feel most tangibly, are those of the state, designated to police a semi-transformed society, and to often refuse, on behalf of capital and the locally powerful, legitimate popular claims for social services and social redress; hence, the tendency for the poor and the "untransformed" to give at least as much importance to "street-level politics" as to work-place contestation in defining the overall texture of the political situation.

Moreover, it is precisely under such conditions, I would argue, that the left must feel compelled, much more imaginatively than ever before (in terms of clear principle and by means of compromise and assiduous political work), to seek to draw the best of various claims and assertions (both street-corner and work-site) as arise from diverse but related contradictions into effectively counter-hegemonic projects.[20] They must become, in short, claims and assertions that represent the "highest common factor" of their protagonists' various social locations. Of course, these will certainly include worker's demands defined quite specifically but, in the Global South in particular, it is the people across quite a broad front and mobilized around (if you like) a kind of revolutionary and eminently progressive populism who can be bring themselves (and be brought by means of effective means of political work) to defy not only oppression but also, collectively, the rule of capital.

But we cannot stop at merely a more expansive class definition of agency. For we must make a positive force in our struggle for liberation of other tensions in society that can be wedded to claims and assertions advanced in the name of class-defined redress if we are imaginative enough to do so. As my former teacher and old friend, Ralph Miliband, has noted, capitalism's grossly uneven development around the world has produced "extremely fertile terrain" for the kind of "pathological deformations" – predatory authoritarianisms and those "demagogues and charlatans peddling their poisonous wares...of ethnic and religious exclusion and hatred"[21] – that now scar the global landscape. As I would add: losing confidence in socialist and other humanely modern, humanly cooperative, projects, people turn for social meaning to more ready-to-hand identities, often with fundamentalist fervour. And yet, despite this, progressives committed to class struggle can and should continue to view such identities as contingent in their socio-political implications and as not being, in many cases, in contradiction with socialist purposes. And we should, when possible, invite the bearers of such identities – alongside feminists, environmentalists, anti-racists, activists around issues of sexual orienta-

---

[20] Note that Barker himself is skeptical about the priority (or even wisdom) of seeking to discover some counter-hegemony to encompass and generalize the diversity of such important and legitimate claims. In my opinion and on this aspect of the question he is effectively answered, also in the pages of Southern Africa Report, by Colin Leys, "Colin Leys Replies," *SAR* 12, 4 (September, 1997) and Veronica Schild, "Their Hegemony or Ours" (see footnote 8, above).

[21] Ralph Miliband, *Socialism in a Sceptical Age* (London: Verso, 1995), 192.

tion and the like – to join us within a broader community-in-the-making and within a universalizing democratic project of global, anti-capitalist transformation.

In fact, as Miliband continues,

> ...everywhere there are common goals and aspirations -- for democratic forms where they are denied and for more democratic forms where these are no more than a screen for oligarchic rule; for the achievement of a social order in which improvements in the condition of the most deprived – often a majority of the population – is the prime concern of governments; for the subordination of the economy to meeting social needs. In all countries, there are people, in numbers large and small, who are moved by the vision of a new social order in which democracy, egalitarianism and cooperation – the essential values of socialism – would be prevailing principles of social organization. It is in the growth of their numbers and in the success of their struggles that lies the best hope for humankind.[22]

But the corollary of this position is equally compelling: those of us on the left had better learn to operate in a complex world of diverse faiths, races and ethnic belongings, to unite such "belongings" to our cause of class liberation, or they will continue to return to haunt us – treated as "merely" divisive "identifiers," only representing claims that can, at their worst, turn rancid and dangerous to humane purpose. So, too, must gender-defined and environmentally-concerned projects be ever more assertively articulated as being, not reducible to, but coequal with and enlarged by an assertion of class considerations.[23]

In short, one of our key goals must be to define "agency" not merely in terms of some rather abstractly defined "working class interest." For that apparently simple slogan – correct but excessively schematic - has presented far too open an invitation to arrogance and high-handedness (in the interest of the "working class," don't you know) to essentialist vanguards of all kinds, ever quick to assert arrogantly just what "the class" must and should do. Instead we need to reach towards embrace of the range of shades of identity within and beyond strict class boundaries that can be won to revolutionary praxis. Not that tensions between diverse goals and purposes will then simply disappear, of course. Yet seeking to realize such an enlarged project of "class struggle" also underlines the requirement of much more democratic methods of negotiation of both the means and the ends of revolutionary work than has characterized most past socialist undertakings – in mobilizing the forces both to launch revolutionary change and to sustain the process of socialist construction in the long run.

---

[22] Ibid, 194-5.

[23] Material in this paragraph is drawn from my book, *Development after Globalization*, especially ch. 3, "Identifying Class, Classifying Difference," where this overall argument is spelled out at much greater length.

III. South Africa: Proletariat and Precariat

Here South Africa is a key case, one that, as suggested in my first footnote (number one, above), I am currently examining in detail for an article complementary to the present one. To complete the present essay I will sketch something of that analysis here while referring the reader to that piece itself should he/she wish to further pursue the matter.[24] For the fact is that South Africa is the country in Africa that has experienced a more "modern" and conventionally capitalist transformation than the rest of the continent - and it has had a greater degree of a recognizable "proletarianization," due, in particular, to its dramatic (and on-going) "mineral revolution" of the past 150 years. But it is also a society marked by the perpetuation and further growth of that "dangerous class" of which we have spoken (those mired, especially in the vast urban townships, in the swamp of "precarious work"...and less).

It is certainly true, for example, that the organized working class has been a key player in the country's politics – a major force for example at the crucial intersection of class struggle and anti-apartheid assertion.[25] It was, in fact, the crucial role played by COSATU as it emerged as the key centre of organized black labour in the 1980s that gave observers who were skeptical from quite early on regarding the revolutionary credentials of the ANC/SACP the sense that that something more radical was afoot in South Africa. But of course the promise was even wider than that epitomized by COSATU, for it also lay in the broader movement of township-based self-assertion on the part of many Africans of different genders and diverse social locations. Though this kind of popular assertion was not facilitated by the ANC's reassertion of its vanguardist mind-set during its ascension to power,[26] it

---

[24] See my "Reviving Resistance: Indices of Opposition in Present-Day South Africa" (op. cit.).

[25] The documentation on this subject is substantial but for a useful overview of COSATU and the organized working-class as it emerged into the post-apartheid milieu and a "neo-liberalizing world" see Eddie Webster and Glenn Adler, "Exodus Without a Map: The Labour Movement in a Liberalizing South Africa," in *Labour Regimes and Liberalization: The Restructuring of State-Society Relations in Africa*, ed. Bjorn Beckman and Lloyd Sachikonye (Harare: University of Zimbabwe Press, 2001). See also, for an analysis of more recent developments, Roger Southall and Eddie Webster, "Unions and Parties in South Africa: COSATU and the ANC in the wake of Polokwane," in *Trade Unions and Party Politics: Labour Movements in Africa*, ed. Bjorn Beckman, Sakhela Buhlungu and Lloyd Sachikonye (Johannesburg: Human Sciences Research Council, 2010) and, inter alia, Carolyn Bassett and Marlea Clarke, "South African trade unions and globalization: going for the 'high-road," getting stuck on the 'low-road'," *World Organisation, Labour and Globalisation* 2, 1 (Spring, 2008) and Sakhela Buhlungu, *A Paradox of Victory: COSATU and the Democratic Transformation in South Africa* (Scottsville, S.A: University of KwaZulu-Natal Press, 2010).

[26] See Rusty Bernstein's revealing 2002 letter to the author, later published as "'The turning point...' Letter from Rusty Bernstein to John S. Saul," *Transformation* 64 (2007).

was to revive in opposition to the policies of state and ruling party in the 1990s and, especially, in the first decade of the new century.

Here some have begun to see the possibility of a dawning of a new kind of self-conscious joining of work-place and street-level assertions of the kind that had – thanks to the saliency and universality of apartheid as shared enemy – underpinned broad-based struggle in the 1980s. Now, of course, the best organized workers were to some degree absent from the promise of counter-hegemonic struggle, having pledged themselves, from quite early on, to a the role of junior partner (as quasi-"labour aristocrats"?) to the ANC/SACP as part of the TriPartite Alliance in objective support of a neo-liberal overall trajectory for the economy.[27] And the wide-spread manifestations of township struggle remained paradoxical as well. For in the broad mass of the impoverished we find a population locked, on the one hand, in almost slavish electoral thrall to the ANC and its liberation-struggle credentials. Yet, on the other hand, this has proven simultaneously, to be a population ready to act out, at "street-level" as it were and in highly dramatic fashion, its resistance to a broad range of governmental policies and activities. Thus, as the abstract preceding a recent important article on what he terms to be the "Rebellion of the Poor" in South Africa phrases it, Peter Alexander has argued:

> Since 2004 South Africa has experienced a movement of local protests amounting to a rebellion of the poor. This has been widespread and intense, reaching insurrectionary proportions in some cases. On the surface, the protests have been about service delivery and against uncaring, self-serving a corrupt leaders of the municipalities. A key feature has been mass participation by a new generation of fighters, especially unemployed youth but also school students. Many issues that underpinned the [initial] ascendancy of Jacob Zuma also fuel the present action, including a sense of injustice arising from the realities of persistent inequality.[28]

Moreover, he notes, "While the inter-connections between the local protests, and between the local protests and militant action involving other elements of civil society, are limited, it is suggested that this is likely to change"!

In effect, then, two schools emerge. One, clearly exemplified by David Harvey and Patrick Bond in their writings, sees in the energies evidenced by these and other assertions of "civil society" the manifestation of a genuinely proletarian reality of struggle – struggle directly linked to other tangibly workplace-centered actions by those of more familiar working-class belonging. For such writers of the

---

[27] On the virtues of a new "small-a" alliance between organized labour and civil society, one that could deplace the presently existing "large-A" Alliance from political centrality in South Africa, see John S. Saul, *Revolutionary Traveller* (Winnipeg: Arbeiter Ring, 2009), 292-6 and Patrick Bond, "South African splinters: From 'elite transition'
to 'small-alliance'," *Review of African Political Economy* 127 (March 2011).

[28] Peter Alexander, "Rebellion of the poor: South Africa's service delivery protests - a preliminary analysis," *Review of African Political Economy* 37, no. 123 (March, 2010).

left, Gillian Hart suggests, "the central task is to rip away the mask that obfuscates neoliberal class power [confident that] such an exposé will help pave the way for a coherent resurgence of mass movements... [moving] beyond race, ethnicity, gender, and other dimensions of difference in order to achieve class-based solidarity in an increasingly dangerous world."[29] But this is not quite good enough, Hart asserts.

As she continues,

> *Pace* David Harvey, the task confronting the left in South Africa and elsewhere is considerably more complex than that of exposing neoliberal class power. Nor is it adequate to posit a shift from race to class apartheid. Most immediately, the ANC government's embrace of GEAR constitutes a re-articulation of race and class that is also part of an activist project of rule.[30]

Note this last sentence: "class," "race," "rule" (and, in another context, she would no doubt add "gender"); small wonder that, for her, "the challenges facing the left are far more complex" than, her view, Harvey countenances.

> The drama that exploded at Polokwane [site of Zuma's challenging of Mbeki] was as much about contesting the meaning of nation and liberation as it was about the fallout from a neoliberal class project and socio-economic structure and we ignore these sentiments and struggles at our peril.[31]

In sum, she is saying, the claims of a left-populism[32] that self-consciously takes the liberatory claims centered on considerations of gender, race and the exercise of democratic voice with great seriousness, must not be obscured by any too exclusive a preoccupation with the simultaneous reality of class determination.

How best to square this particular circle: "class politics" or "a more broadly liberatory politics?" The short answer: both of the above, for the Bonds and the Harts are equally correct, as far as they go. However, it is in making the two pieces of the puzzle – the puzzle as to what can and will drive the "lower orders" in their pursuit of equity - fit together for revolutionary purposes that the real challenge lies. It is easy to see how they might not fit: the most organized of workers going deeper and deeper into the (minimally) gilded ghetto of "privilege;" township dwellers more and more seduced down the blind-alleys of the most "dangerous" of consciousnesses: criminality, xenophobia, ethnic rivalry and the like.[33] But, on both sides of

---

[29] Gillian Hart, "Provocations of neoliberalism: Contesting the nation and liberation after apartheid," in *Zuma's Own Goal: Losing South Africa's 'War on Poverty*', ed. Brij Maharaj, Ashwin Desai and Patrick Bond (Trenton, N.J.: African World Press, 2011), 82.

[30] Hart, ibid., 83. Bond's own characteristic mode of argument is epitomized by Hart, ibid., 96.

[31] Hart, ibid., 96

[32] This is not a phrase that Hart herself uses, it should be noted.

[33] See John S. Saul, "Race, Class, Gender and Voice: Four Terrains of Liberation," being chapter 1 of Saul, *Liberation Lite: The Roots of Recolonization in Southern Africa* (Delhi Trenton, N.J. and Asmara: Three Essays Collective and Africa World Press/Red Sea Press, 2011). On the re-

the equation, such postures remain so far from being the whole story of work-place and township life that many South African activists reach for a different narrative, a different possibility.

Add to this the fact that, on both sides of the equation, claims are, at their best, driven by a demand for equity and fairness, disturbingly liberal-sounding substantives in their vague and potentially windy abstraction, but words with meaning nonetheless. And one thing more: the varied planes of struggle need each other. For "class" preoccupations pursued without full attention to the terrains of struggle for gender and racial equality and for a guarantee of access to the expression of real democratic voice are as unlikely to make a meaningful revolution as are movements based on gender, race and voice that don't take demands based on class considerations sufficiently seriously.[34] Genuine liberation, genuine socialism and genuine liberatory socialism demand all four components.

---

cent success of Julius Malema, head of the ANC's own Youth League, in manipulating what are essentially racist claims in contemporary South Africa in sustaining his own claims to primacy see my "The Transition in South Africa: Choice, Fate...or Recolonization?" first presented as the Harold Wolpe lecture at the University of KwaZulu/Natal, Durban, South Africa, September 29, 2011 and subsequently to be published in the Durban-based Critical Arts (forthcoming).

[34] The complexities of township life, the realities of a real struggle for equity there, and the simultaneous danger of slippage to less than savoury outcomes have been well documented in recent literature, as will be discussed at greater length in my attendant essay anticipated in Footnotes 1, above. See, in addition to Peter Alexander (as cited in footnote 26), the running compilations of township unrest being assembled by John Devenish at the University of KwaZulu/Natal. See too such fine "township insider" accounts as that by Jacob Dlamini and entitled *Native Nostalgia* (Aukland Park, S.A.: Jacana, 2009), a book at once sociological and autobiographical.

Crisis, change and the working class in Argentina

Ruth Felder and Viviana Patroni

Introduction

For many observers, the type of reforms implemented in Argentina since 2003 is greatly indicative of a move away from neoliberalism. This current 'post-neoliberal' stage is marked by a long-lasting and substantial process of economic recovery, the fall of unemployment and poverty and the end of austerity policies, leading some analysts to announce the end of neoliberalism. Yet, others highlight the persistence of policies, institutional arrangements and patterns of wealth distribution in the country's development strategy since 2003 that are still closely related to the conditions that resulted from the neoliberal reforms of the 1990s. A major limitation of most of these views is that they focus on limited sets of indicators, but fail to notice the articulation between structural transformation, economic policies and the balances of forces between capital and labour. Paying attention to this articulation is crucial to interpreting the period and identifying the lines of continuity and change.

In this paper, we will endeavour to analyze precisely those actions on the part of the state that tend to affect the relative power of capital vis-à-vis labour. We propose to do so by considering the transformations in labour markets since the neoliberal reforms of the 1990s. Our argument is that while there are a number of critical discontinuities in terms of the realities faced by workers in Argentina over the last two decades, there is also evidence that the structural change brought about in the 1990s remains deeply embedded in the economic and social fabric of the country. In a similar fashion, since 2003, policies have embodied a number of tensions between continuity and change. The impact of a strong economic reactivation has been felt differently by various sectors of the working class. Economic recovery and a significant political transformation in the country, in short, have so far proven insufficient in reversing the fragmentation of the working class.

Neoliberal reforms in Argentina:

The military coup of 1976 irrevocably changed the Argentinian economy and the arena within which conflicts between workers and their employers had been contained since the 1940s. The military rulers (1976-1983) came to identify the considerable strength of organized labour with the political, social and economic crisis the country faced in the mid-1970s. Accordingly, the core of their policy was aimed at imposing a new discipline on labour, at the cost of thousands of lives, clearing the way for the implementation of the first neoliberal policies. However, it was not until the 1990s that a full and effective package of 'market-friendly' policies was implemented. More particularly, it was the tempering of inflation—one of the country's most taxing problems since the 1960s —through the implementation of a currency board (the Convertibility Plan) in 1991 that established the context for the pursuit of a radical and fast-paced process of neoliberal restructuring.

The Convertibility Plan tied the Argentinian currency to the US dollar and required full backing of the currency in US dollars, gold, or dollar-nominated bonds. It also prohibited indexation and made wage increases conditional upon productivity gains.[1] The Plan gained a very high rate of approval and cemented a broad consensus around the primacy of stability as a target in economic policy-making. But the exchange anchor was much more than a stabilization program. The strict monetary and fiscal discipline necessary to maintain the fixed exchange rate became a central pillar in promoting the process of structural reforms—trade and financial liberalization, privatization, and the re-orientation of the regulatory functions of the state over the economy—known as the Washington Consensus. The shortcomings of this approach, however, were evident from its very inception. One important source of pressure was the growing trade deficit in an increasingly overvalued currency, generated by the combination of the fixed exchange rate and trade liberalization. Because exports were not enough to close the expanding gap in the current account, the sustainability of the currency board was heavily reliant on the inflow of foreign capital, through either investment or loans. In addition to trade deficits, Argentina also faced growing difficulties related to the remittance of profits and interest payments on its foreign debt. Moreover, the major international financial upheavals of the 1990s (most notably the Mexican crisis in 1995 and the Asian crisis in 1997) increased investors' concerns and thus raised the premium they were willing to accept in exchange for more funds.

---

[1] This condition resulted in a virtual wage freeze during the decade of Convertibility.

Without the capacity to depreciate the currency, recession became the main mechanism to balance the current account. Foreign lending could also have solved the problem, but as Argentina became a higher-risk market in the eyes of investors, it became almost impossible for the country to secure new loans. By the time of the Plan's collapse in 2002, Argentina's foreign debt, both private and public, had climbed to US$ 155 billion, up almost threefold since 1991. By March of 2002, the GDP per capita was almost a quarter smaller than it had been in 1976. The social cost of the program was even more calamitous, as we will explore below.

The assault on labour: structural reforms and flexibilization

The program of reforms that President Carlos Menem (1989-1999) implemented in the 1990s in Argentina included, as the common sense of the times dictated, direct measures to undo the 'rigidities' that characterized the functioning of labour markets. The policies were a considerable transgression of the principles of Peronism, Menem's political affiliation, and manifested a pivotal change in the historical weight of labour unions within the Peronist Justicialist Party itself (Partido Justicialista, PJ).

According to the neoliberal dogma, once the artificially high—that is, regulation-imposed—price of hiring and firing workers had been reduced and wages reflected a value set at a point closer to equilibrium, companies were going to respond by increasing their demand for labour. The prevalence of these more 'flexible' conditions in the labour market would secure not only more jobs in general, but more formal work in particular. Greater rates of labour absorption would also multiply the impact of growth, and thus the deregulation of labour markets would be one more conduit in the virtuous cycle of economic expansion. It is worth pointing out that formal employment in this context was not in conflict with growing precariousness, since it was only under conditions of flexibility that firms were expected to increase their number of employees. However, labour deregulation in combination with structural adjustment in Argentina resulted not only in rising levels of precariousness and informality but also in growing unemployment. Even so, as the employment crisis deepened in Argentina during the 1990s, the government gained new ammunition to promote labour reforms as the only possible way to encourage employment generation. In reality, underlying the pressure to push for greater labour flexibilization was the urgent need to control production costs in an economic context that made labour costs the only viable source of adjustment.

Transformations in labour markets during the 1990s were determined by two sets of factors related to one another through a number of economic and political realities that worked together to magnify their pernicious impact on workers. One was the various reforms introduced to labour legislation during the 1990s that were directed at altering the parameters that had organized labour markets in Argentina during its industrialization since at least the 1940s. The other, equally important factor was the direction of economic policies and the periods of stagnation that afflicted the country between 1994 and 1996 and between 1998 and 2002. These economic realities imposed a discipline of their own on workers, which aggravated labour precariousness and reinforced the flexibilizing thrust of the legal reforms.

Although toward the end of Menem's second presidency—and as an attempt to strengthen the support of an embattled PJ—some of the reforms introduced during the decade were reversed, the overall direction of reforms until then was unambiguously toward creating more flexible labour conditions in the country (Marshall 2004: 12). The undermining of individual rights was a common feature of the legislative reforms introduced during the 1990s. These reforms included changes in the legislation to reduce the costs of hiring and firing workers, facilitate the use of temporary and part-time workers and reduce employers' contributions to social security (González 2003, 99-100).

While Menem's initiatives to promote changes in the regulation of collective agreements in order to allow negotiations at the plant level did not prosper, in practice, the decentralization of the bargaining process became the rule. Thus, there was a substantial increase in the proportion of collective agreements negotiated at the plant level, rising from 18.3 percent in 1991 to 88.3 percent in 1998 (Bisio et al. 1999, 157). These kinds of agreements were one more vehicle for flexibilization, in many cases allowing working conditions below the standards established by the existing collective agreement for the activity at the national level.

Moreover, as we have suggested, labour flexibilization was not only the product of labour policy reform but also the de facto result of economic restructuring and the precarious and uncertain conditions this restructuring generated for all workers. Of particular relevance in explaining the changes that operated in labour markets during the 1990s, is the performance of the industrial sector. This was the sector most affected by the conditions imposed by the Convertibility Plan, especially the combination of an increasingly appreciated currency and trade liberalization. To remain competitive and adjust to the terms imposed by artificially low-priced imports, some domestic producers acquired new capital-intensive technology rendered relatively affordable by the overvalued exchange rate. Though improvements in productivity can be seen as a positive aspect of the incorporation of new technology, growing productivity can also, as Leiva (2008, 113-116) argues, be the result of raising the ratio of capital to labour by reducing the number of workers and increasing the intensity of work. This was certainly one of the ways in which productivity improvements operated in Argentina. Finally, many firms did not have access to the financial resources required for the modernization of their plants and thus succumbed to the weight of foreign competition. By 1998, the industrial sector contributed only 17% of the GDP, compared to 22.4% in 1982. This scenario was negative in terms of employment: the industrial sector lost 30% of jobs between 1991 and 2000 (Lindenboim 2003, 78).

The reduction of employment in the industrial sector during the 1990s contrasts with the changes in employment in other areas, most noticeably in construction, retailing, transportation and the public sector, where, in fact, employment increased during the periods of growth. However, the tendency was increasingly for these sectors to absorb workers under conditions of precariousness. With the exception of the early phases of Convertibility, the tendency was also for a momentous growth of unemployment and underemployment. From 6 percent in 1991, unemployment reached 18.3 percent in 2001 and 21.5 percent in May 2002. Underemployment affected an additional 16.3 percent of workers in 2001. These high levels of employment and underemployment were certainly critical variables in explaining the growing power of employers to impose more flexible conditions in the organization of production.

The new shape of labour markets in Argentina:

In reflecting on the momentous transformation of labour markets in Argentina during the 1990s, one factor that stands out is the swiftness and scope with which change materialized. In a context of rapidly and drastically deteriorating working conditions and growing unemployment, a rising sense and experience of precariousness was the reality most workers were forced to face, be they formally or informally employed. Implicit in the claim that neoliberal reforms had finally provided the way out of instability and economic decline was an understanding that unemployment and poverty were only temporary problems. In a somewhat contradictory sense, while economic growth was considered to be key for the resolution of these problems, unemployment and poverty were also explained as consequences of individual failure and socio-cultural characteristics that prevented the poor from participating in the expanding opportunities that a more open and less regulated economy had to offer (Lo Vuolo et al. 1999, 293-294).

The concept of 'informality' has continued to be used within the specialized literature to depict a wide and increasingly diverse universe of employment situations that deviate from standard employment. For example, it has been argued that during the 1990s, the very legal lines that distinguish formal from informal work became increasingly blurred (Olmedo and Murray 2002). Indeed, while informality has traditionally been conceptualized as the realm of the labour market that lies beyond state regulation, the experience of countries like Argentina during the 1990s comes to challenge this proposition. In fact, it was precisely the active regulatory role of the state that dictated the new conditions for workers, which resembled those of informal employment: temporary, poorly-paid and unprotected work and a reduction in employers' contributions to the social security system (Olmedo and Murray 2002, 428-429). That is, the flexibilization of labour markets did not require a 'withdrawal' of the state from excessive regulation but, instead, its active involvement in re-regulating labour relations in a way that provided a solution to what capitalists perceived as impossibly high costs for managing labour under the conditions dictated by globalization.

However, to account for the transformation of labour markets in Argentina since the 1990s, it seems imperative to differentiate the various forms employment has taken in a move away from what the ILO defines as a 'standard employment relationship'. In particular, it is 'precariousness' that better depicts the experience of the large number of workers referred to in the previous discussion (Lindenboim 2003, 76-77). A broad construction of the notion of precariousness includes workers affected by changes in labour legislation that allow the existence of legal contracts that incorporate precariousness in the sense of job insecurity, very low pay and lack of access to social security coverage, union representation and other legal benefits, such as holidays and family allowance. Precarious workers are also those hired as providers of a service; that is, the self-employed, workers hired through employment agencies and interns.[2]

In official statistics, and thus of common use in the specialized literature, precariousness is equated with non-registered work, both in the formal and informal sectors. This notion refers to those salaried workers whose participation in the workplace has not been legally registered as established by labour law and thus whose employment denotes a state of illegality. Workers in this group represent a particularly vulnerable demographic as they lack access to any of the benefits of existing legislation and do not receive the protection of existing social security. Since the 1990s, non-registered workers have played a key role in firms' adaptation strategies to structural transformation, within both formal and informal sectors and in firms of all sizes.[3] These workers tend to be concentrated within microenterprises,[4] most of them within the informal sector, where they represent 66.5 percent of salaried workers. A similar situation exists within small enterprises (Neffa 2010, 65-6). However, between 1980 and 2002, the incidence of precariousness doubled in medium- and large-sized enterprises (Novick et al. 2008, 38).

---

[2] Interestingly, the hiring of workers as service providers became a generalized modality for federal and local states, which speaks to the active involvement of the state in extending labour informality and precariousness.

[3] Non-registered workers encompass the largest segment of workers in private households. However, our discussion here is limited to workers in the private and public sectors.

[4] These are small productive ventures of up to 5 employees, characterized by the use of very limited capital input, achieving only very low rates of productivity and therefore barely surviving as viable enterprises.

The incorporation of non-registered workers into the formal labour market occurs in a counter-cyclical fashion, but it has tended to remain high notwithstanding the rapid rates of growth since 2003 and the high levels of employment generation, as we will discuss below. Thus, while in the second trimester of 2009, non-registered employment dropped to 34.8% of salaried workers from its highest point of almost 49% in 2003, it was still substantially higher than the 27.2% registered in 1990 (Neffa 2010, 68-70). The numbers reached in this category indicate the centrality of this strategy for employers and the lack of commitment, during the 1990s, to the exercise of any kind of protective role on the part of the authorities in charge of enforcing labour legislation. The figures on non-registered work do not reveal, though, the broader incidence of precariousness that is embedded in the other forms of atypical employment, even when they are legal. Thus, some analysts suggest that, at the end of the first decade of the 21st century, approximately half of the economically active population in Argentina face precariousness, informality and underemployment (Observatorio de la Deuda Social 2009, 4).

Finally, another feature of the transformation of employment in Argentina during the 1990s was the devastating lack of options for workers to escape the negative implications of restructuring. As we have suggested above, what the changes in labour legislation did not undercut was chipped away at by economic reforms and recession and their impact on the level and quality of employment. Social programs implemented at the time tended to reinforce and reproduce the precarious conditions that all workers faced. For example, the only unemployment insurance in the country provided coverage, in 1999, to only the 7% of unemployed workers qualified to receive the very low benefits offered through the program (CELS 2003, 16). The government also implemented a number of workfare programs to address the mounting social problems created by unemployment, but they were very limited in their reach. These programs only provided compensation on a temporary basis that was well below the minimum required to satisfy the basic needs of a family and without any social security protection.[5] In many cases, the holders of workfare programs performed the same tasks as other public employees, without any job security or social security contributions and for a small fraction of their wages.

---

[5] Some of the main employment programs were Reinserción Laboral (Labour Reintegration), Empleo Joven (Youth Employment), and Plan Trabajar (Program to Work). These were all targeted programs that only reached a small portion of the population. For example, the most important one, Plan Trabajar, reached 110,000 beneficiaries in 1996 and 350,000 between May 1997 and May 1998 (CELS 2003, 32). According to data from the Ministry of Labour, the total number of unemployed people in 1996 was approximately 2 million, and in 1997 it was 1.9 million (INDEC).

It was only with the uprising of December 2001 that the government sought to increase the number of beneficiaries under workfare programs, in an attempt to contain the high levels of mobilization among the unemployed and poor.

Changes in labour legislation and the reality dictated by the growing reserve army of workers explain the political and social context that has made precarious work a reality for a very large segment of workers. The flexibilization of labour relations thus introduced also implied that all workers experienced some degree of precariousness, both because they could be dismissed with few financial consequences to their employers and because new workers could be hired without difficulty under conditions beneficial to employers. In short, precariousness and growing unemployment played an essential disciplinary role for the whole of the working class.

Sustained economic growth in combination with a shift in economic and labour policies since 2003 has created a new context for addressing some of the challenges of unemployment and precariousness. Yet, the new policy orientation of the government has not been sufficient to eliminate the segmentation of labour markets. We will return to this discussion after considering the several and deep economic transformations that have characterized Argentina in the post-2003 period.

Economy, policies and politics in the crisis and the recovery

As mentioned above, external openness, monetary stability and structural reforms generated the conditions for a deep crisis by the end of the 1990s. By then, the country was dealing with a long-lasting recession, alarming rates of unemployment and impoverishment, social uneasiness along with increasing fiscal hardship and the spiralling growth of public debt. In this scenario, the government made successive attempts to reduce fiscal spending, postpone debt payments and deepen structural reforms. These measures not only failed to reduce the fiscal deficit or regain the confidence of lenders, but they also aggravated the recession, fuelled social tensions and increased international distrust about the capacity of the country to service its debt. During 2001, capital outflows accelerated, putting the domestic banking system on the brink of collapse. Also, the IMF cancelled its assistance program and pushed for a restructuring of the debt, further fiscal adjustment and additional structural reforms. Despite mounting pressures, the government refused to abandon the currency board. Instead, it imposed a new measure to block access to bank accounts, with the purpose of preventing an incipient speculative run against the domestic banking system. The sudden lack of liquidity aggravated the recession and fuelled even more anger among urban, middle-income groups in a context of intense protests by unemployed workers and lootings led by local politicians. Turmoil spread throughout the country, ending in the resignation of the president, Fernando de la Rúa, and the appointment of Senator Adolfo Rodríguez

Saá (2001) as the interim president. Rodríguez Saá resigned after only one week, during which he announced the decision to default on part of the public debt, which would then be renegotiated.

Senator Eduardo Duhalde (2002-2003), who replaced Rodríguez Saá in January 2002, made the difficult decision to abandon the currency board. Predictably, the default and the devaluation unleashed new struggles regarding the allocation of the costs of the crisis. These struggles were expressed in attempts by different capitalist fractions to transfer the costs of the crisis to the state, the spread of social mobilization in the context of an acute fall of the GDP and the re-emergence of inflation.[6] The devaluation was accompanied by efforts to adapt the legal and institutional frameworks to the new economic and political scenario.[7] This period of unprecedented economic, political and social crisis was also marked by the delegitimation of neoliberal reforms and by growing social consensus about the legitimate authority of the state in the regulation of markets—among them, labour markets.

Initially, the Duhalde administration attempted to meet the demands of domestic capitalist fractions while following the requirements of the IMF to deepen economic liberalization, strengthen monetary discipline and resume payments on the defaulted public debt. After failing to meet most of these goals and demands, the economic authorities distanced themselves from the orthodox macroeconomic policies demanded by the IMF and other international actors. This 'heterodoxy' (i.e. the regulation of the exchange market and the imposition of controls on capital movements) succeeded in overcoming the acute economic instability that prevailed at the time and created the conditions for a new stage of growth. The improvement of the economic situation was also an important element in the political 'normalization' of the country. However, the evolution of the political crisis had its own dynamics, marked, on the one hand, by growing social mobilization and protests and, on the other, by demands for order and repression from members of the government, politicians and business representatives. In June 2002, police repression ended with the killing of two members of a movement of unemployed workers. The subsequent political scandal, compounded with very high pressure from dif-

---

[6] During 2002, the GDP fell 10.9%. Despite this fall, the CPI increased 40.9%, accompanying the abrupt devaluation of the peso.

[7] Large numbers of debts and loans nominated in dollars had to be restructured such that neither creditors nor debtors were forced to bear the full brunt of the devaluation, and bankruptcy proceedings were postponed to prevent massive company failures. The prices of public utilities (that had been dollarized during the previous decade) were frozen. To improve the difficult fiscal situation and control the rise of the price of basic goods, taxes on oil and agricultural exports were imposed. Amidst growing unemployment and poverty, the legal amount of severance pay was doubled to discourage layoffs, and a workfare program offered minimum income to a large number of unemployed and poor heads of households.

ferent capitalist fractions and the failure of the government to obtain assistance from the IMF, led Duhalde to announce early presidential elections.[8]

Néstor Kirchner, the governor of the southern province of Santa Cruz, became the candidate fielded by the party in power. He was in favour of a competitive exchange rate as the means to promote exports and import substitution and advocated for broader state intervention in the economy. Kirchner and his team vindicated an active role of the state, blamed neoliberal reforms for the crisis and refused to accept the recommendations to implement adjustment policies. Kirchner also criticized the proposals for a Free Trade Agreement of the Americas (FTAA) and announced his interest in building economic and political alliances within Latin America. To the chagrin of political and economic actors demanding 'responsible economic policies' and law-and-order actions, Kirchner announced that his government would not criminalize social protests and that sovereign debt servicing would not be prioritized over the needs of the most impoverished groups of the population. Kirchner's initial statements were an acknowledgment of the deep political crisis that affected the legitimacy of the state, the government and political parties and made it impossible to resume the path of neoliberal adjustment. Accordingly, the government negotiated with creditors to restructure the defaulted public debt and succeeded in exchanging the defaulted bonds for new ones with a considerable reduction of principal of the debt and longer maturities. After two years of tense negotiations, the government cancelled the IMF's assistance program, freeing itself from IMF surveillance and gaining autonomy to carry out expansionary macroeconomic policies and regulations.

The devaluation, the renegotiation of the public debt and the new degree of freedom to carry out macroeconomic policies created conditions for a period of sustained growth. The high exchange rate fuelled a process of import substitution and gave further impulse to exports. Through the imposition of a tax on the exports of primary commodities, the state appropriated part of the foreign exchange windfall. This in turn helped to solve the twin deficit (external and fiscal) that had affected the country during the previous decade of currency overvaluation. The reversal of the decade-long fiscal hardship and the political crisis of the fiscal austerity discourse gave the state a renewed role in subsidizing diverse economic activities and expanding welfare and social security benefits. At the same time, devaluation and the inflationary surge that followed resulted in a sudden reduction of labour costs that, together with a freeze imposed on the prices of public utilities, further reduced domestic production costs.

---

[8] When Eduardo Duhalde was appointed as a provisional president, it was decided that his administration would last until December 2003, but in June 2002 he announced that he would resign by May 2003.

Macro policies and growth

The shift from a free float adopted in early 2002 to a dirty float by mid-2002 was instrumental in stopping the run against the peso and controlling the rising inflation that had followed the devaluation.[9] In turn, the incipient stabilization was central for the economic recovery experienced later in that year. Relative prices were then extremely favourable to tradable goods, a change that coincided with high international prices for Argentinian exports and low international interest rates.

The use of the exchange rate as a key tool to enhance growth would prove successful in a favourable domestic and international context. But in its initial stage, it involved a drastic redistribution of wealth away from some fractions of capital that had been largely privileged during the period of neoliberal reforms (namely banks and public utility operators). More importantly, devaluation also affected workers negatively—a trend that began to be reversed, as we will see below, through the implementation of comprehensive social programs, the promotion of wage increases and the reduction in unemployment.[10] Later, when both domestic and international variables took a turn for the worse, balancing the requirements of the export and import-substituting sectors proved increasingly challenging and, unsurprisingly, exacerbated historical class tensions in the country.

The shift from a free exchange rate regime to a dirty float was part of a broader departure from the blueprint of the 1990s that also included the restructuring of the public debt with a major reduction of the principal of the debt, the end of the IMF's assistance program, the nationalization of several privatized public utilities and the reversal of austerity policies, among other changes. This shift should be understood as the result of the failure of the option to deepen the path of fiscal discipline and liberalization, following IMF requirements, as this course of action, pursued in early 2002, only aggravated instability; this was not due only to the technical shortcomings of policies. In fact, these results only make sense when considered in the socio-political context in which policies were implemented. In the heated political context of 2002-03, social mobilization limited the viability of an orthodox way out of the crisis.

---

[9] In January 2002, the decision to abandon the currency board was accompanied by the adoption of a regulated exchange rate, and the exchange rate between the US dollar and the Argentinian peso was 1 = 1.40. Shortly after, the government adopted a floating exchange rate regime, following an IMF requirement to grant assistance to the country. The price of the dollar grew quickly, reaching its peak by the end of June 2002 (1 = 3.860).

[10] Not only did wages not follow the pace of inflation, but also the prices of some wage goods grew more than the general rate of inflation. During 2002, the CPI grew 41 % while the price of food grew 74.9% (INDEC). The purchasing power of the minimum wage is a clear example of this. In December 2001, the minimum wage covered 45.1% of the standard basket of goods], and in December 2002 it covered only 29.5% (Secretaría de Política Económica).

Between 2003 and 2008, the Argentinian economy experienced unprecedented rates of growth that left five years of uninterrupted recession behind. Exports grew in an international scenario of rising prices and demand for the foodstuffs and agricultural products that constitute the core of the country's exports. Reversing the trend of the 1990s, in which manufacturing lagged behind the growth of the GDP, in the 2000s, manufacturing expanded at a rate above the average (Campos, González and Sacavini 2010, 60). This in turn led to a drastic reduction of unemployment and to moderate wage increments that have alleviated workers' hardship and gradually improved, albeit not uniformly, the purchasing power of some wage earners. This in turn has strengthened domestic consumption and has worked to secure high profits. This virtuous cycle has been instrumental in rebuilding the legitimacy of the state as an essential economic player.

But the recovery has not been free from tensions and contradictions. It was agricultural activities that led the export boom (soybeans, cereals and beef), along with their industrial products. Most of them were produced with little care for the negative social and environmental consequences of population displacement, deforestation, pollution, etc. Likewise, the extensive use of land for export crops increasingly displaced the production of foodstuffs for domestic consumption and made domestic production increasingly unable to meet growing demand.

Furthermore, growth did not reverse the persistently high levels of inequality and precariousness, providing clear evidence of the limits imposed by the structural transformation of the country over the previous decades.

Economic growth and labour: post-convertibility's premises and promises

When the recession reached its lowest point in mid-2002, poverty affected 53% of the population. The recession of the late 1990s and early 2000s compounded with labour market flexibilization and their detrimental consequences for employment levels and the protection of workers' rights explains a large part of the social problems then faced by Argentina. As an emergency response to this situation and to address a highly volatile political moment, then President Duhalde implemented an assistance program titled Program for Unemployed Heads of Households (*Programa Jefes y Jefas de Hogares Desocupados,* PJJHD). It reached 2,000,000 beneficiaries across the country by the end of 2002, but it did not overcome the limitations of previous social programs, namely the extremely low levels of benefits, and it did not provide health care or social security coverage.

This program provided some relief to beneficiaries, but it is the growth of employment resulting from economic reactivation after 2003 and the policies advanced by the Kirchner administration to affect employment and salaries that can account for considerable improvements in poverty indicators since then. In 2002, salaries were severely eroded by currency devaluation and the price increases it prompted. In 2003, salaries reached a historic low, standing at only 54.8 percent of the level in 1970 (Graña and Kennedy 2008). The pattern of wage decline was altered by the intervention of the government through the implementation of presidential decrees granting lump-sum wage increases, and salaries started to grow (Orovitz Sanmartino 2010). Between 2002 and 2005, these across-the-board increases partially offset the effects of inflation and improved the wages of formal workers as well as some sectors among the precariously employed.

Starting in 2004, the evolution of wages began to be more closely connected to the acceleration of growth, the intensification of labour conflicts and the reactivation of collective bargaining between workers and employers with the mediation of the state. This development has given unions a new and critical role in the negotiation of moderate salary increases and has accorded the CGT a renewed political primacy. The main outcome of the reactivation of wage negotiations was the consolidation of a trend toward the improvement of salaries among registered workers, although at a slower pace since 2007, when the contradictions and tensions of the new accumulation pattern became evident. However, the performance of salaries has exhibited significant variation among salaried workers, basically because not all of them can protect their salaries against inflation with the same effectiveness. For salaried workers in general, wages have remained practically stagnant between 2007 and the second trimester of 2010 and have yet to pass the levels reached before the crisis of 2001. The performance of wages for non-registered workers can be inferred from these measures: this sector has seen its income undermined by the effects of inflation (Campos et al. 2009, 5).

In comparing the labour demands that registered workers made through their unions during this period and in the 1990s, it is in fact the focus on wage improvements that has been at the centre of labour conflicts after 2003, as opposed to a concern for the preservation of jobs, which characterized the decade of Convertibility. This focus and, very importantly, the momentous increase in the number of collective agreements that have been negotiated are the key features of developments in labour markets since 2004 (Palomino 2007, 26).

Precarious workers have also benefited from some wage improvement in connection to increments in the legal minimum wage and the rise in salaries, but this has not prevented their wages from remaining lower than the salaries of formal workers (Chitarroni and Cimillo 2007, 7-8) or from falling in real terms as we mention above.

High rates of economic growth since 2003 resulted in a remarkable rate of employment generation and a concomitant reduction of unemployment and underemployment. For the country as a whole, unemployment fell 57 percent between 2002 and 2008 (Panigo and Neffa 2009, 9). Also fundamental was the transformation in the quality of jobs that the economy generated: while during the 1990s only 6% of new jobs were registered, between 2003 and 2008 85% of new jobs satisfied this requirement (ibid., 14). Although the government implemented a number of programs to protect employment during the crisis of 2008, it could not fully prevent the negative impact of the economic slowdown on workers.[11] Nonetheless, by 2010, unemployment began to fall once again, closing the year at 7.3 percent (INDEC). Importantly, however, since 2008 there has been a deceleration in the rate of labour absorption.[12] We shall return to this point in the last section of the chapter.

Social policy has also contributed to addressing some of the most pressing demands of poor sectors, although the decline in unemployment created a new context for the formulation of assistance programs. An estimated 500,000 beneficiaries of the PJJHF have entered the labour market since 2003 (Weisburd Halperin 2007), and the remaining beneficiaries considered employable have been gradually transferred to programs administered by the Ministry of Labour, in particular to a new Employment and Training Insurance program (*Seguro de Capacitación y Empleo).* Other groups of beneficiaries defined as structurally disadvantaged and 'unemployable' were transferred to programs offered by the Ministry of Social Development, the most important being Families for Social Inclusion (*Programa Familias por la Inclusión Social).* Approximately 300,000 former beneficiaries of PJJHD had been transferred to this program by the end of 2007 (Casanova 2008). Families for Social Inclusion forms part of a number of social programs aimed at addressing not the issue of unemployment directly, but rather poverty and social exclusion. In a similar category is the National Program of Food Security (*Programa Nacional de Seguridad Alimentaria*), which reached a total of 1 million families in 2004. While these programs have contributed in various ways to providing assistance to the most vulnerable groups, it was the implementation in 2009 of the Universal Allowance for Children (*Asignación Universal por Hijo*), a child subsidy for families of the unemployed, informally employed or self-employed with salaries below the minimum wage, which has had the greatest impact on raising family income. As with wages, the critical issue in terms of poverty is to prevent inflation from undermining the real value of this child subsidy.

---

[11] These programs consisted of different forms of assisting and rewarding companies that committed to maintaining their staff without firing workers.

[12] In another contrast with the experience of the 1990s, the rate of labour absorption was considerably higher between 2003 and 2008. The decline in the relative cost of labour, the reactivation of some labour-intensive industrial sectors prompted by the devaluation and the high idle capacity that existed by the end of Convertibility are all important variables accounting for the growth of employment and production without a concomitant increase in investment (Campos et al. 2010, 60).

The combined effect of rising employment, improvements in salaries and the implementation of a much more encompassing set of social programs has been to significantly reduce poverty and indigence. But most available statistical data on these issues are conflictive in Argentina because of well-founded questions about the accuracy of official statistics from 2007 on.[13] Nonetheless, it is undeniable that the government's policies in the area of employment and poverty alleviation have rendered positive results. In turn, a reduction in poverty and improvements in the purchasing power of salaries have been instrumental in maintaining the momentum in terms of a pattern of economic growth that once again gives attention to the health of the domestic market. None of this was originally too costly for most employers, as the devaluation dramatically reduced the wage bill.

Unfortunately, poverty remains very high, and that this continues to be the case is, as it was in the 1990s, related in a number of ways to the performance of labour markets. In particular, the very high incidence of precarious work, in all its forms, is at the core of the problem. To fight informality, the government has concentrated its efforts on simplifying the procedures for registering workers, on implementing a tax moratorium for employers that registered their workers and on intensifying audits. There has also been a sustained commitment to increasing the ability to enforce compliance with labour legislation. These policies have been effective for unregistered workers within formal firms. However, many other precarious workers, who form segments of the informal sector, remain trapped in situations of vulnerability. They are part of the growing number of very small companies, family firms and self-employed workers linked to larger firms in the formal sector through the outsourcing of activities (Gioza Zuazúa 2007, 332-334). Thus, although 85 percent of the jobs created between 2003 and 2008 were registered formally, precarious workers still represent 36.5 percent of the workforce (Orovitz Sanmartino 2010). This figure is still considerably higher than the level in 1991, when informal workers represented 30 percent of the workforce, which was already a major increase from the 19 percent in 1980 (Chitarroni and Cimillo 2007, 6).

The shades of the light at the end of tunnel:

The case of Argentina makes explicit the limited ability of economic growth by itself to address the problem of precarious work. Improvements in the rate of registered work have been the result of a number of new regulations that both sanction the evasion of labour legislation and facilitate the registration of workers as required by law. Notwithstanding these positive changes, precariousness has remained an intractable problem. As can only be imagined, explanations for this pre-

[13] See below.

dicament cover a broad range of theoretical and political stands. According to some, the key variable is time. Simply stated, the issue is that policies implemented to correct the problem will eventually reduce precariousness to more manageable levels. The benchmark to assess what these levels should be is not all that clear; however, given Argentina's track record of social inclusion, a return to figures from the mid-1970s would be a very good start. The key point is that in this understanding of the problem, the very dynamic of the new developmentalism in the country will generate the conditions for the consolidation, again, of an integrated labour market. There are some merits to this view, particularly because the consistent and remarkable improvements for a large segment of workers in Argentina since 2003 are undeniable. As we have suggested, though, the recovery of levels of employment, real salaries and the reduction of precarious work appears to have reached a plateau since 2007, prior to the effect of the world crisis on domestic economic activity. Also, state intervention aimed at guaranteeing some minimum income even to the most marginalized groups among the poor has contributed to bolstering the power of labour to resist the pressure to accept ever degrading working conditions. It is very likely, as some critics suggest, that more could have been done. However, it is extremely unlikely that, as representatives of concentrated capital protest, the labour policies the government has employed in the post-Convertibility period have undermined the country's growth potential and sustainability.

As we say above, the virtuous cycle initiated by the combination of agricultural and agro-industrial exports and import substitution has not been free from tensions. First, as unemployment fell, workers' strength to demand wage improvements grew. Second, the state has made increasing efforts to maintain the competitiveness of the exchange rate eroded by the same trade surplus that the exchange regime had helped to build. To intervene in the exchange market without running into debt or increasing the monetary supply, it had to maintain strict fiscal discipline. What was at stake was the dispute for the appropriation of wealth on the part of actors whose bargaining position has been strengthened by the new prosperity. Especially, growing workers' demands threatened the extraordinary profits accumulated after 2003. The result of this dispute was an acceleration of inflation and a cycle of inflationary struggles that gradually eroded the competitive advantages of the high real exchange rate.

Starting in 2006, the economic authorities attempted to regulate prices and to negotiate price truces with business, with only partial and short-term results. By 2007, the positive effects of the competitive exchange rate showed the first signs of exhaustion. Moreover, as inflation accelerated, the exchange rate started to be used as an anti-inflationary anchor (Campos, González and Sacavini 2010, 67). When price agreements showed their limitations, the *Instituto Nacional de Estadísticas y Censos* (INDEC, National Institute for Statistics and Censuses) changed its methods to measure inflation in a way that has seriously damaged the reliability of official statistics. Speculation about the actual figures has become a central axis of political conflict. It may also have helped to increase inflationary expectations and has resulted especially problematic in processes of collective bargaining. In addition, the acceleration of inflation strengthened arguments about the need to 'cool down the economy' made by economists and politicians.

In March 2008, the government made the decision to introduce a sliding-scale tax for the export of soybeans and sunflower seeds that would fluctuate along with changes in international prices. Its purpose was to de-link the domestic prices of foodstuffs from the unprecedentedly high international prices of export crops and transfer to the state part of the extraordinary rents accrued to agricultural producers because of the fertility of Argentinian soil and high international prices. This, in turn, was expected to alleviate inflationary pressures and create incentives for farmers to switch from export crops to staple foods. Instead, the immediate response from the four main landowner organizations of the country was a lockout that lasted more than three months, produced serious difficulties in the supply of food and triggered additional price rises. After widespread protests that managed to gather broad social support from both rural and urban groups, the government sought congressional support for its tax reform. The proposal was defeated, and the project was left aside. From then on, the task to control the rise of the prices of foodstuffs became much more difficult. In addition, the political consequences of this conflict outlived the proposal, as the rebellion strengthened and unified political, economic and social actors strongly opposed to a government they saw as populist, authoritarian and irresponsible. This coalition gathered groups with very diverse and even contradictory interests, which have so far been unable to offer an alternative to the development strategy of the government. Nonetheless, they have been effective in challenging the anti-neoliberal consensus of the immediate post-crisis period, bringing arguments about fiscal indiscipline, market confidence and the distortive intervention of the state back into the public arena and political debate. The defeat of the incumbent party in the mid-term election of 2009 was a clear indication of this shift.

The crisis raised to the second power

While this domestic crisis was unfolding, the effects of the global crisis were also felt in the country. The latter did not translate into financial shortages for the state—as had been the case in the international crises of the 1980s and 1990s—because access to voluntary credit markets was already restricted due to the default. More importantly, the reduction of the public debt burden and the taxes on exports have helped to reverse long-term budgetary deficits and have made the state less dependent on external borrowing. The crisis manifested itself in a sudden deceleration of growth, falling exports, rising unemployment and deteriorating state revenues. 2009 put a temporary stop to the high rates of GDP growth in an economy with some worrying signs since 2007. On the other hand, the fall of the international prices of Argentinian exports combined with the deceleration of growth resulted in a temporary reduction of inflation.

During this critical juncture, economic policies followed increasingly contradictory paths. On the one hand, a number of policies seemed to be oriented by concerns about reintegrating the country into international finance and regaining access to external borrowing. Accordingly, the government let the exchange rate fall and announced its intention to negotiate with the Paris Club and the holdouts of the 2005 restructuring of the public debt, to give a definitive closure to the default. On the other hand, some decisions have deepened the challenges to 'pro-market orthodoxy', generating irate criticism from economists and politicians that warn about the consequences of violating 'market imperatives'. Thus, facing a less favourable international scenario, the government also made the decision to annul the independence of the Central Bank with the immediate goal of using the international reserves—rather than new borrowing—to service the public debt. The debate led to the institution of new forms of coordination between the economic authorities and the Central Bank and new growth-related goals assigned to the latter. Also, pension funds that had been partially privatized in 1994 were nationalized in 2008.

Conclusion: tension, contradictions and new options

As we have suggested, 2007 marks a point of inflection in the trajectory of the country. Also since that year—first because of the global slowdown and its impact on the country but also because of deeper structural conditions—there have been some noteworthy transformations in the performance of key variables in labour markets. Although registered employment continued to show substantial rates of growth, since 2007—that is, before the effects of the world crisis reached the country late in 2008—it did so at a slower rate, from 12 percent at its most dynamic point in the last quarter of 2004 to 6.8 percent in the second quarter of 2008 (Campos et al. 2009, 6).[14] The change in the rate of employment growth was more accentuated in the industrial sector and less so in services (ibid., 6-7). The tendency we are identifying here is evident in the strong recovery of 2010, when the economy grew at a very robust 9.2 percent but was not sufficient to reverse the low dynamism in new employment generation.[15]

---

[14] During this period, registered work has also grown faster than employment, a fact that can be explained by noting that some of the formal jobs were not new but rather conversions from non-registered positions.

[15] The growing gap between GDP and employment growth might be overestimated because of the under-estimation of the inflation rate in official statistics.

The significant reduction in non-registered work we identify above has also slowed since 2007. The tendency has continued to be toward the creation of better quality work, but the reduction in the incidence of precariousness has become substantially smaller: 0.2 percent down in the third quarter of 2010 from its level in 2009 and only 0.5% over the two years. Moreover, workers in this segment of the labour market have also been structurally limited in their ability to protect their income against inflation. Thus, the dispersion in incomes within the working class is also a problem that remains to be solved.

The pattern of accumulation taking shape since 2003 is dependent on a modern agri-business sector to procure the hard currency that made possible the sustainability of both state spending and an industrial sector mostly geared toward the domestic market. In many ways, this pattern mirrors the structural contradictions of the import-substituting model but now under a more open and globally integrated national economy. The unifying factor among these dissenting capitalist interests is the concern about labour costs and state spending.

The persistent fragmentation of the working class is one of the key characteristics in this development experience. The rapid pace of economic growth since 2003 has not sufficed to reverse this fragmentation. On the contrary, informality and precariousness have outlasted the neoliberal policies and economic context in which they grew exponentially. In this sense, it is reasonable to conclude that the fragmentation of labour markets is a structural feature of the country today, whose resolution lies beyond the confines of Argentina's current economic strategy.

References:

Bisio, Raúl, Osvaldo Battistini and Juan Montes Cató. "Transformaciones de la negociación colectiva durante la vigencia de gobiernos constitucionales a partir de 1973." In *Política y relaciones laborales en la transición democrática argentina,* edited by Arturo Fernández and Raúl Bisio, 135-179. Buenos Aires: Lumen/Humanitas, 1999.

Campos, Luis, Ana Laura Fernandez, Mariana González, Federico Marongiu, and Marcela Sacavini. *La situación de los trabajadores en argentina frente a la crisis económica actual*. Working Paper N° 11, Buenos Aires: Centro de Estudios para el Desarrollo Argentino (CENDA), September 2009.

Campos, Luis, Mariana González and Marcela Sacavini. "El mercado de trabajo en los distintos patrones de crecimiento." *Realidad Económica*, no. 253 (Jul-Aug 15 2010).

Casanova, Luis. "Informe sobre los programas de empleo provinciales 2007." Working paper. Buenos Aires, Dirección de Análisis de Gasto Público y

Programas Sociales. Secretaría de Programación Económica. Ministerio de Economía y Producción, October 2008. http://www.mecon.gov.ar/peconomica/basehome/programas_empleo2007.pdf

Centro de Estudios Legales y Sociales (CELS). *El estado frente a la protesta social: 1996-2002*. Buenos Aires: Siglo XXI Editores, 2003.

Chitarroni, Horacio and Elsa Cimillo. "¿Resurge el sujeto histórico?: cambios en el colectivo del trabajo asalariado: 1974-2006." *Lavboratorio. Estudios sobre Cambio Estructura y Desigualdad Social* 9, no. 21 (2007): 5-11.

Cufré, David and Alfredo Zaiat. "Trabajamos para sacar a la economía del riesgo de híper." *Página 12*, May 5, 2002. Accessed June 13, 2010. http://www.pagina12.com.ar/diario/economia/2-4762-2002-05-05.html.

Delpech, Cecilia, Marita Gonzalez, Berta Horen, Juan Antonio Labiaguerre, Guillermo Muller, Jose Villadeamigo, and Leopoldo Weisburd Halperin. "*Políticas Sociales en la Argentina. Entre la ciudadanía plena y el asistencialismo focalizado en la contención del pauperismo*." Buenos Aires: CEPED, 2007.

Dirección Nacional de Programación Macroeconómica. *Información Económica al Día. Empleo e Ingresos. Información General*. Buenos Aires, Ministerio de Economía y Finanzas Públicas. Accessed March 9, 2011. http://www.mecon.gov.ar/peconomica/basehome/infoeco.html

Giarraca, Norma, Miguel Teubal and Tomás Palmisano. "Paro agrario: crónica de un conflicto alargado." *Realidad Económica*, no. 237 (July 1-Aug 15 2008): 33-54.

Gioza Zuazúa, Noemí. "Transformaciones y tendencias del mercado de empleo en la Argentina. Entre el desempleo y el empleo precario." In *Transformaciones recientes en la economía argentina. Tendencias y perspectivas*, edited by Karina Forcinito and Victoria Basualdo. Buenos Aires: Prometeo, 2007.

González, Mariana. "Transformaciones de hecho y de derecho en las relaciones laborales en los 90." In *Entre el Trabajo y la Política. Las Reformas de las Políticas Sociales Argentinas en Perspectiva Comparada*, edited by Javier Lindenboim and Claudia Danani, 89-104. Buenos Aires: Biblios, 2003.

Graña, Juan and Damián Kennedy. *Salario real, costo laboral y productividad, Argentina 1947-2006. Análisis de la información y metodología de estimación*. Buenos Aires: Centro de Estudios sobre Población, Empleo y Desarrollo (CEPED), 2008.

Leiva, Fernando. *Latin American Neostructuralism: The Contradictions of Post-Neoliberal Development*. Minneapolis and London: University of Minnesota Press, 2008.

Lindenboim, Javier. "El mercado de trabajo en la Argentina en la transición secular: cada vez menos y peores empleos." In *Entre el Trabajo y la Política. Las Reformas de las Políticas Sociales Argentinas en Perspectiva*

Comparada, edited by Javier Lindenboim and C. Danani, 57-85. Buenos Aires: Biblios, 2003.

Lo Vuolo, Rubén, Alberto Barbeito, Laura Pautassi and Corina Rodríguez. *La pobreza… de la política contra la pobreza*. Buenos Aires-Madrid: Miño y Dávila Editores, 1999.

Marshall, Adriana. *Labour market policies and regulations in Argentina, Brazil and Mexico: Programmes and impacts*. International Labour Organization, 2004. Accessed March 12, 2011. http://www.ilo.org/public/english/employment/strat/download/esp13.pdf

Neffa, Julio César. "El trabajo no registrado como modalidad límite de precariedad." In *La corrosión del trabajo: Estudios sobre informalidad y precariedad laboral*, edited by Mariana Busso and Pablo Pérez, 55-77. Buenos Aires: Miño y Dávila, 2010.

Novick, Marta, Ximena Mazorra and Diego Schleser. "Un nuevo esquema de políticas públicas para la reducción de la informalidad laboral." In *Aportes a una nueva visión de la informalidad laboral en la Argentina*, edited by Ministerio de Trabajo, Empleo y Seguridad Social, 23-42. Buenos Aires: Banco Mundial, 2008.

Observatorio de la Deuda Social. *Deudas y progresos sociales en un país que hace frente a su bicentenario. Argentina: 2004-2010*. Buenos Aires: Universidad Católica Argentina, 2009.

Olmedo, Carla and Martin J. Murray. "The Formalization of Informal/Precarious Labor in Contemporary Argentina." *International Sociology* 17, no.3 (2002): 421-443.

Orovitz Sanmartino, Jorge. "Crisis, acumulación y forma de estado en la Argentina post-neoliberal." *Cuestiones de Sociología* (2010): 5-6.

Palomino, Héctor et al. "De la protesta social al conflicto sindical." Paper presented at First International Conference on Labour Relations, Buenos Aires, 2007.

Panigo, Demian and Julio César Neffa. "El mercado de trabajo argentino en el nuevo modelo de desarrollo." Working Paper, Dirección Nacional de Programación Macroeconómica Dirección de Modelos y Proyecciones, Ministerio de Economía, República Argentina, 2009. http://www.econ.uba.ar/www/institutos/economia/Ceped/publicaciones/cuadernosceped/Cuaderno10_CEPED.pdf

The Future of China: Crisis and Class Struggle

Minqi Li

China has overtaken Japan to become the worlds' second largest economy and measured by purchasing power parity, China may overtake the US to become the world's largest economy in a few years. The future of China is thus one of the most important determinants that will help to shape the direction of global transformation in the 21st century.

This chapter argues that in the coming decades, China is likely to face insurmountable economic, social, and ecological crisis. The combination of these crises will lead to the breakdown of China's existing social structure and possibly pave the way for a new Chinese revolution. Given China's significance, a new Chinese revolution could significantly influence the global balance of class power, and possibly turn it to the favor of the global working classes.

China and the Semi-Periphery

Back to the early 19th century, China remained the world's largest economy. The relative gap between China and the advanced capitalist countries in term of per capita income was about 2 to 1. After the Opium War, China was forcibly incorporated into the capitalist world system. After a century of imperialist invasions and civil wars, by the mid-20th century, China was reduced to one of the poorest countries in the world. The income gap between China and the most advanced western country (the United States) widened to about 20 to 1. The gap between China and the advanced capitalist countries started to narrow in the late 20th century. By the early 2000s, the income gap between China and the United States narrowed to less than 10 to 1 (Maddison 2003).

What could these dramatic turns in the relative historical fortunes of China and the West tell us about the long-term historical trajectory of the capitalist world system? Until recently (the late 20th century), there had been a long-term tendency for inter-state income inequality to widen in the capitalist world system. With the economic rise of China and India, this long-term tendency seems to have been reversed. Is this reversal good or bad for the future of the capitalist world system?[1]

According to the conventional wisdom, a system with a large middle layer should contribute to the system's stability. This argument, however, is in contradiction with both historical evidence and careful theoretical reasoning. After all, all the long-lasting historical class systems were based on highly unequal, pyramid like class structures. That is, those at the social "bottom" tended to make up the great majority of the population. This should not be surprising. A necessary condition for any class system to exist and function is to have economic surplus concentrated in the hands of a small group of elites.

In a capitalist world system, world surplus value needs to be concentrated in a small number of states (the core states). This concentration is necessary to maintain high profits in the "leading industries" (that is, the monopolistic industries). The large profits in the leading industries provide incentives for the core states to make large capital investment, which in turn serves as the driving engine for global capital accumulation.

Thus, as a first approximation, the capitalist world system is divided between the core and the periphery. The core states are politically and militarily strong and specialize in high profit, high wage, and monopolistic economic activities. The peripheral states are politically and militarily weak and specialize in low profit, low wage, and highly competitive economic activities.[2]

In the actual historical evolution of the capitalist world system, there has been a third layer or the "middle layer" of states between the core and the periphery,

---

[1] China and India are the two most dramatic cases of economic rise, with a combined share of 40 percent of the world population. But as is to be explained below, the rise of China and India has been a part of the general rise of the semi-periphery of the capitalist world system, including China, India, Brazil, Russia, and many commodities exporters.

[2] Because the world surplus value is concentrated in the core, the core states could use some of the surplus value to maintain internal political and social stability, creating a comparatively large "middle class" (in Lenin's analysis, the imperialist states could use the "super profits" from colonies to buy off the labor aristocracies, see Lenin 1916). This in turn leads to misconception that a large middle layer is consistent with political and social stability. But at the world system level, the so-called middle classes in the core states belong to a privileged minority.

known as the "semi-periphery". What is the semi-periphery about and what has been its function in the normal operation of the capitalist world system?

In economic terms, while the surplus value produced by a peripheral state is mostly transferred to the core (reflected by the very income gap between the periphery and the core), a semi-peripheral state is able to retain roughly the same amount of surplus value as it produces (thus the income level of a semi-peripheral state is roughly around the world average).

As the semi-periphery receives a significant portion of the world surplus value, it has some stake in the system. The semi-peripheral states thus tend to play by the rule of the system (mainly by promoting world-wide capital accumulation). This helps to undermine a possible political rebellion by the unified periphery.[3]

Historically, the semi-periphery tended to be a minority of the global population. In the 20th century, the core, the semi-periphery, and the periphery roughly accounted for one-fifth, one-fifth, and two-thirds of the world population respectively. The limited size of the semi-periphery made it possible for the bulk of the world surplus value to be concentrated in the core. Moreover, the low levels of material consumption of the great majority of the global population helped to alleviate the pressure on the global ecological system.

However, with the economic rise of China and India, these conditions have been or will be dramatically changed. In the early 21st century, the current and potential semi-peripheral states include (but not limited to) China, India, much of Southeast Asia, much of Latin America, the Middle East oil exporters, South Africa, Russia, and Eastern Europe. These countries represent roughly two-thirds of the world population and currently about two-fifths of the world GDP. Under the current trend, it will not take much longer before the combined share of the semi-periphery in the world GDP exceeds 50 percent.

For the capitalist world system, this represents a fundamentally destabilizing transformation. First of all, with about two-thirds of the world population in the semi-periphery, what remains of the periphery? How could the much reduced periphery provide the necessary surplus value to sustain both the core and the much expanded semi-periphery?

Secondly, with global political power now dispersed between a large number of core and semi-peripheral states, it becomes much more difficult to undertake system-level coordination to solve system-level problems. The system thus faces the

---

[3] For more discussions on the core, the periphery, and the semi-periphery in the capitalist world system, see Wallerstein (1979, 18-23; 69-72).

prospect to sink into permanent chaos where every state pursues its own short-term national interest at the expense of the system as a whole.[4]

Thirdly, as the general population of the semi-periphery demands a much higher level of material consumption, the pressure imposed by the capitalist world system on the global ecological system will become unbearable, leading to global ecological collapse.

The economic rise of China, thus, is part of the world historical process of the expansion of the semi-periphery and the economic, political, and ecological contradictions of the Chinese capitalism are a part of the current structural crisis of the capitalist world system.

But why was the long-term tendency towards inter-state inequality reversed and how has the internal logic of the capitalist world system led to the great expansion of the semi-periphery?

The Chinese Model

As capitalist development proceeds, there has been a historical tendency for both wage costs and ecological costs to rise over time. With capitalist development, a growing proportion of the labor force is transformed into proletarianized working class living in the cities. The proletarianized working class is much more likely to organize for economic and political struggles. These struggles have forced the capitalist class to make concessions at different historical stages, leading to rising wages as well as growing government spending on socialized forms of labor power reproduction (such as healthcare, education, unemployment benefits, and pensions).

Moreover, capitalist accumulation requires consumption of material resources and generation of material wastes on increasingly larger scales. The demand of accumulation is in fundamental conflict with the inherent limits of the earth's eco-

[4] Related to this argument, historically the effective functioning of the capitalist world system has required the leadership of a hegemonic power, such as the Dutch hegemonic power in the 17th century, the British hegemonic power in the 19th century, and the US hegemonic power in the 20th century. However, by the early 21st century, as the US power is in decline, none of the other major powers (including China) is in a position to replace the US to serve as the next hegemonic power. On the one hand, none of the major powers is likely to establish overwhelming advantages over the other powers in industrial, financial, and military powers, which would be required for the rise of a hegemonic power. The inherent conflicts between nation-states rule out the possibility of a stable, enduring alliance of several big states to function effectively as a "co-operative" hegemonic power and if such an alliance does form, it could be so powerful that it turns itself into a world empire or a world government, leading to the end of the capitalist dynamics. For more detailed arguments, see (Li 2009, 113-138).

logical systems. With the depletion of resources and environmental degradation, either the capitalist class would have to spend a growing amount of financial resources to clean up the environment, or the rising costs of resources and deterioration of environmental conditions would impose limits on accumulation.

Historically, the capitalist world system has responded to the pressure of rising wage and ecological costs through geographic expansion and geographic relocation. As the core states suffer from declining profit rates and the old monopolistic industries no longer generate high profits, the core state's capital needs to move out of the old monopolistic industries and into certain new "leading" sectors, recreating conditions of monopoly and high profits.

The old industries, however, need to be relocated somewhere. It is the semi-peripheral states that have served as the "reserve army of states for global capital relocation". With lower labor costs and minimal environmental regulation, industries that are no longer profitable in the core states could generate an acceptable level of profit in the semi-periphery. On the other hand, compared to the peripheral states, the semi-peripheral states are more effective and could provide the necessary physical and social infrastructure for capital accumulation.

China was the major beneficiary of the last round of global capital relocation. In the 1960s, all the core states were faced with growing working class militancy and falling profit rates. In response, the western capitalist classes undertook a counter offensive led by Thatcher and Reagan. In the neoliberal era, capital was relocated from the West to the rest of the world with lower labor and regulation costs.

After the 1976 counter-revolutionary coup, the Chinese bureaucratic capitalist class consolidated political power. The Chinese ruling class dismantled the rural people's communes. The agricultural privatization created a pool of hundreds of millions of workers that formed the world's largest reserve army of cheap labor force. This pool of reserve army of cheap labor force not only provided the basis for the rapid expansion of capitalist production in China but also helped to undermine the global working class's bargaining power, contributing to global profit rate recovery.[5]

---

[5] It is well known to students in Marxism that by maintaining a reserve army of labor (a pool of labor force that is unemployed or underemployed), capitalists could use the threat of unemployment to discipline the employed labor force, forcing them to accept lower wages and increase labor productivity, so that to maintain certain profit rates. At the global level, by relocating capital to the periphery and semi-periphery where the wages are generally much lower than the core, the core capitalists could exploit the so-called "thereat effect," forcing the core working classes to accept lower wages and worse working conditions as well as weakening the unions. China, with its huge demographic size and comparatively very low wages relative to the core wages,

The contradiction between the production of surplus value and the "realization" of surplus value is one of the permanent contradictions of the capitalist mode of production. High rate of exploitation allows the capitalists to have high profit rate and sustain rapid pace of accumulation. However, under certain conditions, excessive exploitation, by undermining the working class bargaining power, reduces the "effective demand" that would be required for the normal operation of capitalist economy. If the capitalist market fails to expand as rapidly as the capitalist production, overwhelmed by overproduction, the capitalist economy could sink into crisis or prolonged stagnation.

For the Chinese capitalism, this contradiction has been "solved" through the absorption of its very large surplus value through exports and investment. Before the 2009 Great Recession, investment accounts for about 45 percent, net exports about 10 percent, and the total exports about 40 percent of China's GDP. By comparison, household consumption was only about 35 percent of GDP, reflecting the depressed purchasing power of the Chinese working people.[6]

For China to run large trade surpluses, some other big economy has to run large trade deficits. Indeed, before the 2009 crisis, the US has been running large trade deficits, absorbing exports from China and other economies that pursued export-led growth (such Germany, Japan, South Korea, and Southeast Asian countries).

With the burst of the US housing bubble, this pattern of growth collapsed. For the moment, the US government is running large fiscal deficits, keeping the economy afloat. Both the US and the Euro-zone will struggle with stagnation in the next few years. As the government debt-GDP ratios keep rising in the core states, the core states may face a major fiscal crisis in the not too distant future. In this case, China can no longer rely upon exports as one of the two leading engines of economic growth.

Could the future Chinese economic growth continue to be led by investment? Investment is already about 50 percent of China's GDP. Excessive investment leads to excess production capacity and potentially devastating nonperforming loans in the banking sector. More importantly, very high investment in fixed assets requires the consumption of massive amounts of energy and mineral resources, deepening the ecological crisis in both China and the world.

From a social reformist point of view, this is the time for China to pursue income redistribution. If a portion of the national income can be redistributed from the capitalists to the workers (but leaving enough for the capitalists to make large

---

offers an ideal site for global capital relocation that could provide an almost inexhaustible cheap labor force within a certain historical period. In this way, China had played a decisive role in undermining the global working class's bargaining power in the neoliberal era.

[6] China's macroeconomic data are from National Bureau of Statistics (2009).

profits and pursue rapid capital accumulation), it may be possible for the Chinese economy to be restructured to be led by working class consumption. Indeed, the western core states had undertaken a similar restructuring after the Second World War, paving the way for the so-called "golden age" of capitalism.

If China's trade surplus were to be replaced by balanced trade and investment falls to a more sustainable level of 35 percent of GDP, then the working class consumption should rise by 20 percent of GDP. This would require either the working class income or government spending on social programs rise relative to GDP by a similar magnitude. But will the Chinese capitalist class accept a redistribution from capital to labor on the order of 20 percent of GDP?

The Logic of Class Struggle

How did China turn from a revolutionary socialist state in the 1960s and 1970s into a major pillar of global capitalism today? After the counter-revolutionary coup in 1976 (when radical Maoist leaders were arrested), the emerging bureaucratic capitalist class took over and consolidated the political power.

In the 1980s, the state sector working class continued to enjoy many of the socialist rights and remained strong at the factory level. Instead of organizing a direct, frontal attack on the working class which would be politically costly and might not succeed, the Chinese bureaucratic capitalist class adopted a strategy of "surrounding the cities with the countryside".

China's "economic reform" started with the privatization of the agriculture. With the dismantling of the collective people's communes, hundreds of millions of "surplus workers" in the rural areas were made available for capitalist exploitation. Foreign and domestic capitalist enterprises grew explosively, profiting from China's cheap labor force, low taxes, and lack of social and environmental regulations.

By the 1990s, the capitalist sector has overtaken the state sector to become the dominant economic force. The Chinese government was ready to push for massive privatization in the cities. Tens of millions of state workers were laid off. Those who were employed were deprived of the remaining socialist protection.

However, the very success of the Chinese capitalism has prepared the conditions for its eventual downfall. First of all, the state sector working class (including the laid off state sector workers) has developed political experience in both the socialist period and the capitalist period. This rich historical experience has contributed to a dramatic increase in class consciousness and organizational capacity among China's state sector workers. In recent years, the state sector workers have organized many anti-privatization struggles and many are led by activists influenced by Marxist-Leninist-Maoist ideas.

By contrast, the migrant working class (the workers who have their origin in the countryside and work in the new capitalist sector) remains politically inexperienced. However, in recent years, the migrant workers have also developed the consciousness to demand more economic and social rights (not yet political rights or socialism). As China's capitalist accumulation continues to deplete the rural surplus labor force and a new generation of the migrant workers increasingly consider themselves as "workers" rather than "peasants", the objective balance of power will increasingly shift to the favor of the working class, encouraging the migrant workers to get organized fighting for economic and social rights.

In addition, under the capitalist development, many among the petty bourgeoisie (or the urban "middle class") have also suffered from declining living standards. Many cannot afford to buy an apartment in the cities. College graduates cannot find jobs and have to live in slum-like conditions. The proletarianization of the petty bourgeoisie has contributed to the rise of the intellectual left in China. A growing number of young people have turned into Marxist-Leninist-Maoists.

The future of China depends on whether political unity can be developed between the state sector workers, the migrant workers, and the proletarianized petty bourgeoisie. If such a unity does take shape, it will become a political force that the Chinese capitalist class cannot defeat.

Is it conceivable that the Chinese capitalist class could undertake certain social reforms to accommodate the rising class tensions and redirect the Chinese capitalism onto a more "sustainable" path? Over the past few years, the Hu Jintao-Wen Jiabao administration has been talking about building a so-called "harmonious society" with less inequality. In reality, despite some minor policy adjustments, economic and social inequality has continued to widen. For several reasons, meaningful social reform is unlikely to be achieved.

First of all, much of the Chinese capitalist wealth has its origin in the theft of state and collective assets left from the socialist era. The entire ruling class is thoroughly corrupt and at the local level, political power increasingly rests upon cooperation with local mafias. In this context, the central government has little ability to discipline the ruling class. Even if the central government cares about the long-term sustainability of capitalism, it does not have the ability or will to force any significant capitalist group to make major concessions.

Secondly, despite the rapid growth of the Chinese economy, China has failed to make inroads into the truly high value added segments of the global commodity chains. China now relies upon foreign capital for almost all key technological areas in industry. Without access to the monopolistic profits associated with the high value added activities, the Chinese capitalism will have to rely upon cheap labor force to maintain its global "competitive advantage". In the future, as the Chinese working class gets organized and demands a growing range of rights, the Chinese capitalism will no longer be able to maintain social stability without undermining capitalist accumulation.[7]

Thirdly, and potentially the most important, both the Chinese capitalist accumulation and the global capitalist accumulation have rested upon the relentless exploitation of the environment. As the global ecological system approaches total collapse, any further expansion of capitalism is now in fundamental conflict with the long-term survival of the humanity.[8]

China and Peak Oil

In the neoliberal era, global capitalist classes organized a general attack on the economic and social rights won by the working classes in the previous decades. Moreover, with financial deregulation and liberalized flows of capital across national borders, virtually all national governments are under pressure to lower costs for capital accumulation. This has led to a global "race to the bottom" in term of wage costs as well as social and environmental regulations.

While depressed working class income helps to improve national capitalist "competitive advantages" in the global market, the general depression of the global working class income undermines global effective demand. The situation potentially leads to global economic stagnation and destructive financial crises.

In this context, many national economies (China, Japan, Germany, South Korea, Southeast Asia, and to a less extent, India and Latin America) have relied upon exports to overcome the limits of insufficient internal demand to sustain economic growth. Before the Great Recession of 2009, it was the US private consumption that had helped to absorb the exports from the rest of the world and led the expansion of the global effective demand.

Since then, the US households have been forced to reduce spending, increase saving, and repair their own balance sheets. The global economy currently relies upon two pillars. On the one hand, the US economy is still running a significant trade deficit (about 3 percent of US GDP). As the US private sector has turned

---

[7] On how China has failed to rise to the technology frontier, see Hart-Landsberg (2010).

[8] It may be argued that capitalism could over come the ecological limits through technical innovation. I believe that it is beyond the practical technical possibility to simultaneously achieve ecological sustainability and endless capital accumulation. For detailed arguments against the technical solutions to ecological crisis, see Li (2008; 2011).

into a net saver, the US now relies upon a very large fiscal deficit (about 10 percent of GDP) to sustain economic recovery.

On the other hand, while China continues to run a large trade surplus against the US, China increasingly depends on investment as the sole driving engine for its economic growth. China's investment in turn generates large amounts of demand for energy, raw materials, and capital goods for the rest of the world. This situation is inherently unstable.

From 2005 to 2008, despite surging oil price, world oil production had failed to grow rapidly in response to world oil demand. The current evidence suggests that world oil production is likely to peak in the near future and start to decline in a few years. Thus, from now to about 2015, in practical terms there will be little growth in world oil supply.[9]

On the other hand, the oil demand from China, India, and other so-called "emerging markets" is likely to continue growing rapidly. If the daily oil consumption by China and India grows by one million barrels a year from now to 2015, then by 2015 there will be a cumulative increase in oil demand of five million barrels, equaling about one quarter of the current US oil consumption.

With global oil supply staying flat, where will the extra five million barrels of oil come from? It seems that the extra oil consumption in China and India will have to be at the expense of western countries. By comparison, from 2007 to 2009, as a result of the deepest economic crisis in the postwar history, the daily oil consumption in OECD (Organisation of Economic Co-operation and Development) countries declined by about four million barrels.[10]

Thus, quite likely, the surging oil demand from China and India against the background of peak world oil production will lead to another major surge of oil price. This, in combination with the long-term fiscal crisis that is now confronting virtually every western country, will send the entire western world into another major economic crisis, around 2015.

As the western economies struggle with persistent stagnation and successive economic crises, China and export-led economies will lose their main export markets. As China's imports continue to grow (given its demand for energy, raw materials, and advanced capital goods) but its export markets stagnate or shrink, China could run increasingly large trade deficits after 2015.

Given the current pace of oil demand growth, China's daily oil consumption will increase to 15 million barrels by 2020 and daily imports will rise to 10 million

---

[9] For theory and empirical evidence of peak oil, see Campbell (2005) and Mckillop (2005).
[10] Data for world oil consumption are from BP (2010).

barrels. Assume a likely future oil price of 200 dollars a barrel, China's annual oil imports will cost more than 700 billion dollars. Unlike the United States, China does not have a globally accepted reserve currency and cannot finance its trade deficit by printing money. Once China's foreign exchange reserves are depleted, China will have to face either a dramatic slowdown in economic growth or a major economic crisis. Either way, it could trigger a major social crisis or revolution.

China and Climate Change

An international scientific consensus has been established that, fossil fuels consumption from human economic activities has been the primary factor that is responsible for the emissions of greenhouse gases which have in turn contributed to global warming (IPCC 2007a).

The global average temperature is currently about 0.8°C higher than the pre-industrial level. If global warming (relative to the pre-industrial temperature) reaches 2°C, then much of the world will suffer from widespread drought and up to 40 percent of the plant and animal species could go extinct. Moreover, certain climate "tipping points" may be reached so that the earth's oceans and terrestrial ecological systems could enter into carbon feedbacks that would release more greenhouse gases, leading to run away global warming. For this reason, scientists now consider 2°C warming as the upper limit, beyond which the worst climate catastrophes may not be prevented.

If global warming reaches 3°C, then the world will become nearly ice free, global sea level could rise by 25 meters, and the world's rainforests are likely to be destroyed. If the atmospheric concentration of carbon dioxide rises above 500 parts per million (ppm), then the Algae in the oceans may start to fail, leading to a further jump of global temperature by several degrees. In that event, only a few pockets of the world's land surfaces may remain suitable for human inhabitation and the human civilization as we know it will practically cease to exist (Spratt and Sutton 2008).

Table 1 compares the alternative scenarios of global warming and the corresponding levels of carbon dioxide emissions. According to the Intergovernmental Panel on Climate Change, to prevent global warming by more than 2°C, it is necessary to stabilize the atmospheric concentration of carbon dioxide and other long-lived greenhouse gases at below 450 ppm of carbon dioxide equivalent. After making allowances for non-carbon dioxide greenhouse gases, the atmospheric concentration of carbon dioxide needs to stabilize at below 350 ppm. This in turn requires global cumulative emissions of carbon dioxide over the 21st century to be no more than one trillion metric tons.

Currently, land use changes (mainly deforestation) result in emissions of carbon dioxide of about six billion metric tons a year. Assuming that over the 21st century, the average annual emissions from deforestation may be reduced to about half of the current level, the total emissions from deforestation would amount to 300 billion metric tons over the century. This leaves a "budget" of 700 billion metric tons for the cumulative emissions from fossil fuels consumption.

From 2000 to 2009, about 300 billion metric tons of carbon dioxide had already been emitted due to fossil fuels consumption, leaving only 400 billion metric tons in the remaining budget. Currently, the world economy is generating about 30 billion metric tons of carbon dioxide each year. At this rate, the global carbon budget required to prevent global warming by 2°C will be exhausted in about 13 years.

Since 2000, China's carbon dioxide emissions from fossil fuels have grown at about 10 percent a year. In 2007, China overtook the US to become the world's largest greenhouse gas emitter and now China accounts for about 25 percent of the world total emissions.

At the United Nations Conference at Copenhagen, the Chinese government made the pledge to reduce China's "emission intensity" (that is, the ratio of emissions to GDP) by 40-45 percent from 2005 to 2020. Given China's rapid economic growth, this pledge in fact amounts to a commitment to triple China's greenhouse gas emissions during this period.

Although there may be multiple ways to define a country's "fair" share in the global carbon budget, given China's economic size and the fact that China is already the world's largest emitter of greenhouse gases, it is highly unlikely that the rest of the world will accept China's emissions share to be more than China's population share in the world. Assume China's fair share of carbon budget is roughly the same as China's population share, or about 20 percent, China's carbon budget consistent with less than 2°C global warming needs to be no more than 140 billion metric tons of carbon dioxide emissions.

From 2000 to 2009, China had already emitted about 50 billion metric tons and is currently generating about 8 billion metric tons of emissions a year. Thus China is on track to exhaust its own carbon budget in only about 10 years.

The current relentless capitalist accumulation in China and the world thus constitutes unprecedented threat to the human civilization. Unless the humanity liberates itself from the chains of capitalist exploitation, the rest of this century will witness global ecological catastrophes that threaten the life of billions.

Under the unlikely scenario, at some point between now and 2020, under the enormous pressure from the rest of the world, China may be forced to drastically reduce emissions. However, given the magnitude of the emission reduction required, it is likely to have devastating impact on China's capital accumulation and the collapse of the Chinese economy would be followed by the general collapse of the global capitalist economy.

Alternatively, the fate of humanity depends on whether the Chinese working class can unite with the global working classes to lead a successful global revolution in the first half of the 21st century.

China and the Global Class Struggle

In the *Communist Manifesto*, Marx famously predicted that capitalist development would inevitably lead to the growth of the proletarianized working class and prepare the necessary conditions for the working class to organize economically and politically. As the organized working class grows in size and strength, eventually it will prove itself to be the grave diggers of capitalism (Marx and Engels 1978).

About one and a half century after the *Communist Manifesto*, what has happened? The late 19th and early 20th century saw the rapid growth of working class movements and socialist political parties throughout Europe. However, as the western working class movements gained strength politically, their stake in the existing capitalist system has also increased. Reformist tendencies (known as "revisionism") gradually became dominant within the European socialist parties (the "Second International" parties). After the Second World War, the European socialist parties officially abandoned revolutionary objectives and committed themselves to incremental reforms within the capitalist system.

The Russian Bolshevik Party was the only major party within the "Second International" that remained committed to revolutionary overthrow of capitalism. During the First World War, Lenin attempted to analyze and understand the phenomenon of "revisionism". Lenin argued that in the "imperialist" era, western capitalism benefited from "super profits" exploited from colonies and semi-colonies. The western capitalists would then use a portion of the super profits to buy off the working class leaders or the "labor aristocracies". Lenin argued that the colonial super profits constituted the material basis of revisionism (Lenin 1916).

After the Second World War, a growing Marxist literature followed the Leninist tradition and further argued that because of "unequal exchanges" and the operations of the "capitalist world system", the western capitalist wealth had been largely based on the exploitation of the periphery. The so-called "technological revolutions" had basically been different ways to create world market monopolies that would allow a few "core" capitalist states to extract surplus value from the rest of the world (Amin 1974; Wallerstein 1979).

However, neither the super profits nor the unequal exchanges had succeeded in maintaining permanent social peace in the West. Through long-term economic and political struggles, the western working classes had been able to secure important concessions from the capitalist classes, winning a growing range of economic, social, and political rights. By the 1960s, these working class gains had begun to put pressure on capitalist profits, threatening to undermine the basic conditions of capitalist accumulation. Neoliberalism was the global capitalist response to this crisis.

Neoliberalism is a significant world historical development. It clearly demonstrates that global capitalism has developed to such a point that it is no longer possible for capitalism to simultaneously meet the basic requirements of capital accumulation while accommodating the historically determined demands of the working classes in the core capitalist states. In other words, the second international reformism or the social contract that has secured basic social peace within western capitalism since the mid-20th century, has run into irreconcilable contradiction and therefore is historically bankrupt.

Another major development in the neoliberal era has to do with the changing balance of global economic forces. Relocation of global capital to exploit the cheap labor force in the "emerging markets" has been a major component of the neoliberal strategy. However, this has led to the large formations of working classes in the semi-periphery. Over time, the semi-periphery working classes will demand economic, social, and political rights comparable to those enjoyed by the western working classes. This development, once it happens, would dismantle the global system of unequal exchange (which has been based on the super exploitation of the peripheral working classes) and therefore destroy the material foundation of western labor aristocracies.

The current intensification of class struggle in the core states thus could mark the beginning of a new historical era. It is no longer possible for the core states to accommodate both the historically established "social contracts" (most importantly pensions and health care commitments) and the capital accumulation requirements. This contradiction has manifested itself as fiscal crisis throughout the core states.

The core state capitalist classes are now attempting to impose the entire burden of adjustment onto the working classes, to reestablish favorable conditions for capital accumulation by creating a new cheap labor regime. The current struggle is therefore a life-and-death question for both the capitalist classes and the working classes. For the working classes, they will have to either fight back or eventually accept the total loss of the entire historical gains they have made since the 19th century.

If the capitalist classes succeed in depriving the core state workers of their historical gains, their "victory" could yet prove to be no more than a pyrrhic one. If the capitalist classes manage to impose massive declines of living standards onto the core state working classes, this would dramatically reduce the world-wide effective demand. The depression of the global demand could then lead to a global depression. The economic crisis could then evolve into a general social and political crisis.

Under another possible scenario, some effective revolutionary political forces may emerge in the core states in the medium-term. The core state working classes would undertake effective, unified struggles to make a decisive break with the existing capitalist order, moving towards the general socialization of the basic means of production and democratization of state power. The new socialist powers would then redirect the economy towards meeting population's legitimate basic needs and accomplishing ecological sustainability.

The semi-periphery could prove to be the center of global capitalist contradictions. Capitalist development in the semi-periphery has depended upon super exploitation of domestic cheap labor force, intense exploitation of material resources and abuse of environment, and exports to the western markets. None of these factors is any more sustainable.

In the coming years, the semi-peripheral capitalist economies will have to face shrinking western markets, rising tides of working class struggles, resources depletion, and increasingly devastating environmental crisis. The combination of these contradictions will lead to the breakdown of the semi-peripheral capitalist regimes and potentially a general revolutionary crisis.

Given its economic size, its central position in the global capitalist division of labor, its role in the global ecological contradictions, China could very well emerge as the key battleground within the semi-periphery. A revolutionary upsurge of the Chinese working class will destroy not only the Chinese capitalism but also the entire system of global capitalist division of labor, decisively changing the global balance of power to the favor the world's working classes.[11]

---

[11] In this chapter, I discussed the changing historical conditions that together constitute a structural crisis of the capitalist world system that the existing system probably will be unable to overcome. I also discussed the various historical tendencies that are likely to favor the next upsurge of the global revolution. Whether the future global revolution will succeed in not only overthrowing capitalism, but also paving the way for a progressive alternative to the existing world system, will have to depend on the actual historical dynamic of class struggle. On the positive side, capitalist development has created large working classes with a relatively high level of general education and political consciousness in many parts of the world. On the negative side, the impending global ecological crisis may severely limit the viable historical options for any post-capitalist system. The hope is that the future working class revolutions would not only learn from the experiences of the historical revolutions, but also take advantage of the positive technological achievements of capitalism, managing to achieve ecological sustainability while meeting

References:

Amin, Samir. *Accumulation on a World Scale: A Critique of the Theory of Underdevelopment*. New York and London: Monthly Review Press, 1974.

British Petroleum. "BP Statistical Review of World Energy." 2010. Accessed June 16, 2011. http://www.bp.com/statisticalreview.

Campbell, Colin J. *Oil Crisis*. Brentwood, Essex, UK: Multi-Science Publishing Company Ltd., 2005.

Hart-Landsberg, Martin. "The Chinese Reform Experience: A Critical Assessment." *Review of Radical Political Economics* (forthcoming).

IPCC, Intergovernmental Panel on Climate Change. *A Report of Working Group I of the Intergovernmental Panel on Climate Change: Summary for Policymakers*. 2007a. Accessed August 12, 2010. www.ipcc.ch.

____. *A Report of Working Group III of the Intergovernmental Panel on Climate Change: Chapter 3 (Issues Related to Mitigation in the Long-Term Context)*. 2007b. Accessed August 12, 2010. www.ipcc.ch.

Lenin, Vladimir Ilyich. *Imperialism, the Highest Stage of Capitalism*. 1916. Accessed September 5, 2010. http://www.marxists.org/archive/lenin/works/1916/imp-hsc.

Li, Minqi. "Climate Change, Limits to Growth, and the Imperative for Socialism." *Monthly Review* 60, no. 3 (July-August, 2008): 51-67.

____. *The Rise of China and the Demise of the Capitalist World Economy*. New York: Monthly Review Press, 2009.

____. "The 21st Century Crisis: Climate Catastrophe or Socialism" (The David Gordon Memorial Lecture). *Review of Radical Political Economics* (Forthcoming).

Maddison, Angus. *The World Economy: Historical Statistics*. Paris: Organisation for Economic Co-operation and Development, 2003.

Marx, Karl and Friedrich Engels. "Manifesto of the Communist Party." In The Marx-Engels Reader,e dited by Robert C. Tucker, 469-500. New York: W. W. Norton & Company, 1978.

Mckillop, Andrew and Sheila Newman, ed. *The Final Energy Crisis*. London; Ann Arbor: Pluto Press, 2005.

National Bureau of Statistics, People's Republic of China. *Statistical Yearbook of China 2009*. Accessed July 18, 2010. http://www.stats.gov.cn.

Spratt, David, and Philip Sutton. *Climate Code Red: the Case for a Sustainability Emergency*. 2008. Accessed July 30, 2010. http://www.climatecodered.net.

Wallerstein, Immanuel. *The Capitalist World-Economy*. Cambridge: Cambridge University Press, 1979.

---

the basic needs of the general population. This could lay down the material foundations for an ecologically sustainable as well as socially equitable society.

Table 1. Alternative Scenarios of Global Warming and the "Carbon Budget"

Global Warming (relative to pre-industrial temperature)	2°C	3°C	4°C
Atmospheric Concentration of CO2-equivalenta	450 ppm	550 ppm	700 ppm
Atmospheric Concentration of CO2	350 ppm	450 ppm	550 ppm
Approximate Carbon Budgetb	1,000 Gt	2,000 Gt	3,000 Gt
Less: Allowances for Deforestation	300 Gt	300 Gt	300 Gt
Approximate Fossil Carbon Budget	700 Gt	1,700 Gt	2,700 Gt
China's "Fair" Carbon Budget	140 Gt	340 Gt	540 Gt

Gt: billion metric tons of carbon dioxide.

a) Including carbon dioxide and other greenhouse gases.

b) Cumulative emissions of carbon dioxide over the 21st century consistent with the required atmospheric concentration of greenhouse gases.

Sources: IPCC (2007b), Chapter 3.

Turning the Crisis into an Opportunity: Turkish State's Response to the 2008 Crisis*

Sebnem Oguz

Introduction

The global capitalist crisis led to a revival of interest in critical studies of political economy both globally and in Turkey. Despite the theoretical vigour of Marxism in explaining capitalist crises, however, national-developmentalist approaches with Keynesian and/or institutionalist overtones are still quite influential in Turkish studies.[1] These approaches converge on an epistemological position that takes the national economy as the main unit of analysis and assesses the impact of the global crisis as well the Turkish state's response in national rather than class-relational terms. This often leads to the overestimation of the destructive consequences of the global crisis on the Turkish economy and/or the underestimation of the success by which the Turkish state was able to manage the crisis. From a Marxist perspective that acknowledges 'the contradiction between the internationality of accumulation and the nationality of state regulation'[2], however, it can be argued that the Turkish

---

* An earlier version of this paper was published in Amme İdaresi Dergisi (Vol. 44, No. 1, 2011). I would like to thank Fuat Ercan, Greg Albo and Adam Hanieh for their comments and suggestions.

[1] For a critical analysis of these approaches see Fuat Ercan and Sebnem Oguz, "Rethinking Anti-Neoliberal Strategies through the Perspective of Value Theory: Insights from the Turkish Case," *Science and Society* 71, no.2 (2007): 173-202.

[2] Dick Bryan, *The Chase Across the Globe: International Accumulation and the Contradictions for Nation States* (Boulder: Westview Press, 1995), 69. Indeed, this is also one of the most signif-

state indeed managed to 'turn the crisis into an opportunity' in terms of the long-term orientations of the international accumulation process within its borders and the administrative mechanisms needed to manage its contradictions.

At this point a further clarification of the concept of 'crisis as opportunity' is needed. In the mainstream literature, especially in the publications of international financial institutions, crisis as opportunity refers to the ability of national governments to use the crisis to deepen market reforms, with more neo-classical versions emphasising objectives like fiscal stability, and neo-institutionalist versions emphasising improvement of investment climate or regulatory capacities. In the national-developmentalist versions of the institutionalist literature, it refers to the capacity of states to use the crisis as an opportunity to tackle the long-term challenges of development. In the Turkish case, a prominent example of this can be found in a recent article written by Ziya Öniş and Ali Burak Güven, where the authors argue that "Turkish policymakers did indeed 'let the crisis go to waste', rather than using it is as a window of opportunity to tackle the structural challenges of Turkish development."[3] In the Marxist literature, however, crisis as opportunity usually refers to the adoption or consolidation of certain capitalist and/or imperial state strategies. For instance, James Cypher used the concept in reference to the way the U.S. state took advantage of the debt crisis in Latin America to revive its hegemony in the region.[4] Recently, Ursula Huws has used the concept in reference to the way transnational corporations have used the crisis as an opportunity to expand further into the public sector.[5] The way the concept of 'crisis as opportunity' is used also depends on how the state is conceptualised. Instrumentalist approaches tend to view the crisis as an opportunity for the state to promote the interests of certain classes or class fractions (usually capital or capital fractions such as financial capital, but in some cases labour as well). On the other hand, structuralist analyses emphasize the state's role in using the crisis for promoting the conditions

---

icant lessons to be drawn from the crisis: "The crisis vividly demonstrated one of Marx's great insights in The Communist Manifesto: while capitalism is international in substance, its reproduction remains national in form." (Greg Albo, Sam Gindin and Leo Panitch, *In and Out of Crisis: The Global Financial Meltdown and Left Alternatives* (Oakland: PM Press, 2010), 124)

[3] Ziya Öniş and Ali Burak Güven, "Global Crisis, National Responses: The Political Economy of Turkish Exceptionalism," *New Political Economy* 16, no.5 (2011): 604. In a previous article written from the same perspective, Öniş and Şenses attribute the structural weakness of Turkish state capacity to the 'reactive' nature of Turkish developmental state as opposed to the 'proactive' nature of East Asian developmental states. (Ziya Öniş and Fikret Şenses, "Global Dynamics, Domestic Coalitions and a Reactive State: Major Policy Shifts in Post-War Turkish Economic Development," *METU Studies in Development* 34, no.2 (2007).

[4] James Cypher, "The Debt Crisis As "Opportunity": Strategies to Revive U.S. Hegemony," *Latin American Perspectives* 16, no.1 (1989): 52-78.

[5] Ursula Huws, "Crisis as Capitalist Opportunity: New Accumulation through Public Service Commodification," in *The Crisis and the Left: Socialist Register 2012*, ed. Greg Albo, Leo Panitch and Vivek Chibber (London: The Merlin Press, 2012).

of capital accumulation process as a whole. In this article, I will broadly follow the latter path and argue that the Turkish state has turned the crisis into an opportunity in terms of the structural requirements of the particular phase of capital accumulation in Turkey in the 2000s, which is marked by the orientation of Turkish capitalism towards global integration on the basis of productive capital accumulation and new mechanisms of labour control. AKP (Justice and Development Party) government managed to do this by using the post-crisis discourse on the necessity of promoting investment and employment as a legitimate basis for tackling the challenges of this particular phase.[6] The government also used the urgent requirements of the crisis management process for consolidating what I will call the 'neoliberal authoritarian state form.'

The concept of 'authoritarian statism' was first used by Poulantzas to define the new state form that emerged to contain the specific contradictions of capitalism in Western Europe in the late 1970s.[7] As such, the concept has its own historical and socio-spatial specificities. However, the core tendencies associated with the authoritarian state form, that is, the decline of the political scene, the strengthening of the executive, and the political role assumed by the state administration - particularly the specialised economic apparatus which is directly linked into the accumulation-reproduction process of capital - have become even more relevant today, and more so after the 2008 crisis, as these tendencies are functional in managing the increasing contradictions of the neoliberal model of globalisation in isolation from the influence of broader masses.[8] But what differs in the current authoritarian state form from what Poulantzas described in the 1970s is its neoliberal content. In this article, therefore, I will use the term neoliberal authoritarian state to refer to the current state form in Turkey.

---

[6] This might seem peculiar at first sight, since AKP is usually perceived as 'exceptional' in its economic policies because of its roots in the Islamic-oriented 'Anatolian bourgeoisie' as well as its fierce style of bargaining with international institutions. The unusual delay in the AKP government's response to the 2008 crisis as well as its rejection of a new deal with the IMF has further enhanced such perceptions. However, as this paper will try to show, the exceptionalism argument misses a crucial point: When AKP came to power in 2002, neoliberal economic policies were already inscribed in the executive branch of the state. Therefore, AKP's peculiarities have not made any significant difference in the long-term economic policy orientations of the state.

[7] Nicos Poulantzas, *State, Power, Socialism* (London: New Left Books, 1978).

[8] Konstantinos Tsoukalas, "Globalization and 'The Executive Committee': Reflections on the Contemporary State", in *Global Capitalism vs. Democracy: Socialist Register*, ed. Colin Leys and Leo Panitch (London: Merlin Press, 1999), 56-75; Bob Jessop, "The Capitalist Type of State and Authoritarian Statism: Poulantzas's State Theory as a Modern Classic," in *Reading Poulantzas*, ed. Alexander Gallas, Lars Bretthauer, John Kannankulam and Ingo Stutzle (London: Merlin Press, 2011).

In this framework, the next section will discuss the historical context in which post-crisis measures should be understood, namely the new orientations of Turkish capitalism towards productive capital accumulation in the 2000s. It will be followed by a detailed account of the major economic policies adopted for this purpose, and how these policies were consolidated through the post-crisis measures. The article will conclude by an analysis of the implications of the crisis management process for understanding the emerging state form in Turkey.

Historical Context of the Post-Crisis Measures

The process of capital accumulation in Turkey has gone through different phases depending upon the historical interaction between domestic and global dynamics. Due to the late development of capitalism, the accumulation process was at the same time the formation and internationalisation of the circuits of productive, commercial and money capital.[9] In this context, the first phase was the formation of commercial capital. By the end of the nineteenth century, the late Ottoman economy was inserted into the commercial circuit of West European capital, and commodity relations were established in agriculture. Following the Great Depression, an internal process of industrialisation became a necessity to domestically recreate markets for the traditional export products, and substitute domestic production for the previous imports of basic consumer goods.[10] Thus, industrialisation started in the 1930s by the transition from commercial to productive capital through massive state investments. In the immediate post-war period, this transition was briefly disrupted by the shift of economic policy priorities from industry to agriculture as a requirement of the Marshall Plan that demanded an increase in Turkey's agricultural exports to Europe. With the recovery in European agriculture in the 1950s, agricultural prices started to decline and Turkey found itself in a foreign exchange shortage. At this point, certain sections of domestic commercial capitalists turned to industrial production in cooperation with foreign capital.[11] The model was based on the production of durable consumption goods with imported inputs serving a relatively high-income internal market. In the 1960s and 1970s, a group of domestic productive capital groups that grew through this model started to gain control over commercial and money-capital through ownership of banks. This led to the formation of conglomerates known as 'holding companies'. By the end of the 1970s, big holding companies, which absorbed most of the potential of inward-oriented accumulation, sought new openings through integration with the

---

[9] Fuat Ercan and Sebnem Oguz, "Rescaling as a Class Relationship and Process: The Case of Public Procurement Law in Turkey," *Political Geography* 25, no.6 (2006): 646.

[10] Haldun Gülalp, "Patterns of Capital Accumulation and State-Society Relations in Turkey," *Journal of Contemporary Asia* 15, no.3 (1985): 329-348.

[11] Gülalp ibid.

world market. To be able to do this, they needed new financial sources in the form of foreign exchange, and this required a change in the economic policies towards an increased export orientation. Internationally, this demand coincided with the search of globally expanding capitals for new areas for expansion. The transition to export-oriented accumulation in 1980 came into being as a result of these internal and external dynamics.[12]

In the post-1980 period, capital accumulation process in Turkey went through three main phases: accumulation through export promotion and wage suppression (1980-1989); accumulation based on the inflow of international money-capital (1989-late 1990s) and a new orientation towards global integration on the basis of productive capital accumulation (late 1990s onwards).[13] The key variable of the export-oriented accumulation model in the first phase was to participate in the international division of labour by specialising in the production of labour-intensive goods.[14] Accordingly, the economic program accepted in January 1980 aimed at a profound restructuring of industrial capital in order to render its structure consistent with the new international division of labour; as well as the suppression of wages for the purpose of lowering both production costs and the domestic consumer demand, thereby encouraging Turkish capital to invest in foreign markets. As the gains of the working-class in the 1960s and 1970s were attained in the context of organisational freedoms outlined in the 1961 Constitution, however, the control of wages could only be possible through the dismantling of that structure. On September 12, 1980, General Kenan Evren, Chief of the General Staff, announced a military coup. The military regime of the 1980s was successful in establishing strict control over wages by prohibiting all trade-union activity. As a result, there was a phenomenal growth in Turkish exports in the early 1980s,[15] However, this export boom was essentially based on the productive capacities established during the preceding decade. The failure to achieve an investment boom led to an inability to diversify manufactured exports, and an over-dependence on certain types of labour-intensive manufacture.[16] Due to these limitations as well as

---

[12] Fuat Ercan, "The Contradictory Continuity of the Turkish Capital Accumulation Process: A Critical Perspective on the Internationalisation of the Turkish Economy," in *The Ravages of Neoliberalism: Economy, Society and Gender in Turkey*, ed. Sungur Savran and Nesecan Balkan (New York: Nova Publisher, 2003).

[13] Fuat Ercan, "Actuality of Marx's Capital and Marxian Political Insight: The Turkish Case" (paper presented at the Historical Materialism Conference, London, 2006).

[14] Ercan, "The Contradictory."

[15] Korkut Boratav and Erinç Yeldan, "Turkey, 1980-2000: Financial Liberalization, Macroeconomic (In)-Stability, And Patterns of Distribution" in *External Liberalization in Asia, Post-Socialist Europe and Brazil*, ed. Lance Taylor (London: Oxford University Press, 2006).

[16] Ziya Öniş, "The Turkish Economy at the Turn of A New Century: Critical and Comparative Perspectives," in *Turkey's Transformation and American Policy*, ed. Morton Abramowitz (Washington D.C.: The Century Foundation Press, 2000), 100.

the new wave of labour militancy that made wage suppression polices unsustainable[17], the export drive lost its momentum by the end of the 1980s. At this point, external financial liberalisation was seen as a unique opportunity to overcome the difficulties faced by domestic capital and the state. Through the transition to the convertibility of the Turkish Lira in 1989, international money capital was lured in order to meet the need for money capital.

Throughout the 1990s, financial liberalisation worked as a mechanism of resource transfer to big capital groups, as the holding banks became the central agent in the domestically mediated external borrowing of the state.[18] These banks found an immense opportunity in attracting short-term international money-capital through benefiting from the relationship between the exchange rate and the interest rate. Financial investments by banks with funds obtained on international markets as credit denominated in dollars, later converted into Turkish lira, and then loaned to the government with high interest rates was the distinguishing character of this period. As almost all private commercial banks were part of holding companies with industrial-commercial bases, banks directed the money capital derived from state debts to the expansion of their holding companies. In this way, the profits of big capital groups increased tremendously in the 1990s.[19] However, the orientation of capital towards money capital resulted in a decline in the production of new surplus value. Although the option of adopting the short-term interest-oriented accumulation dynamics of money capital in place of the long-term profit-oriented dynamics of productive capital could be an alternative for individual capitals, the eventual limits of the money-capital option implied crisis for capital accumulation as a whole.[20] The economic crises in Turkey of 1994, 1998, 2000 and 2001 should be understood in this context. As a matter of fact, throughout the 1990s fixed investments linked to the manufacturing industries virtually stagnated and did not exceed their real 1990 levels as of 2001. Consequently, the share of manufacturing

---

[17] Following the transition to full electoral competition after the referendum of September 1987, the limitations on the rights of labour unions were relaxed. These conditions led to a new wave of labour militancy that made wage suppression polices unsustainable. From March to May of 1989, over half a million public sector employees were engaged in numerous non-violent actions across the country, known as the 'Spring Actions'. Finally, the government agreed with TÜRK-İŞ to make significant wage concessions. The wage rises amounted to 140% for 1989 and 60% for 1990 (Nilgün Önder, "Integrating with the Global Market: The State and the Crisis of Political Representation: Turkey in the 1980s and 1990s," *International Journal of Political Economy* 28, no.2 (1998).

[18] Derya Karakaş, *Global Integration of Turkish Finance Capital: State, Capital and the Banking Reform in Turkey* (Berlin: VDM Verlag Dr. Müller, 2009), 82.

[19] Ercan, ibid., 2003.

[20] Ercan, ibid., 2003.

investments as a share of total had receded continuously.[21] By the end of 1990s, there was a clear realisation that the economy was on an unsustainable course and a crisis would break out sooner or later if the situation continued to remain unchecked. Consequently, under the close supervision of the IMF[22], a new phase of capital accumulation towards global integration through increased productive capacity emerged.

It is important to note that this new orientation was not an outside-in imposition by the IMF, as it was equally an outcome of the systematic efforts of major business associations in Turkey. The efforts of TÜSİAD, the association representing big capital groups, to change the direction of the economy through a number of reports and press releases from the late 1990s onwards were remarkable in this sense.[23] The reforms demanded by both IMF and TUSIAD centred on the capacity of large domestic companies to expand internationally and engage in partnerships with global capital. This meant that capital groups which previously relied basically on the extraction of absolute surplus value or the redistribution of surplus value by the state would have to reorient themselves towards relative surplus value production through higher technology and increasing labour productivity.[24] The economic measures adopted after the 2008 crisis should be considered as an extension of the long-term policies initiated in this phase. Therefore it is necessary to look at the major elements of these policies in more detail.

---

[21] Ümit Cizre and Erinç Yeldan, "The Turkish Encounter with Neo-liberalism: Economics and Politics in the 2000/2001 Crises," *Review of International Political Economy* 12, no.3 (2005), 387-408.

[22] A stand-by agreement was concluded with the IMF in December 1999, which entailed long-term structural and institutional reforms. It was a novel phenomenon in the sense that Turkey, for the first time in its post-war history, was willing to accept IMF disciplines in the absence of an explicit crisis (Ziya Öniş, "Beyond the 2001 Financial Crisis: The Political Economy of the New Phase of the Neo-liberal Restructuring in Turkey," *Review of International Political Economy* 16, no.3 (2009): 409-432).

[23] The interventions of TÜSİAD gained a much more professional character through the research forums that it established in partnership with universities, such as the Competitiveness Forum formed jointly with Sabancı University, the Economic Research Forum formed jointly with Koç University, and the Foreign Policy Forum formed jointly with Bosphorus University (Özlem Tezcek, "1980 Sonrasında Türkiye'de Düşünce Fabrikalarının Yapısal Değişimi: TEPAV Örneği" (Structural Transformation of Think-Tanks in Turkey in the post-1980 Period: The Case of TEPAV), *Praksis* no.19 (2009): 363-84).

[24] Öniş, ibid.

Policies towards global integration on the basis of productive capital accumulation

The primary objective of the economic policies adopted from the late 1990s onwards was to improve the global competitiveness of Turkish economy through production based on higher technology and labour productivity. For this purpose, five basic policies were adopted: i) a comprehensive banking reform by which the relations between banking and industry were reconfigured to shift money-capital from state debts into fixed capital investments; ii) removal of the legal-institutional barriers to private investment through the 'reform program for the improvement of the investment climate'; iii) the shift in the sectoral composition of productive investments from labour-intensive to capital-intensive sectors; iv) transformation of the socio-spatial organisation of production through regional policies that aim to increase global competitiveness; v) the establishment of new mechanisms of control over labour in line with these structural transformations.

The first among these policies was the banking reform. In order to achieve a productive capital-based accumulation, the banking sector had to be transformed accordingly. To orient industrial production towards high-tech sectors, funds had to be shifted from state debts into fixed capital investments. For this purpose, a new banking law was passed in June 1999, establishing an independent regulatory agency called the Banking Regulation and Supervision Agency (BRSA). The aim of the BRSA was to end the rent transfer to banks through state borrowing, and restructure the banking system according to international standards. Those banks which could go back to traditional banking activities instead of financing state debt were allowed to exist, whereas the banks which could not adapt to the change were eliminated. This transformation necessitated a fundamental shift in banking-industry relations; that is, in the ownership structure of holding banks. Holding companies had to revise their sectoral range for higher competitiveness, implying specialisation on strategic areas and withdrawal from uncompetitive businesses. In this context, some holding companies gradually started to restructure themselves in line with the state regulations bringing international banking standards and aiming to convert banks to independent profit-making units within holding structures. However, some other holding companies, mostly the rising capital groups of the 1980s and 1990s, continued to use their banks in order to finance their expansion policies and this stance ended up with the confiscations of their banks by the state. The banking reform, therefore, became a means by which the relations between banking and industry were reconfigured for a productive capital-based economy.[25]

The second major step was the *'Reform Program for the Improvement of the Investment Climate'*, a comprehensive program which aimed to remove the regulatory barriers to private investment and increase the productivity and competitive-

[25] For a detailed account of this process see Karakaş, ibid.

ness of firms operating in Turkey. The program came to the agenda as a result of domestic and international factors. Domestically, an investment-oriented strategy was demanded by all major business associations, since the potentials of accumulation through the inflow of money capital had reached its limits in the late 1990s. Internationally, this demand coincided with the new competitiveness agenda promoted by organisations such as the IMF, the World Bank, the EU, and the OECD, which were "all busy urging governments everywhere to reform the 'business climate' in order to promote investment and domestic entrepreneurship and stimulate competition".[26] In this conjuncture, the government enacted a 'Decree on Improving the Investment Environment in Turkey' on December 11, 2001, which established a coordinating body with the mandate to remove regulatory barriers to private investment. Technical committees were formed in eleven areas: Company registration; employment of foreigners; sector licenses; taxation and state aid; customs and technical standards; land access and site development; intellectual property protection; foreign direct investment legislation; investment promotion; small and medium enterprises; and corporate governance. Throughout the 2000s, a series of laws, including the foreign direct investment law were enacted in accordance with the workings of these committees.

Thirdly, new industrial policies were adopted for the purpose of improving global competitiveness through a shift in the sectoral composition of investments from labour-intensive to capital-intensive sectors. These policies were reflected in the State Planning Organisation (SPO)'s long-term development plans. For instance, the Eighth Five Year Development Plan for 2001-2005 stated that "it is of great importance that private sector give emphasis to investments towards attaining productive power to create high value added, enhancing competitiveness of the economy, increasing employment, productivity and exports and development and/or transfer of appropriate technologies."[27] In accordance with this perspective, an 'Industrial Policy for Turkey' document was prepared in 2003 under the coordination of the SPO. In this document, "policies ensuring a transition of the industrial structure from consumer goods, raw material and labour intensive goods towards information and technology intensive goods and increasing market share by creating new technologies" were proposed.[28] Along the same lines, the Ninth Five Year Development Plan for 2007-2013 stated that the integration of China and India into the world trade system has made it difficult to sustain competition based on costs in basic products.[29] Therefore, the Plan stated, Turkey's manufacturing industry

---

[26] Paul Cammack, "The Politics of Global Competitiveness," Papers in the Politics of Global Competitiveness no.1 (Manchester Metropolitan University, 2006).
[27] SPO, *Eigth Five-Year Development Plan: 2001-2005* (Ankara: State Planning Organization, 2001), 31.
[28] SPO, *Industrial Policy for Turkey* (Ankara: State Planning Organization, 2003), 46.
[29] SPO, *Ninth Development Plan: 2007-2013* (Ankara: State Planning Organization, 2006), 43.

should "move towards areas where information and innovativeness constitute the determining factor of competition in the value chain."[30] All these policies aimed at increasing the relative surplus value through shifting investments to high-technology sectors. However, this did not mean that competition based the labour-intensive sectors would be totally eliminated.[31] Instead, the companies in these sectors were encouraged to relocate to cheap labour regions such as the Eastern and South-eastern Anatolia[32], which brings us to the fourth point.

In the early 2000s, there was a fundamental change in the regional development policies in the context of the global competitiveness agenda. The Regional Development Report prepared for the Eighth Five Year Development Plan (2001-2005) argued that subnational regional economies with strong linkages, interdependencies between different sectors and reflexive relations provide the best case for benefiting from the global flows of economy. Accordingly the Plan suggested that the traditional planning for development based on the aspatial sectoral analysis is no longer adequate in the face of competitive economic relations involving complex spatial specificities.[33] The Plan also stated that Turkish regional policies would be developed in cohesion with EU regional policies. Accordingly, 10 subnational regions were defined in line with the EU regional statistics system in 2002. The Law No. 5084 that became effective in 2004 put new incentive measures into practice with the aim of "accelerating the increase in investments and employment and increasing the contribution of the private sector to regional development."[34] In 2006, The Law on the Regional Development Agencies came into force, with the aim of "improving collaboration among the public sector, the private sector and non-governmental organisations in local and regional development".[35] What the regional differentiation strategy actually implied, however, was the establishment

---

[30] SPO, ibid., 44.

[31] Ece Kocabıcak and Fuat Ercan, "New Industrial Policy and New Roles in Production and Reproduction of Gender in Turkey," (paper presented at the International Association for Feminist Economics Annual Conference (Boston, 26-28 June 2009).

[32] The Report on Industrial Policies, prepared for the Ninth Development Plan (2007-2013) proposed an even more 'creative' solution: "Rather than underselling their equipment and machinery", The report suggested, "Turkish companies in the textile sector can relocate some parts of their production to the Qualifying Industrial Zones in Jordan and Egypt, thereby preserving their competitive advantage" (SPO Report drawn up by Special Ad Hoc Committee on Industrial Policies (in Turkish), Ankara: State Planning Organization, 2007), 152.

[33] For a detailed account of this change, see İbrahim Gündoğdu, Rescaling of Social Relations towards Subnational Regional Space: An Investigation of Turkish Case (Unpublished Master Thesis, METU, Ankara, 2006).

[34] SPO, ibid., 56.

[35] Law No. 5444 on the Establishment and Duties of Development Agencies, National Gazette, 08.02.06.

of different mechanisms of control over labour at different socio-spatial scales so as to enhance the competitiveness of each scale.[36] This brings us to the final point.

The new competitiveness agenda required the establishment of new and variegated control mechanisms over labour. In the 1980s and 1990s, labour was mainly controlled through policies of wage suppression, which was made possible through a series of restrictions on labour unions. From the late 1990s onwards, policies towards increasing labour productivity required the establishment of new mechanisms of control over labour in the sphere of production and reproduction as well.[37] As the transformation of the sectoral composition of production towards capital-intensive sectors required more qualified labour power, policies emphasising the re-skilling of labour through education came to the fore. The definition of education as a strategic field led to a series of regulations that linked education and employment more closely. For instance, a protocol was signed between the Ministry of National Education and Ministry of Labour and Social Security on the improvement of the effectiveness of the vocational training programs of Turkish Employment Agency, and the strengthening of the links between vocational training and employment.[38] 'Increasing the sensitivity of education to labor demand' through active labour policies was emphasised by the SPO in the Ninth Development Plan for 2007-2013 as well.[39]

The focus on higher skilled, higher value-added production meant a new emphasis on relative surplus value extraction. Yet this did not mean a lessening significance of absolute surplus value extraction. Rather, the new orientation of Turk-

---

[36] This could be most clearly seen in a report prepared by the Ankara Chamber of Industry in 2005, which proposed that Turkey should be divided into three regions in terms of minimum wage practices and that minimum wages should vary in amounts in these three regions. Zafer Çağlayan, the Chairman of the Chamber at that time (and Minister of Economy since July 2011) defended the proposal as follows: "We shouldn't forget that even the most distant part of Turkey is closer to EU markets than China or India. By introducing regional minimum wages in our low-income regions, we can turn these regions into Turkey's own China; and by relocating our labour-intensive sectors to these regions, we can both reduce unemployment and improve our competitiveness in exports." (Zafer Çağlayan, *İşsizlik ve Bölgesel Gelir Dağılımı Eşitsizliğiyle Mücadele için Yerel Asgai Ücret Uygulaması* (Regional Minimum Wage Practice to Fight against Unemployment and Unequal Regional Income Distribution), (Ankara Sanayi Odası, 2005), 2. The proposal was immediately supported by the former Turkish State Minister responsible for foreign trade, Kürşad Tüzmen and the IMF vice President Anne Krueger. Due to the strong opposition from labour unions, however, it was laid aside.

[37] Ercan and Oguz, ibid.

[38] Fuat Ercan and Ferda Uzunyayla, "A Class Perspective on the New Actors and Their Demands from the Turkish Education System," in *The Developing World and State Education: Neoliberal Depredation and Egalitarian Alternatives,* ed. Dave Hill and Ellen Rosskam (London: Routledge, 2008).

[39] SPO, 2006, ibid., 48.

ish capitalism necessitated the intensification of both absolute and relative surplus value extraction.[40] A major part of this process was the flexibilisation of labour in both the private and public sector. In the private sector, the main step in this direction was the adoption of a new Labour Law in 2003, which aimed to legitimise contingent and flexible work through the legal recognition of part-time, temporary and contract labour, as well as increased working time and the right of employers to discharge workers collectively 'in times of crisis'. The law introduced a 'destandardised, fragmented, plural employment system' that basically aimed the intensification of absolute surplus production.[41] It also gave the employer the ability to socialise the responsibility to pay wages in times of recession. According to the Law, in the case of an economic crisis, the employer could reduce weekly working hours significantly or suspend work altogether. If the period of suspension exceeded four weeks, the worker would be entitled to unemployment remuneration and compensated by the unemployment security fund, which would be supplied by the cutbacks in the wages and by a minor contribution from employers. Thus, the employers would be able to shrug off the responsibility of paying wages through application to the unemployment security funds.[42] In the public sector, on the other hand, labour flexibility was introduced within the framework of public personnel reform. From the late 1990s onwards, public employment in civil servant positions was limited, and many civil servant positions were transferred to the contractual personnel category, especially in education and health sectors as well as municipalities.[43] Besides the growing contractual personnel employment, another type of flexible work which increased rapidly in this period was the temporary staff category. This category was originally used for exceptional cases where temporary services were needed in areas that did not require specific skills, such as polling or election registration. However, with the introduction of a new legislation in 2004, workers who lost their jobs in the process of privatisations were also entitled to be temporarily employed under this category. These temporary jobs would be provisional for up to one year and salaries were tied to legal minimum wages. The new jobs would not necessarily be related to the workers' expertise, and workers could

---

[40] Derya Karakaş and Fuat Ercan, "The Strategic Choice between Money And Productive Capital in the Internationalisation of Turkey's Holding Companies" (paper presented at the Association for Heterodox Economics 8, Annual Conference Economics, Pluralism and the Social Sciences, London, 14-16 July 2006).

[41] Ali Özdemir and Gamze Yücesan-Özdemir, "Labour Law Reform in Turkey in the 2000s: The Devil is Not Just in the Detail but also in the Legal Texts," *Economic and Industrial Democracy* 27, no.2 (2006): 311–331.

[42] Özdemir and Yücesan-Özdemir, ibid., 2006.

[43] Burçak Özoğlu Poçan, "The Restructuring of the Turkish Public Sector as Part of the Strategy for Europeanisation," *South-East Europe Review* 2, (2005): 111-130.

be relocated anywhere.[44] In this process, flexible labour models gradually became the rule rather than the exception for public sector employees.

To sum up, the policies towards increasing global competitiveness required the establishment of new mechanisms of control over labour in the spheres of circulation, production and reproduction as well as the diversification of these mechanisms at different sectoral and socio-spatial levels. While policies towards relative surplus extraction through re-skilling strategies come to the fore in high-technology sectors and regions, strategies based on absolute surplus value extraction such as the extension of the working hours, reduction of holiday breaks, etc. were predominantly used in labour-intensive sectors and regions. Furthermore, policies of labour flexibility were put into effect in across all sectors and regions, thereby devalorising labour-power into a replaceable commodity.[45]

The Post-2008 Crisis Measures

The government measures in response to the 2008 crisis consolidated all these policies. However, there was a serious time lag between the crisis and the government's comprehensive reform package. The AKP government denied the significance of the impact of the crisis on Turkey and the necessity of a comprehensive economic package until the local elections in March 2009. In the wake of the 2008 crisis, Erdoğan claimed that "the crisis would touch Turkey only tangentially." This claim was based on the fact that the financial sector in Turkey had emerged largely 'safe and sound' when compared to the advanced capitalist countries where the crisis revealed itself as a financial crisis. This was because Turkey had already completed its banking reform in the early 2000s, therefore the banks were in 'relatively good health' during the 2008 crisis. Still, the lack of a financial crisis did not mean that the crisis touched Turkey only lightly. It was only an indication of the fact that the crisis - in contrast to advanced capitalist countries - revealed itself as a long-term recession in the real sector rather than a sudden market crash. The first reflection of the global crisis in Turkey was the decrease in exports by 30 per cent

---

[44] It was this category to which 12,000 workers of TEKEL, the former state-owned alcohol, cigarettes and tobacco monopoly, were transferred after its privatization. TEKEL workers resisted this legislation by occupying one of the central squares in Ankara from 15 December 2009 to 2 March 2010. For a detailed account of the TEKEL resistance, see Metin Özuğurlu, "The TEKEL Resistance Movement: Reminiscences on Class Struggle," *Capital and Class* 35, no.2 (2011): 179-187.

[45] Fuat Ercan and Sebnem Oguz, "The New Regime of Control over European Labor and the Response of Turkish Unions," (paper presented at the Globalisation and European Integration: "The Nature of the Beast" Conference, University of Warwick, June 5-6, 2009).

in response to the declining export demand from the EU countries[46], leading to a decline in capacity utilisation rate in the manufacturing sector from 74.3 per cent in October 2010 to 59.2 per cent in March 2009.[47] Industrial activity fell by 40 per cent and unemployment rate rose by 5 percentage points to 15.4 per cent by the first quarter of 2009; and GDP contracted by 4.7 over 2009.[48]

The contraction in export markets also led to an outflow of money-capital in the amount of $5.6 billion between October 2008 and March 2009.[49] Under these conditions, big conglomerates which were deeply integrated to the global financial markets borrowed large amounts of funds from international markets where the interest rates were lower than domestic interest rates. Soon, these conglomerates wanted the government to become the guarantor of their foreign debts and losses. That's why, following the crisis, TUSIAD, the big business association in Turkey, pushed the government to sign a new stand-by agreement with the IMF, claiming that a new IMF deal would provide financial resources to ease choked financial channels.[50] On the other hand, small and medium sized capital groups producing export goods sought government support through public expenditures and measures such as reductions in corporate tax and exemption from the payment of social security interest premiums.[51] A new IMF deal would deprive the government from such tools, as it would bring conditionalities such as stricter control of local government finances and the creation of an autonomous tax administration. Therefore, these capital groups repeatedly opposed a new IMF, claiming that such a deal was not a prerequisite for recovery.52

Torn between these contradictory demands, the AKP government tried to please both sections of capital by keeping the IMF deal on the agenda while trying to de-

---

[46] The share of European buyers of Turkish exports declined from 66.4 % in the pre-crisis period to 56.3 % in 2010, whereas the exports shares of Near and Middle Eastern countries increased. For an analysis of how the crisis provided the context for new spaces of accumulation for certain sections of Turkish capital, see Yasin Kaya, '"Turkey's Turn to the East" and the Intra-Class Contradictions in Turkey", *Global Discourse* 2, no.2 (2011). As Kaya acknowledges, however, Turkey's close economic ties with the European countries are still intact.

[47] Mustafa Sönmez, *Teğet'in Yıkımı (Destruction of the Tangential)* (İstanbul: Yordam Yayınevi, 2010), 73.

[48] Hakan Ercan, Erol Taymaz and Erinç Yeldan, *Crisis and Turkey: Impact Analysis of Crisis Response Measures* (ILO Office for Turkey, Ankara: ILO, 2010), 9.

[49] Sönmez, ibid., 73.

[50] Bülent Eczacıbaşı, the chairman of one of Turkey's largest conglomerates would express these concerns as follows: "An interruption in the inflow of financial resources from abroad is an especially big problem because the industry will face trouble meeting its external financing needs. External financing is necessary both for importing and for paying external debt. This is indeed why the business world is so insistent on signing a new stand-by deal with the IMF." (Available at: www.seeurope.net).

[51] Sönmez, ibid., 78.

[52] Sönmez, ibid., 77-78.

lay it until the aftermath of the local elections in March 29, 2009. By delaying the IMF deal, Erdoğan was hoping to give confidence to big capital groups about the continuation of the negotiations with the IMF, while at the same time having the 'flexibility' to deal with the crisis in line with the demands of the small and medium capital groups that formed its own support basis. It was in this context that Erdoğan objected to an IMF condition that Turkey should adopt strict tax auditing measures requiring a comparison of individuals' wealth and their spending. Erdoğan challenged the IMF by saying "we will not sign such a thing".[53] Finally, with the resumption of capital inflow from March 2009 onwards, Erdoğan declared that there is no longer a need to make a new deal with the IMF.[54] After its victory in the local elections, the AKP government started to change its discourse on the crisis, emphasising Turkey's potential to turn the crisis into an opportunity through new policies.[55] The following remarks by the Deputy Prime Minister Ali Babacan summarize this discourse quite clearly: "As the saying goes "*good policies are done in bad times*". The current crisis is providing an opportunity for all of us to address long-term issues. This is true both for countries and corporations. We should exploit this opportunity."[56] When we look at the contents of the policies adopted by the AKP government from March 2009 onwards, we can say that it indeed managed to turn the crisis into an opportunity by using the "bad times" for tackling the long-term challenges of the structural reforms adopted since the late 1990s. In sum, after a period of deliberative faltering between different sections of capital in the beginning, the AKP government accepted the significance of the crisis and used the post-crisis discourse on the necessity of promoting investment and employment as a legitimate basis for consolidating the policies towards productive capital accumulation on the basis of new mechanisms of control over labour.

In this context, the most important step was the announcement of a new incentive package for investment and employment on 4 June, 2009. In the press release

---

[53] NTV News, April 1, 2009, available at: www.ntvmsnbc.com.tr.

[54] Sönmez, ibid., 74-75.

[55] In his speech on "The Global Economic Crisis and Turkey", Prime Minister Erdoğan expressed this quite clearly: "We say that whatever you call it, money or capital or labour does not have a religion, does not have a country, and does not have a nationality. Money is like mercury: whenever it finds the proper environment, a good environment for itself, it immediately flows there. That is a reality. If you prepare that environment it will flow to you, and if you fail to do that then it will turn its direction and go somewhere else. This is why we were determined to provide that environment. For that purpose we also try to increase the flexibility of the labour market and to increase and strengthen the R&D and innovation capacity to expand knowledge and communication, the IT technologies, and to ensure a high value-added production capacity in the industrial and service sectors." (Transcript of the Speech delivered by Recep Tayyip Erdoğan, Prime Minister of the Republic of Turkey, Chatham House, April 3, 2009).

[56] Minister of State and Deputy Prime Minister Ali Babacan's Speech at European Business Leaders Convention, July 3, 2009.

concerning the package, Erdoğan made the following remarks: "We are initiating this incentive package in order to turn the crisis into an opportunity...With this new incentive system, we will support those investments that will increase the competitiveness of our country, improve its productive potential, create permanent employment areas and reduce regional development disparities."[57] As mentioned before, there were two dimensions of this package: 1) investment promotion policies that aim the transformation of the sectoral and socio-spatial dimensions of production; 2) employment policies that aim the establishment of new mechanisms of control over labour. In what follows, I will have a closer look at each of them.

Measures for Promoting Investments

The investment-promotion policies of the new incentive package were put together in the *Decree on Government Subsidies for Investments*, which was accepted on 14 July, 2009. Among the major purposes of the decree were the following: "to orient savings to investments with higher value added investments, increase production and employment, ensure continuity of investment propensity, encourage large investments contributing to international competitiveness and employing high technologies.[58] In the Decree, encouragement of the investments was differentiated into three categories with respect to encouragement measures to be provided: Regional and sectoral implementation, large investments, and general investment encouragement mechanism. The decree defined four regions on the basis of NUTS 2 classification as determined in the Board of Ministers Decree No.2002/4720. Encouragement measures to be provided were differentiated with respect to the development status of the region where the investment would be located. In the first region that included İstanbul and its surroundings as well as İzmir and Ankara, high-technology based investments such as automotive, electronics, pharmaceuticals and medical equipments would be supported. In the second region that mainly included the Mediterranean provinces, relatively lower technology based sectors such as intelligent multi-functional textile, non-metallic mineral products, paper, food and beverage production would be encouraged. And in the third and fourth regions which particularly covered the Eastern and South Eastern provinces, labour intensive sectors such as agriculture and agriculture based manufacturing industry, confection, leather, plastic, rubber, metal goods, and also tourism, health and education investments would be encouraged. The incentives included exemption from customs and duties, value added tax exemption, interest expenditure support, reduced corporate/income tax, payment of employer's social security interest premiums by the Treasury, and land allocation for investors. The investors would benefit from the incentives according to their scales and regions. Thus, con-

[57] Full text of the Speech by Recep Tayyip Erdogan on the New Incentive Package for Investment and Employment, July 14, 2009, www.basbakanlik.gov.tr.
[58] Decree No: 2009/15199, Official Gazette, July 16, 2009.

trary to the professed aim of diminishing regional development differences, the Decree clearly encouraged increasing differentiation among regions. The real motive of regional differentiation was to move labour-intensive sectors to the Eastern and South Eastern regions, which are traditional Kurdish areas, and establish the forms of cheap labour and mass exploitation which characterised the 'Chinese export model' within these regions.[59] In this way, policies adopted in the 2000s towards the reorganisation of the sectoral and socio-spatial structure of production so that the declining labour-intensive sectors would still preserve their competitive power by being relocated to cheap labour regions, were rapidly put into practice under the pretext of the need to increase investments in the post-crisis period.

Measures for Increasing Employment

The new incentive system for investments was accompanied by a new 'employment support package.'[60] In a speech at OECD Council, Deputy Prime Minister Ali Babacan revealed the main elements of this package as follows: "In the short-term, active labour market policies, temporary employment schemes and temporary reductions in tax wedge on employment could play an important role. Our government has recently introduced a comprehensive employment support package that includes all of these elements."[61] Thus the major strategy adopted for employment recovery was the enhancement of "active labour power policies" by Turkish Employment Agency (İŞKUR). Along this strategy, a temporary public employment programme through public infrastructure investment came into effect in July, 2009. The programme had two components: one was direct creation of temporary public employment (renovating schools and hospitals, refurbishing public parks, etc.); and the other was support for vocational schools, apprenticeship schemes, and job training with a view to boost employment. Participants were paid the legal minimum wage and their social security premiums were paid by the state. The jobs were created for a maximum of 6 months only, and lacked formal channels for fur-

---

[59] The following comments by Michel Akavi, DHL Express regional director of Europe are quite interesting in this regard: "The post-crisis economy will be more "regional," he said. "China is now the world's factory, thanks to its low-cost labour force and cheap oil. But the difference in salaries between Eastern Europe and China is now decreasing and with oil rising again, it will no longer be convenient to transfer goods from China to Europe. Instead of a global approach, companies will precisely tend to regionalize production." (Hürriyet Daily News, June 30, 2009)

[60] For a detailed account of the impact of the crisis on employment in Turkey, see Ercan et al., ibid.

[61] Minister of State and Deputy Prime Minister Mr. Ali Babacan's Speech at the OECD Council at Ministerial Level, June 24, 2009.

ther follow-up towards formal employment.[62] The *active* employment programmes provided guidance towards job applications but they offered little opportunity for guaranteed job for the attendees. Furthermore, the major bulk of the expenditures were transfers to the central budget for regional development. This was made possible due to the relaxation of the requirements on the utilisation of the state-run Unemployment Insurance Fund so that it could be used for other purposes. According to a new law passed on August 11, 2009[63], sources from the Unemployment Insurance Fund could be transferred to the Treasury to be used in the new incentive package for investors, payment of the workers' social insurance and health insurance premiums, and even infrastructure investments in economic and social developments, especially in the Southeastern Anatolia Project. As such, the only resource left in the hands of workers was also transferred to capitalists. Another important change introduced by the same law was related to the establishment of companies to hire temporary workers through 'private employment agencies.' The new system was defined as "the transfer of a worker, who signed a temporary contract with a private employment agency to another employer in return for a fee." According to the law, the private employment agencies could lease workers to employers for 18 months and around one in four of the total labour force could be consisted of rental workers. Thus, the Law made it possible for companies to hire temporary workers without having to cover their social security and severance payments. The law also included a provision that would turn rental workers against regular workers. According to the law, in case of a strike in transferred work, if the private employment agency could not employ the rental workers in another workplace, it would have to pay half of the fees mentioned in the contract. Thus, in case of a strike, rental workers would either be hired to another workplace or they would get half of their regular wages. Therefore the rental workers would not only be against strike notion from the beginning, but also increase the pressure on regular workers, who would be threatened by the presence of co-workers who worked more cheaply. Due to the strong reaction of labour unions, this regulation was vetoed by the President, but it is still on the agenda.

It is possible to see all these measures as an extension of the policies of labour flexibility introduced in the 2000s, including the expansion of temporary and short-term work as well as the policies of adaptability and employability. The crisis was used as an opportunity to transfer the costs of these policies from capital to the state. The policies of labour flexibility were emphasised in the Medium Term Programme (2010-2012) of the SPO as well. The programme stated the importance of

---

[62] Erinç Yeldan, "Global Crisis and Turkey: A Macroeconomic Assessment of the Effects of Fiscal Stimulus Measures on Employment and Labour Markets," in *Crisis and Turkey: Impact Analysis of Crisis Response Measures* (ILO Office for Turkey, Ankara: ILO, 2010).

[63] Law No.5921 on Amending the Labour Law, Unemployment Insurance Law and Social Insurance and General Health Insurance Law, Official Gazette, August 11, 2009.

the continuation of short-term, active labour market policies, temporary employment schemes, life-long learning programs as well as flexible working models within the concept of 'flexicurity'. The concept of flexicurity, which emerged in Europe in the mid-1990s, was first brought to the agenda in Turkey by Turkish Employers Association in 2006, to legitimise the policies of labour flexibility with the prefix of security –defined narrowly in terms of the provision of retraining between two jobs. It regained currency after the veto of the regulation on the private employment agencies by the President, and recently reappeared in the 'National Employment Strategy' draft announced by the government in June 2010. The Strategy covers the period until 2023, and includes proposals such as the removal of severance payments and the regional differentiation of minimum wage, which were laid aside in response to strong reactions of labour unions. In sum, the post-crisis measures on employment have served to reinforce the establishment of new mechanisms of control over labour under the pretext of 'a new employment support package.'

Crisis Management Mechanisms and the State

The last point that needs to be discussed is the implications of the Turkish crisis management process for state restructuring. At this point, it is possible to say that all the major decisions concerning the crisis were made in the 'Economic Coordination Council' meetings where the top bureaucrats came together with representatives of various sections of capital. In that sense, the major mechanisms of the neoliberal authoritarian state form that was mentioned in the begining of the paper, namely the management of capitalist contradictions directly by the executive branch of the state apparatus rather than mediations of the political scene, were quite relevant for the Turkish crisis management process.

In Turkey, the formation of neoliberal authoritarian state form was crystallised in the 1980s and 1990s through three major steps.[64] First, the political sphere was narrowed through a series of legal restrictions on political parties, which consolidated a monolithic, de-ideologised political structure. This effectively transferred the management of contradictory class issues from the political scene to the state apparatus. Second, the executive branch of the Turkish state was strengthened *vis-à-vis* the legislative branch through a tremendous increase in the number of governmental decrees in the force of law that were used to bypass the Parliament in controversial economic reforms.[65] Third, key economic policy decisions were cen-

[64] For a detailed account see Sebnem Oguz, "Globalization and the Contradictions of State Restructuring in Turkey"
(PhD diss., York University, Toronto, 2008).
[65] Önder, 1998, ibid.

tralised in the hands of a single state agency (the Undersecretariat of Treasury and Foreign Trade) directly accountable to the Prime Ministry, thereby making it possible to implement neoliberal policies without the interference of other layers of the state.

By the end of the 1990s, the new orientation of Turkish capitalism towards global integration on the basis of increased productive capacity of capital necessitated a more comprehensive transformation of the institutional and legal structure of the state. There were two main objectives of this transformation. The first objective was to end the intra-state conflicts over neoliberal reforms, which had paralyzed the process in the 1980s and 1990s. This was achieved through the Constitutional amendments in 1999 that 'locked-in' privatisation and internationalisation as general principles of the state; and the establishment in the early 2000s of independent regulatory agencies that disconnected the neoliberal reform agenda from the political choices of the government of the day.[66] The second objective was to establish a closer relationship between the state and capital in the process of formation of new industrial policies.[67] The first step in this direction was the formation of YOİKK (Coordination Council for the Improvement of the Investment Environment) in 2001, which brought together the top level economic bureaucracts with the chairmen of four major business associations. In 2004, the Investment Advisory Council (IAC), was established to advise the government on measures to stimulate investment. The IAC brought together top government leaders with the senior executives of the World Bank, IMF and European Investment Bank, as well as executives of multinational corporations to consult on reform priorities. Along the same lines, the Ninth Development Plan (2007-2013) stated that "an advisory mechanism, which includes both public and private sector, will be developed in the manufacturing industry to determine sectoral development strategies and priority

---

[66] For a detailed account of this process, see Ümit Sönmez, "The Political Economy of Market and Regulatory Reforms in Turkey: The Logic and Unintended Consequences of Ad-hoc Strategies," *New Political Economy* 16, no.1 (2011): 101-130.

[67] Theoretical premises of this orientation can be found in the institutionalist approaches that attribute a pro-active role to the state in regulating the industrial policies in close cooperation with capital, especially in Peter Evans's argument that the state in the global economy should be autonomous but embedded in the accumulation process in order to provide the institutionalised channels for the continual negotiation of industrial policies (Peter Evans, Embedded Autonomy: States and Industrial Transformation, Princeton, NJ: Princeton University Press, 1995). It is important to note that these approaches actually guided the content of the major economic policies and regulatory reforms adopted in Turkey in the 2000s, especially through the reports prepared by think tanks such as TEPAV (Economic Policy Research Foundation of Turkey). Established in 2004 by TOBB (Union of Chambers and Commodity Exchanges of Turkey), the umbrealla organisation of local chambers of commerce, industry and commodity exchanges, TEPAV worked as a collective of organic intellectuals who guided policy formation, especially for the "real sector'. A prominent example of this was the Report on Industrial Policies, prepared for the Ninth Development Plan (2007-2013) by a Special Ad Hoc Committee, chaired by Güven Sak, the director of TEPAV.

areas as well as perform sectoral monitoring and evaluation."[68] The Report on Industrial Policies, prepared for the Ninth Development Plan (2007-2013) also pointed out the importance of public-private sector dialogue in the formation of economic policies as well as the need for 'strategic coordination' in their implementation, adding that "this must be brought to the agenda of dialogue mechanisms such as the Economic Coordination Council".[69]

Following the 2008 crisis, the Economic Coordination Council (ECC) came to the fore in line with these suggestions. The ECC was established in 2004 for closer monitoring of economic developments and better communication among ministers. However it was given legal status and endowed with new duties and authorities after the 2008 crisis. Its duties included research and evaluation of the recent developments in the global and national economy and coordination of new economic policy decisions.[70] For this purpose, the ECC was authorized to invite representatives of the private sector, NGOs and universities to its meetings. Accordingly, all the major post-crisis measures were discussed in the ECC meetings where the top bureaucrats came together with representatives of various sections of capital and their organic intellectuals. Furthermore, the ECC met frequently in different regions so that it could make decisions in line with the rapidly changing and locally varying conditions of capital accumulation in constant interaction with local representatives of various sections of capital. In that sense, it marked a distinctive step in the mechanisms of neoliberal authoritarian state form.[71]

Conclusion

This essay has argued that, after a brief period of deliberate faltering between different sections of capital, the AKP government has turned the 2008 crisis into an opportunity in terms of the long-term orientations of the accumulation process within its borders and the administrative mechanisms needed to manage its contradictions. Here the opportunity not only refers to the promotion of the interests of certain sections of capital (e.g. capital groups that form the government's support

---

[68] SPO, ibid., 93.
[69] SPO, ibid., 151.
[70] Law No.5838, Official Gazette, February 28, 2009.
[71] A report prepared by the World Bank in cooperation with YOİKK and TEPAV in May 2010 praised the steps taken by the Turkish government to improve regulatory reforms, especially "the creation of public-private mechanisms to deal with the business environment", and argued that it is time for Turkey to establish the appropriate institutions at the centre of government to lead a "whole-of-government" approach to regulatory management (World Bank 2010, ÈInvestment Climate Assessment: From Crisis to Private Sector Led Growth,È Report No. 54123-TR, May 2010, 127). The recent transformation of the State Planning Organisation into a full Ministry of Development with large coordinating powers can be seen as a part of this process.

basis) or capital in general; but more broadly to the promotion of the specific requirements of a certain phase in the accumulation-reproduction process of capital. This shows that the relationship between the state and accumulation process has assumed a more structural character than before, whereby the policies necessary for the reproduction of the accumulation process have been inscribed in the executive branch of the state through the consolidation of the neoliberal authoritarian state form in the last three decades.

Institutionalist approaches miss this point as they idealise the state as an institution that serves national developmental and even social-distributional purposes. Paradoxically, it is precisely this idealisation that also gives them the ability to guide the content of the actual national economic policies. By taking national economies as their unit of analysis and inflict the responsibility of increasing the competitiveness of national economies upon their nation-states, they serve a practical function of making it possible for nation-states to make the regulations that serve the public needs of capitals operating in their territory. On the other hand, by emphasising competition among national economies instead of competition among capitals, they mask the conflicts among different sections of capital and legitimise the regulations for competitiveness as progressive policies aiming at the strengthening of national economies.

From a Marxist perspective, however, the increasing regulatory role of the nation-states in the global competition process stems from the increasing complexity of managing the new contradictions among different sections of capital. The uneven integration of individual capitalists into international economy is the irrevocable context of their conflicting demands on state policy and the increasing complexity of state's role of mediation. While in the period of global integration on the basis of commercial capital, the mediating role of the states is mainly seen in customs and trade policies; in the period of global integration of capital markets, monetary policies related to interest rates and exchange rates have also become contradictory areas that require mediation by the states.[72] In the Turkish case, in the 1980s, when the global integration of Turkish capitalism was based on export promotion, customs and trade policies were the most contentious policy areas. With financial liberalisation in the 1990s, conflicts over exchange rate and interest rate added upon these, and with the new industrial policies introduced in the 2000s, conflicts over investment promotion policies also came into the picture. Since the new investment promotion measures were differentiated according to size, sector and region, the conflicts among capital groups diversified along the same lines as well, and further increased the mediating role of the state. This meant that economic policy decisions would have to be made both in closer interaction with capital groups differentiated according to size, sector, region and form of integration

[72] Bryan, ibid., 84.

with the global accumulation process, and in more centralized fashion, involving further concentration of power in the specialized economic apparatuses of the state. By theorizing this process as regulations aimed at increasing the competitiveness of national economies, institutionalist approaches mask the contradictory nature of the process as well as the transformation of the state towards a more authoritarian form.

References:

Albo, Greg, Sam Gindin and Leo Panitch. *In and Out of Crisis: The Global Financial Meltdown and Left Alternatives*. Oakland: PM Press, 2010.

Boratav, Korkut and Erinç Yeldan. "Turkey, 1980-2000: Financial Liberalization, Macroeconomic (In)-Stability, And Patterns of Distribution." In *External Liberalization in Asia, Post-Socialist Europe and Brazil*, edited by Lance Taylor. London: Oxford University Press, 2006.

Bryan, Dick. *The Chase Across the Globe: International Accumulation and the Contradictions for Nation States*. Boulder: Westview Press, 1995.

Cammack, Paul. "The Politics of Global Competitiveness." Papers in the Politics of Global Competitiveness, no. 1. Manchester Metropolitan University, 2006.

Cizre, Ümit and Erinç Yeldan. "The Turkish Encounter with Neo-liberalism: Economics and Politics in the 2000/2001 Crises." *Review of International Political Economy* 12, no. 3 (2005): 387-408.

Cypher, James. "The Debt Crisis As 'Opportunity': Strategies to Revive U.S. Hegemony." *Latin American Perspectives* 16, no 1 (1989): 52-78.

Çağlayan Zafer. *İşsizlik ve Bölgesel Gelir Dağılımı Eşitsizliğiyle Mücadele için Yerel Asgai Ücret Uygulaması (Regional Minimum Wage Practice to Fight against Unemployment and Unequal Regional Income Distribution)*. Ankara, Ankara Sanayi Odası, 2005.

Ercan, Fuat. "The Contradictory Continuity of the Turkish Capital Accumulation Process: A Critical Perspective on the Internationalisation of the Turkish Economy." In *The Ravages of Neo-liberalism: Economy, Society and Gender in Turkey*, edited by Sungur Savran and Nesecan Balkan. New York: Nova Publisher, 2003.

Ercan, Fuat. "Actuality of Marx's Capital and Marxian Political Insight: The Turkish Case." Paper presented at the Historical Materialism Conference, London, 2006.

Ercan, Fuat and Sebnem Oguz. "Rescaling as a Class Relationship and Process: The Case of Public Procurement Law in Turkey." *Political Geography* 25, no.6 (2006): 641-656.

Ercan, Fuat and Sebnem Oguz. "Rethinking Anti-Neoliberal Strategies through the Perspective of Value Theory: Insights from the Turkish Case." *Science and Society* 71, no.2 (2007): 173-202.

Ercan, Fuat and Sebnem Oguz. "The New Regime of Control over European Labor and the Response of Turkish Unions." Paper presented at the Globalisation and European Integration: 'The Nature of the Beast' Conference, University of Warwick, June 5-6, 2009.

Ercan, Fuat and Ferda Uzunyayla. "A Class Perspective on the New Actors and Their Demands from the Turkish Education System." In *The Developing World and State Education: Neoliberal Depredation and Egalitarian Alternatives*, edited by Dave Hill and Ellen Rosskam. London: Routledge, 2008.

Ercan, Hakan, Erol Taymaz and Erinç Yeldan. *Crisis and Turkey: Impact Analysis of Crisis Response Measures*. ILO Office for Turkey, Ankara: ILO, 2010.

Evans Peter. *Embedded Autonomy: States and Industrial Transformation*. Princeton, NJ: Princeton University Press, 1995.

Gülalp, Haldun. "Patterns of Capital Accumulation and State-Society Relations in Turkey." *Journal of Contemporary Asia* 15, no. 3 (1985): 329-348.

Gündoğdu, İbrahim. *Rescaling of Social Relations towards Subnational Regional Space: An Investigation of Turkish Case*. Master's Thesis, METU, Ankara, 2006.

Huws, Ursula. "Crisis as Capitalist Opportunity: New Accumulation through Public Service Commodification." In *The Crisis This Time: Socialist Register 2011,* edited by Greg Albo, Vivek Chibber, and Leo Panitch, 64-84. London Merlin Press, 2010.

Jessop Bob. "The Capitalist Type of State and Authoritarian Statism: Poulantzas's State Theory as a Modern Classic." In *Reading Poulantzas*, edited by Alexander Gallas, Lars Bretthauer, John Kannankulam and Ingo ,Stutzle. London: Merlin Press, 2011.

Karakaş, Derya. *Global Integration of Turkish Finance Capital: State, Capital and the Banking Reform in Turkey*. Berlin: VDM, 2009.

Karakaş, Derya and Fuat Ercan. "The Strategic Choice Between Money And Productive Capital In The Internationalisation Of Turkey's Holding Companies." Paper presented at the Association for Heterodox Economics 8. Annual Conference Economics, Pluralism and the Social Sciences. London, 14-16 July, 2006.

Kaya, Yasin. "Turkey's Turn to the East" and the Intra-Class Contradictions in Turkey." *Global Discourse* 2, (2011): 2.

Kocabıcak, Ece and Fuat Ercan. "New Industrial Policy and New Roles in Production and Reproduction of Gender in Turkey." Paper presented at the International Association for Feminist Economics Annual Conference, Boston, June 26-28, 2009.

Oguz, Sebnem. *Globalization and the Contradictions of State Restructuring in Turkey*. PhD diss., York University, Toronto, 2008.

Önder, Nilgün. "Integrating with the Global Market: The State and the Crisis of Political Representation: Turkey in the 1980s and 1990s." *International Journal of Political Economy* 28, no.2 (1998): 44-84.

Öniş, Ziya. "The Turkish Economy at the Turn of A New Century: Critical and Comparative Perspectives." In *Turkey's Transformation and American Policy*, edited by Morton Abramowitz. Washington D.C.: The Century Foundation Press, 2000.

Öniş, Ziya and Fikret Şenses. "Global Dynamics, Domestic Coalitions and a Reactive State: Major Policy Shifts in Post-War Turkish Economic Development." *METU Studies in Development* 34, no.2 (2007): 251-286.

Öniş, Ziya. "Beyond the 2001 Financial Crisis: The Political Economy of the New Phase of the Neo-liberal Restructuring in Turkey." *Review of International Political Economy* 16, no.3 (2009): 409-432.

Öniş, Ziya and Ali Burak Güven. "Global Crisis, National Responses: The Political Economy of Turkish Exceptionalism." *New Political Economy* 16, no.5 (2011): 585-608.

Özuğurlu, Metin. "The TEKEL Resistance Movement: Reminiscences on Class Struggle." *Capital and Class* 35, no.2 (2011): 179-187.

Özdemir, Ali and Gamze Yücesan-Özdemir. "Labour Law Reform in Turkey in the 2000s: The Devil is Not Just in the Detail but Also in the Legal Texts." *Economic and Industrial Democracy* 27, no. 2: (2006) 311–331.

Poçan, Burçak Özoğlu. "The Restructuring of the Turkish Public Sector as Part of the Strategy for Europeanisation." *South-East Europe Review* 2 (2005): 111-130.

Poulantzas, Nicos. *State, Power, Socialism*. London: New Left Books, 1978.

SPO. *Eigth Five-Year Development Plan: 2001-2005*. Ankara: State Planning Organization, 2001.

____. *Industrial Policy for Turkey*. Ankara: State Planning Organization, 2003.

____. *Ninth Development Plan: 2007-2013*. Ankara: State Planning Organization, 2006.

____. Report drawn up by Special Ad Hoc Committee on Industrial Policies (in Turkish). Ankara: State Planning Organization, 2007.

Sönmez, Mustafa. *Teğet'in Yıkımı (Destruction of the Tangential)*. İstanbul: Yordam Yayınevi, 2010.

Sönmez, Ümit. "The Political Economy of Market and Regulatory Reforms in Turkey: The Logic and Unintended Consequences of Ad-hoc Strategies." *New Political Economy* 16, no. 1 (2011): 101-30.

Tezcek, Özlem. "1980 Sonrasında Türkiye'de Düşünce Fabrikalarının Yapısal Değişimi: TEPAV Örneği (Structural Transformation of Think-Tanks in Turkey in the post-1980 Period: The Case of TEPAV)." *Praksis* 19, (2009): 363-84.

Tsoukalas, Konstantinos. "Globalization and 'The Executive Committee': Reflections on the Contemporary State." In *Global Capitalism vs. Democracy: Socialist Register 1999*, edited by Colin Leys and Leo Panitch, 56-75. London: The Merlin Press, 2000.

Yeldan, Erinç. “Global Crisis and Turkey: A Macroeconomic Assessment of the Effects of Fiscal Stimulus Measures on Employment and Labour Markets.” In *Crisis and Turkey: Impact Analysis of Crisis Response Measures*. ILO Office for Turkey, Ankara: ILO, 2010.

World Bank. *Investment Climate Assessment: From Crisis to Private Sector-led Growth*. Report No. 54123-TR, May 2010.

Financialization as the development of fictitious capital: the international financial crisis and its consequences in Brazil

Maria de Lourdes Rollemberg Mollo
Translated by: Guio Jacinto

Introduction

The current crisis marks the end of a period in which finance grew out of proportion to real production, giving rise to the process known as the *financialization of the economy*. This process has not only driven the development of the global economy over the past two decades; it is also the underlying cause of the financial crisis that occurred in late 2008, with effects that continue to spread globally.[1]

In this chapter, the financialization of the economy will be analyzed as a process that is centred on the development of so-called *fictitious capital*. The chapter will begin by theoretically defining the concept of fictitious capital in Marx's terms (1974; 1972). This definition draws attention to the decoupling of profit in circulation from its creation in the process of production, an approach to financialization that provides a starting point for the theoretical analysis of financial crises in general.

Next, through a brief literature review, this chapter will examine the role played by the development of fictitious capital in the financialization of the economy and the onset of financial crises.

---

[1] The author would like to thank Alfredo Saad-Filho for comments on an earlier version of this article.

Lastly, the chapter will explore the process of financialization in Brazil, focusing in particular on the financial side of the post-2008 crisis and recovery of the Brazilian economy.

1. The accumulation of capital, credit and fictitious capital: the relative autonomy of circulation in relation to production

Marx (1971) defines capital as money that valorizes itself through the purchase of labour-power. Labour-power, or the human capacity to labour, produces a surplus over and above the necessary costs of its reproduction in other modes of production, but only in capitalism is it transformed into a commodity. Only in a system in which buying to live and selling to buy has become a generalized necessity, and where it is not possible to produce to sell without access to the means of production (which is denied by the institution of private property itself), can this special type of commodity emerge. Labour-power is a special commodity because its use-value is its potential to generate exchange value. In this sense, we can agree with Postone (2008, 134) that "the dialectic of value and use value reconstitutes the necessity of proletarian labour."

This illustrates the domination of these social forms under capitalism. These forms have a central role in the articulation of distinct processes and stages of production, and, above all, in the insertion of social classes: workers, who must sell their labour-power in order to live; and capitalists, who must sell the commodities they have produced in order to realize the surplus-value contained within them, for a profit, and so remain part of the dominant class.

Profit maximization, which is the objective of capitalism as a system, is imposed on individual capitalists through competition. The competitive pressure to continuously increase output and productivity is the *modus* of growth under capitalism. As Marx made clear,

> Competition makes the immanent laws of capitalist production to be felt by each individual capitalist, as external coercive laws. It compels him to keep constantly extending his capital, in order to preserve it, but extend it he cannot, except by means of progressive accumulation. (Marx 1974, 554)

As a result, credit tends to grow rapidly. On the one hand, capitalists can use credit to purchase labour-power and other means of production prior to the realization of surplus-value, thus accelerating or short-circuiting the circuit of capital. On the other hand, credit allows for the centralization and concentration of capital through competition, increasing the scale of production and facilitating technical progress (Brunhoff and Foley 2006). As Albuquerque (2010a, 153) argues, "the development of credit is the cause and effect of big industry": it expands the development of the accumulation of capital in terms of the creation of wealth, technical progress, and the application of science to production.

The compulsory drive to maximize profit and accumulate capital leads to a situation in which, on one hand, capitalists' idle money is deposited in the coffers of the banks, while, on the other hand, the banks re-direct some of that money into the process of production via loans. A few capitalists come to specialize in the exchange of money, becoming what Marx called finance capitalists.

The capital that is lent out by the finance capitalist takes the form of *interest-bearing capital.* The return on interest-bearing capital is a portion of the surplus-value generated in the process of production: the lender receives the loan principal plus an interest payment, while the borrower receives the remaining profit on his or her investment.

But credit also leads to the emergence and development of what Marx called *fictitious capital.* Once the use of interest-bearing capital has been generalized, an investment can generate a return even if it has not been employed in the purchase of labour-power – which, as Marx reminds us, is the only way that it can create surplus-value. In Marx's conception, fictitious capital is fictitious because is not effectively associated with capitalist production and the creation of surplus value.

It is this conception that leads Marx to distinguish between interest-bearing capital and fictitious capital (Mollo 1989a). The first, as Marx says, has the use-value of "serving as capital" (Marx 1972, 338) and "in this capacity of potential capital, as a means of producing profit, it becomes a commodity, but a commodity *sui generis*" (Marx 1972, 339). As such, it "is weighted with surplus-value" (Marx 1972, 342), because the "loaning of money as capital – presupposes… that it will be actually employed as capital, and that it actually flows back to its starting-point" (349) and "interest-bearing capital remains as such only so long as the loaned money is actually converted to capital and a surplus is produced with it, of which interest is a part" (381).

But fictitious capital functions differently, because "the money income is first converted into interest, and from the interest one can determine the capital from which it arises" (Marx 1972, 464). In other words, capital's valuation loses its relation to the real production process and the creation of surplus-value. Marx gives the example of public debt instruments, wherein "the amount loaned to the state no longer exists, but it was never intended that it be expended as capital and only by investment as capital could it have been transformed into a self-preserving value" (Marx 1972, 465). He also refers to stock prices, whose "market-value is determined differently from their nominal value, without any change in the value (even though the expansion may change) of the actual capital" (467).

The distinction Marx makes between interesting-bearing capital and fictitious capital is not universally accepted among Marxists. Meacci (1998, 194), for example, asserts that "the money capital lent to (deposited at) a bank is in turn turned into nothing but a claim on the bank, and therefore again into fictitious capital." However, in characterizing credit as a form of fictitious capital Meacci neglects the role that credit plays in production: accelerating its pace; increasing its scale; anticipating investments; tying together the various stages of production and circulation; in other words, stimulating, *de facto*, the real productive process.

Nelson (2008, 1) also equates fictitious capital with financial capital, claiming that:

> Marx stressed that stocks and shares are often exchanged at 'prices' at variance with the value of the real assets that they represent. In other words, financial capital circulates relatively autonomously of the productive process from which it arises and on which it depends, an endless tango, contributing to capitalist cycles and financial crises.

It should be apparent, though, that in reality financial capital consists in two distinct forms: on the one hand, interest-bearing loan capital; and, on the other hand, fictitious capital, which we can define by the fact that it does not return to real production in order to valorize itself (Mollo 1989a).

Foley (2005), using a definition of fictitious capital similar to that defended here, observes that "loans to productive capitalists are 'real capital'…The value of existing stock…is largely fictitious capital, and bears only a very loose relation to the value of the corporate assets that it legally represents (45)." The relation between the "value of existing stock" and the "value of the corporate assets" is lost because the value of the shares is derived from expected returns (dividends, selling for a higher price in the future) that are not directly related to real production. This is to say their valuation is purely speculative.

We can see that an initial offering of shares would not necessarily be considered fictitious capital, since it raises funds to be invested in the productive process. Thus, as de Paula, Cerqueira and Albuquerque (2001) point out, "the mobilization of capital seems to open more manoeuvring room for capitalist accumulation than pointed out by Hilferding." The authors draw our attention to the fact that it was Marx himself who, in analyzing the role of credit, observed that the formation of the stock market brought about a "tremendous expansion of the scale of production" by permitting the capitalist to have access to capital much greater than his own.[2] Although the authors highlight the connection between finance capital and real production, they nevertheless continue to refer to it as fictitious capital, seemingly without regard for the fact that it may actually contain labour-value.

It would be more appropriate to conceive of financial capital as consisting in both interest-bearing loan capital and fictitious capital – that is, as two different types of capital. Viewed in this light, all the examples that de Paula, Cerquiera, and Albuquerque (2001) provide of money capital that is destined to industrial corporations, "money capital to start a new cycle of valorization of capital" (27), money capital that finances innovative firms, or money capital that provides "an alternative for the financing of a firm" (28) – that is, all the examples of money capital applied to the productive process and the employment of labour-power that has the capacity to create value and surplus-value – should be considered interest-bearing loan capital rather than fictitious capital. In contrast, the valorization that is obtained from shares that are sold in the secondary market, "used as collateral in loans" (27), or forwarded to pay for "takeovers" in place of money is in fact fictitious capital because, as Marx suggested, these are all duplications or multiplications of the same capital and they do not return to or stimulate real production; they do not have any labour-value content.

With the circulation of commodity and money capital and, in particular, the accelerated development of credit and fictitious capital, Marx calls attention to the increased autonomy of prices relative to values and of circulation relative to production.

In reality, Marx's analysis of the value-form in the *Grundrisse* (1980) demonstrates that only with the mediation of money is it possible to conceive of such a separation. In analyzing the price-form, Marx calls attention to the possibility of a divergence between prices and values even before he addresses the transformation of values into prices of production. For Marx "this is no defect" (Marx 1971, 115) but "on the contrary, admirably adapts the price-form to a mode of production whose inherent laws impose themselves only as the means of apparently lawless irregularities that compensate one another" (Marx 1974, 104). In analyzing simple commodity circulation, he emphasizes the possibility of crises emerging due to the use of money and the separation of buying and selling. This possibility, according to Marx, is amplified with the use of credit because the autonomy of circulation increases relative to production as soon as it becomes possible to buy without selling. With the development of fictitious capital this autonomy is accentuated to an

---

[2] Albuquerque (2010b) also presents a detailed analysis of the relations between financial and productive capital highlighting "the role of joint stocks as facilitators of the investments required (477)."

even greater extent. This is why it fictitious capital is so often at the centre of financial crises.

Almost by definition, fictitious capital implies a distortion of the law of value since its valuation is not related to labour. As de Brunhoff (2006, 13) reminds us, "the notion of 'fictitious capital', employed by Marx, designates the manner in which financial income from money capital is formed and grows, within the system of credit, independently of all productive labour." The development of fictitious capital is not an accident: it emerges out of the normal development of credit, the concentration and centralization of capital, and all of capital's attempts to overcome the barriers to its own valorization. The increasing pace and scale of production that is permitted by credit allows capital to overcome these barriers, but it simultaneously opens up the potential for the development of fictitious capital.

The development of fictitious capital is not merely the creation of illusory profits because it does, in fact, enrich its owners. The articulation of production, circulation, and distribution, which continues even as the concrete linkages among these moments in the circuit of capital grow increasingly tenuous, leads to a situation in which profits that have no apparent relation to labour-value must somehow be compensated. Since these profits must be subtracted from the returns from productive activity, there are necessarily compensating losses elsewhere as commodities are sold at prices below the labour-values contained within them. But fictitious profits cannot be maintained indefinitely if the returns coming from production cannot cover its valorization. In this context, crisis intervenes to reveal the limits of the separation between price/value and circulation/production. The irruption of a crisis corrects the disjunction between circulation and production, imposing, albeit in a blind and brutal fashion, the law of value.

In this vein, Marx observes (1975, 605), in analyzing the possibility of crises induced by credit that:

> "The possibility of crises, which became apparent in the simple metamorphosis of the commodity, is once more demonstrated, and further developed by the disjunction between the (direct) process of production and the process of circulation. As soon as these processes do not merge smoothly into one another, the crisis is there." (Marx 1969, 507)

Fictitious capital, as we have seen, is a typical case of the disjunction or autonomy of circulation relative to production, as distinct from interest-bearing loan capital or the primary issuance of shares, which can stimulate production and even delay or defer crises through planning and the coordination of production and consumption.

The development of fictitious capital, in amplifying the disjunction between circulation and production, occupies a central place in crises, and particularly in financial crises, which Marx (1974, 152) perceived as:

> a particular form of crisis, which also is called a monetary crisis, but which may be produced by itself as an independent phenomenon in such a way as to react only indirectly on industry and commerce. The pivot of these crises is to be found in moneyed capital, and their sphere of direct action is therefore the sphere of that capital, viz., banking, the stock exchange, and finance. (Marx 1974, 137)

Production and circulation are parts of the same social process, and for this reason they should be seen as constituting a unity. For Marx (1980, 84), "it is absolutely necessary that the elements which are separated by force but which in essence together manifest themselves through the means of violent explosions of separation of elements which are essentially united. Unity is established through violence." Therefore, crisis re-imposes the unity of production and circulation as parts of one social process.

2. The development of fictitious capital and the current crisis

The crisis of late 2008 emerged largely as a result of the process of financialization we have been exploring on a theoretical level in this paper. As the term itself suggests, financialization involves the predominance of finance over real production, evident in the increasingly tenuous relation between real production and circulation that, as we have seen, defines fictitious capital. This trend can be discerned, for example, in inflated asset prices that lack any clear counterpart in real production, in the priority that is accorded to interest and dividend payments over investments in productive capital, and more generally in the financial sector's ever-increasing economic and political dominance.

Financialization is the driving force behind many of the processes that have defined the so-called globalization of capital. This section will review some of the literature on globalization, with a view to clarifying the links between globalization and the development of fictitious capital.

The period that is conventionally referred to as the era of globalization began as an attempt to overcome two barriers that had complicated the valorization of capital throughout the postwar era of the welfare state. Chesnais (2004) and Dumenil and Levy (2004) draw our attention to two central facts with regard to the origins of globalization. First, the Eurodollar market emerged in a context of weakening regulation, meaning that there existed a market for a currency, the US dollar, that was beyond the control of the issuing country. Nor could the major European states effectively regulate the Eurodollar market, as the dollar remained a foreign currency. Second, Volcker's Federal Reserve raised US interest rates, initiating the liberalization of rates that had long been managed according to a Keynesian vision.

These facts are evidence of a significant growth in the power of the market mechanism and the ideology of neoliberalism that was deployed to legitimize it. This is not, however, to imply a withdrawal of the state. Deregulation and reduced state intervention were accomplished with the full support of governments, not only because they initiated the liberalization of their economies, but also because they benefited from the sale of public bonds that played an important role in the development of global financial markets.

The predominance of finance depended, in the first place, on the search to guarantee real financial earnings. The generalization of restrictive monetary policies contributed to this. In the 1980s, the increase in American interest rates drew savings from the rest of the world to the US and permitted a restructuring of investments, a renewed emphasis on advanced technology, and a massive accumulation of financial assets, stimulating centralized financial management while exerting pressure to control the cost of labour-power (Guttman & Plihon 2008). These changes prepared the American economy for the lowering of interest rates that began in the early 1990s.

This reduction of interest rates helped to sustain demand and consumption within the US, which have continued to grow in spite of three decades of stagnating wages and growing inequality. It is for this reason that Palley (2010, 5) claims "finance is visibly present in the crisis because the expansion of finance played a critical role supporting demand growth and countering stagnationist tendencies within the neoliberal model."

On the other hand, the continuous liberalization of markets that started in the 1980s intensified the competition between capitals. This led to a deregulation of financial markets that encouraged, in the first case, a search for quick (and largely speculative) profits and, in the second case, gave rise to a wide array of increasingly risky financial innovations. This process facilitated the rapid development of fictitious capital.

The development of fictitious capital could be sustained over time due to the massive volume of funds mobilized via the merging of global credit markets. This was a result of the liberalization of national economies or, more specifically, the growing mobility of capital, the generalized deregulation of financial systems, the privatization of pension systems,[3] and technological innovation. An enormous volume of funds drawn from the rest of the world was invested primarily in a few developed countries and, to a lesser extent, in emerging markets.[4] This great volume of capital concentrated in a few markets sustained the development of fictitious capital and an inflation of the value of financial assets relative to real production.

To delve more deeply into an analysis of the aforementioned process of decoupling, we can see that the development of stock derivatives (pieces of paper derived from paper, or, without any doubt, fictitious capital) opened up the path leading to the crisis a full two years before it occurred in 2008. Derivatives traded in over the counter markets (OTC), as reported by the Bank for International Settlements (BIS) (Fahri and Cintra 2009) had a notional value of US$414.8 trillion in 2006 and US$595.3 trillion in 2007. The value of world production in these years, as reported by the IMF, was, respectively, US$48.1 trillion and US$55 trillion. This means that the value of derivatives was 8.6 times greater than that of real production in 2006 and 10.8 times greater in 2007.

Fierce competition forced capitalists into a search for short-term profits and purely speculative financial returns (Epstein 2005; Chesnais 1994, 1996; Brunhoff, et al. 2006) that were not rooted in or re-directed into the sphere of production – that is, into fictitious capital. The spread of flexible exchange rate regimes and free capital mobility exacerbated the fluctuation of exchange rates, offering innumerable opportunities for speculation. This is why Michel Aglietta (1986) called such a combination of flexible exchange rates and free mobility of capital an "explosive mixture."

This is how the logic of maximizing short-term profits through speculation (fictitious capital) became generalized. Capitalists acted under the pressure of fierce competition; consumers reacted to previous gains in their portfolios; and pension

---

[3] The privatization of public pensions created an enormous volume of funds that rushed into the institutional funds (pension funds and mutual funds) that played a fundamental role in the financialization of the economy (Farnetti, 1996 and Sauviat, 2004).

[4] As Prates observes (2005, 285) "The second dimension of financial asymmetry is the particular form in which emerging countries were inserted into the flows of international finance. On the one hand, despite growth in absolute terms of flows directed to those countries in the 1990s, only a marginal share of the funds controlled by global investors is invested in emerging markets." In fact, she mentions that, in December of 2003, "the countries of the centre absorbed about 90% of stock from international bank loans; and in March of 2004, 94% of the total stock of securities negotiated in the international market of capitals had come from those countries." In December of 2005 and 2006 the quantity of securities in the international market (bonds, notes and money market instruments) held by residents from the developed countries was about 86% of the total, according to BIS.

funds moved into profitable short-term investment instruments as a ploy to attract new clients. The hedge funds followed, confident that they would be forgiven if the predictable losses were generalized and no one in particular could be considered guilty (Parenteau 2005).

American consumers were encouraged to invest in the stock market. Interest rates that started out at elevated levels in a controlled inflationary environment stimulated financial investments (Sauviat 2004). Initial gains in the stock market encouraged yet more investments. The availability of information and ease of trading via the internet encouraged more speculative investments.

From the point of view of firms, the market for initial offerings in the stock exchange (IPOs) broadened, increasing the number of firms that could finance themselves through the issuance of securities. The market for high yielding securities grew along with the market in debentures (Guttman and Plihon 2008). In the meantime, wages stagnated while consumption, financed by credit, continued to grow, especially in the United States.

The generalized process of deregulation, especially the de-segmentation of banking systems, with the end of specialized banks (commercial banks, investment banks, etc.) and the generalization of universal banks (banks specializing in multiple functions) has made it more difficult to police banking operations. This has facilitated increasingly risky financial innovations that lose any relation to real production and so drive the growth of fictitious capital. As Guttman and Plihon (2008) emphasize, the banks, as an example, began to offer new types of deposits and different types of loans. In particular, we can highlight the adjustable-rate mortgages that started with artificially low rates and increased abruptly in the subsequent period; negative amortization loans with parts of interest income added to the principal; cheap refinancing; home equity loans; and the securitization of debt through mortgage backed securities. The latter were re-sold by the originating banks, transferring risk to distant third parties. Other mortgage products included the infamous subprime mortgages, marketed to borrowers with a history of credit problems.

All of these financial products shared one feature in common: they were only weakly related to labour-value generated in real production. Whether it was due to the absence of verification at the time the loan was made, or, more importantly, for lack of any relation to the productive process, the only way to guarantee the continued growth of production and income was to defer payment. As a result, the valuation of these products was purely fictitious.

The fictitious nature is even clearer in the so-called *shadow banking system*, as described by Fahri and Cintra (2009). This is the system created by financial institutions that were legally excluded from access to insurance deposits and to rediscounting operations with monetary authorities, although they were bailed out and saved by them with the crisis. The shadow banking system was joined to the banking system because the latter sought to remove the risk from their balance sheets and flee the capital ratios required by the Basel agreements, operating with these institutions ("acquiring protection against credit risks in derivatives markets, securitizing credits with income tied to reimbursements owed by borrowers and creating various special investment vehicles (SIV's " with various types of risk, some "with high leverage (40 to 70 times depending on the collateral" (Fahri and Cintra 2009, 283).

The short-term logic of speculation tended to spread throughout the economy as a whole. As Bellofiore (2002, 65) demonstrates, the criteria for the management of institutional funds

> are those which maximize the value of shares and establish a high level of a 'minimum' return on capital on internal funds, which leads, on the one hand, to promote occupational and wage cuts, reducing productive capacity, and, on the other hand, secondly, to increase the debt to equity, making the financial structure fragile and creating, as a result, the basis for financial crises ever more severe.

The disconnection to the productive process has been analyzed in various ways over the last twenty years. As Crotty (2005) highlights, the prices of financial assets were inflated by growing demand at the same time that the growth of the economy as a whole stagnated. He calls this the 'neoliberal paradox', in which non-financial corporations, to remain competitive, were compelled to drive down wages (thus lowering demand) and to conjure up fraudulent profits. Operating profits fell or grew slowly, forcing non-financial corporations to pursue profits in the financial markets. The slowdown in growth can be traced to the Volcker shock and the disincentive to the launching of shares to increase productive investment privileging speculative gains with the repurchasing of the same (Duménil and Lévy 2004).

Growth in the US was therefore driven by a growth in consumption that could only be sustained by the expansion of credit.[5] Meanwhile, the rest of the world experienced a stagnation or outright decline in wages along with reductions in demand and productive investment (Duménil and Lévy 2004; Epstein and Jayadev

---

[5] In this sense, we agree with Palley (2010) that a financial crisis will have a real counterpart in the early stages because credit developed in order to resolve problems of insufficient demand or under-consumption. Marx himself (1974) called attention to the role of credit in the postponement of crises which, once they begin, grow deeper and more severe. But this is not to deny the financial character of the present crisis, which is a "crisis of money… exerting its action in the immediate sphere of banks, stock exchanges and finance", which emerges "independently, imposing its repercussions over commerce and industry" (Marx 1971, 152).

2005). This is how the world entered 2007 with such an acute imbalance between production and circulation. As Fahri and Cintra (2009) demonstrate, starting in June 2007 the crisis became apparent in the banks' difficulties in refinancing, the reclassification of certain securities, a wave of bank failures and bailouts, and widespread last-resort lending by central banks. The late-2008 failure of Lehman Brothers triggered a widespread process of asset deflation and de-leveraging. The fall of prices in general and financial assets in particular does nothing more than call attention to overproduction, which is rooted in the absence of adequate demand to realize profits, and along with it the elimination of the fictitious nature of capital.

3. Crisis and Recovery in the Brazilian Economy

Financialization in Brazil proceeded much as it did in other countries. In particular, finance's predominance over production can be traced to a high threshold level of interest rates, which stimulated speculative financial investments and inhibited real production, leading to historically low growth, an elevated rate of unemployment, and acute vulnerability to external shocks.

The liberalization of the Brazilian economy began at the end of the 1980s, nearly a decade after the developed countries had begun to liberalize. In the beginning, liberalization centred on the *Plano Real* (Real Plan) of stabilization, which kept the prices of imports low and put downward pressure on domestic prices. In this context, higher interest rates were designed to attract sufficient capital to maintain the value of the currency within a pre-established target range. The resulting appreciation of the currency helped to control prices. After the late-1990s liberalization of the exchange rate, higher interest rates were left in place to sustain the central bank's inflation-targeting strategy and to attenuate currency fluctuations and capital flight.

The elevated rates of interest on public debt instruments, which were among the highest in the world, caused a number of problems for the Brazilian economy. Rates of growth throughout this period were very low, both in comparison to other developing countries and by historical standards.

In fact, even when compared to the 1980s, widely considered a "lost decade" in terms of economic growth due to the global debt crisis, the rate of growth since 1990 has been very low. The median yearly rate of growth between 1980 and 1989 was 2.6%, whereas in the 1990s it was only 1.6% (Table 1). During Fernando Henrique Cardoso's first (1995-8) government the rate of growth was comparable to that of the "lost decade" (2.5% per year), while in his next (1999-2002) government it fell even further (2.1% per year). In the first Lula government (2003-6) the rate of growth improved slightly to 3.4%, but this was still substantially lower than global growth during the same period (4.5%). It is only in the first two years of the second Lula government (2007 and 2008) that significant growth is seen, averaging 5.6% a year. The result of this meager growth is that between 1990 and 2008 Brazil's average growth rate is 2.97% per year in comparison to global growth of the same period of 3.62%. The average rate of unemployment in the major metropolitan regions between 1990 and 2002 was 6.4% in comparison to a lower rate of 5.9% in the 1980s. The situation in São Paulo is even worse: the unemployment rate was 6.82 % between 1984 and 1989 while between 1990 and 2008 it was 10.18%.

Throughout the entire period, as might be expected, the rate of investment was very low as a result of high interest rate levels. During the 1990s the rate of investment reached an average level of only 18.24% of GDP. Between 2000 and 2008 that rate was even lower, 15.05%, compared to an average rate of investment of 22.5% over the "lost decade" of the 1980s. The influence of high SELIC[6] interest rates on central government bonds has been negative, and bank rates for individuals and corporations are even higher. The artificially high returns on liquid securities such as government bonds have absorbed resources that might otherwise have gone toward investment. Capital is drawn to government bonds instead of productive investment. Although, as we have seen, returns from government bonds could be re-invested in a way that would stimulate real production, in Brazil this is usually not the case. A large portion of these returns is used to repay interest – that is, it is used as fictitious capital.

This becomes more apparent when we examine the fate of public revenue and expenditure. Table II shows that, over the years the primary results of public sector borrowing requirements are negative which means that there is a surplus of resources in the balance between public revenue and expenditure excluding interest payments. These payments are very high, and this is the reason why nominal fiscal deficits arise with some regularity. This nominal fiscal deficit, in turn, creates a need for new debt issues in the future. Therefore, the public debt in Brazil is largely fictitious in nature, not because it is public but because it does not lead to increases in real production.

High interest rates also attract speculative capital, overvaluing the currency. This, in addition to inhibiting exports and stimulating imports, which discourages domestic production and job creation, has systematically deteriorated Brazil's current account balance. According to data from IEDI (2010) the participation of in-

[6] An acronym for Sistema Especial de Liquidação e Custodia (Special System of Clearance and Custody), SELIC is the Brazilian Central Bank's overnight lending rate.

dustrial exports, particularly those with high, medium-low and medium-high technology, has fallen consistently since 2000. Industrial imports, particularly those with medium-low and medium-high technology, have grown at the same time, especially since 2004. This deteriorates the Brazilian trade balance and makes Brazil more dependent on commodity exports and more vulnerable to adverse shifts in the terms of trade.

This is precisely the problem dealt with in the 1950s and 1960s by economists from ECLAC.[7] The ECLAC economists identified various problems associated with the development of the periphery.[8] The periphery's specialization in primary products requires imported inputs. These contain a high technological content and a technological standard dictated by the centre. This, in and of itself, increases dependency on technologically advanced imports.

At the same time, the structure of export markets and import tariffs in the periphery deteriorates the peripheral countries' terms of trade. The products that are normally exported tend to be those that have a more competitive market structure. On the other hand, by their intrinsic characteristics, imported products tend to come from more concentrated markets. This allows for a greater control over prices in central countries vis-à-vis the peripheral countries and, consequently, deterioration of the terms of trade for the periphery. In addition, the structure of the labour market is more competitive in the periphery due to lower skill requirements and the relative weakness of labour organization. This contributes to the transfer of surplus value from the periphery to the centre via international trade.

Technological progress is always expensive, tending to concentrate in the hands of those who benefited from it first because they have more resources and previous profits to invest. This by itself is a source of inequality between the countries of the periphery and the centre, reinforcing the deterioration of the terms of trade and reproducing inequality in terms of technology and development. It also makes the periphery more dependent on the developed world and more vulnerable to what occurs there.

Another type of vulnerability is related to international cycles of liquidity. The openness to capital movements articulates Brazil with world speculative finance

---

[7] The United Nations' Economic Commission for Latin America and the Caribbean.

[8] In these analyses, the less-developed countries of the periphery were defined by their specialization in the production and exportation of primary products and by the heterogeneity of their productive structures (different levels of productivity, pay, technological development and general development between sectors), while the more developed countries of the center were seen as having more diversified productive systems as well as more integrated and homogenous societies (Rodriguez 2009).

and, despite the high internal interest rates, leaves the country subject to great fluctuations related to the availability of foreign liquidity. This is why Brazilian growth over the years has been subjected to reflexive cycles (Amado and Resende 2007), where growth is possible if and when international liquidity is abundant and optimism is generalized. In these phases, capital migrates to emerging economies like Brazil more easily. In these moments of euphoria, structural restraints on foreign currencies within peripheral countries are loosened and they grow with greater ease. Nevertheless, growth is accompanied with the deterioration of trade balances which places countries in a more vulnerable position with regards to the cycles of international liquidity. According to the authors, in moments of the reversal of expectations in international finance markets the restriction on liquidity and the flight of capital reaches, in the first place, and in an intense way, those very same peripheral countries, which are seen and understood as Ponzi units, more risky, by the international financial system and its agents, given the greater uncertainty associated with their development. This greater uncertainty is the product of lower incomes and mass consumption as well as a greater dependency on both imports and exports (Amado 1997).

This vulnerability is, as we have seen, is related to the liberalization of the economy and high interest rates which overvalue the national currency and stimulate the entry of speculative money. These capital movements are responsible for accentuated fluctuations in the financial markets of emerging countries, because they are small in comparison to the international speculative funds. Thus, these flows of financial capital already constitute an important element in explaining fluctuations of the Brazilian economy before the crisis, especially because international instability was accentuated during the last twenty years through the general liberalization of exchange rates and capital movements. As a result, it is not surprising that the crisis had serious effects in Brazil.

3.1 The crisis and its contagious effect

The crisis which began in the middle of 2007 in the securities market, linked to subprime mortgages, spread rapidly through the entire international economy after the bankruptcy of the Lehman Brothers investment bank at the end of 2008 (IMF 2009). This crisis began in the most advanced country of the world and imposed its effects on less developed and developing countries like Brazil through falling demand for their exports. In addition, there was an increase of profit repatriation and a reduction of inward investment and capital flows.

The contraction of international liquidity has particularly affected the less developed countries, given their openness to capital flows and the vulnerability of their currencies, which are usually the first to be abandoned in times of crisis (Prates 2005). This liquidity contraction occurred with the onset of the crisis and led to the valorization of the dollar, after a prolonged period, as mentioned, of the overvaluation of the national currency. The exchange rate went from R$ 1.60 at the end of August of 2008 to 2.30 in the middle of October. The growing vulnerability of the country due to the liberalization and financialization of its economy thus becomes apparent. With an open capital account and interest rates that had already been elevated for a long period, growth was highly vulnerable to the effects of the crisis. Only in the last two years preceding the crisis did the growth of the country begin to improve, with interest rates falling from the end of 2005. In the middle of 2008, the resumption of growth was used by the advocates of neo-liberal monetary policy as an argument for raising interest rates, under the allegation of inflationary pressures. Even when the crisis spread towards the end of 2008, interest rates continued to increase until the beginning of 2009 despite the climate of deflation around the world. The result was a fall of output by 0.6% in 2009, which, after the long period of mediocre growth in Brazil, resulted in high social costs.

The fragility of growth in the face of the crisis is, therefore, a consequence of the liberalization of the economy, aggravated by neoliberal monetary policy. The Brazilian banking system did not have the same problems as the developed nations. This is due, in part, to a Brazilian regulatory apparatus that is more strenous than the international standard, which prevented Brazilian banks from taking on such highly leveraged positions. For example, the minimum capital ratio (net worth of banks' assets weighted by risk) established by the BIS[9] in 1988 (Basel I) is 8%. Brazil adopted this standard in 1994, but already in 1998 and 1999 the required minimum ratio was raised to10% and 11% respectively. In other words, Brazilian standards have exceeded the proposals currently being discussed to make world standards more prudent (Basel II, which aims to raise the current minimum capital ratio by 2.5%) since the end of the 1990s.

Despite Brazil's more prudent regulatory framework, exporting firms nevertheless suffered substantially once the crisis hit, exposing the accentuated development of fictitious capital in the preceding years. During the extended period of currency overvaluation it was poorly understood how exporters could continue operating in the market. Once the crisis began it became clear that they had been making financial investments and using the profits to compensate for their operational losses in the export sector. As a rule, in order to protect themselves, the exporters purchased foreign exchange derivatives contracts from banks that, in turn, borrowed short-term abroad in order to fund these contracts. With the appreciation of the Real, firms acquired forward loans, doubling down on their already lever-

[9] Bank for International Settlements.

aged positions (Oreiro and Basílio 2009). On the one hand, they sold dollars forward to the banks earning interest. In normal conditions, these operations are covered with revenue coming from exports. However, in these operations, firms would sell dollars forward again. As a result of these operations, when the dollar appreciated abruptly after the crisis, the demand for dollars increased rapidly in order to honour these contracts. The firms suffered losses estimated by the market at up to R$50 billion (Oreiro and Basílio 2009).

This demonstrates the vacuity of the neoliberal argument according to which countries can avoid crises by submitting to market discipline and adopting an orthodox fiscal and monetary policy. On the contrary, the crisis demonstrates the fragility of the Brazilian economy once it had been opened up to the international process of financialization. At the same time, Brazil's relatively rapid recovery also reveals the extent to which the neoliberal macroeconomic policy in place since the 1990s has been reversed.

3.2 The recovery from the crisis:

The crisis situation in the Brazilian economy was reversed relatively quickly with the aid of countercyclical policy measures. Their adoption was delayed due to a perception that they would undermine the country's fragile growth, particularly with a labour government that was facing criticism from its base as a result of the problems associated with growth during 2003-2006. In fact, the *Partido dos Trabalhodores* (PT) lost many of its supporters and founders in this period, as many objected to its embrace of orthodox economic policy. This criticism, as well as the gains from growth without inflation obtained between 2006 and 2007 led to a further reduction in the interest rate and the economy grew in 2010 by 7,5%. The elements that contributed to this recovery are, on the one hand, the increase in employment over the 2007-8 expansion and the increase in the minimum wage, which grew 29.9% in real terms during the two governments of Fernando Henrique Cardoso and 57.7% in the two governments led by Lula.

On the other hand, minimum income programs also contributed to the recovery, reducing inequality and poverty and thereby increasing the domestic demand of low income classes and in turn stimulating the economy. The poverty rate[10] de-

---

[10] The percentage of people in total population with a per capita household income below the poverty line. The poverty line here considered is double that of extreme poverty line, an estimate of the value of a food basket with a minimum of calories needed to adequately supply a person, based on the recommendations of the FAO and the WHO. Series are calculated from responses

creased from 35% in 1995 and 34% in 2002 to 27% at the end of the first Lula government and 21% by the end of the second. Inequality, measured by the Gini index, has also been reduced, from 0.60 in 1995, 0.59 in 2002 and 0.54 in 2009. The average income of employed persons, in turn, which fell until 2004, has systematically increased until 2010, which explains the quick exit from the crisis.

For the success of the minimum income programs which reduced poverty and inequality, we have the particular contribution of not only the *Bolsa Família* program but also the so- called *Benefício de Prestação Continuada*. Soares et al. (2006) note that 28% of the fall in the Gini index calculated for income transfer programs are due to those specific programs, with the contribution of the *Bolsa Família* being 21% and the *Benefício de Prestação Continuada*- BPC 7%[11]. They point out that this contribution is significant in view of the small participation of these programs in the total income of Brazilian families. The *aposentadorias*[12] higher than the minimum wage, on the contrary, increased inequality, negatively influencing the calculation of the Gini index.

The BPC, pensions, and *aposentadorias* equivalent to the minimum wage can lift families out of extreme poverty and poverty, while other programs have been shown to mitigate but not eliminate poverty. Although the *Bolsa Família* has not been able to eliminate poverty, its impact at the local and regional levels has been significant. This is because poverty is regionally concentrated (Barros and Mendonça 1995). As a result, these programs function as an important local and regional injection of income, stimulating growth, production, and employment that, in turn, contributes to the reduction of another type of inequality, regional inequality.

Conclusion:

In this article we have analyzed the financialization of the economy, understood as the predominance of finance over production, starting from the development of fictitious capital. As against credit, or interest-bearing loan capital, which can encourage the accumulation of capital and production, fictitious capital, by definition, has a price without relation to labour-value and implies the autonomy of circulation relative to production.

---

to the Pesquisa Nacional por Amostra de Domicilios (Pnad/IBGE), a country-wide household survey.

[11] A program created by the Constitution of 1988 of continuous and unconditional benefits for seniors and people with disabilities.

[12] Monthly income paid out through the BPC.

Credit can encourage production and even delay crises by anticipating consumption and investment, although when the crises inherent within capitalism hit, credit can serve to aggravate crises by extending their effects widely. Fictitious capital, therefore, is at the centre of financial crises because it does not stimulate production. Its valorization implies, on the contrary, a siphoning of resources that would otherwise flow to investment in the productive process. The earnings obtained with fictitious capital are generated through increases in demand for bonds and shares and this demand is sustained by income from actual production. Therefore, the valorization of fictitious capital implies the non-valorization of commodities created in production or in non-sales or sales below the value of real production, giving rise to problems of capital accumulation continuing in the same or greater proportion.

When the incomes that sustain the demand for bonds and shares are reduced, fictitious capital fails to appreciate and the sales of the former spark a deflationary process that marks the onset of a crisis. This process rebounds back, then, upon real production, industry, and commerce.

The development of fictitious capital was analyzed in the developed economies with the liberalization and financialization of the very same from the end of 1970s and in the emerging economies, in particular Latin America and Brazil, from the end of the 1980s.

For the world as a whole, the funds coming from all over the world were invested in few developed markets and in lesser proportion in emerging countries. The concentration of investment in a few financial markets gave rise to a rapid valorization of fictitious capital. However, the growth of real production and investment lagged behind the growth of finance, leading to a divergence of the value in circulation relative to the value generated in production. The valorization of fictitious capital was interrupted when revenue coming from production was insufficient to sustain the demand for shares and financial assets. This gave birth to the deflationary processes that characterized the crises of 1990 and the generalized crisis of 2008.

In Brazil the linked processes of financialization and liberalization led to acute economic fragility and vulnerability. The predominance of finance and the development of fictitious capital are evident, in particular, in the high interest rates paid on government bonds and in a public debt which grown to pay off those financial returns, resulting in restricted investment, employment, and growth. This explains the pattern of growth that is known in Brazil as *voô de galinha* (flight of the chicken), a slow and hesitant growth, over the last two decades.

In addition, liberalization linked the Brazilian economy to international finance, and artificially high interest rates attracted speculative capital flows from the world economy, overvaluing the domestic currency while deteriorating the trade balance in quantitative and qualitative terms and increasing Brazil's dependence on higher technology imports. The country also grew more dependent on the cycles of international liquidity and on the "mood" of the market, even with high interest rates. This explains the impact of the crisis on the Brazilian economy, whose output fell 0.6% in 2009 and whose financial losses from currency devaluation were enormous as a result of bad bets on the maintenance of a strong Real.

The Brazilian recovery, all things considered, was relatively rapid. This is due to the countercyclical policies that were adopted and, in particular, to the fall in interest rates, income support programs, the reduction of inequality and poverty, and stimuli to public credit and investment, particularly during the second Lula government. This has sustained demand, especially of low-income classes, providing internal growth alternatives. In these circumstances, recent demands to once again increase interest rates are worrying because, even if it is true that high growth does not necessarily reduce inequality and poverty, lower growth will exacerbate them because it necessarily leads to a reduction in employment and income with devastating social costs.

Table 1 – The Brazilian Economy: Basic Indicators of Growth, Investment, Profitability, and Inequality

Variable	1995	1996	1997	1998	1999	2000	2001	2002
Annual % Change in GDP	3,3	3,7	4,0	2,6	3,6	4,8	2,3	2,9
Rate of Investment as % of GDP	18,32	16,87	17,37	16,97	15,66	16,80	17,03	16,39
Rate of unemployment as % of economically active population	6,7	7,6	8,5	9,7	10,4	-	10,0	9,9
Interest Rate, Over-night/SELIC, annual %	3,61	2,04	1,86	2,13	1,92	1,35	1,34	1,47
Real Minimum Wage in R$	255,27	266,26	273,03	284,01	286,63	296,45	323,38	331,64
Poverty Rate as % of all Households	35,08	34,73	35,17	33,97	35,26		35,17	34,40
Gini Coefficient	0,601	0,602	0,602	0,,600	0,594		0,596	0,589
Average Real Wage in Constant 2010 R$								1.376,43

Variable	2003	2004	2005	2006	2007	2008	2009	2010*
Annual % Change in GDP	3,6	4,9	4,5	5,1	5,2	3,0	-0,6	7,5
Rate of Invest-ment as % of GDP	15,28	16,10	15,94	16,43	17,44	19,11	16,91	19,00
Rate of unem-ployment as % of economically active population	10,5	9,7	10,2	9,2	8,9	7,8	9,1	
Interest Rate, Overnight/SELIC, annual %	1,76	1,26	1,46	1,18	0,94	0,99	0,79	0,76
Real Minimum Wage in R$	333,95	346,38	370,49	422,56	448,10	461,89	495,24	592,88
Poverty Rate as % of all Households	35,78	33,70	30,82	26,75	24,24	22,59	21,42	
Gini Coefficient	0,583	0,572	0,569	0,563	0,556	0,548	0,543	
Average Real Wage in Constant 2010 R$	1.204,83	1.206,73	1.235,41	1.289,92	1.335,66	1.387,96	1.419,51	1.473,59

(*) Estimate Source: BCB, IBGE, IPEA (http://www.ipeadata.gov.br)

Table 2 – Public Finances - % of GDP

Variable	1995	1996	1997	1998	1999	2000	2001	2002
Primary Surplus	0,26	-0,10	-0,96	0,02	3,23	3,47	3,38	3,21
Nominal Interest	7,54	5,77	5,15	7,95	13,21	7,95	8,14	12,82
Nominal Deficit	-7,28	-5,87	-6,11	-7,93	-9,98	-4,48	-4,76	-9,61
Annual Interest Rate (%)	3,61	2,04	1,86	2,13	1,92	1,35	1,34	1,47
Net Public Sector Debt								56,2

Variable	2003	2004	2005	2006	2007	2008	2009
Primary Surplus	3,34	3,81	3,93	3,24	3,37	3,54	2,05
Nominal Interest	7,14	6,42	7,10	6,69	5,97	5,55	5,29
Nominal Deficit	-3,79	-2,62	-3,17	-3,45	-2,59	-2,01	-3,23
Annual Interest Rate (%)	1,76	1,26	1,46	1,18	0,94	0,99	0,79
Net Public Sector Debt	56,4	52,6	48,7	47,5	45,8	42,5	41,8

Source: BCB, IPEA (http://www.ipeadata.gov.br)

Table 3 – Balance of Payments - millions of US$

Variable	2005 1s	2005 2s	2006 1s	2006 2s	2007 1s	2007 2s	2008 1s	2008 2s	2009 1s	2009 2s
Current Account	874,8	1.455,9	462,2	1.811,6	403,5	-145,1	-2.811,8	-1.886,8	- 1.196,2	-2.854,2
Commercial Balance	3.274,8	4.175,6	3.255,5	4.487,2	3.430,7	3.241,2	1.883,7	2.255,6	2.318,1	1.896,9
Exports	8.946	10.772	10.176	12.792	12.202	14.573	15.107	17.883	11.659	13.841
Imports	5.671,4	6596,2	6920,6	8304,5	8771,6	11.331,3	13.223,8	15.627,3	9.340,5	11.943,7
Services and Trans-fers	4.200,8	4.718,8	5.260,9	5.248,7	6.028,8	6.964.0	8.427,5	8.274,7	6.695,0	8.219,0
Services	-592,6	-792,1	-699,5	-907,2	-1.003,1	-1.200,0	-1.357,1	-1.424,5	- 1.352,5	-1.855.1
Transfers	-2.087,9	-2.240,0	-2.433,2	-2.146,7	-2.348,0	-2.533,9	-3.652,8	-3.107.5	- 2.439,1	-3.174,9
Capital Account	727,8	-2.305,1	969,1	1.747,4	10.113,1	4.734,5	6.702,3	-1.810,3	3.115,1	8.768,3
Foreign Direct Investment	1.419,0	1.092,1	1.230,2	1.906,9	3.475,4	2.288,8	2.785,0	4.724,7	2.110,9	2.213,8
Portfolio Investment										
Portfolio Investment-Stocks	418,4	656,8	690,1	595,8	1.263,9	3.105,6	804,7	-2.065,6	505,0	5.673,5
Portfolio Investment-Bonds	505,7	-471,7	-978,2	1.204,8	2.765,9	881,9	1.409,1	-276,0	-127,9	1.642,5
Portfolio Investment-Derivatives	31,6	-38,2	7,7	-0,9	-41,3	-77,1	-63,4	11,3	35,4	-9,3

Source: BCB, IBGE, IPEA (http://www.ipeadata.gov.br)

References:

Aglietta, Michel. *La Fin des Devises Clés: essai sur la monnaie internationale.* Paris: La Découverte, 1986.

Albuquerque, Eduardo da Motta e. "Darimon, bancos e crédito: notas sobre os Grundrisse e a transição para o socialismo." In *O Ensaio Geral : Marx e a Crítica da Economia Política (1857-1858),* edited by João Antonio de Paula, Belo Horizonte: Autêntica, 2010.

_____."Causa e efeito: contribuições de Marx para investigações sobre finanças e inovação." *Revista de Economia Política* 30, no. 3 (July-September 2010).

Barros, Ricardo Paes de and Rosane Silva Pinto de Mendonça. "Os determinantes da desigualdade no Brasil." Discussion paper, no. 377, IPEA (1995).

Bellofiore, Riccardo. "O Capitalismo dos Fundos de Pensão." *Revista Outubro*, no. 7 (2002): 61-76.

Brunhoff, Suzanne. "Finance, Capital, États." In *La Finance Capitaliste*, edited by Suzanne de Brunhoff, François Chesnais, Gérard Duménil, Michel Husson and Dominique Lévy. Paris: PUF, 2006.

Brunhoff, Suzanne and Duncan K. Foley. "Karl Marx's theory of money and credit." In *A Handbook of Alternative Monetary Economics*, edited by Philip Arestis and Malcolm Sawyer. Cheltenham,UK/Northampton, MA: Edward Elgar, 2006.

Chesnais, François. *La mondialisation du capital*. Paris: Syros, 1994.

_____. *A Finança Mundializada*. São Paulo: Boitempo, 2004.

Crotty, James. "The Neoliberal Paradox: The Impact of Destructive Product Market Competition and 'Modern' Financial Markets on Nonfinancial Corporation Performance in the Neoliberal Era." In *Financialization and the World Economy*, edited by Gerald A. Epstein. Cheltenham, UK. Northhampton, MA: Edward Elgar, 2005.

Duménil, Gerald and Dominique Lévy. "O Neoliberalismo sob a Hegemonia Norte-Americana." in *A Finança Mundializada*, edited by François Chesnais. São Paulo: Boitempo, 1996.

Epstein, Gerald A., ed. *Financialization and the World Economy*. Cheltenham, UK/ Northhampton, MA: Edward Elgar, 2005.

Epstein, Gerald A. and Arjun Jayadev. "The Rise of Rentier Incomes in OECD Countries: Financialization, Central Bank Policy and Labor Solidarity." In *Financialization and the World Economy*, edited by Gerald A. Epstein. Cheltenham, UK/ Northhampton, MA: Edward Elgar, 2005.

Farhi, Maryse and Marcos Antonio Cintra. "A arquitetura do sistema financeiro internacional contemporâneo." *Revista de Economia Política* 29, no. 3 (2009): 274-294.

Farnetti, Richard. "Le role des fonds de pension et d'investissement collectives anglo-saxons dans l'essor de la finance globalisée." In *La mondialisation fi-*

nancière – gênese, coûts et enjeux, edited by François Chesnais. Paris: Syros, 1996.

Foley, Duncan. "Marx's Theory of Money in Historical Perspective." In *Marx's Theory of Money – Modern Appraisals*, edited by Fred Moseley. London/New York: Palgrave Macmillan, 2005.

Guttmann, Robert and Dominique Plihon. "O endividamento do consumidor no cerne do capitalismo conduzido pelas finanças." *Economia e Sociedade* 17, Special Issue (2008).

IEDI. *Sem Paralelo na História Econômica Brasileira Recente*. Carta IEDI no. 438 (2010).

IMF. *World Economic Outlook: Crisis and Recovery, April 2009*. Accessed July 18, 2010. http://www.imf.org.

Marx, Karl. *Manuscrits de 1857-1858 ("Grundrisse")*. Paris: Editions Sociales, 1980.

_____. *Capital, Volume I*. London: Lawrence & Wishart, 1974.

_____. *Capital, Volume III*, London: Lawrence & Wishart, 1972.

_____. *Theories of Surplus Value*. London: Lawrence & Wishart, 1969.

Meacci, Ferdinando. "Fictitious Capital and Crises." In *Marxian Economics – A Reappraisal*, edited by Riccardo Bellofiore. London/New York: MacMillan/St. Martin's Press, 1997.

Mollo, Maria de Lourdes Rollemberg. *Monnaie, Valeur et Capital Fictif*. PhD diss., Paris-X, Nanterre, 1989.

Nelson, Anitra. "Fictitious Capital and Real Compacts." *Radical Notes* 15 (October 2008).

Oreiro, Jose Luis and Flavio Augusto Correa Basilio. "A crise financeira brasileira: uma análise a partir do conceito de fragilidade financeira à la Minsky." *Revista de Economia Política* 29, no.1 (2009).

Palley, Thomas I. "The Limits of Minsky's Financial Instability Hypothesis as an Explanation of the Crises." *Montly Review* 61, No. 11 (April 2010).

Parenteu, Robert W. "The Late 1990's US Bubble: Finacialization in the Extreme." *Financialization and the World Economy*, edited by Gerald A. Epstein. Cheltenham, UK/ Northhampton, MA, USA: Edward Elgar, 2005.

Paula, João Antonio de, Hugo Eduardo Araujo da Gama Cerqueira and Eduardo da Motta e Albuquerque. "Finance and industrial evolution : introductory notes on a key relationship for the capitalist accumulation." *Econômica* 3, no. 1 (2001).

Postone, Moishe. "Rethinking Capital in the light of the Grundrisse." In *Karl Marx's Grundrisse*, edited by Marcello Musto. London/New York: Routledge, 2008.

Prates, Daniela Magalhães. "As Assimetrias do Sistema Monetário e Financeiro Internacional." *Revista de Economia Contemporânea* 9, No. 2 (May-August 2005).

Sauviat, Catherine. “Os Fundos de Pensão e os Fundos Mútuos : Principais atores da finança mundializada e do poder acionário.” In *A Finança Mundializada*, edited by François Chesnais. São Paulo: Boitempo, 2004.

Food Security as a Neo-Liberal Discourse

Mustafa Koc

Introduction: Conditions of food provisioning under capitalism

As an essential for human life, food has also been one of the key commodities in capitalist economies. Food has played a very important role during the primitive accumulation process in earlier phases of capitalism; it has been a key instrument of "development" in nation building phases of many emerging states; it has been fundamental in the transfer of rural surplus labour to the dominant domestic and international ruling classes; and it has been vital for the reproduction of labour. For all these reasons, food provisioning has been one of the key concerns of the state in capitalist societies. Increasing segments of the population became alienated from the means of production and lost skills to provide for their own subsistence they became dependent on availability and accessibility of food through market and non-market mechanisms. This made food provisioning a key function of the state. This function included maintenance of the proper conditions of the accumulation process, legitimation of modern market practices of access to food and securing political stability.

Expansion of capitalist economic relations around the world has resulted in generalization of commodity relations, destruction of traditional rural livelihoods and forced changes in conditions of food production, distribution, access, and dietary practices. Dynamics of urbanization, industrialization and globalization shaped by this transformation have created new life styles, new tastes, new consumptions patterns, and new forms of inequalities and entitlements and affected conditions of food provisioning and access to food in unique ways. However, as

Albritton argues, capitalism has never effectively managed agriculture and food provision because its basic operating principles have not permitted to it (2009). Agriculture and food provisioning has remained as a crucial anomaly whether in the form of slave economies during the primitive accumulation stage of capitalism or in the form of persistence of peasant or simple commodity production until the 21st Century.

As Mann and Dickinson (1980) argued earlier, peculiar aspects of certain spheres of agricultural production that are characterized by relatively fixed and lengthy total production time, and a significant gap between total production time and labour time created obstacles for the real subsumption of the labour process in agriculture. The susceptibility of prices to due to violent climatic and market fluctuations were further disincentives for capital's direct involvement in the production process in certain sectors of agriculture. For these reasons modern factory farming/plantation operations remained limited to certain geographies or certain commodities. Formal subsumption through vertical or horizontal integration and forms of contract farming arrangements has continued to survive in the agri-food sector until the present.

However, with its crucial role in the reproduction of labour, food provisioning or providing "cheap food" literally and metaphorically has become crucial for capital. As wider segments of the population have lost their ability to produce their own food, food provisioning has become a never-ending concern for the modern state as this task was not only crucial for the accumulation process but also for the stability of the political regimes. This made exploitation of slave labour, indentured labour, peasantry, simple commodity producers and farm labourers doubly important for the accumulation process for appropriation of the surplus value produced in agriculture, while at the same time reducing the cost of reproduction of labour. The countryside has also provided the reserve army of labour and remained as the breadbasket of the urban populations who lost their ability to produce their essentials of life and became totally dependent on capital's capacity to provide the link between rural and urban workers/consumers of a different sort. These peculiar tendencies may in part explain the interventionist role of the state in the twentieth century over the conditions of food production and distribution.

Emergence of the food security discourse:

Since the early 1970s the discourse of "food security" defined the conditions of food provisioning in modern capitalist societies and legitimized social inequalities in access to means of production and food. Despite its wide use, food security has been a rather confusing concept with multiple definitions, and different priorities that kept changing over time (Maxwell and Slater 2004; Shaw 2007).

One of the most commonly used definitions of food security is that it is a condition "that exists when all people, at all times, have physical, social and economic access to sufficient, safe and nutritious food that meets their dietary needs and food preferences for an active and healthy life" (FAO 2002). Adopted by the United Nations Food and Agricultural Organization (FAO) at the World Food Summit of 1996, this definition is one of over 200 different definitions of the concept (Maxwell and Smith 1992). As a report by the FAO stated, food security "is a flexible concept as reflected in the many attempts at definition in research and policy usage. Whenever the concept is introduced in the title of a study or its objectives, it is necessary to look closely to establish the explicit or implied definition" (FAO 2002). Meaning different things to different people, food security appears as a wish list rather than an analytically robust construct.

A recent scholarly scrutiny of the food security discourse is bringing much needed critical perspective to our comprehension of the concept (Allen and Guthman 2006; Fairbairn 2009; Holt-Gimènez and Shattuck 2011; Jarosz 2009 and 2010; Koc 2006 and 2010; Martin 2010; McMichael 2009; Mooney and Hunt 2009). Reflecting insights of the political economy and political ecology literatures, these studies offer us a review of the conditions of production, distribution and consumption of food in modern agri-food system; impacts of globalization and neo-liberal reforms on the livelihoods of people; and the role of ideologies and discourses in legitimizing of or resisting to these conditions.

Examining the changes in the discourse of food security, these recent studies point out that the perplexity of food security is not accidental, but is reflecting shifts in the social organization of the economy and the food system in the latter half of the twentieth century. These studies relate the changes in food security discourse to the specific ways the food system is organized, the policies and practices that define conditions of food provisioning, and the politics of food (Fairbairn 2010; Jarosz 2009; Koc 2006).

Allen defines discourse as "the ensemble of social, political, and cultural languages and meanings and codes and relationships that construct, maintain or challenge the social order" (Allen 2004, 7). As such, discourses by nature are contested ways of understanding particular realities that preoccupy public awareness. Discourses reflect historical processes and public discussions and interpretations of these processes by various social forces and ideologies. Food security as a discourse, in this sense, refers to ideas, attitudes, courses of action, beliefs and practices that define conditions of food provisioning in modern society.

Recognizing the discursive context of different meanings attached to the same phrase by different claim-makers, Mooney and Hunt (2009) identify food security "as an elaborate master frame encompassing at least three different action frames" associated with hunger and malnutrition, community food security and intentional or accidental food safety risks. Using Goffman's musical analogy of keying, Mooney and Hunt (2009) suggest distinct sets of interests and power differentials among major actors in endorsement or critique of major institutional practices: flat keys represent dominant practices; sharp keys, critical ones. They demonstrate that these variations are not just due to analytical differences in defining what food security is about, but reflect inequalities of power within the food system and changing visions of food provisioning and entitlements to food. Unfortunately, the keying metaphor (as flat and sharp) unnecessarily limits their analysis into a dichotomous framework, ignores internal conflicts among the dominant interests and turns the struggles for resistance and change into an abstract policy debate.

Fairbairn (2010), Juhasz (2009; 2010) and Koc (2006; 2010; 2011) argue that while the food security concept emerging in response to the accumulation crisis during the 1970s presented some of the earlier developmentalist and rights-based arguments, in later years it reflected a clear neo-liberal vision. The scalar shift from national to household food security as well as the shift from a welfare model to an emphasis on the role of civil society organizations and philanthropy in providing food security reflected the influence of the dominant neo-liberal vision and the shift to a global/corporate food regime.

Emergence of the Global Food System in the post-World War II Era

Although food security as a concept emerged in response to the food crisis during the early 1970s its origins can be found in the post-World War II developments that shaped the global food system.

Observers of the modern capitalist economy argue that while reflecting the general laws of motion of the capitalist accumulation process, there are certain historical stages in the economic and political organization of the society. Each of these stages present unique arrangements in terms of the organization of production, distribution and consumption, labour regimes, patterns of socio-political arrangements, and laws and policies (Aglietta 1982; Koc 1994; Lipietz 1987). Several observers have pointed out that similar stages can also be observed in the modern food system, labeled as "food regimes" (Friedmann and McMichael 1989; Le Heron 1993; McMichael 2009). Food regimes recognize a correspondence between changes in the food system and dominant economic trends, regulatory characteristics and national and international policy arrangements. In this paper I will be focusing on the changes in the food system during the post-1970s period, a period that is identified with a global or corporate food regime (McMichael 2009).

Before elaborating on the changes during the global food regime, however, I would like to identify some key characteristics of the modern food system that had prevailed in the previous decades. These key characteristics are important for our understanding of the structures, processes and institutional practices of the modern food system, and the factors that led to the rise of the food security discourse in mid-1970s.

One of the most significant developments that played a key role in shaping the conditions of food provisioning was the rise of the nation state. Emerging first in Western Europe, the number of nation states multiplied throughout the twentieth century, especially after the collapse of the colonialist regimes in the post-World War II era. Most of the nation-building projects considered food provisioning a domestic priority and encouraged agricultural production for domestic food security as well as the financial base for the domestic development projects.

However, anarchy of production in the global markets and tensions among imperial powers led to frequent economic and political crises such as the Great Depression and the World Wars. The Great Depression, in particular, played a key role in the adoption of interventionist policies in agriculture. In the US, farm-support policies resulted in the formation of huge food stocks. Subsidized cheap grain as animal feed played a crucial role in the expansion of the livestock/meat complex. The surplus food was also used as food aid to entice newly emerging nation states in the former colonies to undermine peasant based subsistence production and specialize in the production of agricultural commodities for exports. In 1954 the US Agricultural Trade, Development and Assistance Act (Food for Peace) was signed to provide US food aid to assist war-torn Europe and the emerging new nations in the global South. In 1963, the World Food Program (WFP) was established to use food aid for social and economic development. Commodification and food aid policies mostly benefited large landowners who could afford required investments in large scale monocrop farming and agricultural implements and inputs in the developing countries, and forced increasing numbers of subsistence-based peasants out of agriculture.

Food provisioning was not only a national, but also an international priority. In the post-World War II era, the prevailing international food policy priority in the West has been the modernization and rationalization of production and removal of obstacles to international trade. As early as 1941, the Atlantic Charter, an accord between the US and British governments, included policy frames such as "freedom from want," "lowering of trade barriers," and "global economic cooperation and advancement of social welfare" (Cépède 1984). John Boyd Orr, the man who would become the first Director-General of the United Nations Food and Agricultural Organization (FAO), defended the need for increased production of food, expansion of the world economy to provide purchasing power for all and control of the world food supply (Orr 1943, 34-36). One of the most significant outcomes of the developmentalist modernization of the agri-food system was the spread of high-yield hybrid seeds and intensive agriculture known as the Green Revolution in the developing world.

The Green Revolution, which started in the 1940s and continued throughout the 1960s and 1970s, led to further modernization of agriculture in many developing countries. The Green Revolution relied on intensive agricultural production, using high-yield hybrid seed varieties and farm inputs, such as fertilizers, herbicides and pesticides. Supported by irrigation and the mechanization of production, it led to significant increases in yields in grains. However, these technologies were not accessible to poor rural families and resulted in the concentration of production in the hands of mechanized farmers, pushing millions of impoverished poor peasants into the cities.

The 1950s and 1960s were the golden era of consumerism in North America. Shaped by the Fordist accumulation strategy that emphasized mass production for mass consumption (Baca 2004), durable food and intensive meat commodity complexes expanded (Atkins and Bowler 2003; Le Heron 1993; Koc 2009; McMichael 2009). The consumerist tendencies that peaked in the 1950s became the driving engine of economic growth, creating new markets for processed food industry and food retailers on a global scale. Fordism, by promoting mass consumption while "democratized" the market place by making consumer goods accesible to wider segments of the population created further strains on the environment and resources. One of the best examples of the Fordist obsession with efficiency in delivering cheap food for the wider masses was the rise of fast food industry, what Ritzer (1996) calls McDonaldization.

McDonaldization brought assembly line technology to fast food production. With its emphasis on efficiency, calculability, predictability, and control, rationalization of production in the fast food sector soon transformed other major segments of the value chain from meat processing to frozen fruits and vegetables (Ritzer 1996; Schlosser 2001). In its pursuit of large profits, the fast food industry worked towards lowering the cost of production by using unskilled non-union workers and automation, and emphasizing quantity instead of quality. The fast food revolution not only transformed the modern food system, but its managerial structure also set a model for the economic restructuring of the 1980s.

The speed of rural-urban migration limited employment opportunities in cities, and the lack of infrastructure and social services put further strain on the already overburdened services in countries with limited resources and extreme income inequalities. Urban populations of many of the developing nations grew dramatically in the post-WW II era. Between 1950 and 1990, urban populations of developed countries doubled from 448 million to 875 million. In the same period, urban populations in developing countries more than quintupled from 280 million to 1.6 billion. The discourse of population explosion emerged in the 1960s, both legitimizing the importance of the Green Revolution, and also covering up its role in turning large segments of the rural population into "surplus" humanity.

Crisis in the 1970s and the Emergence of the Food Security Discourse

By the early 1970s, a major global economic slump created a serious accumulation crisis. The Bangladesh famine of 1971, the oil crisis of 1973, the collapse of the Bretton Woods agreement in 1971, and a sudden rise in grain prices following a historical deal between the US and USSR in 1975 marked the end of the post-War economic recovery. For developing nations the rapid rise of the price of oil worsened their trade balance, started a cycle of foreign debts. Securing foreign credit became tied to the approval of the International Monetary Fund (IMF). The tight monetary and austerity policies imposed by the IMF meant significant cuts in social programs, increasing integration with the global economy, and rise in poverty and hunger.

A series of important international conferences took place to deal with the crisis. The Third World Population Conference organized by the United Nations, held in Bucharest, Romania (August 19-30, 1974) addressed the consequence of the rising world population, especially in the underdeveloped South. The UNEP/UNCTAD Symposium on Patterns of Resources Use, Environment and Development Strategies, in Cocoyoc, Mexico (October 8-12, 1974), highlighted the uneven distribution of resources as the cause of poverty and environmental degradation. At the FAO World Food Conference in Rome (November 5-16, 1974) the focus was food insecurity.

In 1974 FAO sources announced that out of a world population of 3.7 billion, 400 million people were hungry. The World Food Conference's definition of food security reflected its traditional concern with food supply, expansion of consumption and international trade: "Availability at all times of adequate world food supplies of basic foodstuffs to sustain a steady expansion of food consumption and to offset fluctuations in production and prices" (United Nations 1975). The Universal Declaration on the Eradication of Hunger and Malnutrition adopted on 16 November 1974 by the World Food Conference underlined the importance of international cooperation for food security:

> The well-being of the peoples of the world largely depends on the adequate production and distribution of food as well as the establishment of a world food security system which would ensure adequate availability of, and reasonable prices for, food at all times, irrespective of periodic fluctuations and vagaries of weather and free of political and economic pressures, and should thus facilitate, amongst other things, the development process of developing countries. (FAO 1974)

By incorporating elements from earlier "rights" discourses and addressing criticisms about existing inequalities, this new definition was a significant advance from earlier food security discourses that primarily stressed availability through productive capacity and food aid and market stability through prices policy and stocks. The early food security frame reflected the post-war vision about economic growth through market economies, leadership of nation states as key actors in securing conditions of accumulation and food security domestically, and international cooperation for food security through effective management of global stocks, commodity prices and food aid.

Increasing protests all around the world throughout the 1960s and 70s were challenging the post-War hegemonic order demanding expansion of citizenship rights, including the right to food, opposing imperialist wars, underdevelopment of the global South, and the role of transnational corporations and international financial institutions such as the International Monetary Fund (IMF) and the World Bank in this process. Critics of these policies were pointing to the ill effects of the global expansion of commodity relations, productionist strategies, and dependency relations (Frank 1967; George 1976; Lappé and Collins 1977; Mamdani 1972). As critics would argue, however, the reason for lack of food security was not shortage of food, or overpopulation, but unequal access to means of livelihoods including food. Amartya Sen (1981), for example, in his analysis of famines, would argue that food insecurity reflected differences in power and entitlement. Responding to these criticisms, the FAO (1983) adopted a definition of food security by including an emphasis on accessibility: "Ensuring that all people at all times have both physical and economic access to the basic food that they need."

The Neo-liberal Alteration

The two decades between the World Food Conference of 1974 and the World Food Summit (WFS) of 1996 were marked by free market liberalism, the intensification of global economic relations, and the restructuring of the economy and the state (Araghi 2003; Barndt 2002; Bonanno et al. 1994; Friedland 2004; Koc 1994; McMichael 2005; Moreira 2011; Pritchard 2005; Tilzey 2006). Corporate response to the crisis included measures such as a shift to the new information technologies, decentralization and privatization, emphasis on increasing rationalization and efficiency; deskilling, use of cheap labour and intensification of the work process; and global sourcing of resources. Globalization of the industrial and agricultural production was accompanied by an even more dramatic trend in the globalization of the financial markets (Harvey 2005; Inglis and Gimlin 2009; Lipietz 1987; Thornton 2004).

These changes were justified by the dominant neo-liberal ideology. Neo-liberal ideology justified these changes and emphasized the free movement of goods and services across borders, the shrinking of the role of the state in the economy, the dismantling of social programs and changes in the conditions of work. Neo-liberal reforms adopted by many governments around the world, including Canada, aimed to dismantle government-run social programs, and brought changes in public policies, programs and institutions such as minimum wage laws, trade union rules, environmental protection acts, unemployment insurance, public medicine, marketing boards, supply management and co-operative structures (Bonanno 2004; Burch and Goss 1999).

The immediate impacts of these changes reflected a decline in well-paying unionized jobs with rising employment in the service sector, precarious and part-time employment and the rise of the informal sector. Decline in social programs made the situation worse, resulting in higher rates of poverty and food insecurity.

The neo-liberal food security discourse included a shift from a rights-based language to a market-oriented one that defined food as a commodity and food insecurity as a personal failure of not having enough income to purchase food. A World Bank document in 1993 would clearly reflect this shift:

> In practice, however, food is a commodity. Access to it is largely a function of income and asset distribution, as well as the functioning (or malfunctioning) of food production and marketing systems. From this perspective, access to food is governed by the same factors that govern access to any other commodity. (134, cited in Fairbairn 2010, 25)

Another important change in the food security discourse during the neo-liberal era was a shift from an autarchic, state centric model to market liberalism and shifting food security objectives from the national level to the household level. As World Bank experts suggested, "food security is achieved only if all households have the ability to buy food. There is no necessary link between self-sufficiency and food security (1986, 31, cited in Jarosz 2011, 125)."

These changes paralleled a new emphasis on the role of decentralization of the state (regional and local governance), civil society organizations such as community-based organizations, NGOs and charities in service delivery to fill the gap left by the shrinking of the nation state (Bonanno et al. 1994; Koc 1994; Moreira 2011).

In this environment driven mostly by market priorities, civil society organizations (CSOs) have tried to be the voice of the marginalized and defend the priorities of social justice and development. Governments and industry representatives have been inviting CSO representatives to consultative meetings to get their feedback on various issues dealing with international and domestic policy. The so-called consultations have often been criticized by civil society representatives as mere lip service, simply serving to legitimize existing structures rather than being a transparent, participatory and democratic process (Hodgson 2004; Koc et al. 2008).

As national social programs shrank or were downloaded to provincial and local governments, often the burden of care was transferred to families and CSOs. Philanthropic organizations, such as food banks, started filling the gap left from government-run social programs (Power 2005; Riches 1997; Tarasuk and Eakin 2005). In Canada, the first food bank opened in Edmonton in 1981 in response to what was then thought as the worst recession since the Great Depression. In March 2011 number of people going to food banks was 851014 in a single month, with over 800 food banks and 3000 associated food programs. As Tarasuk and Eakin (2005) argue, food banks became not only an adjunct to the social assistance system in Canada but also contributed to 'corporate welfare' by distributing industry-donated unsellable products with the unpaid labour in food banks.

Another significant characteristic of the global food regime has been increasing corporate concentration and control through mergers and buy-outs. In the US, for example, the market share of the top four companies in beef processing increased from 72% in 1990 to 83.5 % in 2007. In pork packing the control of the top four companies increased from 37% in 1987 to 66 % in 2007. Similar trends could be seen in broilers (an increase from 35 in 1986 to 58.5% in 2007) (Heffernan and Hendrickson 2007).

In Canada, the concentration ratio of the top four companies (CR4) reached 76.2% in pork packing, 73.2% in beef packing, 64% in grain handling, and 78.76% in wheat flour milling in 2003/2004. In retail, CR4 for 2004-2005 was 77.99 %. In fertilizers, CR4 varied from a low of 81.3% in nitrogen to 100 % in nitric acid, ammonium nitrate, ammonium sulfate and nitrogen solutions. From banking (CR5=82.41) to transportation (CR2 in railways=100) farmers faced oligopolistic markets (Koc 2009; Market Share Matrix Project 2006).

Through new strategic alliances, vertical and horizontal integration strategies global agri-food corporations managed to control various sectors of the market. Changes introduced by information, communications and transportation technologies such as giant purchasing centres, electronically enabled supply chains, radio frequency identification (RFID), bar-code system, and nanotechnologies, allowed agro-food transnational corporations to control wider segments of the markets (Moreira 2011). By connecting diverse segments of production, processing and retailing, vertical integration, on the other hand, allowed corporations to control their upstream suppliers and downstream buyers, creating virtual monopolies. In this scheme, farmers were forced to keep producing with ever-declining returns.

Like hunger, the farm crisis became a permanent feature of the modern food system in the neo-liberal era (Qualman 2001). In Canada, between 1985 and 2004, net farm income declined in real terms by an average of $104 million per year (at 1992 dollar rate), although output prices slightly increased by about $90 million annually. National Farmers Union claimed that the net market income in the early 2000s fell even below the Great Depression levels in Canada (NFU 2005).

Dealing with victims of corporate and state restructuring has increasingly been left to community-based civil society organizations (CSOs). However, lacking the legitimacy of the state and political parties, CSOs have often been dismissed as self-serving interest groups. Instead, they have been expected to work with limited financial resources, while competing among themselves, and expected to assume the eroding functions of the welfare state. Running from project to project, they were under constant pressure to seek funding often from corporate donors or private foundations, relying on volunteer labour, dealing with high labour turnover rates, running from project to project with shortage of trained personnel and funding (Koc and Bas 2012; Koc et al. 2008).

The community food security (CFS) frame that has been identified by many observers as a progressive alternative food initiative (AFI) in challenging the dominant food system (Bellows and Hamm 2003; Mooney and Hunt 2009; Slater 2007; Winne, Joseph, Fisher 1997) needs to be understood within this neo-liberal context of the shrinking welfare state, and shifting of the burden of care to families, communities, and civil society organizations. While CFS initiatives, like food banks, were genuine community based initiatives to respond to the crisis, they were neither seen as serious threats to the institutional practices of the global food regime, nor were on a collision course with the dominant neo-liberal ideology.

By the 1990s food insecurity was on the rise not only in the underdeveloped countries but even in advanced industrial countries such as Canada (Riches 1997; Tarasuk and Beaton 2003). According to the FAO estimations, there were approximately 800 million people around the world suffering from hunger and malnutrition (Koc and MacRae 2001).

In response to increasing public criticism, the FAO called for the World Food Summit in Rome (WFS) in 1996 to formulate a global food security agenda. The Rome Declaration on World Food Security and the WFS Plan of Action adopted in 1996 called for each nation to develop and implement a national plan of action to achieve food security domestically and internationally. A commitment was signed "to eradicate hunger in all countries with the target of reducing by half the number of undernourished people by no later than the year 2015 (FAO 1996)."

A parallel civil society meeting held by the WFS offered considerable criticism of corporate concentration, global trade policies, and widening social inequalities. Via Campesina, the new organization representing peasants and small family farmers offered an alternative discourse of food sovereignty as the right of peoples to define their own food and agriculture and to protect and regulate domestic agricultural production and trade in order to achieve self-reliance and sustainable development objectives (Desmarais 2007; Wittman, Desmarais Wiebe 2011).

> Long-term food security depends on those who produce food and care for the natural environment…Food is a basic human right. This right can only be realized in a system where food sovereignty is guaranteed. Food sovereignty is the right of each nation to maintain and develop its own capacity to produce its basic foods respecting cultural and productive diversity. …Food sovereignty is a precondition to genuine food security. (Via Campesina 1996)

Possibly in an attempt to partially incorporate these criticisms, the Rome Declaration included phrases recognizing the significance of partnership with civil society actors and their role in enhancing food security. But critics of FAO argued that in reality, civil society partnership really meant community organizations filling service gaps left by shrinking government programs; sharing the burden but not the decision-making power (Koc et al. 2008). As Patel (2009) states however, recognition of the role of civil society

> [….] marked the success of activists and the NGO and policymaking community to [….] include non-state actors and to shift the discussion away from production issues toward broader social concerns, it was also an intervention in a very different world and series of debates. No longer was there a Non-Aligned Movement. Nor was there, at least in the world of state-level diplomacy, the possibility of an alternative to US-style neoliberal capitalism. It was an intervention at a time when neoliberal triumphalism could be seen in the break away from a commitment to the full meeting of human rights, to the watered down Millennium Development Goals, which provided, under the mantle of 'realistically achievable goals', a much more elastic time frame for the achievement of goals that were intended by the authors of such goals to be delivered with all due haste. (Patel 2009, 664)

At the WFS, food security was defined as a condition "when all people, at all times, have physical and economic access to sufficient, safe and nutritious food to meet their dietary needs and food preferences for an active and healthy life (FAO 1996)." This definition is further refined in The State of Food Insecurity 2001: "Food security [is] a situation that exists when all people, at all times, have physical, social and economic access to sufficient, safe and nutritious food that meets their dietary needs and food preferences for an active and healthy life."

Deepening Crisis of Accumulation and Food Security in the early 2000s

Following the recessions of 1974-75 and 1980-82 global restructuring and reorganization of finance resulted in a new wave of economic growth which lasted till the crisis in Asian markets in 1997 (McNally 2009; Panitch, Albo and Chibber 2011; Panitch and Leys 2004). The neoliberal era resulted in a severe decline in the countryside, resulting in further movement of the marginalized rural populations into urban areas (Klein 2007; Panith and Gindin 2009). For the first time in human history, the number of people living in cities exceeded the number of people living in the countryside by the early 2000s. Following the WFS, many countries, adopted national action plans for food security, following the language of the Rome Declaration (Koc and Bas 2012). The follow up meeting, which was supposed to be held in Rome in November 2001 five years after the original summit was cancelled due to security concerns following September 11 that year.

Unregulated financial markets deepened the crisis of global finance and the number of people living in poverty began to rise again. When the World Food Summit-Five Years Later (WFS-FYL) meeting was held in Rome in June 2002, global priorities had again changed. As a result of the post 9-11 atmosphere, people in many parts of the world could be more easily convinced to accept military expansionism and the replacement of the discourse of human securities with national security and war against terrorism.

At the WFS-FYL meeting the FAO announced that the 2015 target was unreachable. The new target was reducing the number of hungry to 440 million by 2030. By 2004 "food security" was now used in reference to the prevention of intentional contamination of the food supply through tampering or other malicious criminal or terrorist actions or threats (ASTHO 2006). In the US, for example, USDA has identified a set of new biosecurity challenges to prevent, detect, and act in response to food safety emergencies, including: biosecurity of Food and Food Supply, food Security and Emergency Preparedness, along with a number of diseases such as the Exotic Newcastle Disease (END), Avian Influenza, Hoof and Mouth Disease (FMD), Bovine Spongiform Encephalopathy (BSE), and Soybean Rust (SBR).

Seeking "sustainable solutions" to environmental catastrophes created by global Fordism that sustained increasing production and consumption, to the threat of peak oil, global warming and to deal with its environmental critics, global capital decided to "go green" by using part of the global grain and oil seed stocks as biofuel (Weis 2007). Between 2004 and 2010 the amount of grains used as biofuel rose from 2 percent to 6.5 percent of the global production (Searchinger 2011). When speculations in the global commodity markets and plans to use grains and oil seeds as bio-fuel raised food prices, riots spread throughout the world (Clapp and Cohen 2009). Deregulation of the Commodities Futures Trading Commission in 1999 allowed global finance organizations such as Goldman Sachs and the Deutsche Bank to develop commodity indexes and speculating from fluctuations in the futures market (Kaufman 2011). Oil rich countries aiming for long-term food security and investment firms seeking better returns through large scale grain and oil-seeds production in a world of increasing commodity prices, began purchasing or leasing large tracks of land in the South (Vidal 2010). By 2008, "stability" was added to the conventional lists of food security priorities (FAO 2006). The Human Security Unit at the UN Office for the Coordination of Humanitarian Affairs claimed that "[food] insecurity is inherently interlinked with political security, socio-economic development, human rights and the environment. Consequently, a sharp rise in food prices can have a significant impact on human security reaching far beyond the immediate effects of hunger and malnutrition" (UNOCHA 2009, 1). Interestingly, this time stability was not just stability of the commodity prices as in 1974, but was political stability, in an era of global re-colonization.

Increasingly, food came to be used as a legitimate tool of punishment or discipline toward unfriendly regimes. Sanctions, in Iraq, Yugoslavia, North Korea, Palestine, Libya, Zimbabwe and elsewhere included denial of food and turned into collective punishment for millions of people while the global commitment to food security continued to reduce the numbers of hungry (Koc, Das and Jernigan 2007).

Conclusion

The global food system is organized according to the principles of efficiency, productivity, and profitability. Concerns about safety, social justice, local and regional development, and national sovereignty are only important as far as they do not become a categorical threat to the reproduction of labour, and to the conditions of accumulation (Desmarais 2007; Koc 2009; McMichael 2005; Patel 2007). As some of the critics of the modern food system argue, many of the chronic or periodic problems that are associated with the food system, such as the farm crisis, hunger and malnutrition, and obesity epidemic, are not anomalies but are reproduced by structures and institutions of the modern food system (Lang, Barling and Craher 2009; Lang and Heasman 2004; Nestle 2002).

Food security emerged as a discourse during the accumulation crisis in mid-1970s. While it reflected the international recognition of the need for cooperation to address humanitarian crises that condemned part of the world population to poverty and hunger, it also defined the conditions of food provisioning and addressing causes of the problems, priorities of action, and the role of institutional actors in seeking solutions to food insecurity. Its perplexity has reflected shifting priorities in the global economy and the contested nature of food provisioning in market economies.

The food security discourse was effective in underlining shortages in this process and offering policy solutions to improve availability, accessibility and effective utility of food. The most significant shortcoming of the concept, however, has been its lack of a critical focus on the food system and of the absence of an analytical approach to explain how food insecurity has been created by everyday practices, structures and institutions of the modern food system.

Many observers such as Albritton (2009) have argued that the capitalist economy has not only been incapable of addressing food security, but by its very nature has been the source of food insecurity. Nevertheless, food security has served as an effective discourse for both legitimizing market relations and disciplining the public by giving the impression that food security can be achieved within the capitalist agri-food system, while at the same time ensuring compliance of subordinate populations with the threat of food insecurity. As Patel (2009) states the concept of food security ignores discussing the social control of the food system (665). Food security discourse identifies problem of food provisioning as mostly a matter of availability and accessibility. It does not provide any critical inquiry on ownership of means of production, access to commons (such as land, water, seeds) and ignores the concentration of decision making process on conditions of food production and access to food in the hands of a few corporations.

Although food security sounds like a noble objective, it inherently implies that food insecurity is the norm and food security is the ideal by identifying lack of optimum conditions (in production, distribution and utilization) as problems. There is also a bleaker side to the food security discourse. Through aid and philanthropic programs, such as food stamps in the US or food banks in Canada, poverty and food insecurity are contained to a level that does not threaten the stability of political regimes around the world. This containment also serves as a disciplining tool. Like the prison system, persistence of islands of hunger and food insecurity creates a threat for the rest of the population with hunger, causing people to feel grateful for what they have and securing their compliance.

Since the mid-1970s, the period in which the food security discourse has emerged as an international priority, the world has suffered one of the worse assaults on social citizenship rights that resulted in the deterioration of the conditions of access to healthy food for ever larger segments of the global population. As a result of the neo-liberal restructuring, around a billion people remained without access to means of livelihood to produce their own food or did not have sufficient income to purchase it in the market place. Another billion, who had to look for cheap processed foods to feed themselves, suffered serious health problems. As the global economy is going through another major accumulation crisis in early 2000s, we can expect ever-widening segments of the world population to suffer food insecurity while the gap between the rich and the poor gets wider. One thing is certain: a more sustainable, equitable and healthy food system cannot happen in isolation. The emerging food sovereignty movement is connecting farmers, workers, and eaters in the effort to work towards a better food system.

References:

Aglietta, Michel. "World Capitalism in the Eighties." *New Left Review* 136, no. 1 (1982): 5–41.

Albo, Greg, Panitch, Leo and Vivek Chibber, ed. *The Crisis this time. Socialist Register 2011*. London: The Merlin Press, 2010.

Albritton, Robert. *Let Them Eat Junk: How Capitalism Creates Hunger and Obesity*. New York: Pluto Press, 2009.

Allen, Patricia. *Together at the Table: Sustainability and Sustenance in the American Agrifood System.* University Park, PA: The Pennsylvania State University Press, 2004.

Allen, Patricia and Julie Guthman. "From 'old school' to 'farm-to-school': Neoliberalization from the ground up." *Agriculture and Human Values* 23, (2006): 401–415.

Araghi, Farshad. "Food Regimes and the Production of Value: Some Methodological Issues." *Journal of Peasant Studies* 30, no. 2 (2008): 41–70.

Association of State and Territorial Health Officials. *States of Preparedness: Health Agency Progress*. Washington DC., 2006. Accessed April 12, 2010. htpp:// www.borderhealth.org/files/res_714.pdf.

Barndt, Deborah. *Tangled Routes: Women, Work, and Globalization on the Tomato Trail*. Lanham, Maryland: Rowman and Littlefield, 2002.

Bellows, Annie C. and Michael W. Hamm. "International Effects on and Inspiration for Community Food Security Policies and Practices in the USA." *Critical Public Health* 13, no. 2 (2003): 107–123.

Bonanno, Alessandro. "Globalization, Transnational Corporations, the State and Democracy." *International Journal of the Sociology of Agriculture and Food* 10, no.1 (2004): 37–48.

Bonanno, Alessandro, Lawrence Busch, William H. Friedland, Lourdes Gouveia, Enzo Mingione. *From Columbus to ConAgra: The Globalization of Agriculture and Food*. Lawrence, KS: University of Kansas, 1994.

Burch, David and Jasper Goss. "Global Sourcing and Retail Chains: Shifting Relationships of Production of Australian Agri-Foods." *Rural Sociology* 64, no. 2 (1999): 2334–2350.

Cépède, Michele. "The Fight Against Hunger: Its History on the International Agenda." *Food Policy* 9, no.4 (1984): 282-290.

Clapp, Jennifer and Mark Cohen. *The Global Food Crisis: Governance Challenges and Opportunities*. Waterloo: Wilfrid Laurier University Press, 2009.

Desmarais, Annette A. *La Vía Campesina: Globalization and the Power of Peasants*. Halifax and London: Fernwood Publishing and Pluto Press, 2007.

ETC Group. "Oligopoly Inc. 2005." *Communique* 99. Accessed August 22, 2007. www.etcgroup.org.

FAO. "An Introduction to the Basic Concepts of Food Security." *EC - FAO Food Security Programme*. Accessed March 7, 2010. http://www.fao.org/docrep/013/al936e/al936e00.pdf .

FAO. "Reducing Poverty and Hunger: The Critical Role of Financing for Food, Agriculture and Rural Development." Paper Prepared for the International Conference on Financing for Development Monterrey, Mexico, 18-22 March 2002. Accessed March 7, 2010. ftp://ftp.fao.org/docrep/fao/003/y6265E/Y6265E.pdf.

FAO. "Rome Declaration and Plan of Action for Food Security." FAO, Rome, 1996. Accessed March 7, 2010. http://www.fao.org/docrep/003/w3613e/w3613e00.HTM.

FAO."World Food Security: A Reappraisal of the Concepts and Approaches. Director General's Report." Rome, 1983.

FAO. Universal Declaration on the Eradication of Hunger and Malnutrition. FAO, Rome, 1974. Accessed March 14, 2010. http://www2.ohchr.org/english/law/malnutrition.htm.

Frank, Andre Gunder. *Capitalism and Underdevelopment in Latin America*. New York and London: Monthly Review Press, 1967.

Friedland, William. "Agrifood Globalization and Commodity Systems." *International Journal of the Sociology of Agriculture and Food* 12, (2004):5-16.

Friedmann, Harriet. "What on Earth is the Modern World-system? Food-getting and Territory in the Modern Era and Beyond." *Journal of World-System Research* 6, no.3 (2000): 480-515.

Friedmann, Harriet and Philip McMichael. "Agriculture and the State System: the Rise and Decline of National Agricultures, 1870 to the Present." *Sociologia Ruralis* 29, (1989): 93-117.

George, Susan. *How the Other Half Dies: The Real Reasons for World Hunger*. Harmondsworth: Penguin Books, 1976.

Guthman, Julie, Amy W. Morris, and Patricia Allen. "Squaring Farm Security and Food Security in Two Types of Alternative Food Institutions." *Rural Sociology* 71, no.4 (2006): 662-684.

Harvey, David. *A Brief History of Neoliberalism*. New York, NY: Oxford University Press, 2005.

Heffernan, William, and Mary Hendrickson. "The Global Food System: A Research Agenda." Report to the Agribusiness Accountability Initiative Conference on Corporate Power in the Global Food System. Hertfordshire, UK: High Leigh Conference Centre, 2005. Accessed August 21, 2007. http://www.foodcircles.missouri.edu/global.pdf.

Hodgson, Lesley. "Manufactured Civil Society: Counting the Cost." *Critical Social Policy* 24, no.2 (2004): 139-164.

Holt-Giménez, Eric and Annie Shattuck. "Food crises, food regimes and food movements: rumblings of reform or tides of transformation?" *The Journal of Peasant Studies* 38, no.1 (2011):109–144.

Inglis, David and Debra Gimlin, edit. *Globalization of Food.* Oxford, New York: Berg, 2009.

Jarosz, Lucy. "Defining World Hunger: Scale and Neoliberal Ideology in International Food Security Policy Discourse." *Food Culture and Society* 14, no.1 (2011): 117-139.

Jarosz, Lucy. "Energy, Climate Change, Meat, and Markets: Mapping the Coordinates of the Current World Food Crisis." *Geography Compass* 3, no. 6 (2009): 2065-2083.

Kaufman, Frederick. "How Goldman Sachs Created the Food Crisis." *Foreign Policy*, April 27, 2011. Accessed May 3, 2011. http://www.foreignpolicy.com/articles/2011/04/27/how_goldman_sachs_created_the_food_crisis.

Klein, Naomi. *The Shock Doctrine: The Rise of Disaster Capitalism.* New York: Metropolitan, 2007.

Koc, Mustafa, Jennifer Summer, and Anthony Winson, ed. *Critical Perspectives in Food Studies*. Toronto: Oxford University Press, 2011.

Koc, Mustafa. "Hyphenated Alternatives: Discourses of Food Security." Paper presented at the Joint Annual Meetings of the Agriculture Food and Human Values Society, Association for the Study of Food and Society and Society for Anthropology of Food and Nutrition The University of Montana, Missoula, Montana, US, June 10, 2011.

Koc, Mustafa. "Conceptual Perplexity of Food Security: A Critical Examination of Alternative Food Discourses." Paper presented at the Sociology of Agriculture and Food, International Sociological Association, XVII World Congress of Sociology, Gothenburg, Sweden, July 14, 2010.

Koc, Mustafa. "Hunger and Plenty: Fragmented Integration in the Global Food System." In *The New ISA Handbook in Contemporary International Sociology: Conflict, Competition, Cooperation*, edited by Anne Denis and Devorah Kalekin-Fishman, 323-335. New York: Sage, 2009.

Koc, Mustafa, Rod MacRae, and Kelly Bronson, ed. *Interdisciplinary Perspectives in Food Studies*. Toronto: McGraw-Hill, 2008.

Koc, Mustafa. "Changing Discourses of Food Security, and the Role of Civil Society in the Neo-liberal Era." Paper presented at the Annual Meeting of the Canadian Association for Food Studies, York University, Canada, June 1, 2006.

Koc, Mustafa. "Globalization as a Discourse." In *Colombus to Conagra: Globalization of Agriculture and Food*, edited by Alessandro Bonanno, Lawrence Busch, William H. Friedland, Lourdes Gouveia, and Enzo Mingione. Lawrence, KS: University of Kansas Press, 1994.

Koc, Mustafa and Japji Anne Bas. "Canada's Action Plan on Food Security: The interactions between Civil Society and the State to Advance Food Security in Canada." In *Health and sustainability in the Canadian food system: Advocacy and opportunity for civil society,* edited by Elisabeth Abergel and Rod MacRae. Vancouver: UBC Press, 2012.

Koc, Mustafa, Rupen Das, and Carry Jernigan. "Food Security and Food Sovereignty in Iraq: The Impact of War and Sanctions on the Civilian Population." *Food, Culture and Society* 10, no. 2 (2009): 317-348.

Koc, Mustafa and Rod MacRae, ed. *Working Together: Civil Society Working for Food Security in Canada.* Toronto: MSWG, 2001.

Koc, Mustafa, Rod MacRae, Ellen Desjardins, and Wayne Roberts. "Getting Civil About Food: The Interactions Between Civil Society and the State to Advance Sustainable Food Systems in Canada." *Journal of Hunger & Environmental Nutrition* 3, no. 2/3 (2008): 122-144.

Lang, Tim, David Barling, and Martin Craher. *Food Policy: Integrating Health Environment and Society.* Oxford: Oxford University Press, 2009.

Lang, Tim and Martin Heasman. *Food Wars.* London: Earthscan, 2004.

Lappé, Frances Moore and Joseph Collins. *Food First: Beyond the Myth of Scarcity.* Boston: Houghton Mifflin Company, 1977.

Lipietz, Alain. *Miracles and Mirages: The Crises of Global Fordism.* London: Verso, 1987.

Mamdani, Mahmoud. *The Myth of Population Control.* New York and London: Monthly Review Press, 1972.

Maxwell, Simon and Rachel Slater. *Food Policy: Old and New.* Oxford: Overseas Development Institute and Blackwell Publishing, 2004.

Maxwell, Simon and Marisol Smith. "Household food security: a conceptual review." In *Household Food Security: Concepts, Indicators, Measurements: A Technical Review*, edited by Simon Maxwell, Timothy R. Frankenberg. New York and Rome: UNICEF and IFAD, 1992.

McMichael, Phillip. "A Food Regime Analysis of the "World food Crisis"." *Agriculture and Human Values* 26, (2009): 281-295.

McMichael, Phillip. "Global Development and the Corporate Food Regime." In *New Directions in the Sociology of Global Development*, edited by Frederick H. Buttel and Phillip McMichael. Amsterdam: Elsevier, 2005.

McNally, David. "From Financial Crisis to World-Slump: Accumulation, Financialisation, and the Global Slowdown." *Historical Materialism* 17, (2009):35-83.

Mooney, Patrick H. and Scott A. Hunt. "Food Security: The Elaboration of Contested Claims to a Consensus Frame." *Rural Sociology* 74, no.4 (2009): 469-497.

Moreira, Manuel Belo. "Changes in Food Chains in the Context of Globalization." *International Journal of Sociology of Agriculture and Food* 18, no.2 (2011):134-148

Orr, J.Boyd. *Food and the People*. London: Pilot Press, 1943.

Panitch, Leo and Collin Leys, edit. *The Globalization Decade: A Critical Reader*. Halifax, N.S and London: Fernwood/Merlin Press, 2004.

Panitch, Leo and Sam Gindin. "The Current Crisis: A Socialist Perspective." *Studies in Political Economy* 83, (2009): 7-31.

Patel, Raj. "What does food sovereignty look like?" *The Journal of Peasant Studies* 36, no. 3 (2009): 663–706.

Patel, Raj. *Stuffed and Starved: Markets, Power and the Hidden Battle for the World Food System*. London: Portobello, 2007.

Power, Elain M. "The unfreedom of being other: Canadian lone mothers' experiences of poverty and 'life on the cheque." *Sociology* 39, no.4 (2005): 643–660.

Pritchard, Bill. "Implementing and Maintaining Neoliberal Agriculture in Australia Part 1: The Development of Policy." *International Journal of the Sociology of Agriculture and Food* 13, no. 1 (2005): 1-12.

Qualman, Darrin. *The Farm Crisis and Corporate Power*. Ottawa: Canadian Centre for Policy Alternatives, 2001.

Riches, Graham, ed. *First World Hunger: Food Security and Welfare Politics*. London: McMillan, 1997.

Searchinger, Tim. "How Biofuels Contribute to the Food Crisis." *Washington Post*, February 11, 2011. Accessed February 16, 2011. http://www.washingtonpost.com/wpdyn/content/article/2011/02/10/AR2011021006323.html.

Sen, Amartya. *Poverty and Famines: An Essay on Entitlement and Deprivation*. Oxford, UK: Oxford University Press, 1981.

Shaw, John D. *World Food Security: A History since 1945*. Houndsmill, Basingstoke, Hamshire: Palgrave Macmillan, 2007.

Slater, Joyce. *Community Food Security. Position of Dietitians of Canada*. Public Policy Statement. Ottawa: Dietitians of Canada, 2007.

Tarasuk, Valerie and George H. Beaton. "Household Food Insecurity and Hunger among Families Using Food Banks." *Canadian Journal of Public Health* 90, (2003): 109-13.

Tarasuk, Valerie and Joan M. Eakin. "Food assistance through "surplus" food: Insights from an ethnographic study of food bank work." *Agriculture and Human Values* 22, (2005): 177–186.

Thornton, William H. "Neoglobalism: The Fourth Way." *Antipode* 36, no.4 (2004): 564-74.

Tilzey, Mark. "Neo--liberalism, the WTO and New Modes of Agri-Environmental Governance in the European Union, the USA and Australia." *International Journal of the Sociology of Agriculture and Food* 14, no. 1 (2006): 1-28.

United Nations. *Report of the World Food Conference*, Rome, 5-16 November 1974. New York: United Nations, 1975.

UNOCHA, Office of the United Nations High Commissioner of Human Right. "Rising Food Prices and its Implications on Human Security." *Human Security at the United Nations*, Newsletter. Issue 5, Spring 2009.

Vidal, John. "How food and water are driving a 21st-century African land grab." *The Guardian*, March, 7, 2010. Accessed March 8, 2010. http://www.guardian.co.uk/environment/2010/mar/07/food-water-africa-land-grab.

Weis, Tony. *The Global Food Economy: the Battle for the Future of Farming*. Winnipeg: Fernwood Publishing, 2007.

Winne, Mark, Joseph Hugh and Fisher Andy. *Community food security: A guide to concept, design and implementation*. Venice, CA: Community Food Security Coalition, 1997.

Wittman, Hannah, Annette A. Desmarais and Nettie Wiebe. *Food Sovereignty in Canada*. Halifax and Winnepeg: Fernwood Publishing, 2011.

Via Campesina. "The right to produce and access to land. Voice of the Turtle." Accessed June 12,2011. http://www.voiceoftheturtle.org/library/1996%20Declaration%20 Of%Food%20sovereignty.pdf

Excellence, Quality, and the Lowering of Higher Education and Research: The Neoliberal Program in Review

Eric Newstadt

It is increasingly clear that in the midst of what Anwar Shaikh has referred to as the "first Great Depression of the Twenty First Century" (Shaikh 2011), governments around the world will attempt to slash government spending, apparently in a bid to stabilize the global economy through austerity. Of course, 'austerity' will not involve across-the-board cuts to government budgets, but will rather involve draconian cuts to public services coupled with a dense mixture of both across-the-board corporate tax-breaks, targeted incentives, and the strategic expansion of the state in key areas, all aimed at driving economic growth in the so-called "knowledge based economy". This programmatic agenda, which is correctly understood as neo-liberal in its orientation, is based on four ideas: 1) 'knowledge' is the key to success in the global economy; 2) markets and market-based competition are the most efficient means to affect the allocation of capital and therein both the valuation and production of new knowledge; 3) knowledge is a commodity; 4) human beings are radically limited such that the failure to recognize knowledge as a commodity is a "fatal conceit" (De Angelis and Harvie 2009b; Mirowski 2011, 29).[1]

[1] These ideas are foundational to the work of too many to list here. Philip Mirowski provides an excellent overview in his book, *The Road from Mont Pelerin* (2009). It is nonetheless vital to recognize that such ideas are fundamental to the work of more than just the neo-classical core – they re-appear in the work of New Growth Theorists, of the new and post-Keynesians, of the mainstream of economics and public policy.

In what follows, we examine the credibility of these ideas by examining those measures of research and teaching quality that have been most frequently relied upon to both evidence the success of neo-liberal restructuring, and to assure us of the promise held by broadening and deepening that same program. What will become clear as this examination proceeds is that the neo-liberal program has been – and will continue to be – an abject failure, even on its own terms. In fact, the degree to which the neo-liberal program has been a failure suggests that perhaps "success" is not about the creation of so many knowledge commodities as it is about building the socio-economic and political conditions necessary to create and maintain highly flexible labour markets.

Before we can begin the aforementioned evaluation we must establish two things: 1) an outline of the neo-liberal agenda for higher education; and, 2) some indication of the degree to which that program has already been tried and tested. These first tasks are under-taken immediately in sections one and two. In the third section we examine the "evidence", and in the fourth section, we offer some conclusions concerning the utility/viability of the neo-liberal program, the contradictions that are undermining the same, and the opportunities that oppositional movements might exploit in seeking to press beyond neo-liberal forms of higher education. For the most part, the 'evidence' we analyse will be culled mainly from studies of higher education in Canada, the United States and Great Britain. Our focus on these three jurisdictions should not be taken to mean however that the arguments made below apply to those contexts alone. The United States and Britain are arguably the clearest and paradigmatic examples of neo-liberal restructuring (Dumenil and Levy 2005; Panitch and Gindin 2004); Canada, on the other hand, offers a window into the kind of restructuring now taking place in "subordinate states" around the world (Panitch and Gindin 2004). And as is indicated below, the neo-liberal program has been assiduously pursued throughout both Eastern and Western Europe through declarations and treaties, like the Bologna Process, which aims to create the European Higher Education Area (Lorenz 2006); neo-liberal restructuring in Australia and New Zealand are also often pointed to as other examples of neo-liberal "policy-borrowing" (Schwartz 2000); and studies of higher education in the developing world also point to the secular pursuit of neo-liberal restructuring (Samoff and Bidemi 2004).

Institutionalizing the Neo-liberal Agenda for Higher Education and Research

At the highest level of analysis, the neo-liberal agenda for higher education and university research is straightforward: the agenda seeks to create deep, broad, and intensely competitive markets for what are conceived of as educational and research commodities. This agenda flows from the simple and persistent assertion that market-based competition is *the* most efficient method for the allocation of capital. As such, markets will facilitate the mass production of relatively high-quality and low-cost educational and research commodities. In so far as such educational and research commodities are and will not be identical, it is necessary to render them both suitable for particular kinds of uses in the knowledge based economy and, at the same time, commensurable. Accordingly, the neoliberals maintain that by supporting the development of markets and/or market-type price signalling in post-secondary education and university research, governments can support competition, and, in turn, specialization such that labour and research markets will be flush with precisely the skills and knowledge necessary to drive economic growth in the "knowledge-based economy" (Mirowski 2011, 35-37; Botwinick 1993; Schultz 1961; Becker 1962).[2],[3]

At lower levels of analysis, the neo-liberal agenda is decidedly more complex: because it seeks to leverage the state's resources and power so as to bolster the ability of capital to direct investment. The state is therefore fundamental to the neo-liberal agenda, but in different ways in different places; where deep and broad markets do not exist, the state is called upon to provide financial incentives to help develop new fields of accumulation. And the state is also relied upon to provide the juridical backdrop in front of which such programs can happen – claims on ownership must be protected in particular ways, oppositional forces must be controlled and corralled, the rules of the game, as it were, must be re-made to force the universities and students to compete, to understand themselves as competitive firms and/or agents (Lucas 1988; Romer 1990; Lipsey 2000). Thus, policy is everywhere and always adjusted to account for the particularities of place and time. For instance, where tuition-fees have been historically regulated by the state, the neo-liberal program has been to support the progressive raising of regulated ceilings alongside the expansion of state-backed student loan programs and the development of market-type signalling systems most frequently based upon some forms

---

[2] With such policies and programs in place, neo-liberals foresee the development of a system(s) of higher education within which a variety of specialized institutions "naturally" evolve: research-intensive institutions; liberal-arts colleges; trade and skills colleges; and poly-technical institutes. Within each tranche, institutions are organized hierarchically based upon the returns that "investors" (students and private-sector benefactors) are able to realize on their "investments". This hierarchy of differentiated institutions is itself subject to change as competitive private institutions vie to beat-out their competitors so as to attract more money and students.

[3] This approach to the production of "knowledge commodities" and "human capital", have a lengthy theoretical pedigree. Mirowski (2011) does an excellent job of discussing how contemporary approaches to knowledge production are rooted in the work of F.A. Von Hayek. Schultz (1961) and Becker (1962) are regarded as pioneers. Lipsey presents a more contemporary representation that brings these strands together under the auspices of New Growth Theory, thereby raising the spectre of Lucas's (1988) and Romer's (1990) work, which must also be seen as part of the neo-liberal canon.

of assessment and ranking procedure.[4],[5]. On the research side, policy has been adjusted to fill in gaps, for example, in credit markets by having the state provide seed capital where venture capitalists are not as plentiful as they are in the United States (Mirowski 2011, 114-128; Sears 2003). The state has also been called upon to fund research through programs that press universities closer to industry, generally by making access to funds conditional upon the conclusion of research agreements with private-sector "partners", and/or by simply allowing for the results of publicly funded research to be held privately (OECD 2005, 14-33; Scarpetta and OECD 2003, 84-85; OECD 2010, 5).

In as much as the neo-liberal agenda for higher education has not been fully implemented in any jurisdiction (as an ideal-type, it is simply impossible to *fully* realize), there should be decidedly less doubt than there continues to be, that neo-liberal policy has touched – and largely transformed – every nook and cranny of the university, and higher education more generally.[6],[7] The aforementioned varie-

---

[4] Tuition-fees have been increased in too many jurisdictions to list or reference; since 1980 tuition-fees have been introduced and consistently raised in the UK, Australia, New Zealand, and Germany (Paton 2012; Jongbloed). Throughout Canada, tuition-fees have increased precipitously since the mid-1990's (Macdonald and Shaker 2011), as have levels of Student Debt (Trick 2005).

[5] Rankings operate as price-type signaling systems by providing what is most frequently a numeric representation of what the market evaluates as "quality". As such, quality assessment can facilitate the process of commodification and specialization even in jurisdictions where prices are regulated and more or less the same at different institutions. This kind of argument is advanced by De Angelis and Harvie (De Angelis and Harvie 2009a).

[6] On the left, thinkers like Simon Marginson and Gary Rhodes have argued that the daily rhythms of research and teaching are, for many academics, largely unchanged. While this assertion is itself contested, the more important issue has to do with the degree to which the ideological spectrum has narrowed and been instrumentalized, used in the (re)production of commercializable research commodities, flexible labour markets, and contemporary capitalism more generally. (That academics still read, write, lecture, publish and sit on committees is quite besides the point, perhaps even symptomatic of it; the pressure to perform the work-related tasks ever more productively has intensified the workplace, led to the industrialization of taught-programs, been accompanied by the growth of huge bureaucratic managerial structures, and, most fundamentally exemplifies a process of proletarianization of academic work.

[7] The persistence of ignorance in this regard is perhaps rooted in several related issues: first, levels of state involvement remain high. Even though the state has cut back on monies transferred to higher education for operating purposes, most states in the developed world have actually increased, however mildly, the amount of support available for research.[7] Even more so, the state's tendency to make research funding conditional is hardly new. Of course, as Sears, Mirowski and others have clarified, the nature of such conditionality has indeed changed considerably (Sears 2003; Mirowski 2011). Second, neo-liberal policy has been incredibly variegated, both between and within jurisdictions.[7] Simply put, the reduction of higher education to the status of commodity with mass appeal (i.e. the instrumentalization of higher education and university research), has sometimes required neoliberalism to assume a "human-face". Third and finally, neo-liberal policy has often times sought to effect a "culture change", by which is meant the so-

gation of neo-liberal policy has occurred in the context of other policy shifts that are in many cases near-universal and which are arguably of a more fundamental nature. In other words, there are key areas within which neo-liberal policy has been institutionalized in virtually every jurisdiction and which have significant knock-on consequences for *everything* that goes on inside the university and higher education.

For instance, arguably the single most significant change has had to do with legislation that deals with the protection of intellectual property (IP) and patent. Though not always directed specifically at the university or institutions of higher education, such legislation, which has become ubiquitous nationally and internationally, has completely transformed the process of research and development. While this impact will be discussed in detail below, the legislation of which we are speaking has enabled private firms (including the universities themselves) to take ownership and control of knowledge discovered in publicly funded research protocols performed in publicly funded and/or owned laboratories (Coriat 2002, 1492-1499; Polster 2001, 87-88; Mirowski 2011, 117). Scholars working in the area have most frequently cited Bayh-Dole (1980) as the key piece of legislation, but as Mirowski and others have made clear, Bayh-Dole was but one piece in a series of legislative moves that made it possible for private firms to monopolize the results of publicly funded research in the US. Mirowski and others have also outlined that such legislative moves have been emulated everywhere *and* reproduced at the international level via the Trade Related Aspects of Intellectual Property (TRIPs) agreement and the World Intellectual Property Organization (Mirowski 2009; Slaughter and Rhodes 2004; Naidoo 2003, 250-251).

Against this altered juridical backdrop, states have developed various programs that have tended to both discipline researchers who do not pursue closer links with industry and which provide generous forms of financial support to those researchers and universities that do develop such links. In other words, the state has not just made it possible for the university to leverage public funding to generate privately held intellectual property; it has gone much further and made it utterly necessary for them to do so (OECD 2005, 28-30; Scarpetta and OECD 2003, 84-85; Advisory Panel on Science and Technology 1999, 1-2). For example, in 1989 Canada's federal government started the "National Centres of Excellence" program with the express goal of changing the culture within Canada's academy by providing extra research funding to multi-year projects that both offered the promise of commercialization and brought in private co-sponsors. This national program mim-

---

cial reproduction and embedding of neo-liberal ideology. The evidence of programmatic success is, in this regard, less the transformation of what happens on a day-to-day basis within the university than it is the re-direction and refocusing of that activity.

icked several provincial projects then already underway in the country, all of which sought to do precisely the same thing: offer private firms access to public funds and research infrastructure to generate privately owned IP. And as has been variously documented, such programs have been consistently expanded since their introduction in the mid to late 1980's (Trick 2005, 22-26; University of British Columbia. and Fisher 2006, 77-99; Fisher, Atkinson-Grosjean, and House 2001). Much like the United States' Bayh-Dole, such policies have been avidly supported by international organizations like the OECD, and duplicated with incredible alacrity in myriad other jurisdictions (OECD 2010; Mirowski 2011, 133-135).[8]

In terms of both teaching and research, governments around the world have instituted a huge and ever-increasing swathe of policies and programs intended to inspect and establish the level of quality of the educational and research commodities being provided in, and put out by, universities. In fact, to coordinate and manage the imposition of quality assurance in higher education, states have often established quality assurance "QUANGO's" (quasi non-governmental organizations), which have since 1991 begun working internationally via their own non-governmental organization, the International Network of Quality Assurance Agencies in Higher Education (INQAAHE).[9] These systems of quality assessment have tended to be introduced alongside: 1) cut-backs to operating transfers for higher education; 2) the deregulation of state-controlled tuition-fees (or else progressively raised regulated ceilings); and, 3) the expansion of government funded student loan programs (Finnie 2005; Johnstone 2004). The stated intent of such quality assurance programs has been to impose a price-type signalling system in publicly funded systems of higher education; by reducing the quality of a higher education to something that can be measurably assessed in what are always quantitative terms, current programs of quality assurance have sought to prove publicly the efficacy of on-going state funding and to provide would be customers (students and potential employers) with the information necessary to make decisions about attendance and hiring (Shore and Wright 1999; De Angelis and Harvie 2009a; Lang 2005).

In sum, then, governments around the world have pursued the neo-liberal agenda for at least the last twenty-five to thirty years. In part, the evidence of such pursuits is the institutionalization of neo-liberalism via: 1) changes to laws that deal with intellectual property and patent; 2) changes to the mechanisms through

---

[8] The OECD also publishes scorecards and other data on different national "innovation" programs. These can be accessed on-line at http://www.oecd.org/document/34/0,3746,en_41462537_41454856_41471586_1_1_1_1,00.html.

[9] In 1991 the International Network for Quality Assessment and Agencies in Higher Education was formed with a membership of 8. Today, INQAAHE holds a membership of over 200 such agencies.

which governments support the basic operations of universities as well as university-based R&D; and, 3) the use of "quality assurance" / price-type signalling programs, as the primary means by which to verify the efficacy of the overall program. It makes sense therefore that we turn our attention to a review of what has been established as 'quality' within the neo-liberal university (Shore and Wright 1999; Slaughter and Rhodes 2004; Slaughter 1997; Harvie 2006; De Angelis and Harvie 2009b).

Pricing Teaching and Research: Indicators of "Quality" in the Neo-liberal University

In terms of teaching and learning, the aim has been to provide evidence of quality by assessing both individual teachers and their output: students. To this end, university and college administrations, ideologically disposed researchers and teachers, and many governments have developed a huge bulwark of indicators that examine everything from teaching quality to learning quality, and literacy. Most frequently teaching quality has been assessed using "Student Evaluation of Teaching" forms (SETs).

SETs, which were pioneered by student activists in the 1960's and 1970's, have since the 1980's and 90's become a staple in most universities and colleges (Gray and Bergmann 2003; Seldin 1993). The mainstream literature on the utility of SETs is intensely contradictory, and generally expressive of the sentiment that the results of SETs are dependable to a limited extent and in a limited number of circumstances (Gravestock and Gregor-Greenleaf 2008, 29). For example, according to a report prepared for the Higher Education Quality Council of Ontario, research indicates that student evaluation surveys [SETs] are valid in so far as students are deemed good judges of how much they have learned, of how well information is presented (clarity, organization etc.), the degree to which active learning techniques are used, the ease or difficulty of their learning experience, the workload in a course, and the value of the assessment used in the course. Though these claims are in and of themselves dubious (research also indicates that students are greatly influenced by age, sex, colour, the enthusiasm of the instructor in presenting the information, etc.) the report also details that students cannot dependably assess the accuracy of course content, an instructor's knowledge of or competency in his/her discipline, grading practices and methods of delivery, the appropriateness of selected readings, and whether an instructor indicates bias. The report also notes that "global" or overall indicators of teacher performance are highly questionable in terms of their accuracy and usefulness. What this leads to is a cautionary endorsement wherein universities are directed to pay close attention to the myriad factors that could upset the SET applecart:

> Evaluations must be designed to carefully match their institutional context and be accompanied by substantial institutional support. Policies must be comprehensive and equitable. Education for evaluation users – students, faculty and administrators – must dispel myths and misperceptions and improve skill and transparency. Evaluations must be accompanied by ongoing dialogue and support mechanisms, including consultation, to ensure that they contribute to the support and improvement of teaching within the institution. Our research has clearly identified that evaluations are valuable and important tools for the assessment of teaching – but only if they are developed and supported with the understanding that validity is determined by much more than simply the ways students respond to individual items on a survey. (Gravestock and Gregor-Greenleaf 2008, 61)

Of course, it is worth bearing in mind that almost nowhere are SETs so cautiously employed. Indeed, the report itself notes the tendency to rely far too heavily on "global" measures (Gravestock and Gregor-Greenleaf 2008, 31-32). Further, when one considers: that 'valid' results are only obtained when researchers control for a variety of variables (age, sex, race, grade expectations)(Onwuegbuzie et al. 2007; Shevlin et al. 2000); that students' ability to evaluate how much they have learned is unquestioned, at least in absolute terms, even though there is the clear recognition that students cannot assess the degree to which a particular course covers key issues within a discipline/sub-discipline (Gravestock and Gregor-Greenleaf 2008, 28-29); the fact that overall rates of literacy, even amongst university and college graduates are appalling (Statistics Canada and OECD 2005) (see below); and, the fact that there are precious few academics well enough trained to understand and correctly use the results from such teaching evaluations (Gravestock and Gregor-Greenleaf 2008, 36), we must pause to consider whether most of the research on the subject is worth its weight. Simply put, we can only really judge the efficacy of SETs as they are currently, and have historically been used, not in terms of the potential they *might* hold were they to be employed in an ideal and supportive environment. And we should also pay close attention, as at least one commentator has done, to what it is SETs themselves teach students: the short-hand evaluation of intellectual work and learning undermines the goal of supposedly "higher education" and helps to construct students as consumers (Platt 1993).[10]

In terms of learning outcomes and the measurement thereof, the lion's share of the indicators presently in use are based upon a series of assumed correlations between self-reported data and direct, but seldom actually administered, literacy tests.

---

[10] Outside of the mainstream, SETs have been subject to much stronger criticism: first, it is argued that SETs actually undermine the teaching/learning process by themselves teaching that teaching and the evaluation of teaching is a relatively straightforward and easily accomplished task. Second, SETs, which are really just revised customer-satisfaction surveys, function to undermine the teacher-student relationship, and to support neo-liberal ideas about higher education as a commodity to be obtained at service-oriented institutions.

For instance, the National Survey of Student Engagement (NSSE), which is widely regarded as the cutting edge in the assessment of learning outcomes[11], presumes a direct correlation between the frequencies with which students self-report undertaking certain activities, particularly those which are said to be "high-impact". In other words, students who self-report participation in things like group work, or self-study, are said to have participated in so-called "deep-learning" activities, the end result of which is *presumed* to be "high quality learning outcomes"(Chickering and Gamson 1987; Carini, Kuh, and Klein 2006; Coates 2005, 29; National Survey of Student Engagement 2001). However, when NSSE data have been correlated with literacy tests, as they have infrequently been, results have indicated that the overwhelming majority of university graduates demonstrate levels of reading comprehension such that they can, at best, read and follow instructions, even despite relatively high NSSE scores (Baer, Cook, and Baldi 2006, 48). Nonetheless, mainstream scholars have either applauded or ignored such results, claiming, for instance, that the overall number of illiterate students has decreased. While this is true, it is also the case that, through the neo-liberal era (i.e. since the 1980's), the number of students able to demonstrate the highest levels of literacy has similarly decreased (Abrar 2005). To the extent that this has been accomplished in the context of near-constant austerity, and during a period when participation rates (and thereby the absolute number of students) and thus universities have expanded considerably, the mainstream appears to have understood these scores as something of an achievement.

Evidence of Efficiency in Research

If the measurement of teaching and learning quality is a mug's game, then efforts to measure the effectiveness of the neo-liberal program in terms of research is nothing short of miraculous. Perhaps the most apparent problem that plagues neo-liberal forms of quality assessment and measurement around university research has to do with the tendency to equate efficiency (i.e. productivity) with quality. Again, the logic for this equation is straightforward: in a competitive market/market-type environment, firms will be forced to pay top dollar for "excellent" research (i.e. research that private firms are willing to buy or rent, though not necessarily use). Similarly, researchers will be forced to competitively produce such 'excellent' research if they are to earn any support from either the public or private sectors. Thus, by closely tracking resources such as research dollars earned (either

---

[11] NSSE is currently administered at no fewer than 761 colleges and universities throughout North America. All universities in Ontario are required to participate. Ontario's Higher Education Quality Council of Ontario has noted that the NSSE is, "a useful baseline for research on learning quality (Higher Education Quality Council of Ontario 2007)".

from private sources or public bodies), publication counts and citation indices, research awards, licensing revenue, patent counts, and the like, governments and universities are able to track the efficiency with which research is produced, and, at the same time, reproduce the conditions for more such production. If we subscribe to the neo-liberal argument that conflates productivity with quality, then we would find an enormous amount of data available that would allow us to conclusively "prove" the efficacy of the neo-liberal program[12]. On the other hand, if we wish to actually subject this line of reasoning to critique, we are forced to search high and low for dependable data – there has simply been very little support for the development of such. And where such data is available, it, too, is of a rather questionable nature.[13]

One data-set that purports to transcend the neo-liberal equation of productivity and quality is that of bibliometric indices. Such indices track the frequency with which the work of any particular researcher is referred to by other researchers, all within a delimited set of journals. Accordingly, knowledge is said to be of higher quality if it is used more frequently in the generation of other knowledge. Arguably the most widely used source of such data is Thompson Scientific, (formerly Thompson ISI), a subsidiary of global news giant and publishing juggernaut, Thompson-Reuters.[14] Notably, the Thompson ISI citation ("bibliometric") indices cannot be subject to any kind of substantive scrutiny, as the corporation maintains the basis of its selection process and criteria as a trade secret. What this means is

---

[12] There are too many sources here to mention. Both the Association of University Technology Managers (AUTM) and the Association of Association of European Science and Technology Transfer Professionals (ASTP) publish annual reports tracking various measures of gross "output" (patents, licensing dollars etc.). In Canada, a private consulting firm, "Re$earch Money" prepares an annual ratings chart that tracks such aggregate dollars. Many universities also track and publish such results, for instance, the University of Toronto.

[13] The (un)availability of data is itself a subject worthy of study and inquiry. Mirowski (2011) discusses the tendency of government agencies in the US to either stop collecting or stop publishing certain data-sets, particularly those that would seem to challenge the status-quo. Mirowski also looks at the way in which governments have been apt to construct data in such a way as to boost support for programs of conditional finance in, for instance, the biotech sector. Describing such programs as Ponzi schemes, Mirowski argues that such data is fundamental to the neo-liberal program. In Canada, Statistics Canada has cancelled several datasets that track the success of the governments various commercialization initiatives. As well, the efforts of the Agency have been undermined by the current Conservative government, which has cancelled the country's long-form census. But then, Statistics Canada has long been subject to much criticism by users or would-be users who point out that access to key statistics is, in Canada, either not possible or extremely expensive (several such users have formed the "data liberation initiative" see, http://data.library.ubc.ca/datalib/gen/dli.html.

[14] As Mirowski (2011) outlines, Thompson is no longer the only for-profit organization that sells bibliometric data. In fact, several competitors now offer customers up-to-date data drawn from a significantly larger journal-set than does Thompson. However, Thompson's dominant position remains.

that it is simply not possible to test Thomson's claims that its indices are based upon a selection of journals that represent the "highest quality, most relevant materials (Testa 2003, 210)." In considering Testa's claim as to the quality of the journals tracked within Thompson's indices, it is useful to consider that: 1) Thompson in fact publishes many of the journals that are listed on its own index; 2) as a multinational publishing house that owns myriad academic journals, Thompson has a vested interest in preserving those arrangements that would enable private benefactors to maintain ownership of publicly funded research; any effort to make the results of publicly funded research freely available, for instance, via the huge number of open-source electronic journals now in operation, would fundamentally undermine Thompson's business model!

Testa has also clarified that Thompson works hard to select those "core" journals that contain the most frequently cited articles. As such, Thompson's data-set reflects what academics and experts indicate by their citation practices are the most important journals. In the current context, where the most frequently cited journals are also the most generously rewarded, this merely means that Thompson helps to create and disseminate the view that particular journals are relatively more important. Even if this were not the case, bibliometric indices could not usefully act as a measure of quality. Again, context is everything: bibliometric indices merely act as a reflection of the dominant tendencies within both the natural and social sciences; as with peer review, the degree to which one academic's work is cited by other academics could hardly offer a meaningful indication of quality, unless we buy into the assumed correlation (Shore and Wright 1999, 568-570; Roberts 2007, 358; Krimsky 2004). As is suggested below, we have ample reason to question the quality of the academic "outputs" produced under the current regime.

These problems are compounded by a host of others. For instance, it is difficult to gauge either productivity or quality when both multi-authored (in many cases over 50 authors) and ghost-authored papers now occupy a sizeable proportion of what is published within the natural sciences (Sismondo 2007). In both cases, bibliometric indices become decidedly less meaningful or dependable as an indication of any one researcher's contribution. More significantly, different journals expand and contract at different times and at different rates; arguably less a function of quality than of funding, this on-going movement is not caught in bibliometric measurements, which thereby act as a kind of obfuscation of what is happening within a particular discipline. And within some disciplines different journals are hardly representative of the discipline, but instead tend to operate more as a kind of political project with the aim of reproducing extending and/or preserving particular traditions or schools of thought (Mirowski 2009; Mirowski 2011, 259-287; Silva and Slaughter 1984; Lee and Harley 1998, 26-30; Harley 2002).

Government programs designed to evaluate and assess quality in a more thorough manner than is possible with the more simplistic quantitative measures listed above are also seriously flawed. Pioneering among the various research quality assessment programs undertaken by governments around the world has been the UK's Research Assessment Exercise (RAE). The RAE or Research Excellence Framework (REF), as it is now called, was first introduced in 1986 and followed hotly on the heels of legislation that effectively ended tenure in the United Kingdom (Willmott 2003, 132). Every 4-6 years since that time, faculty that have been designated by their departments as "active researchers" have had to submit one paper from each of the preceding years which they or their department feels is representative of their best work. Though the evaluative criteria were initially kept secret, the government has, since the third round of of the RAE, progressively opened things up. Currently, submitted works are subject to evaluation by panels of academics and experts who have in turn been guided in their evaluations by criteria established through consultation with the government's Higher Education Funding Council for England (HEFCE). In this way, peer review, which is problematic for the reasons outlined above, has also been effectively confined and directed via a process that is ultimately decided upon by an agency that has long established its support for commercialization (Shore and Wright 1999, 569-570). The results of panel evaluations are compiled and turned into an overall score on a five-point scale. Government research money has then been apportioned to each department or program based on both that department's score and the number of researchers to which the department is home (Willmott 2003; Lee and Harley 1998; Harley 2002; Morgan 2004; Baimbridge; Elton 2000; Rolfe 2003).

As much as the evaluative criteria used in the initial rounds of the RAE were kept secret, it was nonetheless made clear that higher grades would be given to research that was, "of direct relevance to the needs of commerce and industry (Higher Education Funding Council for England 2011, 48)." [15] To this statement, the HEFCE has recently added other, less instrumental descriptors. Still, this expanded notion of excellence is now placed within a new evaluative category – im-

[15] Recently, this phrase, which first appeared in 1995, has been used in conjunction with other statements which are ostensibly intended to broaden the definition of "excellence". In a way, this change reflects both the efforts of oppositional groups and some of the deleterious consequences that the RAE have had. It is also worth mentioning that recent pronouncements from the Government in the UK have demonstrated that the drive to press universities closer to industry has hardly weakened at all. For instance, the Government's recent "white paper"(need to pay attention to consistency concerning quotation marks), which focused more on teaching and access than on research, indicated that the availability of loan and grant funding to students will depend on whether or not universities can prove that their degrees are 'fit' for their 'purpose', which is understood only as employment. For instance, see (Department for Business Innovation and Skills 2007). For a good overview of the history of the Research Assessment Exercise, see (Willmott 2003).

pact – which will hardly help to prevent the on-going conflation of 'excellent' research with that which is 'useful' (Higher Education Funding Council for England 2011).

Anecdotal evidence suggests that in as much as the RAE/REF has provoked researchers to be more "productive", at least in terms of the number of articles generated, the quality of such research remains an open question. Not only have publishers indicated feeling pressured to publish the work of their British colleagues before it is sufficiently refined, lest their colleagues become un-employed or still more poorly paid, scholars themselves admit to "slicing and dicing" their work, dividing one paper into several so as to meet publication schedules and productivity requirements . Many academics in the UK have also raised concern over the fact the RAE/REF has undermined their ability to undertake long-form work, or to take significant amounts of time to properly gather and reflect on data (Harley 2002, 323–333; Smith 2000; Lee and Harley 1998). The RAE/REF, in other words, has helped to reproduce as normal, the kind of 'just-in-time' science that, as is detailed below, has not been demonstrably linked with meaningful forms of economic growth or innovation (Smith 2000; Willmott 2003; Harley 2002).[16] Others have found that the RAE has worked to create and reinforce a divide between research winners and losers that both undermines the potential expansion of cutting-edge scientific inquiry and punishes those academics and students who work at and attend less resourced institutions (Rolfe 2003; Elton 2000; Morgan 2004). Of course, the results of the REF are most useful when linked to other data, specifically to measures of the apparent utility of the knowledge being generated under the auspices of the RAE/REF regime. Thus, outside of efforts like the RAE/REF, governments and other NGOs have also been apt to want to "prove" the efficacy of the neo-liberal research enterprise by looking at the tendency of universities to produce IP, which is tracked through patent applications and grants or through the income generated by licensing such IP. Here again, more is always and everywhere construed as better – more patents and more revenues are held up as evidence of more quality, more innovation, or so the logic goes.

[16] Recent policy pronouncements from the British government also suggest that there are other ways to skin this proverbial cat. The conservative government has announced plans to make student support available to students so long as their programs are evaluated as fit-for-their-purpose, which is then defined as practically applicable in labour markets (Great Britain 2011). Thus, by both rewarding particular kinds of research and by funding particular kinds of taught programs will the government be able to fundamentally affect the direction of scientific research in the UK.

More Patents, more Licensing, Less Quality

There is a considerable literature that deals with the utility of patent data and licensing revenue as a means by which to prove the efficacy of investment in university R&D (Mowery and Ziedonis 2002; Rasmussen 2008; Lanjouw and Schankerman 2004; Jensen and Thursby 2001; J. Thursby and Thursby 2000). Unfortunately, the bulk of this literature is of questionable value; any apparent decline in patent quality is explained-away as a by-product of such things as truncated datasets or inexperienced market participants (i.e. universities that initially sought to license low-quality IP, only to be disciplined by the market into producing high quality IP). Over time, in other words, marked based incentives will drive necessary adjustments and thereby the production of high-quality research (Mowery and Ziedonis 2002).

Evidence from other sources seems to suggest that the quality of patents has indeed declined since the 1980s. For instance, experts in the field estimate that as many as 30% of new patents are redundant and overlap existing patents (Glass 2011); and the reports by the US's Food and Drug Administration indicate that only about 15% of new drug patents are for truly original compounds (Mirowski 2011, 214-215). Moreover, increased licensing revenue may only be an indication of the increased costs associated with conducting research. For instance, universities now extensively use Material Transfer Agreements (MTAs), as a means to earn licensing revenue by charging each other for the use of patented materials necessary for the conduct of other research (Mirowski 2011, 152-160). Also of note is the fact that the Association of University Technology Managers, only publishes data detailing the amount of gross revenue earned by universities through licensing; no organization or university publishes *net* revenue, which would offer some indication of how much is being spent to develop and manage (litigate) IP, relative to how much is earned licensing the same; what data are available seem to corroborate this very suggestion, that licensing revenue, evaluated on a net basis, makes the whole enterprise appear decidedly less lucrative.[17] In Canada, for example, despite a marked increase in the number of patents being both applied for and granted, patent approvals as a percent of applications are trending downward. And universities are spending ever more to administer this IP (Statistics Canada 2008).

Universities have also become upstream providers of IP to a new breed of downstream "user", so-called, "Non-Practicing Entities" or NPEs. Such NPEs, which are most prevalent in the US, but are present in other jurisdictions too,

---

[17] Data from a now cancelled survey by Canada's national statistical agency, Statistics Canada, made clear that the costs for universities of administering IP have been rising consistently since 1998. Other data suggests that university IP is receiving patent approval less and less frequently, again since 1998. (Statistics Canada 2008)

amass huge arsenals of patents as a means to threaten litigation and generate previously unheard-of rents. Though such firms purport to act as the protectors of scientists lacking business savvy, they appear more so to be the benefactors of the venture capitalists who provide the seed capital for their patent libraries. With a closet full of sufficiently broad patents, these "patent-trolls" either rent out or sell on their patents to tech firms interested in protecting themselves against litigation by other such trolls, or by competitive firms looking to take out main rivals (Mirowski 2011, 148; Glass 2011). Indeed, so immense is the cost associated with the kind of protracted litigation one commonly finds around IP that many tech-based firms have found it more economically sensible to pay licensing fees when they are demanded in order to access patent libraries. Or else firms simply opt to amass their own arsenal of patents, most of which they never intend to use, so as to hold them over the head of litigious competitors and NPEs. Rather than prove the originality of whatever technologies they have developed or brought in-house or demonstrate the frivolity of claims about encroachment, firms pay to access patent libraries as a kind of insurance (Arthur 2011; Mirowski 2011, 148; Glass 2011).

Patenting and licensing, in other words, have become precious hostages worth a healthy ransom at least as much as they have mechanisms to ensure that dedicated scientists and inventors receive well-earned rewards for new ideas. We also have yet to mention the influence peddled by powerful institutional forms that only emerged in the neo-liberal era; the NPEs, huge swathes of the universities' institutional apparatus, new forms of arms length government bodies, private consultants that provide "innovation expertise," and venture capitalists exercise considerable power and their survival simply depends upon their ability to leverage that power to recreate the neo-liberal program that feeds them (Finder 2008; Glass 2011; Slaughter 1997; Slaughter and Rhodes 2004; Pisano 2006). The upshot is simple enough: the "evidence" used to support the neo-liberal program fails utterly to recognize that patents,

> ...bear economic value for all sorts of reasons unrelated to the progress of science: they may be used to block rivals from entering your market or to frustrate anyone the holder wishes to prevent from further researching the area; they may be used as defensive devices against other big holders or patent portfolios; they can be used as defences in antitrust action; they can be pretexts for parasitical litigation by patent trolls. Thus it would almost always be a travesty to try and "impute backward" the scientific significance of a discovery from some market indicator like license revenue, or patent renewal fees, or the extent of litigation. Value need not reliably map into significance or importance from a scientific perspective. (Mirowski 2011, 307)

The "Ice-berg" effect: commercialization and economic growth

Some neo-liberals, rather than become bogged down in the intricacies of patent data or bibliometric indices, have instead attempted to prove the efficacy of the neo-liberal research program by detailing apparent links between investment in university research and economic growth. In this regard, the neo-liberal enterprise has been to demonstrate that each dollar invested in university research has a multiplier effect, such that the rate of return to the overall economy is terrifically high, thus making investment in university research incredibly attractive. Exemplary here has been the work of Fernand Martin whose study of the economic impact of university research has formed the basis of successive reports by lobby groups and government agencies both in Canada and the United States (Martin 1998).[18] Martin's work, which seeks to demonstrate the relative benefits of government investment in university research, builds upon the idea that new knowledge leads to increases in the overall rate of productivity. Simply, new knowledge will, for Martin, "spill-over" from one sector of the economy to another, and, as 'spill-over' occurs, so the productive efficiency of firms' operations increases (as they make use of and apply the new technology). Thus, investment in knowledge is said to have a larger, macro-economic effect, wherein new knowledge increases the overall rate of productivity and is therefore a boost to GDP. In fact, for Martin, the net return on investment in university research is, over seven years, about 200%. Martin refers to this awesome rate of return as an "impact iceberg" both because it is massive and because the process of spill-over makes it hard to actually see; because of the way in which new knowledge is adapted and built upon, the impact of such knowledge, like a line of computer code buried in a larger program, is hard to see.

To get his jaw-dropping return on investment (ROI), Martin makes several assumptions, the most significant of which is the idea that it is possible to dissemble the rate of growth of GDP so as to determine by what it is being driven, be it new knowledge, good weather, the availability of health care, the application of monitoring technologies that help managers punish idle workers and, of course, the rate

---

[18] Martin's work was used first in Canada by the Association of Universities and Colleges Canada (see AUCC 1998). That 1998 report by the AUCC has subsequently been updated in a series of annual reports (the "Momentum Reports) put out by the AUCC to lobby government for research funding. The use of Martin's methodology is also evident in a report prepared by ICF Consulting for the University of California in March of 2003. See the Report, "California's Future it Starts Here" at, http://www.universityofcalifornia.edu/itstartshere/report/fullreport.pdf. Martin's methodology is also used in Lynch and Aydin (2004)'s, "Literature Review of the Economic and Social Impact of Higher Education Research Funding. The 1998 report is available at: http://www.aucc.ca/_pdf/english/publications/researchfile/1997-98/vol2n3_e.pdf, the 2005 and 2008 reports, which both bear the title, "Momentum," can be found: http://www.aucc.ca/momentum/en/.

at which new knowledge spills over from one economic sector to another (Martin 1998, 679-683). Assuming, as mainstream economists do, that this were possible – and it is not – it is still less likely that such analyses could be predicatively accurate, particularly given that there is a host of other assumptions that need to be made in order to reach Martin's conclusion (Fine 2000). For instance, Martin makes assumptions regarding the "productive milieu" within which new technologies are introduced. To do this Martin designates certain values to all manner of variables, which he sees as significant to the process he wants to measure; Martin imputes values for the relative availability of seed capital, the nature of property rights within a given jurisdiction, even the geographic concentration of capital. Such numerical assignments, which ultimately impact on the multiplier-effect that new knowledge is said to have, are in turn built upon the work of other, similarly inclined economists, who have made either the same or a similar set of assumptions regarding economic growth in the hope of demonstrating what has already been assumed to be true (Martin 1998, 682-683).[19]

As has already been outlined, there are many good reasons to doubt that government investment in university R&D has, within the current context, led to so many technological breakthroughs that have in turn triggered productivity increases and overall economic growth. The first has to do with the review of the "evidence" above; the suggested degradation of research and patent quality in the context of a transformed juridical environment suggests that the overall rate of economic growth has been driven less by the spill-over of new technologies from the university into one and then another productive sector of the economy, than it has by the private sector's willingness to invest in and grow a program of accumulation that has presented private sector players with myriad new avenues and devices such as conditional finance programs, material transfer agreements, and other such licensing vehicles, to seize an ever larger portion of the economic growth that such a program thereby produces. There is, in other words, a kind of self-fulfilling prophecy at work here. For instance, it is difficult to estimate with any precision the degree to which consistent increases in drug prices over the last twenty years have been driven by pharmaceutical companies looking to exercise their rights over publicly funded intellectual property developed in publicly built and funded institutions. It is, however, indisputably the case that publicly funded healthcare systems have been taxed by the terminal increase of drug prices since the emer-

[19] To draw conclusions about the efficacy of IP, economists perform "barro-type regressions" in which they attempt to correlate the overall rate of growth of GDP over some historical period (that which fits the model) with factors that are assumed to have a positive or negative impact on that rate of growth. Accordingly, the list of factors that can impact economic growth is both known (they are derived from models in which historical behaviour is "explained" by the presence/absence of the same identifiable factors, like IP protection), and measurable (i.e. Bayh-Dole can be accounted for numerically).

gence of the neo-liberal regime. In other words, states have allowed firms to use public money to perform R&D, to then protect whatever new knowledge is developed, and finally, to then turn-around and charge the state monopoly rents in order to access the same new knowledge that the state paid for in the first place. In this way, neo-liberalism has opened up new avenues for firms to reduce costs, appear to improve productivity, and generate huge profits. Only the most poorly managed firms would not look to invest in such a program.

There are still other more plausible explanations for productivity increases over the last thirty years than measurable improvements caused by the 'spill-over' of university based research and IP. For instance, since the 1980s, productivity increases have happened amidst secular increases to the work-week, overall levels of household debt, unpaid overtime, as well as to declines in the overall rate of unionization throughout the developed world (Baines 2004; Duménil and Lévy 2001; Green 2001; Strazdins and Loughrey 2007; Kotz 2003; Breilh and Centro de Estudios y Asesoría en Salud (Quito) 2005; Panitch and Gindin 2004). In other words, neoliberalism has entailed the removal of institutions that would protect workers' rights and wages, the restructuring or abandonment of state-welfare programs and systems of progressive taxation that provided workers with a basic level of economic security and a format for the progressive redistribution of wealth. Thus, neoliberalism has entailed the creation of so much economic insecurity and inequality such that workers have been willing to do more for less. At the same time, the demand for goods and services has been driven by the ready availability of consumer/household credit, which has reached historically unprecedented levels throughout the neo-liberal era (Wade 2008, 11-13; Cynamon and Fazzari 2008; Papadimitriou et al., 2011). The upshot is that increases to the rate of productivity and the sources of profit under neo-liberalism cannot be plausibly explained with reference merely to "innovation" and the spillover thereof. This is not to say that technological change has not played a fundamental role in the process of economic growth – it has (does); rather than deterministically drive growth (through such mysterious processes as "spillover"), technological change is leveraged socially and politically, as a means through which to find ever more effective/seductive means to squeeze and/or replace wage-labour (Wood 2005). Arguably, this pattern of accumulation is evidenced by the kinds of patterns we have been witnessing throughout the developed world over the last three decades: lengthy periods of economic growth and, simultaneously, secular increases to overall levels of inequality. Again, Martin and mainstream economists like him, ignore such issues and instead presume that the sources of profit can be empirically derived by decomposing aggregate measures of economic activity, like gross domestic product, through complex econometric models that are in turn derived not from reality, but from neo-classical economic theory. Rather than considering the politically unpalatable facts of neoliberalism, which would require an explanation of how dominant patterns of research funding might have contributed to the contemporary context, they have opted for smoke and mirrors: investment in innovation has yielded heretofore unheard-of returns, never-mind the ostensibly unrelated issues of for whom and at what cost (Milonakis and Fine 2009).

As it happens, Martin and his ilk could not be further from the truth: in the context of a global economy where capital is mobile, intellectual property highly protected, and international trade relatively cheap, firms have hardly looked to build more internal research capacity. Nor have they bid-up the price of "high-quality" university-based research. On the contrary, the very firms that have been able to leverage publicly subsidized IP to lower developmental costs of new drugs *and* charge monopoly rents for such drugs when they come to market, have also been able to boost productivity and profits by downsizing their operations in the developed world (i.e. reducing labour-forces, thereby placing downward pressure on wages) (Tempest 2010). This has happened while firms have increased their presence in other jurisdictions.[20] This line of causative explanation becomes more believable still when one considers that key sectors long targeted by generous forms of government investment in and subsidy of university research have consistently failed to generate a profit (Mirowski 2011, 209; Pisano 2006).

The Reproductive Power of the Neo-liberal University

For those who have looked critically at the neoliberal university, it is at this point commonplace to evaluate the overall longevity of the neoliberal project, either in jurisdictional/territorial terms, or globally, given the degree to which such policy has been deployed throughout the world. But whether neoliberal policies around higher education and university research could really affect either innovation or economic competitiveness is really beside the point. First, there is much to suggest that the long-term stability of the current global political economic order will not be undermined by the efficiency with which the neoliberal university is productive of a populace that is only moderately literate, or a scientific base that is generative of so much junk science; we should not mistake the efficient production of the moderately literate for the absence of an ability to train a sufficiently large number of remarkably bright people capable of operating with stunning efficiency within the dominant paradigm. Likewise, we should not mistake the degree to which neoliberalism imperils some idyllic form of science, with the promise that neoliberal

[20] Since the 1980's, Contract Research Organizations (CRO's) have developed in spots all over the Third World. Such organizations perform segments of research, like clinical trials, on contract for big pharmaceutical companies, at a relatively lower cost, and in a relatively looser regulatory environment than is possible in universities throughout the developed world. For more on this phenomenon see, Mirowski (2011, 219-242).

science can efficiently deliver more and more "false wants", or the technologies necessary for the survival – and intensification - of the current world order.

It is also no longer useful to think of any single nation's science base or labour pool as a source of competitive advantage necessary to underscore the durability of the neo-liberal program, particularly if that state happens to be either prominent or pre-eminent within the prevailing world order. Today, the owners of intellectual property are global corporations that enjoy considerable transnational mobility and unprecedented levels of state-support. This should not be taken to mean that states do not – and will not – remain utterly central. Rather, it is to say that the ability of any one state to dominate on the world stage will not necessarily be built on its ability to educate a highly literate domestic labour-force or generate meaningful forms of innovation within its territorial borders. Instead, the projection of power will arguably rest on the ability of key states to maintain a favourable juridical environment, as well as relationships with important firms and segments of global capital.

Put another way, we need to excavate from our analyses of the neo-liberal university those elements of determinism which have often appeared to creep in, if only because the political – and strategic – questions are far more pressing than is the crystal ball gazing we do when we look too broadly at tendencies, analyse by extension, and unwittingly reproduce moribund notions of the state and markets. Indeed, what the preceding implores us to understand is that, however theoretically and empirically weak is the evidence used to support the neo-liberal university, it remains incredibly potent politically. This is at least partly the case precisely because the neoliberal university, and neoliberalism generally, is productive of "sub-optimal" outcomes; the world order within which the neo-liberal university has taken shape is durable and potent because it is effective in the production of popular consent for policies that recreate flexibility in labour markets and particular (consumer) kinds of technologies. Of course, such potency is not absolute – there are cracks and fissures emerging all around which need to be leveraged if we are to get "somewhere else".

The first of these cracks has to do with the persistent inability of neo-liberal forms of education to provide a fulfilling learning experience. This is because the logic of the neo-liberal enterprise conflates economic well-being, which higher education today hardly guarantees, with well-being, enlightenment, fulfilment, and happiness.[21] This is simply not the case. It is crucial to bear in mind that the job

[21] Ryerson University in Toronto, Canada, has recently lauched a new advertising campaign designed to attract new students to its continuing education program. Under the image of a smiling graduate of the program, the campaign's tag line reads: "Be the employee that employers want."

prospects of recent graduates (and not so recent graduates) are dim; not only is unemployment high among recent graduates, but the "return" one earns on an "investment" in higher education is only high if income gains are evaluated relationally, relative to those who have no education. In fact, wage rates, in real terms, have been relatively stable throughout the developed world over the last thirty years (Duménil and Lévy 2011, 46-48; Harvey 2005, 25). That said, employment, throughout the developed world, has shifted to the services sector, where employers have begun to require that potential employees have a degree/diploma, thereby making the average wage available to those that attend neo-liberal higher education. Simply, the neoliberal program cannot deliver on its promise, even when such is evaluated on its own terms; a university degree guarantees access to neither a job nor a high-wage, which again are preconditions to the neo-liberal vision of bliss (for the masses). Moreover, the forms of work that graduates are likely to encounter do not appear to hold the promise of enlightenment. Recent reports from various government agencies indicate that there are high levels of under-employed/ underpaid and overworked young graduates whose work is often highly structured and requires a level of emotional output that is both exhausting and alienating.[22] As patterns of economic dislocation become more stated in unstable and stagnating economies, the neo-liberal university will perhaps become less effective in the reproduction of neo-liberalism, or at least productive of social conditions that can be usefully exploited by oppositional movements.

In the US, unprecedentedly high tuition-fees have also been linked to decreases in the country's higher education participation rate, particularly amongst students from the lower income quartiles (Anon. 2008). It goes without saying that the neo-liberal university can only operate as an effective tool in the reproduction of neo-liberalism if students are willing and able to attend. The secular increase of tuition-fees in other jurisdictions (Canada, the UK, Australia, New Zealand, to name a few) suggests that a similar pattern will eventually develop in those jurisdictions, possibly even if tuition fees do not hit levels seen today in the US. The neo-liberal solution to this potential problem has been twofold: 1) they have relied heavily upon various means-tested forms of subsidy, generally to students from low-income backgrounds; 2) they have made credit more readily available to students (Macdonald and Shaker 2011). While the use of means-testing has been effective at reproducing a "kinder-gentler" neo-liberalism, the upward creep of tuition-fees

---

The image and the line together conflate employment (and docility), with happiness and satisfaction.

[22] Currently, firms evaluated as being top-tier employers are using various forms of social networking software as a kind of employee monitoring device re-packaged and sold as a gateway to employee satisfaction and piece-of-mind. Software like "Rypple" has subordinates, managers and colleagues submit anonymous feedback about their work colleagues. Bentham's Panopticon meets Facebook.

amid persistent and high levels of unemployment suggests that governments may be forced to adjust threshold levels for means-tests in order to make subsidies available to an ever larger proportion of the population. Where they do not so adjust threshold levels, even to the point of making subsidies near-universal, we can expect increasing levels of popular opposition to the neo-liberal program. In the US, where levels of student debt have reached dizzying levels, oppositional movements are already finding a firmer footing in terms of their ability to both organize and mobilize around this very issue. In other jurisdictions, debt is similarly becoming a hot-button issue generative of, in many cases, more discord than is present in the US.

The neo-liberal program has also subjected most academics to a work-regime that is ever-more punishing, alienating, and insecure. This process of "proletarianization" can be linked to more than just the diminution of the quality of research and teaching, as outlined above – it can also be linked to increasing levels of job dissatisfaction and workplace disruptions (Connell and Crawford 2007; Barrett and Meahgan 1998; Levin and Shaker 2011; Shore and Wright 1999, 569-570). While academic work has traditionally provided relatively high salaries, such rates of pay are miserably low when evaluated in terms of tuition-fees paid and overall years spent in school (the neo-liberal tests of return on investment). In fact, those professions that also require lengthy periods of post-graduate study have considerably higher "yields" (Casey 2009; The Economist 2010). The trade-off for most academics has been the flexibility that academic work allows – time to think, explore, and create. As the space for intellectual pursuit becomes more monitored, structured, and limited, we can expect further discord within the professoriate. Historically, universities and government agencies have been able to moderate such discord by effectively dividing the professoriate into myriad different tranches – prolific researchers who earn research awards (and corporate sponsorships) are separated from those that teach, from those that teach on contract, and from those that teach on contract at multiple universities simultaneously. By rewarding the researchers who operate at the pinnacles of the system, both governments and universities have been able to leverage the precariousness of contract faculty to prevent the emergence of militancy within the whole academy (Newson and Buchbinder 1988). While this has often worked, there are signs that such a divide and conquer strategy may be limited, particularly as the precariously employed begin to undertake the majority of teaching on many campuses. This is so because contract and insecurely employed faculty are beginning to organize, develop stronger ties with their tenured faculty. Also, a growing number of academics have become concerned about the quality of education with which such "flexible" work regimes are linked (Schmidt 2011).

Other contradictions relate both to human health and the earth's ecosystem. As a direct result of governments' efforts to press the university ever closer to industry, universities appear less and less willing to question in meaningful ways the efficacy of certain drug treatments, or industrial processes, ones that are potentially devastating to human health and the environment. For instance, in the US, the University of Pennsylvania has consistently appeared relatively unconcerned about the practice of "fracking" (an industrial process used to access stores of natural gas in rock), apparently because the oil and gas industry provides considerable amounts of financial support for research at the university (Glass 2011). Such patterns, which have already produced numerous other serious public health and environmental crises, will most assuredly continue to do so, and in the process will provide important opportunities for oppositional movements to make significant gains.[23]

Finally, it is necessary to consider some of the theoretical considerations indicated by the foregoing analysis. At times it seems unbelievable that in the face of cogent critique anyone could continue to believe in the virtues of the neo-liberal line, at least not in earnest. Indeed, in light of both the available evidence and the fact that neo-liberal organizations like the Trilateral Commission have long sought to leverage higher education to reproduce consent for a renewed and market-based form of authoritarianism[24], seem to belie notions that markets are relatively efficient ways of organizing human relations. It would seem that "the evidence" is really nothing more than a sideshow intended to draw attention away from the

---

[23] By way of another example, recently, questions have emerged about the effectiveness of Tamflu, an antiviral produced by Roche, one of the world's largest pharmaceutical companies, which was claimed would be effective in the treatment of the Avian Flu. During the Avian Flu epidemic in 2009, governments around the world spent billions stockpiling the drug, largely based on Roche's research. Subsequently, and just as stockpiled drugs are about to expire, third party analysts using only a portion of Roche's data (Roche has refused to release the remaining data and in fact claims that it doesn't exist), has thrown Roche's findings into question and even raised additional questions about potential side-effects of the drug (Rattue 2012). Of course, the pressing questions relate to more than just Tamiflu: Roche merely followed regular drug approval protocols in funding the research that would be used by the drug approval agencies to "verify" the efficacy of Tamiflu.

[24] In the 1970's, the Trilateral Commission, a transnational neo-liberal juggernaut, published, "The Crisis of Democracy". In that report, the Commission argued that the university was fundamental to resolving the root cause of the aforementioned crisis, which they argued was a surplus of democracy. Accordingly the university was to be re-tooled; the educational programming was to be tied more closely to the rhythms and demands of the labour market, and simultaneously leveraged to lower what were held by the Commission to be the unrealistically high expectations of graduates. As with all forms of neo-liberalism, the masses are viewed as limited in their ability to transcend the parameters of human existence so as to optimally organize their affairs. Such limitations mean that only the neo-liberal economist is able to see that markets are benevolent mechanisms around which to organize all forms of human activity.

processes that the neo-liberalization of higher education and research have helped to facilitate, namely the wholesale revision of the post-war class compromise. Such a view seems more plausible still when one discovers the degree to which the work of key thinkers such as Milton Friedman and Friedrich Hayek was developed and advanced as a conscious political project (Mirowski 2009). The theoretical exaltation of the economist within neo-liberal theory, which presents him as objective, rational, and exclusively able to judge which conceits are likely fatal, also seems to indicate that the outcomes of neo-liberal policy could hardly be "unexpected".

Of course, in as much as organizations like the Mont Pelerin Society and the Trilateral Commission have been able to corral the loyalty of key decision-makers around the world and foretell the direction of neo-liberal policy rather accurately, they are still but expressions of the underlying system that they have nonetheless helped to create and reform. The neo-liberal university cannot be so usefully understood as merely a by-product of, as it were, "intelligent design". Rather, it must be seen as a part of the unfolding of a renewed global capitalism within which key segments of the ruling class have worked diligently to construct and maintain a political project and an underlying program of accumulation, always in the face of very particular forms of opposition and class conflict. Only in this way can we access and assess the various forms that neo-liberal policy has taken the world over. And only in this way, can we excavate, examine, and seize the roots and mechanisms of power that capital is presently able to leverage so well in its drive to leverage the university ever-more effectively in the recreation of neo-liberalism.

References:

Abrar, Hasan. "International Perspectives on Higher Education." Paper presented at the National Dialogue on Higher Education, Ottawa, Ontario, November 28, 2005.

De Angelis, Massimo, and David Harvie. "'Cognitive Capitalism' and the Rat-Race: How Capital Measures Immaterial Labour in British Universities." *Historical Materialism* 17, no. 3 (2009): 3-30.

Arthur, Charles. "Nortel Patents Sold for $4.5bn." *The Guardian*, July 1, 2011, Online edition. http://www.guardian.co.uk/technology/2011/jul/01/nortel-patents-sold-apple-sony-microsoft.

Baer, Justin, Anthony Cook, and Stephane Baldi. *The Literacy of America's College Students*. Washington D.C.: American Institutes for Research, 2006. http://www.air.org/files/The20Literacy20of20Americas20College20Students_final20report.pdf.

Baimbridge, Mark. "The Return of the Binary Divide? Evidence from the 1992 RAE." *Journal of Further and Higher Education* 20, no. 1 (1996): 3–13.

Baines, Donna. "Caring for Nothing: Work Organization and Unwaged Labour in Social Services." *Work, Employment & Society* 18, no. 2 (June 2004): 267–295. doi:10.1177/0950017200404277O.

Barrett, Ralph, and Diane Meahgan. "Proletarianization, Professional Autonomy and Professional Discourse: Restructuring Educational Work In Ontario Colleges." *College Quarterly* 5, no. 3 (1998). Accessed December 12, 2011. http://www.collegequarterly.ca/1998-vol05-num03-spring/barrett_meaghan.html.

Becker, Gary. "Investment in Human Capital: A Theoretical Analysis." *The Journal of Political Economy* 70, no. 5 (1962): 9-49. Accessed November 9, 2011. http://vanpelt.sonoma.edu/users/c/cuellar/econ421/humancapital.pdf.

Botwinick, Howard. *Persistent Inequalities: Wage Disparity Under Capitalist Competition*. Princeton, N.J.: Princeton University Press, 1993.

Breilh, Jaime, and Centro de Estudios y Asesoría en Salud (Quito). *Latin American Health Watch: Alternative Latin American Health Report*. Quito, Ecuador, 2005.

Canada. Advisory Panel on Science and Technology. *Public Investments in University Research: Reaping the Benefits*. Ottawa: Information Distribution Centre, Communications Branch, 1999. http://www.carlabrc.ca/projects/commercial/pdf/comm_may-e.pdf.

Carini, Robert M., George D. Kuh, and Stephen P. Klein. "Student Engagement and Student Learning: Testing the Linkages." *Research in Higher Education* 47, no. 1 (February 2006): 1–32. doi:10.1007/s11162-005-8150-9.

Casey, Bernard H. "The Economic Contribution of PhDs." *Journal of Higher Education Policy and Management* 31, no. 3 (July 2009): 219–227. doi:10.1080/13600800902974294.

Chickering, Aurthor, and Zelda Gamson. "Seven Principles for Good Practice in Undergraduate Education." *The American Association for Higher Education Bulletin*. 1987. http://www2.honolulu.hawaii.edu/facdev/guidebk/teachtip/7princip.htm

Coates, Hamish. "The Value of Student Engagement for Higher Education Quality Assurance." *Quality in Higher Education* 11, no. 1 (April 2005): 25–36. doi:10.1080/13538320500074915.

Connell, Raewyn and June Crawford. "Mapping the Intellectual Labour Process." *Journal of Sociology* 43, no. 2 (June 2007): 187–205. doi:10.1177/1440783307076895.

Coriat, Benjamin and Fabienne Orsi. "Establishing a New Intellectual Property Rights Regime in the United States Origins, Content and Problems." *Research Policy* 31, no. 8-9 (December 2002): 1491–1507. doi:10.1016/S0048-7333(02)00078-1.

Cynamon, Barry Z., and Steven M. Fazzari. “Household Debt in the Consumer Age: Source of Growth—Risk of Collapse.” *Capitalism and Society* 3, no. 2 (October 2008):1-30. doi:10.2202/1932-0213.1037. http://www.bepress.com/cas/vol3/iss2/art3.

Department for Business Innovation and Skills. *Students at the Hearth of the System*. White paper, 2007.

Dumenil, Gerard, and Dominique Levy. “The Neoliberal (Counter-)Revolution.” In *Neoliberalism: A Critical Reader*. Edited by Alfredo Saad-Filho and Deborah Johnston. London: Pluto Press, 2005.

_____.“Costs and Benefits of Neoliberalism: A Class Analysis.” *Review of International Political Economy* 8, no. 4 (January 2001): 578–607. doi:10.1080/09692290110077593.

_____.*The Crisis of Neoliberalism*. Cambridge, Mass.: Harvard University Press, 2011.

Elton, Lewis. “The UK Research Assessment Exercise: Unintended Consequences.” *Higher Education Quarterly* 54, no. 3 (July 2000): 274–283. doi:10.1111/1468-2273.00160.

Finder, Alan. “At One University, Tobacco Money Is a Secret.” *New York Times*, May 22, 2008. http://www.nytimes.com/2008/05/22/us/22tobacco.html?pagewanted=print.

Fine, Ben. “Critical Survey. Endogenous Growth Theory: a Critical Assessment.” *Cambridge Journal of Economics* 24, no. 2 (March 1, 2000): 245–265. doi:10.1093/cje/24.2.245.

Finnie, Ross. “Student Financial Aid: The Roles of Loans and Grants.” In *Taking Public Universities Seriously*. Edited by Frank Iacobucci and Carolyn Tuohy, 476–497. Toronto: University of Toronto Press, 2005.

Fisher, Donald, Janet Atkinson-Grosjean, and Dawn House. “Changes in Academy/Industry/State Relations in Canada: The Creation and Development of the Networks of Centres of Excellence.” *Minerva* 39, no. 3 (2001): 299–325.

Glass, Ira. "When Patents Attack." *This American Life*. NPR. Chicago Public Media, 2011. http://www.thisamericanlife.org/radio-archives/episode/441/when-patents-attack.

Government of Ontario. Ministry of Research and Innovation. “Seizing Global Opportunities: Ontario’s Innovation Agenda.” Toronto, Ontario, 2008. http://www.mri.gov.on.ca/english/programs/oia/documents/Ontario%20Innovation%20Agenda.pdf

Gravestock, Pamela, and Emily Gregor-Greenleaf. *Student Course Evaluations: Research, Models and Trends*. Research Paper. Toronto: Higher Education Quality Council of Ontario, 2008.

Gray, Mary, and Barbara Bergmann. “Student Teaching Evaluations: Inaccurate, Demeaning, Misused.” *Academe*, Online edition, Sept-October 2003. http://www.aaup.org/AAUP/pubsres/academe/2003/SO/Feat/gray.htm.

Great Britain. *Higher Education : Students at the Heart of the System*. London: Stationery Office, 2011.

Green, Francis. "It's Been A Hard Day's Night: The Concentration and Intensification of Work in Late Twentieth-Century Britain." *British Journal of Industrial Relations* 39, no. 1 (March 2001): 53–80. doi:10.1111/1467-8543.00189.

Harley, Susan. "The Impact of Research Assessment on Academic Work and Identity in UK Universities." *Studies in Higher Education* 27, no. 2 (2002).

Harvey, David. *A Brief history of Neoliberalism*. Oxford: Oxford University Press, 2005.

Harvie, D. "Value Production and Struggle in the Classroom: Teachers Within, Against and Beyond Capital." *Capital & Class* 30, no.1 (January 2006): 1–32. doi:10.1177/030981680608800102.

Higher Education Funding Council for England. "Assessment Framework and Guidance on Submissions". Higher Education Funding Council for England. 2011. http://www.hefce.ac.uk/research/ref/pubs/2011/02_11/.

Higher Education Quality Council of Ontario. *Review and Research Plan*. 2007. http://www.heqco.ca/SiteCollectionDocuments/101_EN.pdf.

Jensen, Richard, and Marie Thursby. "Proofs and Prototypes for Sale: The Licensing of University Inventions." *The American Economic Review* 91, no. 1 (March 2001):240-259.

Johnstone, Bruce. "Higher Education Finance and Accessibility: Tuition-Fees and Student Loans in Sub-Saharan Africa." *Journal of Higher Education in Africa* 2, no. 2 (2004): 11–36.

Jongbloed, Ben. "Tuition Fees in Europe and Australasia: Theory, Trends and Policies." In *Higher Education: Handbook of Theory and Research*, ed. John C.Smart, 241–310. Dordrecht: Kluwer Academic Publishers. http://www.springerlink.com/index/10.1007/1-4020-2456-8_7.

Kotz, David. "The U.S. Economy in the 1990s: A Neoliberal Success Story?" *Monthly Review* 54, no. 11 (2003): 15–33.

Krimsky, Sheldon and Ralph Nader. *Science in the Private Interest*. New York: Rowman and Littlefield, 2004.

Lang, Daniel. "The Political Economy of Performance Funding." In *Taking Public Universities Seriously*. Edited by Frank Iacobucci and Carolyn Tuohy. Toronto: University of Toronto Press, 2005.

Lanjouw, Jean O., and Mark Schankerman. "Patent Quality and Research Productivity: Measuring Innovation with Multiple Indicators." *The Economic Journal* 114, no. 495 (April 2004): 441–465. doi:10.1111/j.1468-0297.2004.00216.x.

Lee, F. S., and S. Harley. "Peer Review, the Research Assessment Exercise and the Demise of Non-Mainstream Economics." *Capital & Class* 22, no. 3 (January 1998): 23–51. doi:10.1177/030981689806600103.

Levin, John S., and Genevieve G. Shaker. "The Hybrid and Dualistic Identity of Full-Time Non-Tenure-Track Faculty." *American Behavioral Scientist* 55, no. 11 (October 2011): 1461–1484. doi:10.1177/0002764211409382.

Lipsey, Richard. "New Growth Theories and Economic Policy for the Knowledge-Economy." In *Transitions to the Knowledge Society: Policies and Strategies for Individual Participation and Learning*, ed. Kjell Rubenson and Hans Schuetze. Vancouver: UBC Press, 2000.

Lorenz, Chris. "Higher Education Policies in the European Union, the 'Knowledge Economy' and Neo-liberalism." *Social Europe* (Autumn 2006): 78-86.

Lucas, Robert. "On the Mechanics of Economic Development." *Journal of Monetary Economic* 22 (1988): 3–42.

Lynch, Tim, and Necati Aydin. *Literature Review of the Economic and Social Impact of Higher Education Research Funding*. Leadership Board for Applied Research and Public Service. 2004.

Macdonald, David, and Erika Shaker. *Under Pressure: The Impact of Rising Tuition Fees on Ontario Families*. Canadian Centre for Policy Alternatives, 2011. http://www.policyalternatives.ca/publications/reports/under-pressure.

Martin, Fernand. "The Economic Impact of Canadian University R&D." *Research Policy* 27 (1998): 667–687.

Measuring Up 2008: The National Report Card on Higher Education. The National Center for Public Policy and Higher Education. http://measuringup2008.highereducation.org/print/NCPPHEMUNationalRpt.pdf.

Milonakis, Dimitris and Ben Fine. *From Political Economy to Economics: Method, the Social and the Historical in the Evolution of Economic Theory*. London, New York: Routledge, 2009.

Mirowski, Philip. *The Road from Mont Pèlerin: the Making of the Neoliberal Thought Collective*. Cambridge, Mass.: Harvard University Press, 2009.

_____. *Science-mart: Privatizing American Science*. Cambridge, MA: Harvard University Press, 2011.

Mirowski, Phillip. *Science-Mart: Privatizing American Science*. Cambridge, MA: Harvard University Press, 2011.

Morgan, K.J. "The Research Assessment Exercise in English Universities, 2001." *Higher Education* 48, no. 4 (December 2004): 461–482. doi:10.1023/B:HIGH.0000046717.11717.06.

Mowery, David C., and Arvids A. Ziedonis. "Academic Patent Quality and Quantity Before and After the Bayh–Dole Act in the United States." *Research Policy* 31, no. 3 (March 2002): 399–418. doi:10.1016/S0048-7333(01)00116-0.

Naidoo, Rajani. "Repositioning Higher Education as a Global Commodity: Opportunities and Challenges for Future Sociology of Education Work." *British Journal of Sociology of Education* 24, no. 2 (2003): 249-259.

National Survey of Student Engagement. "Our Origins and Potential".

National Survey of Student Engagement, 2001
http://nsse.iub.edu/html/origins.cfm.

Newson, Janice, and Howard Buchbinder. "University means business universities, corporations and academic work." 1988. http://catalog.hathitrust.org/api/volumes/oclc/16713088.html.

OECD. *Innovation Policy and Performance: a Cross-country Comparison*. Paris: OECD, 2005.

_____. *The OECD Innovation Strategy: Getting a Head Start on Tomorrow*. Paris: OECD, 2010.

Onwuegbuzie, Anthony J. et al. "Students' Perceptions of Characteristics of Effective College Teachers: A Validity Study of a Teaching Evaluation Form Using a Mixed-Methods Analysis." *American Educational Research Journal* 44, no. 1 (March 1, 2007): 113–160. doi:10.3102/0002831206298169.

Panitch, Leo, and Sam Gindin. "Global Capitalism and Americal Empire." In *The New Imperial Challenge: Socialist Register 2004*, edited by Colin Ley and Leo Panitch, 1-42. London: The Merlin Press, 2004.

Papadimitriou, Dimitri B., Anwar M. Shaikh, Claudio H. dos Santos, and Gennaro Zezza. "Is Personal Debt Sustainable?" *SSRN Electronic Journal* (2011). doi:10.2139/ssrn.1833616. http://www.ssrn.com/abstract=1833616.

Paton, Graeme. "Students 'Face Leaving University with L60 Debts'." *The Telegraph*, January 14, 2012. Online edition, sec. Education.

Pisano, Gary. "Can Science Be a Business?" *Harvard Business Review* 84, no. 10 (October 2006): 114–125.

Platt, Michael. "What Student Evaluations Teach." *Perspectives on Political Science* 22, no. 1 (Winter 1993).

Polster, Claire. "How the Law Works: Exploring the Implications of Emerging Intellectual Property Regimes for Knowledge, Economy and Society." *Current Sociology* 49, no. 4 (July 1, 2001): 85–100. doi:10.1177/0011392101049004006.

Rasmussen, Einar. "Government Instruments to Support the Commercialization of University Research: Lessons from Canada." *Technovation* 28, no. 8 (August 2008): 506–517. doi:10.1016/j.technovation.2007.12.002.

Rattue, Petra. "Tamiflu's Effectiveness Remains Uncertain - Roche Still Not Releasing Vital Trial Data." *Medical News Today*, January 18, 2012, Online edition. http://www.medicalnewstoday.com/articles/240477.php.

Roberts, Peter. "Neoliberalism, Performativity and Research." *International Review of Education* 53, no. 4 (July 21, 2007): 349–365. doi:10.1007/s11159-007-9049-9.

Rolfe, Heather. "University Strategy in an Age of Uncertainty: The Effect of Higher Education Funding on Old and New Universities." *Higher Education Quarterly* 57, no. 1 (January 2003): 24–47. doi:10.1111/1468-2273.00233.

Romer, Paul. "Endogenous Growth Theory." *Journal of Political Economy* 98, no. 5 (1990): 71–102.

Samoff, Joel, and Carol Bidemi. "Conditions, Coalitions, and Influence: The World Bank and Higher Education in Africa." Paper presented at the Annual Conference of the Comparative and International Education Society, Salt Lake City, March 8-12, 2004.

Scarpetta, Stefano, and OECD. *The Sources of Economic Growth in OECD Countries*. Paris France: Organisation for Economic Co-operation and Development, 2003.

Scharpf, Fritz, Vivien Schmidt, and Herman Schwartz, ed. "Internationalization and Two Liberal Welfare States: Australia and New Zealand." In *Welfare and Work in the Open Economy Volume II: Diverse Responses to Common Challenges*. Oxford: Oxford University Press, 2000.

Schmidt, Peter. "Unions Confront the Fault Lines Between Adjuncts and Full-Timers." *The Chronicle of Higher Education* (November 20, 2011). http://chronicle.com/article/Unions-Confront-Fault-Lines/129836/.

Schultz, Theodore. "Investment in Human Capital." *The American Economic Review* 51, no. 1 (1961): 1–17.

Sears, Alan. *Retooling the Mind Factory Education in a Lean State*. Aurora: Garamond Press, 2003.

Seldin, Peter. "The Use and Abuse of Student Ratings of Professors." *The Chronicle of Higher Education* 39 (July 21, 1993): 40.

Shaikh, Anwar. "The First Great Depression of the 21st Century." In *The Crisis This Time: Socialist Register2011, edited by Greg Albo, Leo Panitch and Vivek Chibber, 44-63 (London: The Merlin Press, 2010).*

Shevlin, Mark, Philip Banyard, Mark Davies, and Mark Griffiths. "The Validity of Student Evaluation of Teaching in Higher Education: Love Me, Love My Lectures?" *Assessment & Evaluation in Higher Education* 25, no. 4 (December 2000): 397–405. doi:10.1080/713611436.

Shore, Cris, and Susan Wright. "Audit Culture and Anthropology: Neo-liberalism in British Higher Education." *The Journal of the Royal Anthropological Institute* 5, no. 4 (December 1999): 557–575.

Silva, Edward, and Sheila Slaughter. *Serving Power: The Making of the Academic Science Expert*. Westport, CT: Greenwood Press, 1984.

Sismondo, Sergio. "Ghost Management: How Much of the Medical Literature Is Shaped Behind the Scenes by the PharmaceuticalIndustry?" *PLoS Medicine* 4, no. 9 (2007): e286. doi:10.1371/journal.pmed.0040286.

Slaughter, Sheila. *Academic Capitalism: Politics, Policies, and the Entrepreneurial University*. Baltimore, MD: Johns Hopkins University Press, 1997.

Slaughter, Sheila, and Gary Rhodes. *Academic Capitalism and the New Economy: Markets, State, and Higher Education*. Baltimore, MD: Johns Hopkins University Press, 2004.

Smith, Neil. "Afterword: Who Rules this Sausage Factory?" *Antipode* 32, no. 3 (2000): 330–339.

Statistics Canada. *Survey of Intellectual Property Commercialization in Higher Education Sector*. Data-series. Statistics Canada, 2008. http://dc1.chass.utoronto.ca.ezproxy.library.yorku.ca/cgibin/cansimdim/c2_getArray.pl.

Statistics Canada and OECD. *Learning a Living: First Results of the Adult Literacy and Life Skills Survey*. 2005. http://www.statcan.gc.ca.ezproxy.library.yorku.ca/pub/89-603-x/2005001/pdf/4200878-eng.pdf.

Strazdins, Lyndall, and Bernadette Loughrey. "Too Busy: Why Time Is a Health and Environmental Problem." *New South Wales Public Health Bulletin* 18, no. 12 (2007): 219. doi:10.1071/NB07029.

Tempest, Brian. "A Structural Change in the Global Pharmaceutical Marketplace." *Journal of Generic Medicines* 7, no. 2 (April 2010): 113–117. doi:10.1057/jgm.2010.11.

Testa, James. "The Thomson ISI Journal Selection Process." *Serials Review* 29 (2003): 210–212. doi:10.1016/S0098-7913(03)00063-7.

The Economist. "The Disposable Academic: Why Doing a PhD Is Often a Waste of Time." *The Economist*, December 16, 2010. http://www.economist.com/node/17723223.

Thursby, Jerry, and Marie Thursby. "Who Is Selling the Ivory Tower? Sources of Growth in University Licensing." Working Paper, NBER Working Paper Series 7718, May 2000.

Trick, David. *Continuity, Retrenchment and Renewal: The Politics of Government-University Relations in Ontario 1985-2002*. Toronto: University of Toronto Press, 2005.

University of British Columbia and Donald Fisher. *Canadian Federal Policy and Postsecondary Education*. Vancouver: Centre for Policy Studies in Higher Education and Training (CHET) Faculty of Education, University of British Columbia, 2006.

Wade, Robert. "Financial Regime Change?" *New Left Review* 53, no. 5 (2008): 5–21.

Willmott, Hugh. "Commercialising Higher Education in the UK: The State, Industry and Peer Review." *Studies in Higher Education* 28, no. 2 (2003): 129–141. doi:10.1080/0307507032000058127.

Wood, Ellen Meiksins. *Empire of Capital*. London: Verso Press, 2005.

AUTHORS

Anna M. Agathangelou, Associate Professor of Political Science and Women's Studies at York University, Toronto and Co-Director of Global Change Institute, Nicosia, Cyprus. Author of *The Global Political Economy of Sex: Desire, Violence and Insecurity in Mediterranean Nation-States* (Palgrave Macmillan, 2006) and co-author with L.H.M. Ling, *Transforming World Politics: From Empire to Multiple Worlds* (London and New York: Routledge, 2009). She is also the co-editor (with Nevzat Soguk) of the *Special Forum on the Arab Revolutions of Globalizations* (Routledge, 2011) and with Kyle D. Killian, the Special Issue in *Tensions* entitled "(De) Fatalizing the Present and Creating Radical Alternatives" (York University, 2011).

Gregory Albo, Associate Professor in the Department of Political Science at York University, Toronto. His recent publications include "Contemporary Capitalism," in *Elgar Companion to Marxist Economics*, ed. Ben Fine and Alfredo Saad-Filho (London: Elgar, forthcoming); "The 'New Economy' and Capitalism Today," in *Interrogating the New Economy: Restructuring Work in the 21st Century*, N. Pupo and M. Thomas, ed. (Toronto: University of Toronto Press, 2010); and (with Sam Gindin and Leo Panitch) *In and Out of Crisis: The Global Financial Meltdown and Left Alternatives* (Oakland: PM Press, 2010).

Ruth Felder, Lecturer in Administration and Public Policies at the University of Buenos Aires, Argentina. She is the author of "Turbulent times: structural reforms, crisis and labour policy in Argentina (1990s-2000s)" with Viviana Patroni, in *Comparative Public Policy in Latin America*, ed. J. Diez and S. Franceschet (UTP, forthcoming); and "Austerity and its Aftermath: Neoliberalism and Labour in Argentina" with Viviana Patroni, *Journal of the Society for Socialist Studies* 7, no. 1-2 (2011).

Adam Hanieh, Assistant Professor in the Department of Development Studies at the School of Oriental and African Studies (SOAS), University of London, editorial board member of *Historical Materialism* and member of the board of management for the Council for British Research in the Levant. Author of *Capitalism and Class in the Gulf Arab States* (New York: Palgrave-Macmillan, 2011); "International financial institutions and Egypt" in *African Awakening: The Emerging Revolutions*, ed. Firoze Manji and Sokari Ekine (Pambazuka Press, 2011); and "The Internationalisation of Gulf capital and Palestinian class formation" *Capital and Class* 35, no.1 (2011).

Christoph Hermann, Senior Researcher at the Working Life Research Centre in Vienna and lecturer at the University of Vienna. Co-editor of *Privatization of Public Services Impacts for Employment, Working Conditions, and Service Quality in Europe* (London: Routledge, 2012) and *Privatisation against the European Social Model: A critique of European policies and proposals for alternatives* (Palgrave Macmillan, 2009).

Barış Karaağaç, , Lecturer in the Department of International Development Studies at Trent University. His recent publications include "Marx's Theory of Economic Crisis: A Worldwide Bibliography, 1989-2011" with George Comninel in M. Musto, ed. (Forthcoming 2013); and, "Segregations and Geopolitical 'New' Orders: Turkish Armed Forces as Entrepreneurial Venturist Masters" with Anna Agathangelou in *Uluslararası ilişkiler* (The Journal of International Relations) 8, No.29 (2011): 101-122.

Mustafa Koc, Professor at the Department of Sociology, Ryerson University, Toronto, Canada. His published works include (with Rod MacRae, Luc J.A. Mougeot, and Jennifer Welsh) For *Hunger Proof Cities* (Ottawa: IDRC Books, 1999); (with Rod MacRae and Kelly Bronson) *Interdisciplinary Perspectives in Food Studies* (Toronto: McGraw-Hill Ryerson, 2008); (with Jennifer Sumner and Tony Winson) *Critical Perspectives in Food Studies* (Oxford University Press, forthcoming).

Minqi Li, Associate Professor in the Department of Economics at the University of Utah. Author of *The Rise of China and the Demise of the Capitalist World Economy* (Pluto Press, 2009). His recent publications include "The 21st Century: Is There an Alternative (to Socialism)?" *Science and Society* 77, no.1 (2013):10-43; and "The Rise of the Working Class and the Future of the Chinese Revolution," *Monthly Review* 63, no.2 (2011): 38-51.

Maria de Lourdes Rollemberg Mollo, Professor of Economics at the University of Brasilia, Brazil. Author of "Credit and Financial Crises: the contributions of Marx and Keynes to Understanding the Current Crisis," *International Journal of Applied Economics and Econometrics* 19, no. 4 (2011): 86-111; "Neoliberal economic policies in Brazil (1994-2005): Cardoso, Lula and the need for a democratic alternative" with Alfredo Saad-Filho, *New Political Economy* 11, (March 2006): 99-124; and, "Inflation and Stabilization in Brazil: A Political Economy Analysis" with Alfredo Saad-Filho, *The Review of Radical Political Economics* 34, (2002): 109-135.

Eric Newstadt, Doctoral candidate at York University in Toronto, Ontario. He has worked as an activist and researcher in Canada's students' movement. Newstadt has published "Neoliberalism and the Federal Reserve" in *American Empire and the Politics of Global Finance*, ed. Leo Panitch and Martijn Konings (Basingstoke, New York: Palgrave Macmillan, 2009).

Şebnem Oğuz, Associate Professor in the Department of Political Science and International Relations at Başkent University, Ankara. She is the co-author (with Fuat Ercan) of "Rescaling as a Class Relationship and Process: The Case of Public Procurement Law in Turkey," *Political Geography* 25, no. 6 (2006): 641-656; and "Rethinking Anti-Neoliberal Strategies through the Perspective of Value Theory: Insights from the Turkish Case," *Science and Society* 71, no. 2 (2007): 173-202.

Viviana Patroni, Associate Professor in the Department of Social Science at York University. Between 2000-2003 and 2004-2007 she was the Director of the Centre for Research on Latin America and the Caribbean, York University. Her articles have appeared in *Capital and Class, Research in Political Economy, LABOUR, Capital and Society*, among other journals. She is one of the co-editors (with Liisa North and Timothy David Clark) of *Community Rights and Corporate Responsibility: Canadian Mining and Oil Companies in Latin America* (Toronto: Between the Lines,2006).

John S. Saul, Professor Emeritus of Social and Political Science, York University, Toronto and author of some twenty books on southern Africa and on development issues, including *Essays of the Political Economy of Africa*, with Giovanni Arrighi (New York, London: Monthly Review Press, 1973); *The Crisis in South Africa* (London: Zed Press, 1986); *Namibia's Liberation Struggle: The Two-Edged Sword*, with Colin Leys (London: James Currey, 1995); *The Next Liberation Struggle* (Toronto: Between-the-Lines, 2006); *Revolutionary Traveller* (Winnipeg: Arbeiter Ring, 2009); *Liberation Lite: The Roots of Recolonization in Southern Africa* (Trenton, NJ: Africa World Press, 2011); and *The Thirty Years War for Southern African Liberation,1960-1990* (Cambridge UP, forthcoming).

Ingo Schmidt, Professor and Academic Coordinator of the Labour Studies Programme at Athabasca University, Canada. Author of *Trade Unions and Keynesianism* (Münster: Verlag Westfälisches Dampfboot, 1997); editor of *Our World Isn't a Commodity – Handbook for Globalization Critics* (Köln: Kiepenheuer & Witsch, 2002); *Varieties of Neoliberalism* (Hamburg: VSA Verlag, 2008); and *Social Democracy After the Cold War* (Athabasca: Athabasca University Press, 2012).

Politik, Gemeinschaft und Gesellschaft in einer globalisierten Welt
hrsg. von Thomas Faist (Universität Bielefeld)

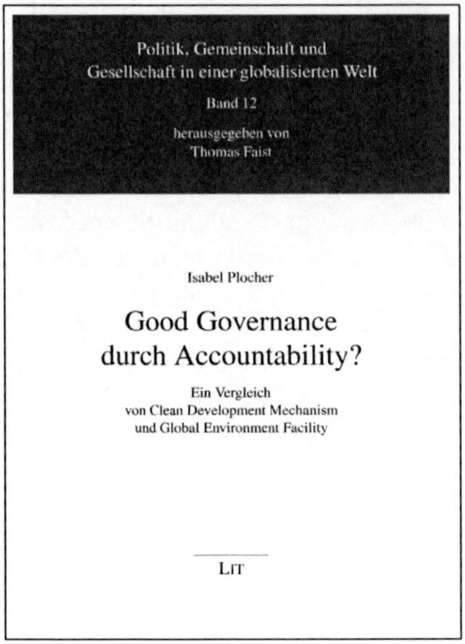

Isabel Plocher
Good Governance durch Accountability?
Ein Vergleich von Clean Development Mechanism und Global Environment Facility
Dieses Buch untersucht Institutionen, über die Umweltschutzprojekte in Entwicklungsländern finanziert werden: den Clean Development Mechanism des Kyoto-Protokolls und die Global Environment Facility. In beiden Institutionen bestehen auch Anreize, Projekte zu registrieren, die nicht genuin zum Umweltschutz beitragen. Die Untersuchung zeigt, welche Entscheidungsverfahren und Accountability-Strukturen die Registrierung derartiger Projekte tendenziell verhindern und stattdessen sachgerechtere Ergebnisse erwarten lassen, und erklärt so Unterschiede im Funktionieren der beiden Institutionen.
Bd. 12, 2011, 328 S., 34,90 €, br.,
ISBN 978-3-643-10975-0

Katharina Hierl
Die Islamisierung der deutschen Integrationsdebatte
Zur Konstruktion kultureller Identitäten, Differenzen und Grenzziehungen im postkolonialen Diskurs
Mittlerweile konzentriert sich der deutsche Integrationsdiskurs vor allem auf Muslime sowie Migrantinnen und Migranten aus dem arabischen und türkischen Kulturraum. Kulturelle Differenzen und insbesondere Religion werden zu den elementaren Faktoren erklärt, die über Scheitern oder Gelingen des Integrationsprozesses entscheiden. Dabei werden postkoloniale Deutungsmuster und Bilder erzeugt und reproduziert. Dieses Phänomen wird als die Islamisierung der Integrationsdebatte bezeichnet werden und ist das Untersuchungsobjekt dieses Buches.
Katharina Hierl studierte Politikwissenschaft, Islamwissenschaft und Soziologie an der Universität Erlangen-Nürnberg.
Bd. 13, 2012, 176 S., 29,90 €, br.,
ISBN 978-3-643-11744-1

LIT Verlag Berlin – Münster – Wien – Zürich – London
Auslieferung Deutschland / Österreich / Schweiz: siehe Impressumsseite